Grace for today

GRACE FOR TODAY

Donald S. Fortner

 EVANGELICAL PRESS

EVANGELICAL PRESS
16/18 High Street, Welwyn, Herts, AL6 9EQ, England

© Evangelical Press 1986

First published 1986

British Library Cataloguing in Publication Data
Fortner, Donald S.
  Grace for today.
  1. Devotional calendars.
  I. Title
  242'.2   BS390

ISBN 0-85234-233-0

Typeset by Wagstaffs Typeshuttle, Henlow, Beds.
Printed in Great Britain by The Bath Press, Avon.

'Teach me thy way, O Lord'

Psalm 1:1–6

There is no better way for us to begin this day and this year than by earnestly seeking the will of God in it. It is certain that God sovereignly accomplishes his will, his eternal purpose, in all things (Isa. 46:9–11). Nothing comes to pass in time except that which God purposed in eternity. Yet nothing is more important, and nothing more difficult, to a believer than seeking the will of God in making responsible choices and decisions about his actions in life. We know by painful experience that it is possible to make the wrong choices. We rejoice to know that God graciously overrules our errors in judgement for our spiritual, eternal good and for the glory of his own great name (Rom. 8:28). And we praise him for that! But when a believer walks contrary to the will of his Lord, he brings grief and trouble to himself. Be wise, therefore, and seek grace both to know and do the will of God in all things.

'Teach me thy way, O Lord.' Do you desire, my friend, to know the will of God in all things? Then ask God himself to reveal his will to you, by his Spirit and by his Word. He alone can teach you his way and he will if you are willing to walk in it. **'I will walk in thy truth.'** In essence, David is saying, 'Lord, if you teach me your way, by your grace I will gladly walk in it. If you will mark out my path in providence, I will stick to it.' This is the attitude of submission and faith before the Lord. And where there is true faith in the Lord Jesus Christ and submission to his will, there will always be an acknowledgement of weakness and sin and the need for divine grace. **'Unite my heart to fear thy name.'** We can walk in God's will only as he gives us grace to do so. When we do make errors concerning the will of God, it is either because we have not earnestly sought his will, or else because we are rebellious to it. Of this one thing we can be sure: God always reveals his will to the person who is willing to do it (Prov. 3:5–6).

'He appeared to put away sin'

Read Isaiah 53:1–8

In his life of obedience to the law of God Christ established righteousness for us. But that righteousness is not sufficient, in and of itself, to make us acceptable to God. Sin must be punished. Justice must be satisfied. Every guilty sinner must be put to death. The only way God could both punish us for sin and save us from sin was by the infinitely meritorious, voluntary and efficacious death, burial and resurrection of the Lord Jesus Christ, our Substitute. For the accomplishment of our salvation Christ became 'obedient unto death, even the death of the cross'.

God made his Son to be sin for us. Christ had no sin of his own. He had no original sin and no actual sin. He was 'holy, harmless, undefiled and separate from sin'. Yet he was made sin. By divine imputation, all the sin of all God's elect was laid upon Christ our Substitute. Christ 'his own self bare our sins in his own body on the tree'. This transfer of sin from us to our Substitute was so real and complete that the Son of God became sin for us! He even claimed our sin as his own, willingly assuming all responsibility for the sins of his people.

God the Son, being made sin, died as our Substitute. When God found sin on his Son, he cried out to his own holy law and inflexible justice: 'Awake, O sword, against my shepherd, and against the man that is my fellow... smite the shepherd!" Then and there all the sin of all God's elect was slain, annihilated for ever and taken away. Justice, being fully satisfied, for ever sheathed its dreadful sword. Wrath, being completely spent upon Christ, is altogether absorbed in Christ for all his people. In so far as God's law and justice are concerned, all of God's elect have died. We died in Christ our Substitute.

In Christ all who believe are completely justified. His precious blood has for ever washed away our sins, so that we are justly pardoned and forgiven. His life of righteousness has been imputed to us, so that we are perfectly holy in God's sight. In Christ we have all that God in his law demands for our acceptance, complete satisfaction for sin and perfect righteousness.

'Enoch walked with God'

Read Colossians 3:1–17

This is an astounding statement: **'Enoch'**, a sinful man like you and me, **'walked with God'!** And 'he had this testimony, that he pleased God'. In his daily life Enoch walked in company with the living God, living in God's presence as his constant Friend, in whom he confided and by whom he was loved. What kind of man was Enoch? What kind of life did he live? The answer is clear: Enoch was a man of faith, and he lived a life of faith. He was not a sinless man. He did not live a higher life, a deeper life or a holier life than anyone else who lives by faith. It was not Enoch's conduct, his personality, or his disposition that pleased God, but his faith in Christ (Heb. 11:5–6).

There was nothing at all remarkable about the character or works of this man Enoch by nature, which caused God to look upon him with pleasure. Enoch did not win God's favour by something he did. God was pleased with Enoch, because Enoch believed God. He believed that which God has spoken. Enoch's faith was the same as Abel's before him and Noah's after him. The faith by which Enoch walked with God and pleased God was the same faith that the dying thief possessed. And it is the faith of God's elect today. My friend, walking with God is neither more nor less than believing God. The only way anyone can walk with God and please God is by faith in the Lord Jesus Christ. No man pleases God, but his Son. No man walks with God, but his Son. And the only way any fallen child of Adam can please God and walk with God is by faith in his Son, the Lord Jesus Christ.

Our sanctification, like our justification, is by faith in the Lord Jesus Christ. We grow in grace as we grow in faith. Having begun in the Spirit, we are not now made perfect by the flesh. We do not begin and go a certain distance by faith in Christ, and then finish our course by the works of the law. To walk with God is to continue as we began – by faith in Christ. 'As ye have therefore received Christ Jesus the Lord, so walk ye in him: rooted and built up in him, and stablished in the faith.'

'If a man die, shall he live again?'

Read 1 Thessalonians 4:13–18

With Paul, I say, 'If in this life only we have hope in Christ, we are of all men most miserable' (1 Cor. 15:19). If there were no eternal life in Christ, no eternal bliss of life with Christ in glory and no resurrection, the believer would be the most miserably frustrated person in the world. We would never have that which we most earnestly desire – Christ. We would never enjoy that for which we are most ambitious – Christ. We would never see the end of our hope – Christ. We would never embrace Christ, or be embraced by him. My mind has never entertained a more cruel or miserable thought. What a tormenting supposition! But it is not so! I live in hope of the resurrection, and my hope is well founded. I have three good reasons for this good hope.

I have already been resurrected representatively (Eph. 2:5–6; Rom. 8:29–30). When the Lord Jesus Christ arose from the grave, he arose as the Representative of his people. We were resurrected with Christ! His representative resurrection necessitates and guarantees the resurrection of his people. Christ was raised as the firstfruits of them that sleep, and the full harvest must follow. Christ was raised as the second Adam and, as we have born the image of our first covenant head, we must bear the image of the second. Our Lord's covenant engagements as the Surety of his elect are not complete until we are raised from the dead (John 6:37–40).

I have already experienced the resurrection of Christ in regeneration. The new birth, regeneration, is the first resurrection. It is nothing less than life from the dead. Those who have experienced the first resurrection must experience the second. The second death has no power over us, because we have been raised to new life in Christ by the power of his grace (Rev. 20:6; John 5:25; 11:25–26).

I believe the revelation of God concerning the resurrection of our bodies (John 5:28–29; 1 Cor. 15:35–41, 51–58; 1 Thess. 4:13–18). 'I know that my redeemer liveth, and that he shall stand at the latter day upon the earth: and though after my skin worms destroy this body, yet in my flesh shall I see God' (Job 19:25–26).

'Three delightful duties'

Read Philippians 4:4–13

Writing by divine inspiration, the apostle Paul admonishes all believers to do three things: **'Rejoice evermore. Pray without ceasing. In everything give thanks.'** Our God is so gracious to his people that he makes delight a duty! What could be more delightful and pleasant than constant joy, prayer and thanksgiving? May God give each of us a heart to engage eagerly in these three delightful duties.

'Rejoice evermore!' Our sins are forgiven. We have the righteousness of God in Christ imputed to us. We are accepted in the Beloved. We are children of God by faith in Christ, heirs of God and joint-heirs with his Son, Jesus Christ. That one who loved us and gave himself for us is the sovereign Ruler of the universe. Why should we mourn? 'My Beloved is mine, and I am my Beloved's.' What then can keep me from rejoicing? I will rejoice in God my Saviour at all times. I cannot rejoice in sorrow, pain and trouble. But I can rejoice in my God in the midst of sorrow, pain and trouble.

'Pray without ceasing!' Paul does not mean that we should always be engaged in audible prayer. His meaning is 'Live constantly before God in conscious, believing dependence upon him.' He is simply telling us to believe God at all times. When you are serving and worshipping the Lord, believe him, acknowledge your dependence upon the blood and righteousness of Christ for acceptance with God. When you sin, trust Christ for pardon. When you are tempted and tried, trust Christ for protection. When you work, trust Christ for strength. When you eat, acknowledge that you are fed by the hand of God's goodness. In all things, willingly submit to and trust the wise, adorable, good providence of your God.

'In everything give thanks!' At all times, in all circumstances, give thanks to God. Faith can give thanks in all things, because faith realizes that whatever comes to pass comes to pass by the will of God. Give thanks, because, whatever your present circumstances, **'This is the will of God in Christ Jesus concerning you.'**

'The precious blood of Christ'

Read Exodus 12:1–14

We who believe know that we have been redeemed **'with the precious blood of Christ'**. To us the Saviour's blood is truly precious. It has become common today for preachers to say very little about the blood. We are sometimes ridiculed for preaching blood atonement. We are told that such preaching is crude, outdated and insignificant in these modern times. And those who do preach about the blood, for the most part, make the blood of Christ to be a vain, insignificant thing, by denouncing its saving, redeeming efficacy.

We reverence the blood of Christ. We know that 'without shedding of blood is no remission' (Heb. 9:22). Why do we place such importance upon the blood of Christ and hold it to be a precious thing? The blood of Christ is precious, because it is the blood of the incarnate God (Acts 20:28). The blood poured out for our redemption at Calvary was the blood of a man, but that man is the eternal God! We have been justified by the blood (Rom. 3:24), reconciled to God by the blood (Eph. 2:13) and cleansed from all sin by the precious blood of Christ (1 John 1:7). The blood of Christ has satisfied the wrath and justice of God's holy law, so that through the blood God is both just and the justifier of every believer (Rom. 3:24–26). Every blessing of God's grace in the everlasting covenant comes to us through the blood of Christ: redemption, pardon, peace, forgiveness, sanctification and glorification (Col. 1:14, 20; Heb. 10:10–14; 13:12). Our consciences are purged from guilt by our Saviour's precious blood (Heb. 9:12–14). Through the blood we have access to God (Heb. 10:19–20). We who believe shall triumph over all our enemies, death, hell and the grave, by the blood (Rev. 12:11). We shall stand before the throne of God purified by the precious blood of Christ (Rev. 7:14). And we shall glorify Christ in heaven, singing his everlasting praise for the precious, redeeming blood (Rev. 5:9).

Nothing is more practical, more important, or more delightful to the people of God than the blood, the precious, effectual, cleansing, redeeming blood of Christ.

'Repentance unto life'

Read 1 Thessalonians 1:4-10

There is a repentance which is no sign or evidence of spiritual life at all. It is not a repentance produced in the heart by the Holy Spirit, but a repentance produced only in the emotions by human power. Legal fear, moral reformation, remorse for sin, a desire for heaven and a mere confession of sin are things often substituted for repentance. You may possess all these things and yet not have repentance unto life. These forms of repentance were found in Cain, Esau, Saul, Ahab, Judas, Simon Magus and Felix, but they all perished under the wrath of God. All temporary repentance is false repentance.

'Repentance unto life' is a gift of God's grace. It is produced in the heart by the regenerating work of the Holy Spirit, through the revelation of Christ in the gospel (Zech. 12:10). This 'repentance unto life' basically involves four essential elements.

Repentance comes by the *conviction* of the Holy Spirit (John 16:8-14). The Holy Spirit convinces men of sin, their evil, vile, corrupt nature, causing the sinner to abhor not only his deeds, but himself as well. He convinces men of righteousness, showing sinners that they have no righteousness and that all righteousness is in Christ. And he convinces men of judgement, revealing God's judgement of sin in Christ, the sinner's Substitute, the accomplishment of redemption through his blood and that all unbelievers must be judged for sin and condemned, even as the prince of this world has been judged. There must also be a *conversion* of the heart to God. The heart is repentant only when it is reconciled to God in his true character (1 Thess. 1:9; 2 Cor. 5:20). When the sinner bows to Christ's sovereign throne in loving adoration and devotion, he has 'repentance unto life'. True repentance is the *commitment* of the heart to Christ (Luke 14:25-33). True conviction always converts and true conversion always produces commitment. The truly repentant heart is committed to the will, the gospel, the church and the glory of Christ. And repentance involves *continuation* (Matt. 10:22; Luke 9:62). God's people do persevere in the faith. They continue in the truth. They go on to the end of their journey following Christ, seeking Christ and trusting Christ.

'The precious things of heaven'

Read Romans 8:16-23

God has blessed all his elect with all spiritual blessings in Christ. He who gave us his Son has given us all things in his Son (Eph. 1:3; 1 Cor. 3:21; Rom. 8:32). Here are five of **'the precious things of heaven'** specifically revealed to us.

1.   *Our precious Saviour.* "Unto you therefore which believe he is precious" (1 Peter 2:7). Christ is the treasure hid in a field, the pearl of great price, for which every believer has gladly sold all that he has to obtain that treasure and have that pearl.

2.   *The precious blood.* 'Ye know that ye were ... redeemed ... with the precious blood of Christ' (1 Peter 1:18-19). The blood of Christ is precious because it is his blood, the blood of the God-man. The blood was foreordained of God as the atonement for our sins. The blood reveals our Saviour's love. The blood satisfies divine justice and removes our sin. The blood secures our forgiveness, pardon, justification and eternal glory. The blood was shed for us. All these things make the blood of Christ precious.

3.   *The precious promises of our God.* In Christ 'are given unto us exceeding great and precious promises' (2 Peter 1:4). The promises of God are precious because they are God's promises. They are unquestionable and sure. And they speak of exceedingly great and precious things: pardon, peace, protection, provision, preservation, providence, perfection.

4.   *Our precious faith.* By the gift of God's grace, we 'have obtained like precious faith' with God's elect (2 Peter 1:1). The doctrine of faith, the gospel is precious. And the grace of faith is precious, precious because it is rare, it honours God and it saves the soul.

5.   *Our precious trials.* 'The trial of your faith, being much more precious than gold' (1 Peter 1:7), proves that your faith is genuine and reveals your Father's love. The trial of faith is precious because it causes your love, faith and joy in Christ to grow, causes you to enjoy and anticipate your inheritance in heaven and will give you great cause to praise and honour God in heaven.

'They had been with Jesus'

Read Matthew 5:1-16

When Peter and John appeared before the Sanhedrin, the Scripture tells us that **'They took knowledge of them, that they had been with Jesus.'** Those men, who had no reverence for God, no regard for Christ and no interest in the gospel, took notice of Peter and John as being men whose lives were evidently under the influence and control of Christ. Their communion and conversation with Christ so influenced their speech and conduct that even their enemies acknowledged them to be followers of Christ.

That fact is of great interest to me. It causes this question to pierce my heart: 'What does my life say about the Christ whom I profess to trust, love and serve?' Of this much I am sure – if I truly know Christ, if I live in communion with Christ by faith, Christ will be, to some degree, manifest in my life. My attitude, my speech and my conduct will, in some measure, reflect him.

The true believer is a person in whom Christ dwells. The new birth is nothing less than Christ coming into a man's heart, taking possession, ruling and causing that man to become a follower of him. Anything less than this is not Christianity. The new birth creates a desire in the heart to be like Christ, causing the person who is born again to seek and strive after the perfection of Christ's character in himself. We know that this perfect conformity to Christ cannot be attained in this life. But that fact in no way hinders us from seeking it. The highest aspiration of the believing heart is to be like Christ. His submission and dedication to the will of God and the glory of God, his patience, love, kindness, tenderness and forgiveness, his self-denial, self-sacrifice, humility and unflinching boldness in the cause of God are things all of God's people seek. Let us ever seek these things ardently. When we close our eyes in death, we shall have this blessed conformity to Christ!

'Thou hast redeemed me, O Lord'

Read Exodus 15:1-19

Redemption is a twofold thing. There is redemption by price and redemption by power. This is beautifully set forth typically by God's deliverance of the children of Israel from Egypt. The Israelites were sealed by blood and kept from the judgement of God. Then God stretched out his mighty arm and redeemed them from the bondage of Egypt.

The Lord Jesus Christ paid *the price of our redemption* at Calvary. God demanded a perfect righteousness. Therefore our Saviour assumed our nature. As a man he became subject to the will and law of God in every point, working out a perfect righteousness as our Representative. But that was not enough. Divine justice demanded a full payment and satisfaction for our transgressions. This could only be accomplished by the death of the sinner. Therefore, 'God made Christ to be sin for us.' And in holy justice the Son of God died in our place upon the cross. God's righteousness and justice were fully satisfied. The price of our redemption was Christ's precious blood. Only by the payment of that price can God both be just and the justifier of the ungodly.

But still his people were under the bondage of sin. We were still under the tyranny of the law. We were still in captivity to Satan and our own lusts. There must also be a *redemption by power*. This redemption by power is the effectual application of the blood to our hearts in the new birth. It is accomplished by our Lord Jesus Christ, through the operation of the Holy Spirit. At God's appointed time he sends forth the Spirit of his Son into the hearts of his people that they might receive the adoption of sons. Mark it down as a sure fact: every soul that Jesus Christ redeemed by the price of his shed blood, he will also redeem by the power of his right arm.

Both are essential to salvation. We must have a suitable Substitute, to redeem us with the price of his own blood. And we must have a sovereign Deliverer to redeem us with the power of his right arm. By virtue of his shed blood, Jesus Christ sets the prisoner free. Let us give praise to our merciful Redeemer.

'The Saviour of the world'

Read John 3:11-21

The apostle John gives us an infallible declaration of our Saviour's purpose for coming into the world: **'We have seen and do testify that the Father sent the Son to be the Saviour of the world.'** Our Lord Jesus Christ left us a marvellous example of faithfulness, love, humility and patience. But our Lord had a far more important reason for coming into the world than that of being a moral example for us to follow. The purpose of the incarnation is the salvation of sinners. 'The Father sent the Son to be the Saviour of the world.' 'This is a faithful saying, and worthy of all acceptation, that Christ Jesus came into the world to save sinners; of whom I am chief' (1 Tim. 1:15). Three things are clear.

This world is sinful, guilty and cursed. This is the true character of the world and all who are in it. 'The whole world lieth in wickedness' (1 John 5:19). When John says that Christ is the Saviour of the world, he is simply telling us that the grace of God is not limited to the nation of Israel alone. God sent his Son to save men and women out of the fallen mass of humanity, Gentiles as well as Jews. Christ came to save guilty sinners (John 3:14-18).

The Lord Jesus Christ is the only Saviour of the world. No one less than God himself could suffice to save us. But when God the Son enters into the world in human flesh to save fallen men, we are sure that the incarnate God cannot fail. 'He shall not fail nor be discouraged, till he have set judgement [righteousness] in the earth' (Isa. 42:4). Christ was sent by the Father, because he volunteered to come into the world to save sinners by establishing righteousness and accomplishing redemption through his obedience as the sinner's Substitute.

Jesus Christ is the Saviour you need. You have no hope of salvation apart from Christ. You are guilty, helpless, perishing in sin. No one but Christ can save you. Christ alone is an all-sufficient Saviour for sinners. His righteousness is all the righteousness you need. His blood is all the ransom God requires.

'When thou prayest'

Read 2 Samuel 7:18-29

In personal, private prayer we commune with the eternal, triune God. Prayer is an acknowledgement of our weakness in the flesh because of sin, and of our need for constant supplies of divine grace. In private prayer we open our hearts to God and pour out our souls before him.

Let us never be pretentious and hypocritical before God in prayer. He sees all and knows all. 'The Lord looketh on the heart.' God is not interested in how we speak to him, the length of our prayers, the frequency of our prayers, or even the words we use in prayer. God looks upon our hearts. He hears what we say in our hearts. He is interested in and has regard for the attitudes, the motives and the desires of our hearts.

True prayer, like all other graces and acts of worship, is a heart work. You may memorize little religious sayings and call them prayers. You may read and recite prayer books and think you are praying. You may repeat the earnest prayers of other people and suppose that you have prayed. But true prayer cannot be taught or learned by men, any more than breathing can be. It is not an art or skill. Prayer is the breath of the renewed soul. Prayer is born in the heart by the grace of God. It is the power and grace of the Spirit in a man's heart that teaches him to pray. Indeed, true faith is prayer and true prayer is faith. We ought to live in an unceasing attitude of prayer, always acknowledging our sin, always seeking God's will, always trusting his grace. In this sense, let us 'pray without ceasing'. But let us never neglect private prayer. Truly, prayer is a source of strength and consolation to the believing heart. Above all things, our prayer life reveals our true heart attitude towards God and ourselves. What we are in prayer before God, we truly are. Our faith in Christ, our sense of our sinfulness and weakness in the flesh, our dependence upon God's providence and our reverence for God are all manifest by our attitude about prayer.

'Surety of a better testament'

Read Jeremiah 32:37-40; Hebrews 8:10-12

The covenant of grace is that solemn agreement between the three persons of the Holy Trinity for the everlasting salvation of God's elect. The covenant was ordered and made sure in all its details before the foundation of the world. The covenant is God's immutable, unalterable purpose of grace towards his elect. It is sometimes called 'the will', sometimes 'the testament' and sometimes 'the covenant' by the inspired writers. But it is clearly revealed, both in the Old and the New Testaments, that our salvation was planned, purposed and made sure in this everlasting covenant of grace by God's eternal decree (Jer. 31:31-34; 32:38-40; Eph. 1:3-14; 2 Tim. 1:9-10).

Our Lord Jesus Christ is the Surety of the covenant. That is to say, God entrusted his glory, his grace and his elect people to his Son, who agreed to assume full responsibility for them, much like a man would entrust his sheep to the care of his son as a shepherd (John 6:37-40). A surety is a representative man, who lays himself under obligation for the one he represents (Gen. 43:8-9). In this sense Christ is our Surety. He drew near to God on our behalf, and laid himself under obligation to God for us, for our eternal salvation (Heb. 10:5-14).

Christ voluntarily became our Surety. Suretyship, to a man of honour, is a voluntary bondage (Prov. 6:1-2); and when Christ became our Surety in the covenant of grace, he voluntarily placed himself in bondage to his Father until his service was performed (Isa. 50:5-7; John 10:16-18). In this sense, he became his Father's Servant. Christ is an absolute Surety. Whatever God required for our salvation, Christ agreed to perform for us. He willingly became responsible to God for his people, for both righteousness and satisfaction. His work as the Surety of the covenant will not be complete until he presents all God's elect before him in glory, 'holy and without blame'. Therefore he says, concerning his elect, 'Them also I must bring.' If so much as one of his elect should perish, he would be a failure and must bear the blame for ever. And that cannot be!

'According to thy word'

Read Lamentations 3:21-26

The apostle Paul, writing by the inspiration of the Holy Spirit, tells us plainly what God's intention, purpose and design are in giving us the inspired volume of Holy Scripture: 'Whatsoever things were written aforetime were written for our learning, that we through patience and comfort of the scriptures might have hope' (Rom. 15:4).

1. The Word of God was written *for our learning*. It was not written simply for us to learn the facts of Bible history, the ways of morality, or even mere doctrinal truth. It is good to learn these things; but the intent of Scripture is far more practical and beneficial. The Word of God has been given to us so that we might learn the way of life, salvation and peace with God through the Lord Jesus Christ. Everything in the book of God speaks about and reveals the Son of God (Luke 24:27, 44-47; John 5:39; Acts 10:43). The purpose of God in giving us his Word is that we might know his Son, the Lord Jesus Christ, and be saved by him.

2. God has given us the Scriptures *to teach us patience*. Patience is that calm, even temper and unruffled spirit with which believing men and women bear the evils of life. Our Lord's admonition to us is 'In patience possess ye your souls' (Luke 21:19). Patience waits upon the Lord. Patience is resignation of the heart to the will of God (James 4:7; 1 Peter 5:6). If we believe God, we can wait upon him with ease and expectation.

3. God has given us his Word *so that we might enjoy the comfort of the Scriptures*. The fact that God is my Father fills me with comfort. The gospel of God, the character of God, the providence of God and the promises of God are wells of consolation for the believing soul.

4. God has given us this blessed volume *so that we might live in the hope of the Scriptures*. Faith primarily looks to the past, trusting what Christ has accomplished. Hope is based upon and arises from faith. Hope looks to the future, anticipating all that Christ has promised.

'They shall never perish'

Read Psalm 89:19-37

Our Lord here makes a blanket, unconditional promise to every true believer. It takes into consideration all times, all circumstances, all contingencies, all events and all possibilities. This promise takes in all the flock. Not one of Christ's sheep will ever perish no, not even one. If you are a believer, if you trust the Lord Jesus Christ, if you have received eternal life, you will never perish. Christ himself has promised it! Nothing in you, nothing done by you, nothing in heaven, earth or hell will ever destroy your soul. Here are seven reasons why Christ's sheep will never perish.

1. *The promise of God must be fulfilled.* God himself says, **'They shall never perish.'** If one promise of God could be broken, no promise could be believed.

2. *The purpose of God cannot be frustrated* (John 6:37-40). God's covenant cannot be made void. His elective purpose cannot be overturned. The suretyship engagements of Christ cannot be broken. The Good Shepherd must save his sheep (John 10:16).

3. *The redemptive work of Christ cannot be nullified* (Isa. 53:10-11). That which Christ purchased, he must have. Otherwise he could never see of the travail of his soul and be satisfied.

4. *The believer's justification by God in Christ is an irreversible act of grace* (Rom. 8:31-34). God will not impute sin to those whom he has justified in his Son (Rom. 4:8).

5. *The work of God's grace in the believer's heart can never be defeated* (Phil. 1:6). That which God has begun he will carry on to perfection. Nothing and no one can halt God's work.

6. *The intercessory work of our Lord Jesus Christ must prevail* (John 17:9-11,15,20; 1 John 2:1-2). Those for whom the Son of God pleads cannot perish.

7. *The seal of the Holy Spirit cannot be broken* (Eph. 1:13-14). God the Holy Spirit has sealed every believer unto the day of redemption, securing our glorious resurrection and eternal inheritance in Christ.

There will be no tears in heaven

Read 2 Corinthians 4:1-18

All who enter eternal glory will shed many tears before they reach their home. Here we weep much because of our sin, our bereavements and our afflictions. Physical, mental, emotional and spiritual pain bring living men to weep. Child of God, do not expect to be free from tears here. But on the other side of the grave, we shall weep no more!

To be sure, there are many things which would cause us to weep in heaven, were it not promised, **'God shall wipe away all tears from their eyes.'** Surely, we would weep over our many sins, the coldness of our hearts, our wasted opportunities and our indifference while we were upon the earth. But God will not allow it. Not one tear shall dim our vision of Christ over there.

The Lord our God will remove us from every source of pain and grief. He will remove us from all sin and remove all sin from us! Well may I cease to weep when I have ceased to sin. And he will give us all that our hearts desire. There will be no weeping over lost reward in that land to which we are going. Our reward will be full, perfect and satisfying. We shall see Christ! We shall be like Christ. We shall love Christ perfectly, serve him unceasingly, worship him without sin, know him fully, rest in him completely and enjoy him entirely! We shall have Christ! All that he is and all that he has will be ours! And we shall cease to weep for ever!

Will you be among that happy company? Not everyone will be there. No one deserves to be there. Yet we are told that there will be a great multitude there which no man can number. All who are washed in the blood of Christ and clothed in his righteousness will be there. All who are chosen of God, for whom the celestial city was prepared, will be there. All who trust Christ alone as Lord and Saviour will be there, but no one else. Will you be there?

'Let these go their way'

Read Romans 3:20-31

Our Lord Jesus Christ was in the garden and the soldiers came to arrest him. When they came to take him away, our Saviour gave this commandment to the soldiers concerning his beloved disciples: **'If therefore ye seek me, let these go their way: that the saying might be fulfilled, which he spake, Of them which thou gavest me have I lost none.'**

Do you see the love and care which our Lord manifested towards his people, even in the hour of his trial? His love is strong as death. He voluntarily gives himself up to the enemy, but demands that his people be set free as a condition of his surrender. As a sheep before her shearers is dumb, he opens not his mouth for his own sake; but for the sake of his disciples he gives a commandment of sovereign authority. This is love, constant, free, self-denying, unchanging love. But there is far more here than is to be found upon the surface.

This is a beautiful picture of our great Substitute in his work of redemption. The Good Shepherd lays down his life for his sheep, but the condition is this: those sheep for whom he died must therefore go free. Our Surety was bound and slain for us and justice demands that those for whom he stands as a Substitute must be set free to go their way. In the midst of Egyptian bondage, that voice rings out as a word of power: 'Let these go their way.' Out of the slavery of sin, out of the bondage of Satan, out from under the curse of the law the redeemed of the Lord must come. He says, upon the merits of his own infinite sacrifice, 'Let these go their way.' With the eye of his justice upon the blood of his Son, the Lord God says of all his elect, 'Let these go their way. Deliver them from going down to the pit: I have found a ransom.' The thunder-cloud of divine wrath burst upon our Saviour's head as he hung upon the cross of Calvary, and God's elect, his chosen sheep, those sinners who, being called by his grace, believe on Christ, shall never be smitten by the bolts of the law's justice and vengeance. They must go free!

'The obedience of one'

Read Romans 5:12-21

The essence of the gospel is substitution. The everlasting salvation of God's elect is in no way dependent upon, or attributed to, anything done by us. 'Salvation is of the Lord!' God's gift of eternal life, all the blessings of grace in this life and all the blessedness of eternal glory in the life to come are freely bestowed upon every believing sinner only as the result of the finished work of the Lord Jesus Christ, our Substitute. We could never earn or merit everlasting salvation. But the Lord Jesus Christ has earned the eternal salvation of God's elect. God in justice, righteousness and truth must reward his Son with the salvation of every soul for whom he lived, died and rose again. **'For as by one man's disobedience many were made sinners, so by the obedience of one shall many be made righteous.'** As we were made sinners in the eyes of God's law and justice by the sin and fall of our father Adam, though we had not yet committed any actual sin of our own, even so we are made righteous by the life and death of our Lord Jesus Christ as our Substitute, though we have no actual righteousness of our own.

By his obedience in life as our Representative, Christ brought in an everlasting righteousness for us. God in his law required that we live in perfect righteousness, entirely without sin, loving God with all our heart, soul, mind and strength, and our neighbours as ourselves. This is what Christ has done for us. In him all who believe have perfectly obeyed God's law. By his obedience in death, the Son of God satisfied the penalty of the law against sin as our Substitute. He was made to be sin for us by divine imputation. And, when he was made to be sin for us, our Substitute received the wages of sin – death. In him all who believe died under penalty of God's law. Now God imputes the righteousness of his Son to every believer. In exactly the same way as Christ was made to be sin for us and was rewarded with death because of sin, we are made to be the righteousness of God in him. Being righteous in Christ, we shall be rewarded for his perfect righteousness with eternal glory.

'Let not your heart be troubled'

Read John 14:18-27

These are words of love and concern. They are the gentle words
of our faithful Friend. But they are words of reproof. Our Lord
is telling us that believing hearts ought never to be anxious,
fearful and worried. He would have us cast our care upon him
and trust him to provide for us and protect us in all things (1
Peter 5:6-7). When our hearts are troubled there is trouble in our
hearts. I know that whenever my heart is troubled with worry,
anxiety and fear my trouble can be traced to some evil thing in my
heart.

Pride is a terrible source of heart trouble. It is pride that causes
us to rebel against God's providence. Most of our sorrows arise
from within. 'When self is conquered, sorrow is to a great extent
banished from the human heart' (Spurgeon). We shall find no
comfort for our hearts until our pride is broken and our hearts
are subdued (Job 1:20-22; 2:9-10).

Unbelief is the root of all heart trouble. Worry, anxiety and fear
are the fruits of unbelief. If I believe God there is nothing I can
reasonably fear, worry about or anxiously consider (Matt.
6:25-34). One old preacher said, 'I dare not fret any more than I
dare curse and swear.'

Covetousness is a real, though unacknowledged, cause of heart
trouble. Our hearts are troubled because we want God to do what
he has not done or give what he has not given. That is
covetousness (Phil. 4:11).

Envy, the desire of another person's ease, wealth or position,
causes a believer's heart great trouble (Ps. 73:1-3). Envy is the
most loathsome, vicious child pride ever sired. As a moth eats
cloth, so envy eats a man. It is the most cruel, destructive passion
of the human heart.

Self-pity is the sum of all these evils. Usually troubled hearts are
peevish, self-willed, self-pitying hearts. The spirit of Christ is
humility, not pride; faith, not unbelief; contentment, not
covetousness; peace, not envy; self-denial, not self-pity. If you
would be free of heart trouble, believe Christ and walk in the
spirit of Christ.

'Walking in the fear of the Lord'

Read Proverbs 1:7-31

Believers are men and women who walk in the fear of the Lord. God's people do not have a slavish dread of God. We are not afraid to speak to him and about him. We are not afraid that he will become angry with us, disinherit us, or punish us for sin. Faith in Christ removes that kind of terrifying fear. Yet the believer does not think, talk about, or speak to God carelessly, flippantly, without reverence for his infinite, glorious, righteous being. A true heart knowledge of the triune God will produce godly fear in a man's heart.

The fear of the Lord is simply reverence for him. It is much like the reverence a son has for his father, involving both love and respect. God has won the admiration of his children's hearts, causing us to reverence him. We reverence his name, his being, his Word and his works. All that God is, all that has to do with him, all that he says and all that he does is held in high esteem by those who know him.

This fear of the Lord shows itself in many ways. To fear God is to hate evil. The man who knows God hates the evil of his own heart and life, hates the evil performed by others and hates the evil of false doctrine, which robs God of his glory. Those who fear the Lord are careful not to offend him. We cherish our fellowship with the eternal God, Father, Son and Holy Spirit. And we take care not to grieve and offend him, because we want nothing to hinder the fellowship we enjoy. The heart that fears the Lord withholds nothing from him, no matter how dear and valuable, when he calls for it. To fear the Lord is to worship him. It is to worship God, as he is revealed in Scripture, in our hearts. Such fear of the Lord is progressive. Believers walk in the fear of the Lord. The more a man knows him, the more he fears him. God grant that I may be found 'walking in the fear of the Lord'. Amen.

'One man should die for the people'

Read 2 Corinthians 5:11-21

The heart of the gospel is redemption and the essence of redemption is substitution. The deepest, most profound, most mysterious and most edifying subject in all the Word of God is set forth in these words: 'He hath made him to be sin for us, who knew no sin, that we might be made the righteousness of God in him!' Substitution is the foundation truth of Christianity. This is the rock upon which our hopes are built. This is the only hope of the sinner and the only true joy of all saints.

The most marvellous thing that ever took place upon the earth, the most stupendous thing ever executed by the power of heaven was this: Jesus Christ, God the eternal Son, was made sin for us, that we might be made the righteousness of God in him!

These two things, Christ being made sin and us being made righteousness, could only be accomplished by substitution. There was no possible way for the Lord of glory to be made sin, except by imputation. And there is no way by which any man can be made righteousness, except by imputation. It is a legal matter. At Calvary Christ became sin for us, and we became righteousness in him. As surely as Christ was made sin, all of those for whom he died are made righteous.

Of this we may be sure: for that multitude of sinners for whom Jesus died there is no possibility of condemnation! 'There is therefore now no condemnation to them which are in Christ Jesus ... For what the law could not do, in that it was weak through the flesh, God sending his own Son in the likeness of sinful flesh, and for sin, condemned sin in the flesh.'

Child of God, we can never understand the depths of wisdom and grace revealed in the substitutionary death of Christ. But we who have seen him dying in our stead should never cease to worship, adore, love and trust our merciful Redeemer.

'Ye cannot do the things that ye would'

Read Psalm 73:1-28

There is a terrible, unceasing struggle in my soul. Being born again by almighty grace, I have a new heart and a new will, a new, heaven-bent nature created in me by the Spirit of God. I long for and seek after righteousness. Above anything in the world, I want to be perfectly free of sin and conformed to the image of the Lord Jesus Christ. This is the desire of every saved sinner. But I cannot do the things I would. I find a law in my members that, when I would do good, evil is present with me. I find in my soul iniquity, transgression and sin far more hideous and ignominious than the profane acts of ungodly men. Lying, theft, drunkenness, adultery and murder are only isolated acts of evil. But my sin is ever before me! I want to pray, but there is too much selfish lust in my prayers to call them prayers. I want to worship God in the Spirit, but there is too much pride in my worship to call it worship. I want to be completely free of all earthly care, trusting God in all things, but there is too much unbelief and selfish resentment towards God's providence to call my faith faith or my submission submission. I want to love God with all my heart, soul, mind and strength, and my neighbour as myself, but there is too much concern for self and love for self to call my love love.

Like all believers in this world, I am a man with two natures, two principles, warring against one another continually; and those two natures are the flesh and the Spirit. The flesh is evil, only evil, and ever seeks evil. The Spirit is righteous, only righteous, and ever seeks righteousness.

This constant warfare between the flesh and the Spirit makes me do three things: (1) I denounce all personal righteousness, for I have none, and confess my sin. (2) I trust Christ alone for all my righteousness before God. And (3) I live in hope of that day when I shall drop this robe of flesh and be like my Saviour, holy, blameless and unreproveable before God.

'Blessed is the man whom thou choosest'

Read Ephesians 1:3-14

Divine election is a constant theme of thanksgiving and praise throughout the Word of God. The blessedness of being one of God's elect fills every believer's heart with praise to God. Those who were chosen by God in eternal love and given to Christ as his sheep in the covenant of grace have been redeemed by the Saviour's precious blood (John 10:11,14,15,26). Divine providence rules all things, sovereignly working all things together for the good of God's elect (Rom. 8:28-30). The Lord Jesus Christ prays and makes intercession for God's elect (John 17:9,20). Satan has no power over the souls and eternal destiny of God's elect, who are kept and preserved by the power of God (Luke 22:31-32; 1 Peter 1:5). Sin will never be charged to God's elect, because all God's elect have been perfectly justified by his grace through the blood of Christ (Rom. 3:24; 4:8). All of God's elect, without exception, will be glorified, presented before the presence of God himself, 'holy and without blame', being perfectly righteous through the imputation of Christ's righteousness to them (Eph. 1:4). In the last day, every one of God's elect will enter into and possess that kingdom prepared for them before the world began, as 'heirs of God and joint-heirs with Christ' (Rom. 8:17). Yes, God's elect people will possess that eternal inheritance to which we were eternally predestinated (Eph. 1:11). When David thought on all these things his heart broke out in praise to God for his eternal, electing love: **'Blessed is the man whom thou choosest!'**

If you are one of God's elect all these blessings, and many more, are yours. If you are not among God's elect none of these blessings will ever be yours. All the blessings of grace flow down to men from the throne of God through the elective purpose of God (Eph. 1:3-6). If you believe on the Lord Jesus Christ, if you bow to Christ as your Lord in faith, trusting his blood and righteousness, you are one of God's elect. If you believe not, you are not elect (John 10:26).

'Who is he that condemneth?'

Read Romans 8:28-39

For some the answer to that question is not hard to find: you are condemned already! It is commonly thought that man is on a sort of spiritual probation. But such is not the case. Hear the Word of God: 'He that believeth not is condemned already, because he hath not believed on the name of the only begotten Son of God ... He that believeth not ... shall not see life; but the wrath of God abideth on him' (John 3:18,36). You are condemned already because of your sin. You must be pardoned, or for ever die! Awake now and flee to Christ. He alone can pardon you and free you from condemnation.

There is no possibility of condemnation for those who are in Christ. There are many who would condemn the true believer if they could. God's people often meet with their enemies in this world and those wicked men would delight to sentence us to condemnation. Satan, that arch-enemy of our souls, would condemn us if it were in his power. Sometimes our own consciences condemn us. But, blessed be God, 'If our heart condemn us, God is greater than our heart, and knoweth all things!'

God alone has the power to condemn us, but he will not. He has declared that he will never condemn any who trust in his Son. He who has the power of condemnation is our Saviour. He knows that we are so perfectly justified that we cannot be condemned.

We raise the bold challenge: 'Who is he that condemneth?' With confident joy we reply, 'No one can condemn us!' With unshaken faith we declare, 'There is therefore now no condemnation to them which are in Christ Jesus.' Does anyone ask, 'What is the grounds of this confidence?' Paul states it plainly: 'It is Christ that died, yea rather, that is risen again, who is even at the right hand of the Father who also maketh intercession for us.' Christ died as our Substitute; we cannot die. Christ has risen for our justification; we are justified. Christ is seated at the right hand of God; the work of our redemption is finished and accepted. Christ makes intercession for us; he must prevail; we must be saved.

'Understandest thou what thou readest?'

Read Acts 8:26-39

It is good to read the Bible regularly, learn the facts of Bible history, memorize as much of the Bible as you can and study the blessed doctrines of the Bible. But it is quite possible to do all of these things and yet gain no spiritual benefit from the Word of God. The Word of God will be of benefit to our souls only to the degree that we understand it. Such understanding in the Scriptures is, and can only be gained, by the gracious instruction of the Holy Spirit (1 Cor. 2:11-16).

A man has understanding in the Scriptures to the degree that *he sees Christ in everything and sees everything in Christ*. Philip gave the eunuch understanding in the Scriptures when he 'preached unto him Jesus'. He preached Christ, nothing but Christ, and that gave the eunuch understanding. In the Word of God, Christ alone is pre-eminent. The Bible is a book about the person and work of the Lord Jesus Christ. Christ is the whole counsel of God, and the whole counsel of God is Christ (Acts 20:26-27; 1 Cor. 2:2; 9:16).

I have understanding in the Scriptures to the degree that *my understanding creates in me a humble, submissive, obedient faith in Christ*. This eunuch showed his understanding in the Word by his willing surrender to believer's baptism, the ordinance of Christ.

We have understanding in the Word of God to the degree that *our understanding causes us to rejoice in Christ*. Once this man understood the Scriptures, 'He went on his way rejoicing.' Spurgeon said, 'The faith of the Scriptures leads joy by the hand, and chases away despair.'

I have understanding in the Scriptures to the degree that *my understanding causes me to seek the salvation of others*. This eunuch carried the gospel with him back to Africa. Once a man learns the gospel, he has got to tell it to others.

And I have understanding in the Scriptures to the degree that *I have a message for all people at all times*. I have a message of salvation, life, comfort, peace and joy to all people, in every circumstance of life. My message to you is the message I have received – Christ crucified.

'Gifts of the Holy Ghost'

Read 1 Corinthians 12:29-13:13

There is much talk today about the miraculous gifts of the Holy Spirit. Many claim to possess these gifts. And some of God's people are confused about them. I want to answer briefly some questions you might have about the gifts of the Spirit.

What miraculous gifts did the apostles possess by the Holy Spirit? As you read through the book of Acts you will see that the apostles had the ability to speak in tongues. (They could preach the gospel to men in foreign languages which they never learned.) The apostles cast out demons. They healed the sick. They did not try to heal the sick; they did it. Every time an apostle of Christ commanded a man to be healed, that man was immediately healed, no matter what his disease. Neither the poison of serpents nor deadly mixtures could harm them, as Paul demonstrated to the astonishment of men on the island of Melita. And they raised the dead to life. All of the apostles possessed all of these gifts. And they all exercised them with absolute efficacy. I defy anyone to find such a man today.

Why were the gifts given? These gifts were bestowed upon the apostles to prove and confirm them before men as the inspired messengers of the enthroned Messiah (Joel 2:28-32; Matt. 11:2-5; Acts 2:14-36; Heb. 2:3-4).

Is there any place for these gifts in the church of Christ today? No, these miraculous apostolic gifts ceased with the apostolic age. In Acts 8:5-18 we read of the apostles coming to Samaria to communicate the gift of the Holy Spirit to the believers there. Philip, though he possessed those gifts, could not communicate them, because Philip was not an apostle. If the gifts could only be communicated by an apostle, they must have ceased when the last of the apostles died. There is no need for such gifts today. We have the complete inspired revelation of God in Holy Scripture (2 Peter 1:9-21). Since there are no forthcoming revelations from God, there is no need for miraculous signs to confirm such revelations. The Word of God is complete, final and sufficient.

'We know him'

Read Romans 10:11-17; Jeremiah 9:23-24

So long as men are ignorant of the Lord Jesus Christ they cannot be saved. It is not enough that men and women be sincere. They must know Christ as he is revealed in Holy Scripture, or they will perish in unbelief. Our Lord himself declares, 'This is life eternal, that they might know thee the only true God, and Jesus Christ, whom thou hast sent' (John 17:3). In order to have true saving faith in Christ a man must have a true gospel knowledge of Christ. Gospel knowledge is essential to saving faith (Rom. 10:9-17).

True faith knows, acknowledges and trusts the Lord Jesus Christ in *the supreme dignity of his person*. Our Lord Jesus Christ is the infinite, incomprehensible, eternal God, who is moved by nothing and touched by nothing. He is also God incarnate, God in our nature, bone of our bone and flesh of our flesh, the man who is touched with the feeling of our infirmities, because he was tempted in all points like as we are, yet without sin.

Faith knows, embraces and trusts Christ, receiving *the salvation done by his performance*. Faith does not, in any way, accomplish salvation. Our salvation was accomplished entirely by the work of our Lord Jesus Christ. Faith, trusting Christ, simply receives what he has done as our Substitute. We receive his righteousness, the righteousness which he performed for us, by faith. We receive redemption and the forgiveness of sins, that which he purchased by his precious blood, by faith.

Saving faith knows Christ as Lord and bows to him in *the sovereign dominion of his position*. Faith submits to the sovereign rule of the sovereign Christ, willingly. Faith does not rebel against sovereignty; it rejoices in it.

True faith knows Christ and rests in *the sure deliverance of his power*. He cannot fail. He is able to save to the uttermost all who come to God by him. All power is in the hands of him who is our Saviour. Therefore our hearts safely trust him.

'It pleased God'

Read Romans 9:11-26

Though to many Paul's conversion, his experience of grace, might seem extraordinary, he tells us that the method of God's grace with him was a pattern, revealing the method of God's grace with all his elect (1 Tim. 1:16). The apostle also tells us plainly what the order and method of God's grace is: **'When it pleased God, who separated me from my mother's womb, and called me by his grace, to reveal his Son in me, that I might preach him among the heathen; immediately I conferred not with flesh and blood'** (Gal. 1:15-16). This is the way God saves sinners. The order of grace never changes. The method of grace never varies.

Salvation begins in the will and pleasure of God: **'When it pleased God'.** The source of saving grace is the will of God. The cause of salvation is not the will of man, but the will of God (Rom. 9:11-18). Having willed to save some of Adam's fallen race, God separated his own elect from the rest of mankind: **'Who separated me from my mother's womb.'** This act of *separation* is God's unconditional election of his people in Christ, before the foundation of the world (2 Thess. 2:13; 2 Tim. 1:9). The phrase **'from my mother's womb'** implies the fact that this election took place before we had done anything good or bad. It is teaching God's sovereignty in election (Jer. 1:4-5). Then, at the time appointed, God calls all of his elect by effectual and irresistible grace: **'And called me by his grace'.** Those who were sanctified in the womb of election are given life by *the call of the Spirit*. This call of the Spirit is always effectual because, in calling his elect to life and faith, God graciously reveals his Son, the Lord Jesus Christ, in his elect: **'To reveal his Son in me'.** Salvation comes when *Christ is revealed*. As the result of this revelation of Christ in the heart, God makes his elect people willingly obedient servants to his Son. God's purpose was that Paul should *willingly serve him*, and serve him he did. Good works will never cause God to be gracious; but God's grace always causes his people to walk willingly in good works.

'The judgement seat of Christ'

Read 2 Corinthians 5:1-11

Though today God is longsuffering with men and is giving the fallen sons of Adam space for repentance, there is a day of judgement and righteous retribution coming (Rev. 20:11-14). God does not delay his judgement because he lacks the will or the power to judge men, but because he has an elect people whom he has determined to save. As soon as he has saved the last of his elect, judgement will come (2 Peter 3:8-15).

According to the revelation of Holy Scripture, the Judge of all men in that great day will be the man, Christ Jesus (Matt. 13:41-43; 25:31-32; John 5:22-29; Acts 10:42; 17:30-31; Rom. 14:9-12; 2 Cor. 5:10). The Judge of the world in that last great day will be the Son of man who is the Son of God. This judgement of men by Christ will be both righteous and impartial. All men will receive the exact penalty or reward of strict justice. The wicked will be judged in strict righteousness according to their works and receive in a body the just reward of their evil deeds. There will be degrees of punishment in hell, because there are degrees of wickedness. Those who sin against greater light will receive greater condemnation (Matt. 11:20-24). The righteous will also be judged in strict righteousness according to their works and receive in body the just reward of their righteous deeds. There will be no degrees of reward for the righteous, because there are no degrees of righteousness. All righteous men are perfect men. These are God's elect, redeemed, justified and sanctified by Christ. There is no evil recorded against them because the righteous obedience of Christ to the law is imputed to them (Rom. 5:19). That same law and justice that demand the eternal punishment of every unbeliever also demand the eternal bliss and glory of every believer, whose names are written in the book of life, because in Christ, by his righteousness and shed blood, every believer is worthy of heaven's eternal inheritance.

'My sin is ever before me'

Read Psalm 32:1-11

Three words are used throughout the Bible to describe the moral depravity of our race. God's judgement falls upon men because of iniquity, transgression and sin.

Iniquity is the perverseness of my righteousness. It is missing the mark, falling short of that which is required by the law of God. How far short do we fall? 'We are all as an unclean thing, and all our righteousnesses are as filthy rags' (Isa. 64:6). My best thoughts, best ambitions, best desires and best deeds are so polluted with sin that in the sight of God they are as vile and obnoxious as discarded menstruous cloths.

Transgression is the perverseness of my evil works. It is the contemptuous disregard of God's law, walking contrary to the law and violating the law by wilful rebellion. Every thought, word and deed that is contrary to the law of God is transgression. It is the breaking of God's law.

Sin is the perverseness of my being. This is what I am. This is the source of all transgression and iniquity. My heart by nature is a foul, polluted cesspool in which every manner of evil imaginable grows (Matt. 15:19). It is a garrison of enmity against God (Rom. 8:7). The evil I do is terrible; but the evil that I am is worse by far. I hate what I do; but I hate what I am more.

If we would obtain mercy from God, *we must confess our sin* (Prov. 28:13; 1 John 1:9). This is more than merely saying, with Judas, 'I have sinned.' It is a heartfelt acknowledgement of our guilt and depravity. We must acknowledge the evil of our righteousness, the evil of our wickedness and the evil of our nature, so that we take sides with God against ourselves (Ps. 51:1-5).

I rejoice to know and to declare to you that *through the merits of Christ's righteousness and shed blood God is faithful and just to forgive iniquity, transgression and sin* (Exod. 34:6-7; 1 John 1:9). This is the good news and glad tidings of the gospel. If we acknowledge and confess our sin God will forgive our sin. The blood of Jesus Christ, the Son of God, cleanses us from all sin.

'The faith of God's elect'

Read Philippians 3:1-14

Almost all men have faith of one kind or another and there are many who profess faith in Christ. But it is evident that the faith produced by modern-day evangelism is not true saving faith, because it does not produce the same characteristics as that faith taught and exemplified in the Word of God. That faith which is produced by the power and grace of God the Holy Spirit through the preaching of the gospel will always be distinguished from false faith by at least five things.

1. *True faith produces a heart truly broken before God over sin* (Ps. 51:1-5, 17). Whenever a man sees himself in the light of God's glory shining upon him through the cross of Christ, he will cry out with the publican, 'God be merciful to me a sinner!' This is where repentance begins. Christ revealed in the heart breaks the heart (Zech. 12:10).

2. *True faith causes the heart to bow willingly to Christ's absolute sovereignty and lordship in all things* (Luke 14:25-33). The believer's submission to Christ is far from perfect; but it is a sincere, willing surrender of the heart to Christ. In our inmost being we voluntarily commit ourselves and all things to the disposal of our gracious Sovereign.

3. *Truth faith looks to Christ alone for all things.* True faith trusts Christ alone. Faith has two hands. With one hand she strips away all the filthy rags of her own righteousness; and with the other she puts on the righteousness of Christ. Faith sees 'Jesus only'. Faith wraps itself up in Christ (1 Cor. 1:30).

4. *True faith will persevere and continue to believe regardless of circumstances* (Heb. 11:13). False faith fluctuates. True faith is steady, continual and relentless. The rougher the storm, the firmer faith clings to Christ. True faith never gives up.

5. *True faith produces a heart of sincere love for the people of God* (1 John 4:8; 5:1). False faith strives to produce love and pretends to love. But love is natural to true faith. Love for the brethren flows as naturally from the believing heart as water flows from the spring.

'I have given you an example'

Read John 13:1-17, 31-35

Believer, never allow anyone to bring you into bondage again.
Having been redeemed by the blood of Christ, and having your
conscience purged .from the guilt of sin by the application of
Christ's blood to your heart, you are entirely, completely free
from the law. You owed the law of God a life of perfect
righteousness. Do you trust Christ? He is the 'the Lord our
Righteousness'. By his obedience to God as your Representative,
Christ did what you could never do. He magnified the law and
made it honourable in his life. That righteous life God imputes to
you. You are perfectly righteous in Christ. You also owed the law
death. Had you died, your death must have been eternal, because
you could never satisfy the law's infinite justice. But Christ, the
God-man, died as your Substitute, bearing your sin and, by his
one sacrifice for sin, he satisfied the very justice of God. So far as
God's law is concerned, you are a dead man. The law has no claim
upon you. You died in Christ. 'There is therefore now no
condemnation to them that are in Christ Jesus!' It would be as
foolish for you to try to obey the law for yourself, as it would for
you to try to atone for your own sins (Rom. 6:14; 7:1-4; 10:4; Gal.
3:24-26; 5:1-4; Col. 2:14-16).

Someone will come along and try to trick you. He will say,
'Well, if you do not live by the law of Moses, you're an
antinomian. You believe every man should do that which is right
in his own eyes.' If you wish to be polite to the legalist (I do not
suggest that you should be), you may reply, 'No my friend, we
have a law to live by. Our Lord commanded us to love one
another. That is our law.' Then the poor bondman will argue,
'But love is a nebulous law. You still must live by the rule of the
Ten Commandments.' If your patience is not worn out, you
might want to answer that objection too: 'Love is not nebulous at
all. We have Christ as our example. He has shown us exactly how
to love. Christ is the pattern we copy and the example we follow. I
am quite sure that I am safe following my Lord.'

'How can I please and honour God?'

Read 1 John 3:1-5, 16-24

Every believer is concerned about this question. I do not think it is beyond reason or revelation to say that this is the heart prayer and desire of every child of God. While we live in this world, we want to please and honour the God of all grace. Is there any clear, biblical answer to this question: 'How can I please and honour God?'

Many tell us that in order to please God we must physically separate ourselves from the world. Every believer understands that God's children are to be separate and distinct from the unbelieving world. We live by principles, motives and desires that the world can never comprehend. But if all it takes to please God is to alter our dress code, change our outward habits and live in seclusion from the world then anyone can please him. It takes only self-discipline, not grace. Moralists and monks have been doing these things for centuries.

Others tell us that to honour God we must live by the law of God. It is true, if anyone could live by the law, God would be pleased with him, for that man would live in sinlessness and righteousness. He would be a perfect man. But God can never be pleased with a mere attempt to live by the law, no matter how sincere that man may be who tries to do so.

Some tell us that the way to please and honour God is to live a holy life. That would be a great thing. But who can do it? Of course, everyone has his own standards of holiness. Some even think they really do live in holiness. But the only true standard of holiness is God himself. When holiness is understood, we see the utter futility of trying to perform holiness for ourselves.

We do not need to search for an answer to this question: 'How can I please and honour God?' We need not be confused by the confused opinions of men. The Lord has not left us in darkness. We please God and honour God by faith. All who believe Christ, trusting his righteousness, his blood, his providence, his grace and his intercession please and honour God, for God is pleased with his Son.

'I give unto them eternal life'

Read Ephesians 1:15-23

Eternal life is the gift of God's grace in Christ. It comes to men freely, as a matter of pure grace. Man does not have eternal life by nature. Eternal life does not evolve from man's sinful heart by some mysterious process of 'spiritual evolution'. It is given to men. It is performed in the heart by the power of God's sovereign grace. It is in no way a matter of debt or reward. 'The gift of God is eternal life.' There was nothing in our hearts or conduct which caused God to bestow eternal life upon us (Jer. 31:3; Eph. 2:1-4). And there is nothing in the believer's heart or conduct which can cause God to take away the gift of eternal life (Isa. 54:10). It is contrary to the nature of God to take away his gifts so freely bestowed upon his people in Christ (Rom. 11:29). This gift of eternal life, so freely given, is an irreversible gift. Acknowledge that eternal life is entirely the gift of God, in no way earned by or dependent upon the goodness of man, and it must be concluded that those to whom eternal life is given are eternally secure in Christ (Eccles. 3:14).

Eternal life must, of necessity, be eternal. Any child, whose reason is not perverted with human religion, readily sees that eternal life cannot be temporary. It cannot come to an end. If I have received from God the gift of eternal life, it is not possible for me, by any act or upon any grounds, to lose it and perish.

The believer's life must be eternal, because it is a life in union with the Lord Jesus Christ. We who believe are so really and truly joined to Christ that we cannot possibly perish unless he also perishes. Our union with Christ is a vital life union, immutable and indestructible. We are married to Christ, bone of his bone and flesh of his flesh (Eph. 5:30). We are members of his body, the church (Eph. 1:23). Can you imagine Christ with a maimed body? Perish the thought! Yet his body would not be complete if so much as one member of his body were lost. All who are in Christ have eternal life; and they are all eternally secure in him.

A word about ministering to your children

Read Psalm 127:1-5

All believing parents are concerned about the souls of their children. We want to see them converted, saved by the grace of God, united to Christ in eternal life. But we must be careful, especially careful with young children, not to push them into a profession of faith before their hearts are renewed by the grace of God.

We dare not set any limitations upon the grace of God. God saves his elect when he will. But the gospel of Christ is not addressed to children and youths who are incapable of making moral, reasonable, responsible decisions for themselves. The gospel is addressed to mature men and women who are capable of understanding their moral responsibility before God. The age of such maturity varies with individuals. But I think that a child who still requires the direction of his parents to determine what he should eat, where he should go, what he should wear and what he can do is incapable of understanding his moral responsibility before God.

Free-willism, easy believism and decisionism are as deadly to children as to adults. Every pastor who honestly deals with the souls of men knows that the vast majority of children who make professions of faith prove to be false. Children are especially susceptible to emotional fears of hell and the pressure to please parents, preachers and teachers. If you try, you can get your children to make a profession of faith. Do not be guilty of such treason to their souls. Wait on God to do his work of grace.

How should we minister to our children? Teach them the gospel. No one can be saved apart from a heart knowledge of gospel truth. Pray for them. Commit your children to the hands of God. Seek his grace for them. Set before them an example of faith in Christ and commitment to the gospel. As our children grow to maturity, nothing will so much influence them as the example we set before them. Wait for God to be gracious. If our sons and daughters are chosen of God and redeemed by Christ they will be born again by the Holy Spirit, at God's appointed time.

'Saul assayed to join himself to the disciples'

Read Ephesians 4:1-16

Saul had been converted by the grace of God on the Damascus Road. He had publicly confessed faith in Christ at Damascus, both by personal testimony and by public baptism. Then he came to Jerusalem and '**he assayed to join himself to the disciples**'. That is to say, he applied for membership in the church at Jerusalem. The despised church of God, which Saul once hated above all people upon the earth, he now loved above all people. No sooner did he return to Jerusalem than he found the place where God's people met in the name of Christ and publicly identified himself with them by uniting with the congregation there

Saul joined the church *voluntarily*. He was not recruited in a 'church membership drive'. No one put any pressure on him, or even asked him, to join the church. Being a believer, Saul wanted to be numbered with God's people. He considered it a privilege and an honour. 'To be joined to a church is to become an open subject of Christ's kingdom, a citizen of the heavenly Jerusalem, one of the family of God, and a member of the body of Christ visibly' (John Gill).

Saul was fully *qualified* to unite with the church at Jerusalem. It is true, he had been a blasphemer and a persecutor, and his former reputation was well known. But God had forgiven him, cleansed him in the blood of Christ and received him. Therefore he was accepted by the church as a brother, beloved in Christ. He professed faith in the Lord Jesus Christ and was baptized as a believer. Nothing more was required to qualify him for membership in the church, and nothing less could be accepted. Church membership is for baptized (immersed) believers only.

By uniting with the local assembly at Jerusalem, Saul publicly demonstrated his *commitment* to those people, to their Lord and to the gospel they were commissioned of God to preach. Uniting publicly with a local assembly, the believer says, 'My heart is joined to you in Christ by the grace of God.' If you are a believer, it is both your privilege and your responsibility to confess Christ by baptism and unite with his people.

'Comfort ye, comfort ye my people, saith your God'

Read Isaiah 40:1-11

This is the charge which God gives to all who preach the gospel. The prophets of God are pre-eminently messengers of comfort (Isa. 52:7). We come to men in the name of God and proclaim to all who will receive it a message of blessed comfort in Jesus Christ.

Here is a word of comfort: the great God calls us '**my people**'! All men and women belong to God. He who created us owns us. But there are some people in this world who are especially loved of God and belong to him, as children to a father, as a wife to her husband. God says, of all who are saved by his grace, you are 'my people'. We belong to him by special election, by particular purchase, by gracious regeneration, by his distinguishing call, by the faith which he has given us and by the bond of love which he has created.

It would seem that nothing could be more blessed than this: God says of us, you are 'my people'. Yet, here is something even more blessed and comforting: the eternal, sovereign, triune God says to us, I am '**your God**'! The almighty, infinite, incomprehensible God condescends to be the personal possession of every believing sinner! He is God. I rejoice in that. But he is my God! That gives me comfort. Child of God, try to get a heart grip on this truth: God almighty is your God!

And our great God desires and delights in the comfort of his people! Just as a father finds happiness in the comfort of his children, our Father delights in our comfort. He sent his Son, the Lord Jesus Christ, into the world to comfort mourning sinners (Isa. 61:1-3; Luke 4:17-21). The primary work of the Holy Spirit in this world is that of a Comforter (John 14:16; 16:17). Our heavenly Father sovereignly arranges all the affairs of providence for the spiritual, eternal comfort of his people. Let every believer grasp this blessed truth: our great God delights in our comfort (John 14:1-3).

'Iniquity is pardoned'

Read Psalm 130:1-8

We are slow to receive it, and preachers are often afraid to proclaim it, but there is blessed comfort for sinners in the gospel. God commands his servants twice to proclaim that comfort. He says, emphatically, 'Comfort ye, comfort ye my people, saith your God.' And he tells us plainly that the only source of comfort for sinners is the gospel of effectually accomplished redemption. **'Speak ye comfortably to Jerusalem** [the people whom he has chosen], **and cry unto her, that her warfare is accomplished, that her iniquity is pardoned: for she hath received of the Lord's hand double for all her sins'** (Isa. 40:1-2). If you trust Christ, if you cast all your hope upon his righteousness and shed blood, if you are a guilty, helpless sinner whose only hope is an all-sufficient Substitute, this gospel is for you.

Your warfare is accomplished. By the sacrifice of his own beloved Son, God has ended his controversy with you. God reconciled his people to himself, satisfying his law and justice in the life and death of Christ as the sinner's Substitute (2 Cor. 5:17-21). He sends his Spirit, applying the blood of Christ to the hearts of men by the gospel, creating faith and reconciling our hearts to him by irresistible grace and power (Col. 1:21). Peace was made by the blood of Christ. Peace is received and enjoyed by faith in that blood.

Your iniquity is pardoned. God has fully put away the sins of all his people by the sacrifice of his Son (Heb. 9:12). God will never hold any believing sinner accountable for sin. He held his Son accountable for us, and punished our sins to the full satisfaction of his justice in his Son.

You have received of the Lord's hand double for all your sins. The justice of God which demanded your eternal ruin has been satisfied by the blood of Christ so that in Christ you are not only pardoned but also made perfectly righteous by divine imputation. Rather than being an enemy of God, subject to and deserving his wrath, grace has made you an heir of God, fully deserving of all his benefits in Christ.

'Who maketh thee to differ?'

Read Matthew 11:20-30

The whole human race is divided by God into two categories: those who are his people and those who are not his people; those who are elect and those who are reprobate; sheep and goats. This distinction between men was made by God in eternity and it is an irreversible distinction. Sheep will never become goats, and goats will never become sheep. The elect of God will never become reprobates and reprobates will never become the elect of God. Between the two there is a great gulf fixed. If any of Adam's fallen race is so infinitely blessed of God as to be numbered among God's people, his elect, his sheep, surely a soul to whom God has been so gracious will gladly acknowledge that the only thing distinguishing between him and those who are damned is the distinguishing grace of God (1 Cor. 4:7). 'Not unto us, O Lord, not unto us, but unto thy name give glory, for thy mercy, and for thy truth's sake,' is the cry of every saved sinner. All who are saved by grace fully recognize, and rejoice in the fact, that grace alone has distinguished them from the rest of Adam's fallen race.

We who believe belong to God, we are Christ's sheep by a distinguishing *election*. We became the Lord's sheep by his own eternal choice. In the covenant of grace, God branded us as his sheep, set a hedge about us and secured our eternal salvation in Christ (John 10:16). The Lord says of his sheep, 'I know them' (John 10:27). And his knowledge of his sheep is that peculiar knowledge of his own elective purpose and omniscient love. We are his, too, by a distinguishing *purchase*. Christ laid down his life for his sheep, in the place of his sheep, in our stead. Christ died as a Substitute for his sheep, to redeem them particularly. He died instead of his sheep dying. Because he died for us, we shall not die (John 10:11, 15). And we belong to him by a distinguishing *call*. 'He calls his own sheep by name, and leadeth them out.' His gracious call is personal, particular and powerful. When he calls, his sheep follow. This call of grace always results in eternal life.

How should the people of God treat those men who preach the gospel to them?

Read Hebrews 13:7-19

The tendency among men is either to treat God's servants with contempt, as the Judaizers at Galatia did Paul (Gal. 4:16), or regard them with an adoring, worshipful reverence, as Cornelius did Peter (Acts 10:25). Both of these attitudes are wrong. The faithful gospel preacher is only a man; therefore he must not be placed on a pedestal to be worshipped and followed blindly. But he is God's man, God's messenger to men; therefore he must not be despised, ignored and treated with contempt. Paul tells us plainly how the people of God should treat faithful preachers (pastors, evangelists, missionaries).

A faithful pastor is one who labours among God's people. He is not a lazy sluggard, but a diligent labourer. His time, energy and attention are consumed by the ministry of the gospel. He studies, prays and preaches, watching over the souls of God's elect as one who must give account. He has little time for anything other than the work of the gospel. Such a man, who spends his life serving the interest of men's souls, should be highly honoured by those for whom he labours (2 Thess. 3:1, Heb. 13:7, 17; 1 Cor. 9:9-14).

'**Know them which labour among you**.' God's people should make it their business to become personally, even intimately, acquainted with faithful gospel preachers, especially their own pastor. Get to know the man who ministers to you. Try to know what his personal needs are, so that you can supply those needs. Try to find a way to assist him and relieve him of unnecessary burdens, so that he may more fully give himself to the work of the gospel. '**Esteem them very highly in love for their work's sake**.' Every faithful gospel preacher deserves and should have the high esteem and sincere love of God's people, because of the work which he performs. He is God's spokesman and representative to you, and he should be treated as such. Those churches which develop such an attitude towards the servants of God will in great measure 'be at peace among themselves'.

'Be not entangled again with the yoke of bondage'

Read Colossians 2:6-23

Legalism is natural to man. And even among those who know better, there is ever a tendency to return to the spirit of legalistic religion. Let us beware of the evils of legalism and resist every tendency of the flesh to return to law religion.

1. The spirit of legalism causes us to seek assurance on the basis of our own works. Assurance that is based on works is false assurance. The believer's assurance is in the person and work of Christ alone. Trusting him, we have assurance.

2. The spirit of legalism causes us to neglect our duties and responsibilities because of our personal feelings of inadequacy and insufficiency. Many refuse to receive the Lord's Supper, as he has commanded us, because they feel unworthy. Many refuse to exercise gifts God has given them to preach, teach, lead the congregation in prayer, or sing, because they do not feel worthy. Who is worthy of such things? No man is in himself. But our worthiness and sufficiency are in Christ.

3. The spirit of legalism causes men to motivate God's people with threats of punishment and promises of reward. We see people beginning to neglect church attendance, fall off in their giving and neglecting other matters of personal responsibility, so we begin to scold them and warn them that they are in danger of being lost. Then they do those things they had previously neglected, not because they love Christ, but out of a sense of duty to prove they are saved. Is this not pure legalism?

4. The spirit of legalism causes us to set up rules of life for God's people which God has not given in his Word. It is the height of self-righteousness and pride for men and churches to add to the Word of God rules of life, 'acceptable Christian behaviour', for men and women who belong to God.

5. The spirit of legalism causes us to set ourselves up as judges of God's saints. Legalism produces such monstrous pride in men that they judge God's people by the inch-long yardstick of their own supposed 'holiness'. May God save us from this spirit of legalism.

'God is no respecter of persons'

Read Colossians 3:1-14

These words do not mean, as many imagine, that God treats all men alike in providence and grace. He does not. 'God's grace is his own; and he dispenses it according to his own sovereign will and pleasure' (Charles Simeon). God sovereignly distinguishes men from one another (1 Cor. 4:7), in election (2 Thess. 2:13), in redemption (John 10:11, 15, 26), in providence (Rom. 8:28) and in his saving grace (2 Tim. 1:9). The illustrations of God's distinguishing grace in the Scriptures are numerous. The Lord accepted Abel but not Cain. He chose Isaac and rejected Ishmael. God loved Jacob and hated Esau. God gives light and withholds light, gives grace and withholds grace entirely according to his own sovereign will, without any regard to man's person (Matt. 11:20-26).

The text simply means that God has no regard for those things that distinguish men from one another in this world: wealth or poverty, morality or immorality, learning or ignorance, race or face. God does not prefer any man or despise any man because of his earthly condition. God's grace is entirely free and sovereign. He says, 'I will have mercy on whom I will have mercy, and I will have compassion on whom I will have compassion. So then it is not of him that willeth, nor of him that runneth, but of God that showeth mercy... and whom he will he hardeneth' (Rom. 9:15-18). No earthly condition, hereditary descent, outward circumstance or religious heritage will secure God's saving grace, or even make a man a likely candidate for salvation. And none of these things will keep God from saving any man, or make him less likely to be saved than others.

'God is no respecter of persons,' and neither should we be. There is no place in the church of God for the honouring of human flesh. We court none and we despise none. We receive as brethren all who worship our God. All are to be treated with equal love, care and esteem. Rich and poor, black and white, male and female — are all equals in Christ.

'My sheep'

Read John 10:1-18

With these two simple words our Lord distinguishes his people from all the rest of mankind. Let men deny it as they will, and let them denounce me for preaching it if that gives them pleasure, but the God of the Bible does distinguish between men. He chooses some and passes by others. He redeems some and leaves others under the curse of the law. He calls some and rejects others. He saves some and damns others. Grace is God's prerogative. He has mercy on whom he will have mercy.

Our Lord makes this very plain. He said to the unbelieving Jews, who refused to believe him, 'Ye are not of my sheep.' And he told them plainly that God had not given them the gift of faith, because they were not numbered among his sheep. 'Ye believe not, because ye are not of my sheep.' The gift of faith, like all other gifts of grace, is reserved for the Lord's sheep, God's chosen, covenant people (Eph. 1:3-6).

If you are a believer, one of that great multitude to whom God has given faith in Christ, it is because you are one of his sheep, elect and precious to the Lord. God our Saviour says of you, you are 'my sheep'. Truly, his grace is 'amazing grace'. In everlasting love, by sovereign, deliberate choice, the Son of God has distinguished you from all other people and made you to be his sheep, his own peculiar possession!

The Lord Jesus Christ has special grace reserved for his sheep. He does many things for his sheep, which he does not do for other men. He agreed in the covenant of grace to save his sheep (John 10:16). He laid down his life in the place of his sheep (John 10:11,15). Our Lord prays for his sheep (John 17:9-11, 15, 20). The Son of God calls his sheep to himself (John 10:3). The Good Shepherd knows his sheep, gives eternal life to his sheep, protects his sheep, provides for his sheep, preserves his sheep and holds his sheep in his almighty hand (John 10:27-30). What a privilege it is for a believing sinner to look upon the incarnate God and say, 'The Lord is my Shepherd,' and to hear him say, 'My sheep'!

'They shall see his face.'

Read Revelation 5:1-14

This is the great object of our hope, the great desire of our hearts, the great joy of heaven and the great fulness of our heavenly reward. The very Christ who died in our place at Calvary, fully satisfying the wrath and justice of God for us, will be seen by us.

We shall literally see his face. It is delightfully true that we shall see and enjoy many things in heaven. But that which is now desired, and will then be enjoyed, above all else is the sight of Christ himself. It seems to me that our text also implies a spiritual sight of Christ, which is far sweeter. In the next world we shall have a greater ability to see Christ than we now possess. We shall see him perfectly and know him fully. And our vision of him will be uninterrupted. The paradise of God is a heaven of pure, intense, eternal, perfect, spiritual fellowship with Christ.

In that future estate of glory and bliss we shall have a clear, undimmed vision of Christ, because everything which now hinders our sight of him will be removed. Our many sins, our earthly cares and our sorrows in this world now prevent us from seeing our Lord as we desire. But then there will be nothing between us and our Saviour. In glory there will be nothing in our hearts to rival Christ. We shall love him as he ought to be loved, perfectly. Christ will not only be supreme, he will be all.

Why do we consider this vision of Christ the greatest bliss of heaven? Why do we place such importance upon this one aspect of our heavenly inheritance? The reason is just this: when we see the Lord's face our salvation will be complete. Every evil thing will be completely eradicated from us. When we see his face we shall be conscious of his favour. And when these eyes see his face a complete transformation will take place. 'We shall be like him, for we shall see him as he is.' We shall see things as he sees them. We shall think as he thinks. Our will will be one with his will. Our hearts will be one with his heart. Then, when we see his face, we shall be perfectly satisfied.

'Behold how he loved him!'

Read 1 John 4:7-19

It might well be said of each blood-bought believer, 'Behold how he loved him!' Child of God, Jesus Christ loves you *eternally*. There never was a time when he did not love you. His love for his own is without beginning and without end. It is eternal.

The Son of God loves his own *peculiarly*. I know that God is good and kind to all men. His benevolence reaches to all his creatures. But there is a special, particular, family love which God has for his own elect. He loved Jacob but not Esau.

The Lord loves his people *perseveringly*. Though we sinned in Adam, were born in sin and lived in sin by deliberate choice, his love for us was never broken. Though we sin still, after experiencing his grace, his love does not cease or grow cold. His love is patient, longsuffering, lasting and enduring. God will never cease to love those whom he has always loved. His love is immutable.

Our Saviour loves us *sacrificially*. 'Hereby perceive we the love of God, because he laid down his life for us.' He so loved us that he voluntarily laid down his life in our place! So mighty is his love that, when he knew the price of our souls was his own precious blood, he willingly poured out his life's blood to redeem us!

The Lord Jesus Christ loves all of his people *savingly*. The love of Christ for us is much more than a wishful emotion. He so loves his own that he desires their salvation. And what he desires he has the power and wisdom to accomplish. His love is not helpless, but powerful. He will not stand idly by and allow one soul whom he loves to perish, when he has the power to save that soul!

And the Lord Jesus Christ loves his people *satisfyingly*. His love will be satisfied. He will never lose the object of his love. The love of Christ will in the end conquer the hearts of all his elect. This special, free and sovereign love of Christ's will satisfy all his people. He will give us all that we can need or desire for all of eternity. He will withhold no good thing from his own. In that great day which is yet to come, God's creation will stand back in awe and wonder and say, concerning his redeemed people, 'Behold how he loved them!'

'To appear in the presence of God for us'

Read Psalm 89:19-36

Everywhere in the Scriptures the work of the Lord Jesus Christ is set forth as the work of a Substitute, one who stands in the place of another.

Christ stood as our Substitute *in eternity past*, as our Surety *in the everlasting covenant of grace* (Heb. 7:22). Before we had ever sinned, he stood as our ransom. Before we ever broke God's law, he stood as our righteousness. God the Father gave our souls, along with all the hosts of his elect, into the hands of Christ as the Surety of the covenant before the world began (John 6:39; 2 Tim. 1:9).

Christ stood in our place as our federal Head and Representative *as he lived in this world.* The sinless life of Christ was as necessary for our redemption as his death. In his life, Christ fulfilled the holy law of God, establishing perfect righteousness for us, without which we could never be accepted before God. By his life, he brought in an everlasting righteousness for his people. His name is 'the Lord our Righteousness' (Jer. 23:6).

The Son of God stood in our place *at Calvary*. He died under the penalty of God's law, bearing our sin, our shame, our guilt and the wrath due to us. He died in our place, so that we should never be required to die (Gal. 3:13; 2 Cor. 5:21).

Jesus Christ the righteous stands in our place *today* as our Advocate in heaven (1 John 2:1-2). His five precious wounds, the merits of his righteousness and the merits of his blood effectually secure our present and eternal welfare. God will not charge us with sin and the law cannot require punishment upon us, because Christ, the risen Lord, our Substitute, stands today as our Advocate with the Father.

And the Lord Jesus Christ himself will stand in our place, as our Substitute before God, *in the day of judgement* (Heb. 2:13). When God examines us, he will behold no spot or blemish in us, because his own Son performed in our place perfect righteousness and obedience, and thoroughly washed away our sins. Trusting Christ as our Substitute, we may fully expect to hear him say to us, 'Well done!'

'The Lord our Righteousness'

Read Isaiah 45:20-25

There are some who teach that Christ was the sinner's Substitute only in his sacrificial work upon the cross. We are told that the righteous life of our Lord Jesus Christ has nothing to do with our redemption and salvation, that his righteousness as a man had no merit and efficacy for his people, but that it only made him a suitable sacrifice for sin. This doctrine is contrary to the plain statements of Holy Scripture. Paul tells us that 'As by the offence of one judgement came upon all men to condemnation; even so by the righteousness of one the free gift came upon all men unto justification of life. For as by one man's disobedience many were made sinners, so by the obedience of one shall many be made righteous' (Rom. 5:18-19).

The righteous life of our Lord Jesus Christ was as necessary for our redemption and salvation as his death. In order for God's elect to be saved, accepted with God, our sin had to be put away and we had to be made perfectly righteous. In his life of obedience as a man, Christ perfectly obeyed the law of God as our Representative and Substitute. The law of God requires not only that we be without sin, but also that we be completely obedient to holiness, that we love God with all our hearts, souls, minds and beings, and our neighbours as ourselves. This righteousness Christ has performed for us as our Substitute. In him we obeyed the law of God perfectly. 'Christ is the end of the law for righteousness.' When God imputed the righteousness of Christ to us, he was 'made unto us righteousness'; and we have been 'made the righteousness of God in him'.

This righteousness which Christ performed is the only righteousness God will accept. It is the only righteousness there is, and we must have it. This is that 'holiness without which no man shall see the Lord'. We delight to renounce all personal righteousness and call him '**the Lord our Righteousness**'. Having established righteousness for us, Christ was 'obedient unto death, even the death of the cross', as our Substitute; and by his death he put away our sins.

'With the heart man believeth'

Read Jeremiah 17:5-14

'If thou shalt confess with thy mouth the Lord Jesus; and shalt believe in thine heart that God hath raised him from the dead, thou shalt be saved.' This is the one thing that is essential: you must 'believe in thine heart'. I urge you to 'examine yourselves, whether ye be in the faith'. I would do nothing to rob any true believer of the joy of confident assurance. But I must warn all men to guard against religious presumption. It is Satan's cheap counterfeit.

False faith can be very deceptive. False faith produces good works. It excites the emotions. It reforms the outward life. It performs deeds of religion. It causes sorrow for sin. It speaks well of Christ. It does works of charity. It trembles under the preaching of the gospel. False faith gains high offices in the church. It secures peace of mind. It walks in the company of great preachers. False faith even holds out to the Day of Judgement (Matt. 7:22-23). My friend, beware of false faith! Remember Lot's wife, Judas, Simon, Demas and Diotrephes. Be not numbered among them.

True faith is the heart knowledge of, trust in and submission to the Lord Jesus Christ. God has revealed Christ to us in the gospel, by which we know our desperate need and his saving power and fulness. Trusting Christ alone as our all-sufficient Saviour, we commit ourselves, body and soul, to him. And where there is true faith, there is the submission of heart to Christ as our sovereign Lord and King. This faith comes not by heredity, nor by the logic and persuasiveness of the preacher. It is the gift of God. Christ is revealed in the heart by the Holy Spirit.

This heart faith can be known by those who possess it. Have we believed? If so, we have firmly, cordially and voluntarily received Christ in all his offices. To them that believe, Christ is precious. Heart faith purifies the heart and weans it from the world. Heart faith works by love, lives in hope and rests in Christ. This is true faith. This is heart faith. F=orsaking A=ll I T=ake H=im.

'Thy God reigneth!'

Read Isaiah 40:12-31

This one thing characterizes every true and faithful preacher of the gospel: in declaring the good tidings of gospel truth and saving grace, he will declare unto men, '**Thy God reigneth**!' Sooner or later, either in mercy or in wrath, God will make all men see and confess that 'The most High ruleth!' (Dan. 4:17, 25, 32.) Any preacher who denies God's absolute, total, universal sovereignty is a false prophet. And any proud sinner who rebels against the gospel revelation of God's sovereign character does not know God. Every sinner who is taught of God will gladly confess with Nebuchadnezzar (Dan. 4:34-35).

1. *The Lord Jehovah is the eternal, self-existent God*: 'I blessed the most High, and I praised and honoured him that liveth for ever.' God alone is eternal. He is before all things and by him all things exist. God alone is independent. All things are dependent upon and affected by God; but he is not dependent upon or affected by anything.

2. *The Lord our God is a God with everlasting dominion*: 'Whose dominion is an everlasting dominion, and his kingdom is from generation to generation.' The God we worship and trust is the sovereign, reigning Monarch of the universe. He sits upon an indisputable, incontestable throne and rules over all things by sovereign right. He is God.

3. *Man is nothing*: 'All the inhabitants of the earth are reputed as nothing.' We are nothing in ourselves, only what God allows us to be. And we are nothing in comparison with God. All men together are only loathsome worms, withering grass and less than nothing.

4. *God's infinite power is at work, sovereignly accomplishing his will*: 'He doeth according to his will in the army of heaven, and among the inhabitants of the earth.' With unexplainable, sovereign, infinite power and wisdom, God so governs all things and all beings that all either willingly or unwillingly accomplish his eternal purpose.

5. *The will of God is irresistible and unimpeachable*: 'None can stay his hand, or say unto him, What doest thou?' God has his way in all things.

'If thou wouldest believe'

Read Mark 5:35-6:6

Every believer's great desire is to see the glory of God. Almost every time we pray, whether in the public assembly of God's church or in private, we repeat the prayer of Moses: 'I beseech thee, show me thy glory' (Exod. 33:18). We do not always use his words, but the prayer is the same: 'Lord, show us your glory.' Is this your desire? It is mine. Why is it then that we seem to see the glory of God so little? Our Lord tells us very plainly. Jesus said, '**Said I not unto thee, that if thou wouldest believe, thou shouldest see the glory of God**?' This was a gentle, but firm reproof. If Martha had simply believed she would have seen the glory of God in her brother's sickness and death, as well as in his resurrection. What a reproof this is to us today! If we did but believe in God, as he ought to be believed, if we implicitly trusted him in all things, as we say we do, we should see his glory in all things.

Faith sees the glory of God in *the gospel* (Rom. 3:23-26). Believing God we see the glory of his wisdom and truth, justice and mercy, righteousness and grace in saving sinners by the doing and dying of the Lord Jesus, the sinner's Substitute.

Faith sees the glory of God in *providence* (Rom. 8:28;11:36). Confident trust and assurance of God's sovereign rule over all things causes the believer to see God's glory in all things. We see his glory either in the immediate event or the prospective outcome. But in all, faith sees the glory of God's wisdom, power and grace in providence. In all that he does, (creation, redemption, providence and salvation), God's glory is seen by those who believe. And faith will see the glory of God in *the resurrection*.

Yet the primary force of our Lord's reproof is this: if we did but believe we should see the glory of God *working in our midst* (Mark 6:5-6). 'Unbelief is so vile and venomous an evil that it transfuseth a kind of dead palsy into the hands of omnipotency' (John Trapp). Christ can do all things by his absolute power. But he can do nothing for unbelievers. He cannot, because he will not. May God give us faith to believe, so that we may see the glory of God working in our midst!

'Fulfilled in us'

Read Galatians 3:1-13

The law of God is holy, just and good. We love the law and honour the law, as the revelation of God's righteousness and justice. But we recognize the fact that fallen men can never fulfil the requirements of God's holy law by their own works. 'Therefore by the deeds of the law there shall no flesh be justified in his sight' (Rom. 3:20). Yet we know also that until the law is perfectly fulfilled, no sinner can be saved. 'The soul that sinneth, it shall die' (Ezek. 18:20). God will not lessen his requirements, or bend his law, even to save his own elect. The law must be fulfilled. Both its requirements of righteousness and justice must be satisfied. The only way fallen, sinful men can ever fulfil the law and be saved is by faith in the Lord Jesus Christ, the sinner's Substitute.

We fulfil *the law's purpose* by faith. The law of God was our schoolmaster. Its one and only purpose was to bring us to the Lord Jesus Christ, that we might be justified by faith in him. Once we come to Christ, once we trust the Son of God, as our Lord and Saviour, the law has nothing more to do with us. Its purpose has been served (Gal. 3:24-26).

By faith in the Lord Jesus Christ we fulfil *the law's requirement* of perfect righteousness. We have no righteousness of our own. But we trust the Lord Jesus who lived in righteousness as our Representative. And trusting him, the righteousness of Christ is imputed to us (Rom. 3:22; 5:19).

And we fulfil *the law's demand* that justice be satisfied by faith in Christ. Sin must be punished. The sentence of the law must be fully executed upon every transgressor. And it is done. Divine justice was fully satisfied for every believer by Christ, the sinner's Substitute (Rom. 8:1-4). Since Christ died, God is both just and the justifier of all who believe (Rom. 3:24-26). Faith in Christ does not ignore the law, defile the law, lessen the law, or make the law void. Indeed, by faith 'we establish the law' (Rom. 3:31).

'A perfect and an upright man'

Read Romans 7:14-25

This is the testimony of God himself concerning his servant Job: **'There is none like him in the earth, a perfect and an upright man, one that feareth God, and escheweth evil.'** I cannot question these facts. Job was God's servant. He feared God and hated evil. He was a perfect and upright man. These things do not describe Job's actions, but the reigning characteristics of his heart, 'for the Lord looketh on the heart'.

I know that Job was a perfect man, because God says he was. But I also know that he was not a sinless man in the flesh, because he confessed, 'I have sinned' (Job 7:20). He said, 'If I justify myself, mine own mouth shall condemn me: if I say, I am perfect, it shall also prove me perverse' (Job 9:20). The doctrine of sinless perfection in the flesh (and those who claim to be without sin claim perfection) is contrary to everything revealed in the Word of God. Those who boast of possessing such perfection expose both their ignorance and their corruption. Those who suppose they are equal to the demands of the law of God are ignorant of the law. And those who claim to be perfect, without sin, are vile, wicked, perverse men. They are liars, claiming what they know is false to be the truth and declaring that God himself is a liar (1 John 1:8-10). What can be more wicked?

What does the Bible mean when it uses the word 'perfect' to describe those who believe God? The word is used in four ways. Usually, as in Job 1:8, it means *'sincere'*. God's people are not deceitful, hypocritical or pretentious. Sometimes perfect means *'mature'* (James 3:2). That person who has learned to bridle his tongue by the grace of God is a mature believer. He is not a babe in Christ, but a man. Frequently, the word 'perfect' refers to the believer's *positional holiness, sinlessness, and blamelessness* before the law of God by the atonement of Christ and the imputation of his righteousness (Ezek. 16:14). And the word 'perfect' describes the ultimate *glorification* of all believers in Christ, when we shall be made entirely conformed to the image of Christ in heaven, body, soul and spirit (Phil. 3:12).

'Christ hath redeemed us'

Read Hebrews 10:1-14

With those four words Paul states the whole doctrine of redemption as it is revealed in the New Testament. *Christ* alone is our Redeemer. Christ bore our sins. Christ endured the wrath of God. Christ satisfied the claims of justice against us, as our Substitute. The work of redemption was fully accomplished. 'Christ *hath* redeemed us.' Nothing is left to be done by us. Christ has done all. The blood of Christ poured out in death for the atonement of sin accomplished an effectual redemption. 'Christ *hath redeemed* us.' Our Lord did not provide for redemption or make redemption a possibility for all men, leaving it into the hands of man's free will to comply with his work and make it effectual. Redemption was performed by Christ alone. Redemption was accomplished at Calvary. And that redemption accomplished at Calvary was an effectual atonement for sin.

The apostle Paul also makes it plain that the benefits of Christ's atonement are designed for and limited to God's elect. 'Christ hath redeemed *us*.' God plainly says, regarding the death of his Son, 'For the transgression of my people was he stricken' (Isa. 53:8). The Bible nowhere states, nor does it anywhere imply, that the Lord Jesus Christ shed his blood and died to redeem all men from the curse of the law. I do not believe that doctrine which says that Judas was redeemed by Christ. It is not possible that our Lord died as a Substitute in Judas' place, bearing the curse of the law for him. Any who embrace such a doctrine must also embrace one of three absurd and blasphemous conclusions: (1) Either Judas is in heaven, which is to deny the Word of God; or (2) Christ failed to redeem the ones for whom he died and failed in his work of redemption as the sinner's Substitute; or (3) the justice of God has fallen to the ground, for if God punishes both the sinner and the sinner's Substitute for the same offence he would mock his own justice. This is the doctrine of Scripture: **'Christ hath redeemed us**!' — all God's elect, all who believe.

'Only believe'

Read John 3:11-21

Self-righteousness is like the mole: drive it out of one hole, and it will quickly find another in which to make its den. We have fairly well beaten it out of the den of good works as a ground of hope before God. But it has found another hiding-place. The dark den where self-righteousness hides with little possibility of detection is called by many names: 'fitness for faith', 'conditions of conversion', 'suitability for salvation', and 'qualifications for grace'. No matter what name you hang over the hole, it is a den of iniquity. It teaches sinners that in order to have true faith in Christ there are certain conditions that must be met. The doctrine goes like this: 'Salvation is by grace alone. It is not what you do, but what Christ has done that saves you. But before you can truly trust Christ and be saved, you must be terrified with conviction, you must weep and mourn over your sin, you must desire holiness, you must repent, you must long for Christ, you must come to see yourself as a lost sinner and then earnestly seek the Lord.'

This doctrine may sound good on the surface, but it is only a roundabout way of preaching salvation by works. There are no prerequisites, no conditions, no qualifications to be met by sinners before they trust Christ. The gospel of Christ is addressed to sinners as sinners, not awakened sinners, not sensible sinners, not convicted sinners, not lost sinners, not repentant sinners — just sinners! God does not command sinners to feel a certain way, experience something or come to realize something about themselves. God commands sinners to 'believe on his Son, Jesus Christ'. The moment a preacher places any condition or qualification of any kind upon the sinner before he can trust Christ and be saved, he ceases to preach a gospel of pure grace. Repentance, conviction of sin, lamentation and sorrow over sin are not prerequisites for coming to Christ and trusting him. These things do not precede faith. They are the results of faith (Zech. 12:10; John 16:7-14).

The mission of Christ's church

Read Romans 1:1-17

We do not need to form a committee to investigate the responsibility of the church in the '80s'. Our Lord has told us exactly what we are to do. He said, '**Go ye into all the world and preach the gospel to every creature. He that believeth and is baptized shall be saved; but he that believeth not shall be damned**' (Mark 16:15-16). The Word of God tells us exactly what we are to do and exactly how we are to do it. Nothing is left to guesswork. Neither our work nor the method by which we are to perform it is to be determined by time, place, circumstances or human opinion.

The singular *purpose* for our existence in this world is *the salvation of God's elect for the glory of his great name*. We are on the trail of Christ's sheep. We have no other object or goal. As our Lord Jesus Christ was sent to redeem God's elect, he has sent his church to gather those redeemed ones to their Saviour (John 20:21). We must never be turned aside from this great work.

The singular *method* of biblical evangelism is *gospel preaching*. When our Lord told us to go into all the world, he did not tell us to entertain the world, to change the world, to provide counselling for the world, to educate the world or to get control of political offices so that we could rule the world. Our Lord said, '**Go ye into all the world and preach the gospel**.' The only method of evangelism that God will own and honour for the salvation of sinners is that which he has ordained: gospel preaching! Other things may charm sinners and console sinners, but only gospel preaching will convert sinners.

And the singular *message* of the gospel is *Jesus Christ and him crucified* (1 Cor. 1:30-2:5). Rowland Hill was correct when he said, 'Any message which does not contain the three 'R's' [Ruin by the Fall, Redemption by the blood, and Regeneration by the Holy Spirit] ought never to have been preached.' It is our business to preach the gospel with simplicity and clarity, declaring to men how that God saves sinners through the merits of his Son, the Lord Jesus Christ.

'Antichrist'

Read 2 Thessalonians 2:1-17

If I understand the Word of God correctly, Antichrist is not a single man who will suddenly appear upon the earth in the last day. Antichrist is a system of religion which is opposed to the gospel of God's free and sovereign grace in Christ. It had already begun in John's day (1 John 2:18). Our Lord told us that the false religion of Antichrist would be such a cunning, crafty deception that were it possible it would deceive the very elect people of God (Matt. 24:24). And the apostle Paul informed us that, as the end draws near, God will take away his restraining hand, allowing the religion of Antichrist to spread throughout the world with signs and lying wonders, 'because they received not the love of the truth, that they might be saved. And for this cause God shall send them a strong delusion, that they should believe a lie: that they all might be damned who believed not the truth, but had pleasure in unrighteousness' (2 Thess. 2:3-12). Without the least hesitancy or fear of error, I warn you that the religion of modern fundamentalism, free-willism, easy-believism and decisionism is the religion of Antichrist.

It is not my desire to stir up strife and division among men. But it is my desire and responsibility to tell you the truth and to warn you of the deceptive delusion of Antichrist religion. Love for the honour of God, love for the truth of God and love for your souls constrains me to speak plainly. Any doctrine that lowers the character of God, his total sovereignty, his absolute righteousness or his strict justice, is Antichrist. Any doctrine that exalts and honours human flesh is Antichrist. Any doctrine that diminishes or adds to the finished work of our Lord Jesus Christ, his righteousness, his satisfaction, his intercession or his efficacy, is Antichrist. And any doctrine that attributes salvation in any measure to the will of man or the works of man is Antichrist.

'Born again... by the word of God'

Read 1 Peter 1:13-25

It is necessary, because God says it is necessary, for sinners to hear the Word of God in order to be saved. In these days, since the completion of the inspired volume of Holy Scripture, God never saves men apart from the hearing of the Word (1 Cor. 1:21; James 1:18; Rom. 10:17). If any dare argue with God, so that he may defend his system of theology, he is a brazenly foolish rebel against God. Those who defy God, I know, will not hear me, but you can be sure of this: where there is no gospel preaching there is no faith in Christ, and where there is no faith in Christ there is no life in Christ. In his own sovereign purpose and grace God has so highly exalted his Word that he will not save his own elect without the preaching of the gospel. Yes, God's elect will be saved, but not apart from the hearing of the Word. If need be, God will have a faithful preacher stoned to death and raise terrible persecution to scatter his people, so that those whom he has ordained to eternal life may hear the Word of life (Acts 11:19-21); but God will not save sinners apart from the ministry of the Word.

God's exaltation of his Word inspires his people in evangelism. We know that without the preaching of the gospel men will perish. We know also that God has a people in this world whom he will save. Therefore we go out into all the world, by whatever means God makes available to us, and preach the gospel to all men. We know that our labour will not be spent in vain (Isa. 55:11). This high value which God places upon his Word, and which we also place upon it, gives us a sense of reverence for the ministry of the Word. To other men, even the most religious, the ministry of the Word is a convenience. If they hear the gospel, that's good; but if they miss hearing the Word of God preached, they think they suffer no great loss. God's people know the Word is vital. It is their soul's food. They cannot live without it. They want to hear God speak, and they know that God speaks through his servants as they preach the Word.

'Of his own will begat he us'

Read Ephesians 2:1-10

Without question, the Word of God plainly teaches us that the source and cause of salvation is the sovereign will and pleasure of God (Rom. 9:16). The will of man is in no way the cause of salvation. Man's will has nothing more to do with the accomplishment of salvation than his works. 'Salvation is of the Lord', entirely of the Lord. Yes, man must believe. Man's will must be inclined towards Christ. The sinner must willingly repent, believe and bow to the Lord Jesus Christ. These things are acts of the human will. They are all necessary for salvation. No man will ever be saved whose will is in rebellion to God. God will have a willing people to worship him. However, man's will is not the cause of God's saving grace. The cause of grace is the will of God alone and it is the grace of God that causes his people to be willing in the day of his power (Ps. 65:4; 110:3). 'Whosoever will', let him come to Christ and be saved, and let him know assuredly that grace has made him willing to come. Otherwise he would never have the will to come.

I contend that every saved sinner gladly acknowledges the fact that the cause of, and reason for his salvation is not his will, but God's will. Paul's experience of grace was a pattern, showing forth the experience of believers (1 Tim. 1:16) and it is certain that Paul's will was not the cause of his salvation. Read Acts 9, and you will see that Paul's will did not even co-operate with God's will in saving him. Paul's will was the destruction of all who worshipped Christ and the utter annihilation of the name of the Lord Jesus Christ from the earth. Grace absolutely arrested Paul. By irresistible power and grace, God made Paul fall to the ground and revealed his Son in him. Not until God had put him down in the dust on the Damascus road was Paul willing to hear his voice and trust his Son. Any man who experiences the grace that Paul experienced will gladly acknowledge what Paul acknowledged: 'When it pleased God ... he revealed his Son in me.'

Why does God save sinners?

Read Psalm 8:1-9

We rejoice to know that God saves sinners. We rejoice to know that God saves sinners by grace through the merits of a Substitute. And we rejoice to know that God's grace is both eternal and immutable. But why does God save sinful men? He had no mercy upon the angels that fell. Why is he gracious to us? Paul gives us the answer repeatedly: '**Blessed be the God and Father of our Lord Jesus Christ, who hath blessed us with all spiritual blessings in heavenly places in Christ... to the praise of the glory of his grace... that we should be to the praise of his glory... unto the praise of his glory.**'

1. God saves us *because it was his eternal pleasure to bless us with his grace.* God passed by the angels that fell; but 'he hath blessed us'. God passed by multitudes of fallen men; but he 'hath blessed us'. The cause of God's blessing upon us is not in us, but in himself alone. Every saved sinner knows and acknowledges that fact. We do not deserve God's favour. 'He hath mercy on whom he will have mercy.'

2. God saved us *so that we might bless him.* Paul is calling us to bless God who hath blessed us. We can add nothing to God's glory, happiness or majesty. God is totally independent and self-sufficient. But we can bless God, that is to say, we can speak well of him 'who hath blessed us'. We bless God by simply trusting him. We bless God by celebrating his many glorious attributes. We bless God by faith in his Son. And we bless God by entertaining great thoughts of him.

3. God saved us *to the praise of the glory of his grace.* The ultimate end of all things is the glory of God. He could as well be glorified in our damnation as in our salvation. Like Pharaoh, we could have been monuments to the glory of God's justice by our ruin. But, blessed be his name, God has chosen to save us, that we might be 'to the praise of the glory of his grace!' (See Ps. 106:8.) May God give us grace even now to praise and magnify his grace.

How does God save sinners?

Read Psalm 116:1-19

In this marvellous doxology Paul gives praise to the three persons of the eternal Trinity, (Father, Son and Holy Spirit), for the infinitely wise and gracious salvation of all the elect. In his adoration and praise to God, Paul proclaims to all men the method of God's saving grace. He tells us how it is that God saves sinners.

1. God saves sinners by *his own sovereign and eternal purpose of grace* (3-6). Here are five things God did for all his elect in Christ before the world was created. He *blessed* us with all spiritual blessings in him. In Christ all of God's elect have every spiritual blessing which holiness can require, which grace can give and which sinful men can need. He *chose* us in eternal election. God's ultimate end in our election is that we (the objects of his love) should be perfectly holy and blameless in his sight. He *predestinated* us to be his own dear children. He *adopted* us into his family. Having adopted us, God sovereignly predestinated all things for us, securing our eternal enjoyment of his grace. He *accepted* us in the Beloved. Before the world was made, before we became sinners, God accepted us in Christ.

2. God saves sinners *by a legal and effectual blood atonement* (6-12). All of those who were chosen by God in eternity were in time redeemed by the blood of the Lord Jesus Christ. In great wisdom, prudence and grace, God found a way to be both just and the justifier of his elect. He made Christ our Substitute. Charging Christ with our sin, and punishing him for sin, God fully redeemed and forgave all his elect when Christ died in our place.

3. God saves sinners *by the irresistible power and grace of the Holy Spirit* (13-14). In the fulness of time every sinner chosen by God and redeemed by Christ is called by the Spirit through the gospel. All who are called believe. All who believe are sealed by the Spirit. And all who are sealed will enter into eternal glory.

'Bear ye one another's burdens, and so fulfil the law of Christ'

Read 1 John 4:7-21

These Galatians had foolishly been trying to bear the heavy burden of the Mosaic law. They had entangled themselves again with the yoke of bondage. They endeavoured to establish righteousness for themselves by the works of the law. None of them said, 'We are saved by our own works.' Satan does not work in such an open manner. These lawmongers at Galatia were saying, 'We are saved by grace, but only if we keep the law.' Others of them said, 'We are saved by grace alone, in so far as our justification is concerned; but in order to be sanctified we must keep the law as a rule of life.' In reality their doctrine was the same. They were attempting to mix law and grace. They had forsaken the gospel way of salvation by grace alone.

Now Paul says to them, 'Do you want a law to live by? Then live by the rule of the law of Christ — love.' Here is a law which is a living principle. It touches the heart, influences the life, honours God and is sympathetic towards and helpful to men. The whole law is fulfilled in this one thing — love. Without it, all the pretentious, self-righteous piety which men claim to possess is hypocrisy.

It seems quite remarkable to me that those self-righteous people who apparently want all men to know that they make the law of Moses their rule of life usually forget that which is the essence and spirit of the law — love. They are so righteous that they become stern, hard, severe, critical and judgemental, which is being unrighteous. Even the righteousness of the Mosaic law is a righteousness of love. But I have never found one of those self-righteous legalists who was tender-hearted, kind and gentle. He looks at the killing letter of the law and becomes as hard and stern as death.

My friends, let this be the law by which we live: 'Love one another.' Reject that which is hard, stern and severe. 'Be ye kind one to another, tender-hearted, forgiving one another, even as God for Christ's sake hath forgiven you.'

'The throne of his glory'

Read Psalm 2:1-12

In my mind's eye, I see the Lord Jesus Christ sitting upon his throne in glory, in the blessed serenity of his total sovereignty. He is not weak, frustrated and anxious, as some have pictured him, not knowing if he will be able to accomplish his purpose. Rather, he is calm, content and peaceful, knowing that by virtue of his sovereign power 'the pleasure of the Lord shall prosper in his hand. He shall see of the travail of his soul, and shall be satisfied.'

Behold his transcendent glory! He is King of kings and Lord of lords. He is the sovereign Monarch of heaven and earth. His empire is as limitless as the universe. His dominion is from everlasting to everlasting. His kingdom rules over all! Everything belongs to him. Everything is governed by him. Everything does his bidding. He is God over all and blessed for ever.

Standing before his throne are all those angelic, heavenly creatures who anxiously worship and serve him. They cast their crowns before him in adoring reverence. In that same great assembly I see all of God's elect who have already entered the heavenly city. They too cast their crowns before his feet and sing the songs of redeeming love. I see beneath his blessed feet the earth, which has become his footstool. His saints upon the earth worship, adore and honour him as the rightful sovereign of the universe and the rightful Lord of their hearts. They live in hopeful expectation of his glorious advent.

But then I see before this great King all the elements of the world, all the beasts of the field, all those fallen sons of Adam who wage their warfare against his throne, all the spirits of the damned in hell, the demons of hell and the prince of darkness himself. My heart begins to melt in fear for the safety of the great King's throne, his kingdom, his glory and my own soul. But all my fears are immediately silenced. All those evil men, the demons of hell, those forces of evil and Satan himself have a bit of iron in their mouths and a bridle of steel; and he who holds the reins of that bridle is the King himself! Christ is on his throne!

'Jesus Christ is Lord!'

Read Isaiah 45:5-25

This is the result of our Saviour's finished work of righteousness and redemption on the earth as our Substitute. Paul is telling us that all the vast empire of God's creation has been placed under the dominion of the God-man, our Saviour. He is telling us that there is no limit to the realm and sphere of our Redeemer's total sovereignty. He is Lord of all! Christ is Lord of all people, Lord of all things and Lord of all events. The Lord God has given to his Son 'a name which is above every name'; and the name he has given him is 'Lord Supreme'.

Jesus Christ is Lord *over all people* upon this earth. He is Lord over the righteous and the wicked, the living and the dead, the believing and the unbelieving (Rom. 14:9). Believers recognize, acknowledge and willingly surrender to his lordship. Unbelievers deny it and rebel against it. But he is none the less Lord. All are under his control, do his bidding, perform his will and accomplish his purpose, always and in all things.

Jesus Christ is Lord *over all the powers of darkness* (Col. 2:15). Those souls damned for ever in hell, the demons of hell and Satan himself are all under the dominion of King Jesus. Not one of our Lord's enemies can breathe or move, except by his permission: and even then their moves are governed by him to accomplish nohing but good for his people and the eternal purpose of God (Job 1:12; 2:6).

Jesus Christ is Lord *over all the affairs of providence* (Isa. 53:10-12; Rom. 8:28; Heb. 1:1-3). I rejoice to tell you that there is no place in this universe, from the throne of God in the highest glory to the lowest pit of deepest hell, where Jesus Christ does not rule in total, absolute, sovereign power. God's creation is not out of control. Nothing is thrown into confusion. Jesus Christ is Lord. His purpose is being accomplished.

And Jesus Christ is Lord *over all the vast regions of heaven* (Heb. 12:10.) The King of the City Beautiful is Immanuel, God in our nature. The light of that city is Christ himself. The reward of heaven is Christ. All the songs of the redeemed in heaven shall be praises to the Lord the Lamb for ever.

The doctrine of the Trinity is an essential element of gospel truth

Read Ephesians 4:1-16

The doctrine of the Trinity is often represented as a speculative point of theology, which must not be pressed too tenaciously. But we cannot place too much importance upon it. It is an essential element of gospel truth. It is interwoven in every aspect of our salvation, all the doctrines of the gospel and the experience of God's people. We cannot do without it. As soon as a man is convinced of his sinful and miserable condition by nature, he perceives that there is a divine person whom he has offended and that there is need for another divine person to make satisfaction for his offences and that there is need for a third divine person to give him life eternal, to regenerate, sanctify and preserve him.

As you read the Bible, it becomes obvious to your mind, if you are a believer, that all three of the divine persons of the Holy Trinity are actively engaged in the salvation of your soul. This fact is nowhere more clearly revealed than in Paul's letter to the Ephesians (1:3-14). *Our salvation was planned by God the Father* in his eternal purpose of grace: 'Blessed be the God and Father of our Lord Jesus Christ, who hath blessed us with all spiritual blessings in heavenly places in Christ: according as he hath chosen us in him before the foundation of the world, that we should be holy and without blame before him: in love having predestinated us unto the adoption of children by Jesus Christ to himself, according to the good pleasure of his will, to the praise of the glory of his grace, wherein he hath made us accepted in the beloved.' *Our salvation was purchased by God the Son* in his substitutionary sacrifice at Calvary: 'In whom we have redemption through his blood, the forgiveness of sins, according to the riches of his grace.' And *our salvation was performed* in our hearts *by* the gracious, effectual work of *God the Holy Spirit* who gave us faith in Christ: 'Ye were sealed with that Holy Spirit of promise, which is the earnest of our inheritance...'

'My Lord and my God'

Read John 20:19-31

There are many who think they do honour to the Lord Jesus Christ when they say that 'Christ is like God', or that 'Christ is a God.' They do him no honour at all. Their pretended honour is naked blasphemy! Their religion is a mockery of the Lord Jesus Christ, for he claimed that he is very God of very God. Did he say, 'Before Abraham was, I AM'? (John 8:58.) Did he not declare, 'I and my Father are one'? (John 10:30.) While our Saviour lived upon this earth, he claimed to possess the attributes of God: righteousness, infinity, eternity, omnipotence, omniscience and omnipresence. And he fully demonstrated the truthfulness of his claims.

The Word of God expressly declares that Jesus Christ is God: 'Thy throne, O God, is for ever and ever' (Ps. 45:6; Heb. 1:8). 'Hereby perceive we the love of God, because he laid down his life for us' (1 John 3:16). 'Christ came, who is over all, God blessed for ever' (Rom. 9:5). 'Without controversy great is the mystery of godliness: God was manifest in the flesh' (1 Tim. 3:16). While he was upon the earth his disciples worshipped the Lord Jesus Christ as God, and were never reproved for doing so. '**Thomas... said unto him, My Lord and my God**' (John 20:28). Had he been merely a good man, or even an angel, he would have surely rebuked any who called upon him and worshipped him as God (Rev. 19:10).

If our Saviour had been nothing more than a good, righteous man he could never have redeemed us and justified us before God's holy law. Only God could render perfect righteousness of infinite merit to the law. Only one who is both God and man in one glorious person could have suffered to full satisfaction the infinite justice of God, so as to merit by one great sacrifice the eternal salvation of God's elect. The Lord Jesus Christ, our Saviour, is 'Immanuel', God with us, God in our nature, the God-man, our Mediator. Were he not God, he would be the greatest impostor who ever lived, and we should all be miserably lost and without hope.

'He gave his only begotten Son'

Read John 3:1-18

The Lord God gave us his Son. We did not earn him. We did not even desire him. And when he came we despised him, rejected him, nailed him up on a piece of wood and mocked him as he died. Yet for all of this, the love, mercy and grace of God were not abated! The purpose of his love was not thwarted. God's love towards fallen, guilty sinners, scattered throughout the whole world, was so great that '**He gave his only begotten Son, that whosoever believeth in him should not perish, but have everlasting life**.'

God gave his Son to be our Saviour in the covenant of grace *before the world began*. Before all worlds, in the mind and purpose of God, he took his own beloved Son, laid him upon the altar of his strict justice as the Substitute of that vast multitude whom he had determined to save and killed him as a sin-atoning, propitiatory sacrifice. In that sense Jesus Christ is the Lamb of God 'slain from the foundation of the world' (Rev. 13:8).

God gave his Son *in the incarnation*. In the fulness of time the divine purpose must be fulfilled. God sent forth his Spirit to prepare a body for his Son in the virgin's womb and Immanuel came, God in our nature! 'God sent forth his Son, made of a woman, made under the law, to redeem them that were under the law' (Gal. 4:4-5).

God gave his Son to die *in the place of sinners at Calvary*. The death of Christ was not the work of Satan, nor even the work of men, for neither Satan nor men had the power to kill God the Son. The death of our Lord Jesus Christ was the work of God the Father, the greatest work ever done by God. It was that work which God had purposed from eternity, for which he created this world. In the crucifixion of his Son by the hands of wicked men God gave his Son up into the hands of his own holy law, to suffer the wrath and vengeance of the law in the place of sinners. Being fully satisfied with the sacrifice of his own dear Son, God now gives salvation and eternal life to every sinner who trusts his Son. Truly, Jesus Christ dying in the place of sinners is the gift of God's love!

'It pleased the Lord to bruise him'

Read John 19:13-30

When the prophet says, '**It pleased the Lord to bruise him**,' he does not mean us to understand that God found a reason for laughter in the agonies of his Son. God did not take delight and joy in punishing his Son. The text might be read like this: 'It gave satisfaction to the Lord to bruise him.' The Lord himself tells us, 'I have no pleasure in the death of the wicked.' In doing so, he is telling us that his wrath and justice can never be satisfied by the death of the wicked. That is the reason why hell is eternal. Men can never satisfy the infinite wrath and justice of God. The torments of the damned in hell can never give God pleasure and satisfaction. But when God bruised his Son, the Lord Jesus Christ, as our Substitute, crushing him beneath the terrible load of our sin, he was pleased with the death of his Son. The sacrifice of our Lord Jesus Christ, pouring out his life's blood unto death, made an infinite satisfaction to the wrath and justice of God. God, in his infinite holiness and justice, could not require more than Christ offered and he could not be satisfied with less than Christ offered for the ransom of our souls.

Surely the prophet also means us to understand that God is pleased with the sure results of his Son's death, The Lord God was pleased to 'make his soul an offering for sin', because he saw more than the blood of his Son being poured out at Calvary. He saw more than the agony and the groans and the ignominious shame that his Son endured. He saw that as a result of his Son's great sacrifice, he would 'justify many'. He saw all the host of his elect standing around his throne, shouting and singing the praises of his Son, throughout the endless ages of eternity. This was 'the joy' which was set before our Saviour, for which he 'endured the cross, despising the shame'. In order to save us, 'to the praise of the glory of his grace', 'it pleased the Lord to bruise him'.

'How shall they believe...?'

Read Romans 10:1-21

In Romans 10:14-17 the apostle Paul tells us four things which are impossible. He has declared, 'Whosoever shall call upon the name of the Lord shall be saved.' And we rejoice to know that it is true. Yet we must not ignore the fact that Paul plainly tells us that certain things must take place before any sinner can call upon the name of the Lord and be saved.

1. No one can call upon Christ for mercy until he believes on Christ. In order for a man to seek the mercy of God in Christ by faith he must believe the testimony God has given concerning his Son: '**How then shall they call on him in whom they have not believed?**'

2. No one can truly believe on Christ until he hears the gospel of Christ. '**How shall they believe in him of whom they have not heard**?' Sinners today are being asked to 'believe on Jesus', but the preachers are not telling anyone who the Lord Jesus Christ is — what he has done — where he is now — or how God in justice saves sinners by the substitutionary sacrifice of his Son. Until a sinner has heard these things faithfully proclaimed he cannot have or exercise true faith in Christ and be saved. No one is saved where the gospel is not faithfully proclaimed.

3. No one can hear the gospel of Christ without a preacher. God has chosen to save sinners by the instrumentality of gospel preaching. God does not call sinners to Christ by the voice of angels or the voice of singers. God calls sinners to Christ by the voice of a preacher, by the voice of a man proclaiming the gospel in the power of the Holy Spirit. '**How shall they hear without a preacher?... Faith cometh by hearing and hearing by the Word of God.**'

4. No man can truly preach the gospel of Christ in the power of the Holy Spirit unless he is sent of God. '**How shall they preach, except they be sent**?' When God intends to call his elect to Christ he always sends a preacher, in the power of the Holy Spirit, to that place where his elect are found, just as he sent Philip to preach the gospel to the eunuch.

'Many of his disciples went back'

Read 1 John 2:15-29

Through the course of our Lord's earthly ministry he had men and women who followed him for a season, but for one reason or another forsook him. This was also the experience of the apostles in the early church. And it continues to be the experience of God's saints today. In every church there are empty seats which were once filled by men and women who were highly esteemed, but who have now forsaken Christ. I have seen many who were so promising, for whom I had such high hopes, forsake Christ. Always, without exception, their apostasy can be traced to one of these four facts.

1. Some forsake Christ simply because *they cannot endure the doctrine of the gospel.* The natural man is highly offended by the gospel of God's free and sovereign grace in Christ. He will not long endure a faithful, consistent declaration of the gospel. Some are offended by the grace of the gospel; others are offended by the simplicity of the gospel.

2. Some forsake Christ because *they received the Word as stony-ground hearers.* Having no root, they wither away as soon as some trial arises because of the Word.

3. Some forsake Christ because *they received the Word as seed sown among thorns.* After a while the cares of this world and the deceitfulness of riches choke out the influence of the gospel.

4. Some forsake Christ because *they do not count the costs of following Christ.* Once they find out what it costs to follow Christ, they determine that the price is too dear and they refuse to pay.

Whenever a professed believer forsakes Christ and the gospel it will be for one of these reasons. We must not be surprised or shaken when it happens. 'They went out from us, but they were not of us: for if they had been of us, they would no doubt have continued with us: but they went out, that they might be made manifest that they were not all of us' (1 John 2:19).

'Will not remember thy sins'

Read Hebrews 10:1-17

God cannot lie. He cannot break his covenant. He cannot forsake his people. He cannot be unjust. He cannot deny himself. And God cannot remember the sins of his people. I do not suggest that God is not aware of the fact that we have sinned, are sinning and will sin. He is. But in so far as the law and justice of God are concerned our sins do not exist. The blood of Christ has blotted them out, washed them away and removed them from us: 'As far as the east is from the west, so far hath he removed our transgressions from us' (Ps. 103:12). Because God himself has removed our sins, he cannot remember our sins. This is his promise to every believer: '**I, even I, am he that blotteth out thy transgressions for mine own sake, and will not remember thy sins**' (Isa. 43:25). What can this promise of grace mean? It means at least these four things.

1. God will never remember our sins so as to treat us any the less graciously because of our sins.

2. God will never remember our sins so as to bring them up and require payment from us for our sins while we live.

3. God will not remember our sins when we stand before him in the Day of Judgement. 'In those days, and in that time, saith the Lord, the iniquity of Israel shall be sought for, and there shall be none; and the sins of Judah, and they shall not be found: for I will pardon them whom I reserve' (Jer. 50:20).

4. God will not remember our sins in the distribution of his heavenly gifts, crowns and rewards. All the limitless bounty of heaven's eternal glory will be given to all of God's elect, because all will be perfect, blameless, sinless and holy through the righteousness and shed blood of the Lord Jesus Christ

Happy the man to whom his God
No more imputes his sin;
But, washed in the Redeemer's blood,
Hath made his garments clean!

'The forgiveness of sins'

Read 1 John 1:1-10

Occasionally I hear preachers make this statement: 'God does not forgive sin.' I understand what they are doing. They are emphasizing the fact that God's justice must be satisfied. But we must be careful not to contradict the plain statements of Holy Scripture. God does forgive sin. He says that he does. He is a God 'keeping mercy for thousands, forgiving iniquity and transgression and sin' (Exod. 34:7). 'God for Christ's sake hath forgiven you' (Eph. 4:32). 'If we confess our sins, he is faithful and just to forgive us our sins, and to cleanse us from all unrighteousness' (1 John 1:9). Yes, marvellous and unbelievable as it may appear, the holy, just and true God does forgive sin! It is true God does not forgive sin as men speak of forgiveness, but he does forgive sin. In faithfulness to his covenant, in faithfulness to his character and in faithfulness to his Son, God forgives sin in a way that is altogether consistent with his justice.

God cannot forgive sin unless he can do so in a way that is honouring to his law and satisfying to his justice. He said, 'The soul that sinneth, it shall die' (Ezek.18:20). He said, 'Cursed is every one that continueth not in all things which are written in the book of the law to do them' (Gal. 3:10). How can God forgive sin and yet be just?

In order for a holy God to forgive sin four things must be done.
1. The law of God must be honoured and perfectly obeyed.
2. The justice of God must be satisfied.
3. The sinner must bear the full punishment of his sin.
4. The sin must be entirely removed.

The Word of God makes it abundantly clear that there is only one way for a holy and just God to forgive sin. God can only forgive sin through the righteous obedience and satisfactory sacrifice of an all-sufficient substitute. The Lord Jesus Christ is that Substitute! In him, and only in him, is there forgiveness with God (Rom. 3:23-26). Trust that Substitute whom God has accepted, and all your sins will be forgiven you. Yes, it is true, 'He delighteth in mercy'! God delights to forgive sin justly, through the blood of his Son.

'Herein is love'

Read Hosea 2:6-20

When the apostle John describes God, he says, 'God is love.' Now that is not all that God is: he is also gracious, just, holy, wise and almighty. But all these attributes are consistent with this glorious truth: 'God is love.' When you and I think about the love of God, we must remind ourselves that God is not a man. His love is not like ours. The love of God is that special affection that he has for his people. It does not arise from anything outside of himself and it does not change. God's love implies his absolute purpose and will deliver, bless and save his people. And that loving purpose of God is never more wonderfully and completely revealed than in the sacrifice of his Son in our stead. In this text, John tells us four things which characterize the love of God.

1. *God loves sovereignly.* '**Herein is love, not that we loved God, but that he loved us**.' There is nothing which compels God to love any of his sinful creatures. But, in his infinite goodness, God says, 'Jacob have I loved.' Our God is infinite and immutable, and so is his love. He loves whom he will, because he will, and he loves them eternally.

2. *God loves sinners.* '**He loved us**.' I preach fully, without reservation, unlimited love, unbounded mercy to the vilest of men. We have nothing in us worthy of consideration. We deserve the utmost terror of God's wrath. Who can express the fulness and magnitude of those words: 'He loved us'?

3. *God loves sacrificially.* '**He sent his Son**.' Do not ever think that Christ died at Calvary in order to win God's love for us. No! Christ died in our place at Calvary because God loved us and he resolved to have us.

4. *God loves savingly.* Brethren, God loved us before the world began. But in order for us to be reconciled to God, justice had to be satisfied. Therefore, our loving Father gave his Son to be the satisfying '**propitiation for our sins**'. Through his substitutionary death, all the sins of God's people were washed away.

'Come unto me'

Read Luke 8:41-56

Coming to Christ is the one essential thing for salvation. He that does not come to Christ, do what he may, or think what he may, is yet in 'the gall of bitterness and in the bonds of iniquity'. Coming to Christ is the very first result of regeneration. The soul that is quickened by the power of God at once realizes its lost condition. Feeling a sense of divine wrath, the quickened sinner flees to Christ and trusts him for salvation. Where there is no coming to Christ, there is no salvation. But how does a poor sinner come to Christ?

1. *Coming to Christ is not a mere physical act.* In our day, men have substituted coming to the front of the church for coming to Christ. Much uproar is made when we say that this is a deception. But I must remind you that during the Saviour's earthly ministry, many came to him with their feet and their lips whose hearts were far from him.

2. *Coming to Christ is not a mere mental act.* Many believe the faith of Christ's words, that is, they give intellectual assent to them, whose hearts are yet unchanged. At heart they are still children of wrath.

3. *Coming to Christ is an act of faith.* It is the response of the heart to the sovereign, life-giving power of God. It is that act of the soul whereby we leave our sins and our self-righteousness and flee to the Lord Jesus Christ. It is simply trusting his righteousness to be our covering and his blood to be our atonement. Coming to Christ is the repentance of sin, the denial of self, and faith in him who is God's salvation. Coming to Christ is the belief of the truth, the crying of the soul unto God and the submission of the heart to Christ's absolute lordship as it is revealed in the gospel. Come now, my friend, away from yourselves, away from your self-righteousness and away from your false refuges – come unto Christ. He alone is able to save poor sinners. Christ is also willing to save poor sinners. Come now to Christ, the true altar, and lay hold of him for eternal life.

'Arise, and be baptized'

Read Romans 6:1-14

It is ever the tendency of fallen man to run to extremes. Nowhere is this tendency more evident than in religious customs, doctrines and practices. With regard to the matter of baptism, almost all men run to one of two extremes. Some make baptism a means of salvation. Anyone who reads the Word of God with honesty immediately recognizes that such doctrine is heresy. 'Salvation is of the Lord.' It is not the water of baptism that washes away sin, but the blood of Christ. We are not saved by baptism, but by grace. There are others who run to the opposite extreme, who make baptism an insignificant thing. Some even neglect it altogether. This too is a perversion of Scripture. Baptism is important. Baptism is essential!

Baptism is essential as a matter of obedience to our Lord Jesus Christ. By example and by commandment our Lord requires that all believers (and only believers) be baptized. To rebel against this ordinance and refuse to be baptized is to expose rebellion, not submission of heart to Christ. Such rebellion is a fair indication that a person is not saved. I have searched the Scriptures carefully and I have not yet found a single believer in the New Testament (other than the penitent thief) who was not baptized. Baptism is an act of obedience to Christ our Lord.

Baptism is essential in confessing Christ before men. This is the New Testament way of confessing faith in Christ. We who believe are symbolically buried with Christ in baptism and we arise from the watery grave with him to walk in the newness of life. Baptism is a vivid picture of the believer's death, burial and resurrection in Christ our Substitute. By this public ordinance we confess to all men our faith in Christ.

Baptism does not save; baptism does not put away sin; baptism has no merit before God. But baptism is essential. It is 'the answer of a good conscience toward God'. If you believe on Christ, obey him and confess him before men in baptism.

'This do'

Read 1 Corinthians 11:23-34

It causes me great concern to see so many who profess faith in the Lord Jesus Christ absenting themselves from the ordinance of the Lord's Supper and neglecting this commandment of Christ. The Lord's Supper is an important part of worship, essential to the spiritual well-being of God's church. The apostle Paul said, 'As often as ye eat this bread and drink this cup, ye do show the Lord's death till he come.'

The purpose of observing the Lord's Supper is that we might symbolically show forth the death of Christ. The Lord Jesus Christ instituted this ordinance just before his death on the cross. The bread and wine symbolically represent the sufferings and death of our Redeemer in our place. The broken bread symbolizes his immaculate body, crushed under the wrath of God beneath the load of our sins. The wine poured out symbolizes his blood, poured out in death, by which our sin was put away. Breaking the bread and drinking the wine, we are reminded of our need of Christ's substitutionary sacrifice to put away sin and we are reminded of God's great love in sacrificing his Son to redeem us.

This is an ordinance which every true believer should observe. Regrettably, many of God's children have been taught to fear coming to the Lord's Supper. They think they are showing reverence for the ordinance by not receiving it. They do not. Our worthiness to take the bread and wine is not in ourselves, but in Christ. We come not with perfection, but with faith. By eating the bread and drinking the wine, we show our confidence in Christ's finished work to make us accepted in the sight of God. No unbeliever is worthy to receive this ordinance, but no believer is unworthy.

The Lord's Supper is to be observed often. A friend recently told me that in his church they had observed the Lord's Supper only once in twelve years! That is utterly inexcusable. We need to be frequently reminded of our Lord's love for us and of the price by which he redeemed us.

'He is our peace'

Read Ephesians 2:1-22

The Lord Jesus Christ is our peace. He is not only the Friend of peace and the Prince of peace, but peace itself. He has not only made peace and proclaimed peace, but Christ is our peace.

Christ is our peace with God. There was a wall of partition separating us from God: our sin and guilt. But Christ came in human flesh to reconcile a holy God and his sinful people. In order to do so, he established righteousness for us, such as God's law required, and satisfied the justice of God against us by pouring out his own life's blood unto death as our Substitute. By his great atonement the Son of God has taken away the sin which separated God and his chosen people. But another wall of partition had to be broken down: our proud, sinful, rebellious will had to be subdued. Christ has done that too. By the power of his Spirit, through the preaching of the gospel, the Lord Jesus Christ has persuaded us who believe to be reconciled to God. 'He is our peace,' because he has reconciled God to us by his effectual blood and reconciled us to God by his irresistible grace.

Christ is our peace with one another. He has made all true believers one in himself. Coming to Christ in faith, we are united in heart and purpose with all other true believers. Faith in Christ destroys all those distinctions of the flesh which alienate sinful men: race, social standing, education, etc. In the kingdom of grace there is neither black nor white, male nor female, rich nor poor: but Christ is all, and in all. 'He is our peace,' because we are one in him.

Christ is our peace within ourselves. When Christ rules in a man's heart, he causes that heart to be at peace. It is written: 'Thou wilt keep him in perfect peace, whose mind is stayed on thee: because he trusteth in thee.' 'For God hath not given us the spirit of fear; but of power, and of love, and of a sound mind.' 'He is our peace,' because he brings peace to the heart.

'The Spirit ... beareth witness'

Read 1 John 2:18-29

In great measure the work of the Holy Spirit is a work of confirmation. He confirms to the hearts of God's elect all the blessings of God bestowed upon us in the covenant of grace and purchased for us by the blood of Christ. He seals the covenant of grace in our hearts and seals our hearts in the grace of God.

The Holy Spirit confirms the faith of God's elect. True faith is the gift of God. It is the product of divine power. And it is the inner witness of the Spirit through the Word of God that assures the believer that his faith is genuine. 'Because ye are sons, God hath sent forth the Spirit of his Son into your hearts, crying, Abba, Father' (Gal. 4:6). '**As many as are led by the Spirit of God, they are the sons of God ... The Spirit itself beareth witness with our spirit, that we are the children of God**' (Rom. 8:14,16).

The Spirit of God confirms God's elect in the truth of God. He is the Spirit of truth. Our Lord said, 'He shall teach you all things, and bring all things to your remembrance, whatsoever I have said unto you' (John 14:26). 'When he, the Spirit of truth is come, he will guide you into all truth: for he shall not speak of himself, but whatsoever he shall hear, that shall he speak: and he will show you things to come. He shall glorify me: for he shall receive of mine, and shall show it unto you' (John 16:13-14). None of God's elect will ever be deceived by the heresy that abounds in these dark days. No true believer will ever be moved away from the hope of the gospel. You who are the sheep of Christ will not hear the voice of a stranger. You will not follow his doctrine, because 'ye have an unction from the Holy One, and ye know all things' (1 John 2:20).

The Spirit of God confirms the ministry of God's servants to the hearts of his people. If a man is called of God to the work of the gospel ministry, God the Holy Spirit will give him the ear of his people (1 John 4:1-6).

'Why stand ye gazing up into heaven?'

Read 2 Peter 3:1-18

Our Lord had plainly told his disciples to stay in Jerusalem until they had received the power of the Holy Spirit, and then to go into all the world to preach the gospel. But they became so engulfed by his ascension that they ignored his command. We have many who make the same mistake among us today. They are so engulfed with their theories and speculations about prophecy that they seldom, if ever, get around to preaching the gospel to any creature.

I spent five years 'studying theology' in two leading Bible colleges, and about all we did was 'gaze into heaven'. Semester after semester was spent trying to unravel the visions of Daniel, Ezekiel and Revelation, but never, not even once, in five years did I hear a professor answer such fundamental, essential questions as these: 'How can a man be just with God?' 'How can he be clean that is born of woman?' 'How can God be just and yet justify the ungodly?'

Be assured, our Lord is coming again. At the time appointed Christ will appear in power and great glory. But no man knows, or can know, when that time is. God has not given us one shred of information to indicate when Christ will come, because he does not intend us to know. Only fools pry into those things which God has kept secret. It is our responsibility, not to speculate about when Christ will come, but faithfully to preach the gospel of his grace, serving the interests of his kingdom and seeking his glory, with hearts full of expectation. It is our business to be about our Master's business.

'**Why stand ye gazing up into heaven**?' Are there no needy ones for you to help? Are there no hungry ones for you to feed? Are there no sick ones for you to visit? Are there no sinners perishing for lack of knowledge? Go and do as the Lord has commanded you, until he comes to take you home. Let us be found in the place God has appointed, doing the work which God has appointed for us, in that hour which God has appointed, when our Lord shall appear.

Imputed righteousness and imparted righteousness

Read Romans 5:12-21; 1 John 3:1-10

Imputed righteousness is an act of God's grace in redemption. Because the Lord Jesus Christ lived in righteousness upon this earth as our Representative and died under the penalty of God's law as our Substitute, the law and justice of God declare that we are righteous. The very righteousness of Christ, his perfect obedience to God as a man, has been imputed to us. That is to say, righteousness has been laid to our account. In exactly the same manner as our sins were imputed to Christ, his righteousness has been imputed to us. When God made Christ to be sin for us, he charged him with our sin. The Son of God became responsible to the law of God for the sins of his elect. And the penalty of sin was exacted from him. He died under the wrath of God. Even so, God having imputed the righteousness of Christ to us who believe, we have become responsible for righteousness in the sight of God's law. And we shall receive the just reward of the law for righteousness, eternal life and everlasting glory. As our works of sin were made to be our Lord's, so his works of righteousness have been made ours. As he received the reward of our sin, we must receive the reward of his righteousness. That is substitution. Our righteousness before God is perfect, unalterable righteousness. It is the righteousness of Christ, our Substitute. Child of God, can you realize this? Your standing, your acceptance with God never varies. God is always well pleased with you in his Son!

Imparted righteousness is an act of God's grace in regeneration. In the new birth God gives his people a new heart, a new will, a new nature, created in righteousness and true holiness. Your standing before God is not improved at all by the new birth. God has given you a heart, nature and will of righteousness so that you now love the things you once hated and hate the things you once loved. By this act of divine grace in regeneration the righteous nature of Christ is imparted to God's elect.

'Leaving us an example'

Read 1 Peter 2:11-25

Some poor people go to Mt Calvary to get salvation and then run back to Mt Sinai to get sanctification. They look to Christ to give them life and look to Moses to rule their life. That will never do. I rejoice to find both salvation and sanctification in the cross of our Lord Jesus Christ. The cross of Christ is our source of life and our rule of life. How can I, as a believer, live in this world for the glory of my God? To find the answer to that question, I must go to the cross of the Lord Jesus Christ. 'For even hereunto were ye called: because Christ also suffered for us, leaving us an example, that ye should follow in his steps' (1 Peter 2:21).

Children of God, we are not under the law. We do not need rules, regulations, threats of punishment or promises of reward to motivate and govern our hearts. In order to live in this world for the glory of God, we must simply follow the example of the one who hung upon the cursed tree, bearing our sins. When I see Christ hanging upon the cross as my Substitute, I see that *self-sacrifice* is essential to honouring God (Luke 14:33). There is a battle for me to fight, a trial for me to endure, a service for me to perform and a cross for me to bear. I cannot serve God without self-sacrifice and self-denial. As Christ hangs upon the cursed tree, bearing our sins, he sets before us an example of *willing obedience* to our heavenly Father. Our Saviour willingly obeyed his Father's will, even unto death (Isa. 50:5-7). This is the way we must serve God. God will never accept any gift, any worship or any service, unless it comes from a willing heart (2 Cor. 8:12). The cross also shows us our Lord's *dedication and perseverance*. He not only agreed to bear our sins and promised to die for us; he actually did it. God requires dedication and perseverance from all who follow Christ. Our Lord's death upon the cross also sets before us an example of real *love* and patient *submission* to the will of God.

'Let us behave ourselves valiantly'

Read Psalm 92:1-15

The Ammonites had come against Israel with a very great army. Even to Joab, a man of great military skill and experience, things looked bad. But he encouraged himself and his brother, Abishai, with these words: '**Be of good courage, and let us behave ourselves valiantly for our people, and for the cities of our God: and let the Lord do that which is good in his sight**' (1 Chron. 19:13). In this time of great difficulty and danger, Joab set before us an example of persevering faithfulness and reverent submission which should be followed by all who seek the glory of God and serve the interest of his kingdom in this world.

Our lives should be characterized by *a persevering faithfulness* to our God and to the work he has committed to our hands. I say to you, 'Be of good courage, and let us behave ourselves valiantly for our people, and for the church of our God.' The Lord has entrusted us with the gospel of his grace. He has given us the means and the opportunity to proclaim the gospel to this generation, and he has commanded us to do so. This is the point of our responsibility. We do not know what God has decreed, but we do know what he has commanded, and what he has commanded we must do. 'Go ye into all the world, and preach the gospel to every creature. He that believeth and is baptized shall be saved.'

And we must serve the Lord our God with *a reverent submission*. '**Let the Lord do that which is good in his sight**.' Joab was saying to Abishai, 'If God saves us, we shall be saved. If we perish, we shall perish. That is up to him. But we will serve him valiantly.' This is our work. We must preach the gospel to all men, as God gives us opportunity. If he is pleased to save men, we shall rejoice and preach the gospel. If God is pleased to harden men, we shall still rejoice and preach the gospel. He is God. We are his servants. Let him do with us what he will. 'Let the Lord do that which is good in his sight.'

'By mercy and truth iniquity is purged'

Read Psalm 85:1-13

How can a holy God forgive sin? How can God be just and yet justify the ungodly? How is iniquity purged? The wise man, Solomon, gives us the answer of divine wisdom to this question: **'By mercy and truth iniquity is purged.'**

The law of God, as it was given at Sinai, proclaims truth without mercy. The law accepts no excuses and makes no exceptions. 'The soul that sinneth, it shall die.' The unrenewed heart desires mercy without truth. Truth without mercy would destroy every transgressor. Mercy without truth would dishonour God and trample his law in the ground. If truth stands alone, this earth must cease to be a place of hope for sinners. If mercy stands alone, heaven would cease to be a place of holiness. There stands God, the Judge of all, in his strict justice. Here we stand, guilty sinners, having broken God's law, deserving eternal damnation. If God gives us our due, there will be no mercy. If he simply passes by our transgressions, there will be no truth. God cannot be merciful at the expense of his justice, and he cannot be just at the expense of his mercy. How can God be both true to his law and merciful to sinners?

Behold the incarnate God, hanging on the cursed tree as the sinner's Substitute, suffering the penalty of God's law in the sinner's place, the Just for the unjust. In the cross of Christ truth and justice are fully satisfied and mercy and grace are righteously bestowed upon sinners. 'Mercy and truth are met together; righteousness and peace have kissed each other' (Ps. 85:10). The truth of God and the mercy of God, the justice of God and the grace of God, have put away the sins of God's elect by the sacrifice of God's own dear Son. 'For he hath made him to be sin for us, who knew no sin; that we might be made the righteousness of God in him' (2 Cor. 5:21).

'The everlasting covenant'

Read Psalm 89:3–4, 19–37

Before the world was, when God dwelt alone in the bliss of his own ineffable glory, the three persons of the blessed Trinity held a council of peace and established an everlasting covenant of grace, by which the everlasting salvation of God's elect and the glory of God in their salvation were guaranteed.

God the Father voluntarily agreed to save a people whom he had chosen in his own everlasting love. *God the Son* willingly agreed to be Surety for those people whom he and his Father loved. He volunteered to come in human flesh to obey the law as our Representative, establishing righteousness in the earth, and to suffer the penalty of the law as our Substitute, satisfying the justice of God for our sins. The Son of God asked the Father for the souls of his beloved people, to trust into his hands their immortal souls, their eternal salvation and the very glory of the eternal Godhead. And the Father, looking on his Son in absolute confidence, gave his Son all the host of his elect and declared them to be in Christ redeemed, justified, sanctified and glorified. *God the Holy Spirit* joyfully agreed to come in the fulness of time to each of those people who were chosen of the Father and for whom the Son had become Surety. He volunteered to regenerate them, call them, give them faith in Christ and preserve them unto the day of resurrection and everlasting glory.

Thus before the world began, God Almighty sovereignly arranged and secured the salvation of every sinner who would be saved by his grace. This is what God promised in that covenant: 'They shall be my people, and I will be their God: and I will give them one heart, and one way, that they may fear me for ever, for the good of them, and of their children after them: and I will make an everlasting covenant with them, that I will not turn away from them, to do them good; but I will put my fear in their hearts, that they shall not depart from me' (Jer. 32:38–40).

'Whether ye be in the faith'

Read 2 Peter 1:1-11

Paul admonishes all of us to make our calling and election sure. He says, '**Examine yourselves, whether ye be in the faith; prove your own selves. Know ye not your own selves, how that Jesus Christ is in you, except ye be reprobates?**' He does not admonish us to examine one another, but he does tell us to examine ourselves. Here are three points by which I examine my own faith. I urge you to do the same.

1. *Is my faith based upon the Word of God?* I know this: 'Faith cometh by hearing, and hearing by the Word of God' (Rom. 10:17). If my faith is genuine, it is born in my heart by the Word of truth. True faith arises from a proper knowledge of God, as he is revealed in Christ, in his holy and sovereign character (John 17:3). True faith arises from a proper knowledge of Christ, the incarnate God, in the glory of his efficacious, sin-atoning sacrifice as our Substitute. And true faith arises from a proper knowledge of ourselves, our guilt, our depravity and our inability. Until a man knows what the Bible says about God, about Christ and about himself, he cannot exercise saving faith.

2. *Does my faith cause me to have a well-grounded hope of a saving interest in Christ?* True faith causes a man to have a good hope through grace. Trusting the merits of Christ's righteousness and shed blood, the true believer has a confident, assured hope of eternal salvation and acceptance with God in Christ. True faith does not depend upon feelings, works or desires. True faith trusts Christ alone and enjoys peaceful hope of eternal glory in him.

3. *Does my faith produce a principle of love in my heart for Christ and his people?* Faith causes a man to love Christ as he is and love the people of God as they are in Christ. This love is a self-denying, self-sacrificing commitment to Christ and his people. Any faith that lacks this love is a false faith.

'Christ is the end of the law'

Read Romans 7:1-13; Galatians 3:19-26

I do not suggest that the law is evil. It is not. God's law is holy, just and good (1 Tim. 1:8-9). I do not say that the believer is free to break the law. Not only is the believer not free to break the law, he has no desire to do so. To those who believe, God's commandments are not grievous (1 John 5:1-3). If we could, we would love God with all our hearts and our neighbours as ourselves. But we do not have the ability to do so. I do say that in Christ the believer is entirely free from the law, because '**Christ is the end of the law for righteousness to every one that believeth**'. 'We are not under the law, but under grace.' We have been crucified with Christ and have 'become dead to the law by the body of Christ'. There is no sense whatsoever in which it may be said that the believer is under the law.

We have no covenant with the law. We live under a covenant of grace. We have no commitment to the law. Our commitment is to Christ, who obeyed the law for us. We do nothing by the constraint of the law. 'The love of Christ constraineth us.'

Christ is the end of the law's purpose. The purpose and object of God's law is to bring us to Christ. Once it has served that purpose, it has no other (Gal. 3:24-25). The law is the sheriff's deputy, who shuts men up in prison for their sin, concluding them all under condemnation, so that they may look to the free grace of God in Christ for deliverance. The law is God's black dog, by which he fetches his sheep home.

Christ is the end of the law in the sense that he has fulfilled it as our Representative. He has magnified the law and made it honourable, establishing righteousness to meet the law's demands as our Representative and dying under the law's just penalty as our Substitute.

By his obedience to the law, *Christ has terminated the law's claims upon the believer* so that in Christ we are entirely free from the law.

Does man have a free will?

Read John 6:35-47

Without question a man is free to do anything he wants to do and has the ability to do. But all reasonable people must acknowledge that a man's desires and abilities are limited by his nature. A mother has the ability to strangle her nursing baby, but she has no desire to do so; it would be contrary to her nature. The Ethiopian may desire to change the colour of his skin, but he has no ability to do so. No, man's will is not absolutely free. It is limited and bound by his nature.

Because man by nature is a fallen, guilty, sinful and depraved creature, altogether without life towards God, our Lord declares that with regard to righteousness, faith and eternal life, man has neither the desire nor the ability to obtain these things. They are altogether contrary to his nature and beyond his ability. The Lord Christ says, 'Ye will not come to me, that ye might have life' (John 5:40). That is to say, in your natural condition, you have no desire to come to Christ. In another place, the Son of God says, 'No man can come to me' (John 6:44). The natural man has no ability to come to Christ. He is spiritually dead. He has no spiritual inclinations, desires or abilities. With regard to the things of Christ, he has no free will.

Yet, in order to be saved, a man must come to Christ in true faith, surrendering to him as Lord with a willing heart. How can this be? God the Holy Spirit sovereignly comes to men and women who are dead in sin and gives them life in Christ. He creates a new heart and a new nature within them. By the preaching of the gospel, he calls them to Christ, with irresistible grace and power, and they always come. Grace makes men willing to come to Christ. Grace gives men the ability to come. And grace sees to it that they do come. Well might every sinner cry out, 'Heal me, O Lord, and I shall be healed; save me, and I shall be saved' (Jer. 17:14).

Five things that are essential
to your salvation

Read 2 Thessalonians 1:1-10

It is plainly written: 'He that believeth and is baptized shall be saved; but he that believeth not shall be damned' (Mark 16:16). Salvation comes to sinners by simple faith in the Lord Jesus Christ. Believe Christ and you will be saved. Yet anyone who reads the Bible, except those whose minds are blinded to all reason by modern religion, knows that true, saving faith is based upon certain revealed knowledge (Rom. 10:13-17). In order for a person to be saved, these five things are essential. The Word of God makes it abundantly clear that true, saving faith involves these five things.

1. *You must know God in his true character* (Exod. 33:19; 34:5-7). Very few people know who God is. The god they worship is but an idolatrous figment of their imagination (Ps. 50:21). God's true character is revealed in the Scriptures. God is absolutely and universally sovereign (Isa. 46:9-11; Dan. 4:35-37; Rom. 9:11-24). God is inflexibly just (Ezek. 18:20; Gal. 3:10). God is infinitely gracious (Micah 7:18-20; Rom. 3:24-26).

2. *You must know yourself in your true character* (Eph. 2:1-3). Man is spiritually dead. His heart is depraved (Matt. 15:19). His actions are evil. He is justly condemned by the law of God. And he has neither the desire nor the ability to change his condition (John 5:40; 6:44).

3. *You must know the Lord Jesus Christ in his true character* (1 Tim. 3:16). Jesus Christ is God in human flesh. He is both God and man in one person. Because he is man, he is able to suffer the penalty of sin. Because he is God, he is able to satisfy the claims of divine justice.

4. *You must know what happened at the cross* (2 Cor. 5:21; Heb. 9:12; Isa. 53:10-11). By his one great sacrifice for sin, Christ satisfied the justice of God for us and put away the sins of his elect.

5. *You must be reconciled to God in your heart* (2 Cor. 5:20). To be reconciled to God is to justify God (Ps. 51:4), willingly bow to Christ as Lord (Luke 14:25-33) and trust Christ alone (Rom. 10:9-13).

The fall of Adam was not an accident

Read Genesis 3:1-24

We who believe the gospel doctrine of absolute predestination do not for a moment entertain the monstrous notion that God forced Adam to sin in the garden, though there are many who delight to accuse us of that evil. Yet we do not accept the preposterous idea that the sin and fall of our father Adam was an accident, which took the eternal God by surprise and shattered his plans for man and creation. A god whose plan and purpose could be shattered, or even shaken, by his creature would be no god at all. Two things must be recognized by all who worship God and receive the revelation of Holy Scripture as the Word of God.

1. If it had been God's will and purpose to do so, he could have kept Adam from sinning in the garden as easily as he kept Abimelech from sinning with Sarah (Gen. 20:6).

2. The sin and fall of our father Adam, like all other things, was predestinated by God in eternity and was brought to pass by the rule of God's sovereign providence for the eternal good of God's elect and the glory of his own great name (Eph. 1:11; Rom. 8:28; 11:33-36).

God did not force Adam, or in any way compel him to sin. But all the circumstances which brought to pass the sin of Adam and the fall of our race were ordained of God in infinite wisdom, goodness and grace. In the same way, God did not force men to crucify his Son. Yet his Son died by the hands of wicked men at exactly the time, and in exactly the way, which God had from eternity predestined (Acts 2:23). God is answerable to no man's judgement. And I certainly do not pretend to have understanding in the mystery of God's purpose and ways. But I do see one glorious aspect of infinite wisdom and grace in the fall of Adam: had Adam not fallen, we could never have known the glory of God's grace in Christ. Adam fell in the garden, according to God's purpose, so that we might know the love, the grace, the wisdom and the glory of God in Christ, the Lamb of God slain from the foundation of the world.

Three great privileges of God's elect

Read Acts 2:41-47; 4:32-37

Baptism — confessing Christ. Baptism is the believer's public confession of faith in Christ. It is a public identification with Christ and his people. It is a public vow of our commitment to the glory of Christ. Being buried with Christ in baptism, the believer says to all the world, 'I belong to the Lord Jesus Christ. I died with him as my Substitute, was buried with him and have been raised up again with him in life. Christ is my life. Henceforth, I live not for self, not for the world, not for Satan, but for Christ' (Rom. 6:3-4).

Church membership — fellowship with Christ in his body. A local church is a body of believers voluntarily gathered in the name of Christ for the worship of Christ, the furtherance of the gospel and the salvation of God's elect. The fellowship of believers in a local church is vital to our spiritual growth in the grace and knowledge of our Lord Jesus Christ. We need one another! (Heb. 10:24-25.) Church membership is an avowed *commitment to the body of Christ* (Phil. 2:1-4.) As a family, we are committed to one another. Church membership is *communion with the body of Christ.* I love the fellowship of God's people, because in the fellowship of God's people I find fellowship with my God and Saviour, the Lord Jesus Christ (Matt. 18:20). Church membership is more than having your name on the same church register. It is *care for the body of Christ.* The true people of God truly care for one another (1 Cor. 12:24-27).

The Lord's Supper — remembering Christ. The Lord's Supper is a symbolic remembrance of Christ. It is a public ordinance in which believers picture their redemption by the death of Christ (1 Cor. 11:23-30). Those who do not trust Christ dare not receive this, or any other ordinance. They do not discern the Lord's body: the need of the incarnation, the righteousness performed in his body, or the sacrifice of his body. But all who trust Christ are to observe this blessed feast in remembrance of him. And we are to observe it often. It is needful for us, so long as we are in this flesh, to be frequently reminded of our Lord's great sacrifice for our redemption.

Four of the most important men in the Bible

Read John 1:35-51

I do not know their names, where they were born, or where they died. The Bible only records one thing that they did. But the one thing which these four men did is the most important work ever performed by men: these four men brought a man to the Lord.

These four men *knew the Lord*. They had true faith in Christ. They believed him to be the Messiah. They recognized his power and authority as the sovereign Lord, the Son of God. They knew that he had power both to heal disease and to forgive sin. They also *knew where Christ was and where he was displaying his power and grace*. He is God. He is everywhere present. But there are certain places where he meets with men and manifests his power and grace to them. These men *had a friend who desperately needed Christ*. Their friend was a hopelessly, helplessly paralysed man. They could not heal their friend or forgive his sin. And they had no way of knowing whether or no Christ would so do. But they knew that if he would, he could. Knowing Christ's power and grace and knowing their friend's desperate need, these four men *determined to bring their poor friend to Christ*. It was not an easy thing to do. The room was crowded with people. No one offered to assist them nor even to make room for them. But they were not deterred. 'They sought means to bring him in and to lay him before him.' At last they got their friend before the Lord. They said nothing; they simply laid the helpless man before Christ. And as a direct result of their labours and faith towards Christ, two marvellous things happened: a sinner was freely forgiven of all his sins and the Lord God was glorified. These four men had been voluntary instruments in the hands of the Lord, and God used them to accomplish his eternal purpose!

I want to be like these four men, diligently labouring to bring sinners to Christ, faithfully giving myself to the work, allowing nothing to stand in my way. And I want you to be like these men — each one doing what he can to get sinners to the Saviour. We cannot save men, renew their hearts, nor give them faith. But we can get men under the sound of the gospel.

'He seemed as one that mocked'

Read Matthew 5:1-15

Lot was a righteous man. He believed God and worshipped God. He was saved, justified and forgiven. But Lot made some very careless decisions early in life that proved most costly for him. In a dispute over a few four-footed beasts, he left his godly Uncle Abraham, took his family and moved to Sodom. The men of that city, who would be his neighbours, were wicked. In Sodom there was no prophet of God, no place where the Lord God was worshipped and not to be found one person who worshipped and served the Lord. In short, there was not one thing in the city that could be of spiritual, eternal benefit to Lot and his family. But Sodom was a wealthy city and offered good business opportunities for a man like Lot. He could provide well for his family, his wife would have the comforts of a nice home and plenty of neighbours and his children would receive a good education and be able to enjoy the social advantages of life in the city. Like most of us, Lot took great care to provide the best for his children in this world and, I am afraid, like most of us, he showed little concern for the eternal welfare of their souls.

At last God sent his servants to Sodom to warn Lot of his impending judgement. They told him to go out and gather his family around him and 'bring them out of this place: for the Lord hath sent us to destroy this city'. Lot knew God; he believed what God's servants told him. Suddenly he was aroused by a sense of divine justice. Fearing for their lives, he went out to warn his sons-in-law of God's judgement. But it was far too late. The actions of his life in Sodom silenced the words of his mouth in their ears. '**He seemed as one that mocked unto his sons-in-law**!' Lot had no influence for good upon his family. Not one soul in his family respected his religion, reverenced his God or regarded his witness. His wife, two of his daughters and his sons-in-law perished with Sodom. And the two daughters who escaped with Lot only had their judgement postponed for a while. They, too, had become Sodomites. Lot is a beacon to warn us of danger. As we love our families and care for their souls, we must avoid the foolishness of Lot.

Some dangers of legalism

Read Acts 15:1-21

Every few days I receive letters and tracts from men trying to persuade me that, though we are free in Christ, we are yet under the bondage of the law. Some of these are good men, men who believe and preach the gospel of God's free grace in Christ. But their error in this point is most serious and grievous.

1. If you seek to be justified by the law, you will surely perish. It is written: 'By the deeds of the law shall no flesh be justified in his sight.'

2. If you seek sanctification or seek to become more holy by obedience to the law, you will become self-righteous. Self-righteousness is neither more nor less than your own righteousness. It is a supposed righteousness performed by you. It is that proud foolishness of heart which supposes that you are more holy than others.

3. If you make the law your rule of life, you will lose the joy of serving Christ. The joy of Christian service is the fact that it is free, unconstrained and spontaneous. It is motivated by love. But when you make the law of God a rule of life the motive becomes fear or desire for reward and all joy is destroyed.

4. If you seek assurance by obeying the law, you will become despondent and fearful. The old Puritans, sound as they were in many points, could never gain any comforting assurance and their congregations were never allowed to enjoy any because they sought it on a legal basis. Some were driven to such despondency by legal fear that they had to be locked away in asylums to keep them from committing suicide. The law breeds fear. You cannot obey it. It can never comfort anyone except a proud, self-righteous man who does not understand it.

5. If you seek acceptance before God in any measure whatsoever upon the basis of the law, you will never be accepted at all. Christ alone is our acceptance before God. He is all our righteousness, all our sanctification, all our holiness, all our redemption and all our peace. To add anything to his finished work is to make his work vain and useless. Christ will be all, or he will be nothing.

'If it be possible, let this cup pass from me'

Read John 12:23-33

The mysteries of Gethsemane are such that we cannot begin to enter into them. I am struck by the fact that Peter, James and John, those disciples who were the nearest to our Lord when he made this prayer, never mention it. They must have realized that the soul sufferings of Christ in the garden were depths into which no mortal could ever dive. This prayer of our Lord is written so that we may wonder and adore the great humiliation of our divine Saviour, but not to supply us with a place of theological speculation. Beloved, we must learn to reverence the silence of Scripture as well as the voice of Scripture. We do not know what the cup was which our Lord prayed to have removed, because the Holy Spirit chose not to tell us. But clearly it is not what most people suppose it was.

Our Lord was not praying here that he might be delivered from going to the cross to bear the wrath of God as our Substitute. The cross was the goal of his life, not the dread of it. Never once do we see any hesitancy on the part of Christ to redeem his people. There was no cowardice in him. He voluntarily agreed to become our Substitute and to die in our place on the cross. And he was resolved to accomplish this mighty work (Ps. 40:7-8; Isa. 50:5-7). Eternally his loving eye was fixed upon the cross.

Besides, our Lord knew very well that it was not possible for the terrible cup of God's wrath to pass from him. He must take this cup, not from the hands of Judas, Pilate, or the Jews — he must take this cup from the hands of his Father and drink its bitter dregs until he had turned it upside down. God's immutable decrees and purposes required it. The covenant of grace required it. The prophecies of the Old Testament required it. His own suretyship engagements required it. The salvation of his people required it. The law, justice and glory of God required the death of our Substitute.

Blessed be his name! Immanuel would not be turned aside from his work, until at the appointed hour he cried, 'It is finished!' And his work was done!

'When ye pray ...'

Read Luke 11:1-13

The wise man gives us this solemn warning: 'Be not rash with thy mouth, and let not thine heart be hasty to utter anything before God; for God is in heaven and thou upon earth: therefore let thy words be few' (Eccles. 5:2). I would do nothing to discourage either public or private prayer. Indeed, we ought all to pray more. But in the act of prayer, we should consider who we are and to whom we are speaking. If we would, I am sure that our prayers would be more earnest, more reverent, more sincere and more effectual.

True prayer is *seeking the will of God*. A believer does not dictate to God what he should do in prayer. Rather, he seeks to know the will of God. This knowledge can be given to us only by the Spirit of God. If we can, at least in measure, know God's will in a matter, then we can pray with confidence about it.

We make our petitions *in the name of Christ*. Praying in Jesus' name is much more than simply tacking the name of Christ on the end of our prayers. It is praying in the conscious awareness that Christ is our only grounds of acceptance before God. It is praying in faith in the righteousness and shed blood of the Son of God. Christ alone merits favour with God. And we pray, asking our favours upon the ground of his merit.

Real prayer is *submitting to the will of God*. Like our Lord, we must learn to pray, 'Thy will be done.' We are all prone to pray that God will heal such and such a person, or save such and such a person, because of our relationship to that person. But what is God's will in the matter? That is what we must seek. When we pray, let us submit our personal desires to the will and glory of God.

Prayer is *an act of the heart*. God cares nothing for the length or eloquence of our prayers. He looks upon the heart. If at heart we are humbled, submissive, reverent and believing, our words might be fewer, but our prayers would be more effectual. 'Lord, teach us to pray!'

'Weep not for me!

Read Psalm 22:1-31

Our Lord was carrying his cross through the streets of Jerusalem. He had been beaten, mocked, abused and scourged. Many were astonished at the hideous sight. 'His visage was so marred more than any man, and his form more than the sons of men.' As Jesus of Nazareth carried his cross through the streets, his temples bled. His face was bruised. And his back was lacerated. The sight was more than some women in the crowd could endure. They felt great sorrow and pity for Jesus. They could not refrain themselves; they wept, bewailed and lamented this suffering man. But Immanuel stopped the procession. Turning to those women, our mighty Saviour said, '**Daughters of Jerusalem, weep not for me, but weep for yourselves, and for your children**.'

Why did our Lord rebuke these weeping women? They were rebuked not because they wept, but because they wept over the wrong thing. They felt sorry for poor Jesus. My friend, Jesus Christ is not a man to be pitied; he is a God to be worshipped and a King to be served! Too many people weep over the story of the crucifixion because they feel sorry for Jesus, thinking that sorrow for Jesus is salvation. Our Lord was not helplessly dragged off to the cross. He marched up to Calvary in triumph. We ought never to lament the fact that Christ died as he did upon the cross. Rather, let us glory in the cross. The death and resurrection of the Son of God is our salvation. Without the cross, we would all perish. The cross is God's remedy for human sin. Weep not over the cure, but over the disease. Weep not over the fulfilling of the law, but over the transgression of the law. Do not ever weep over the fact that Christ died as a Substitute for sinners, but weep over the sin which made the death of Christ necessary for the salvation of his people.

'What shall I render unto the Lord?'

Read Psalm 92:1-15

As believers, we are no longer under the bondage of the law. The legal fears and terrors of the law have no power over us. Paul's language could not be clearer: 'The law is not made for a righteous man, but for the lawless and disobedient.'

But our freedom from the law does not mean that we are without responsibility, obligation or constraint. Paul looked upon himself as the bond-slave of Jesus Christ. We who believe are divorced from Moses, but we are married to Christ. And with marriage comes commitment, responsibility and a certain form of bondage. Yes, we are in bondage to Christ. Ours is a deliberate, wilful, voluntary bondage. Our hearts are bound to Christ by cords of love. 'The love of Christ constraineth us.' This bondage of love is the greatest freedom imaginable.

Now let me reason with you who love the Lord. Surely the motives of love are stronger than any produced by the fear of the law. Think of all the Lord's benefits towards you. Who can count the small dust of God's favours towards us? Just to think of God's daily, temporal mercies of providence is overwhelming. But we have experienced the love, mercy and grace of God in Christ! God gave us his Son! He chose us to be his own. We are redeemed by the blood of Christ and clothed with his righteousness! God the Holy Spirit gave us life, led us to Christ and dwells in our hearts. 'Beloved, now are we the sons of God, and it doth not yet appear what we shall be.'

Surely the consideration of the Lord's benefits towards us will inspire in a loving heart a sense of overwhelming obligation. Out of love to our Saviour and God we ask, '**What shall I render unto the Lord for all his benefits toward me**?' What gift can I bring to my Redeemer? How can I prove the sincerity of my love? How can I show the depth of my gratitude? I will give myself whole-heartedly to my God and Saviour, Jesus Christ, heart, soul, mind and being. Whatever I am, whatever I possess, it belongs to Christ. My time, my property, my talents, my labour all are his. That is the least that I can do. 'Lord, here am I. Use your servant for your glory, however you see fit.'

'Precious in the sight of the Lord is the death of his saints'

Read 2 Corinthians 5:1-10

This statement is true only of the death of a believer. To die without Christ is a terrible thing. For the unbeliever death is the wages of sin, the execution of justice, the beginning of sorrow, the end of all hope, the end of all mercy and the end of all opportunity. To die without Christ is to enter into the torments of infinite, inflexible, insatiable wrath. But for the believer death is a far different thing. For us there is no penalty to be inflicted in death. There is no sin to terrify us. And there is no law to condemn us. Christ, our Substitute, has borne the penalty of our sin, removed our guilt and satisfied every demand of the law and justice of God. To the child of God, it is not death to die. Death for us is a covenant blessing (1 Cor. 3:21-23). It is a departure out of this world unto the Father. It is being unclothed that we might be clothed upon. It is falling asleep in the arms of Christ. It is entrance into the heavenly kingdom. Death to a believer is a happy home-going. There is no limit in this statement; if a man, woman, or child who dies is a believer, one of God's saints, that death is a precious thing in the sight of God.

How can the death of God's saints be precious to him? Why, because they are precious to him. They are the objects of his eternal, electing love, redeemed by the precious blood of Christ and members of his body, the church. The death of God's saints is precious, because then the precious blood of Christ will be satisfied. We are 'the fulness of him that filleth in all'. Without his body, every member intact, the Head cannot be complete. As members of his body, we must be where our Head is — in glory. A believer's death is precious in the sight of God, because it answers the prayer and satisfies the desire of God's well-beloved Son (John 17:24).

Children of God, let us learn to look upon our death and the death of our believing relatives and friends as the Lord does. We may sorrow because we miss them and feel our need of them. But we have no reason to weep for their sakes who die in the Lord. Death to a believer is a precious thing. To be absent from the body is to be present with the Lord!

'There came a leper'

Read Luke 17:1-19

The cleansing of this leper is recorded by Matthew, Mark and Luke. Surely the Holy Spirit intends us to learn some specific lesson from it. This leper is held up as an example of the way in which a sinner must approach the Lord in order to obtain mercy. Let me show you how this man came to Christ.

1. This leper came to Christ *with a deep sense of his personal need*. He was a leper. According to the law, he was unclean, corrupt and defiled. He was an outcast of society. Luke tells us that he was 'full of leprosy'. There was no covering for his disease. From head to toe, he was defiled. The sure result of his disease was death. He could not help himself and no one else could or would help him. Do you need Christ?

1. This leper came to the Lord *in great humiliation*. Mark says, he came 'kneeling'. Luke tells us that he fell on his face at the Saviour's feet. He saw who and what he was. He saw who and what Christ is. And he was humbled. The way to Christ is the road of humiliation. If you would go up to heaven, you must come down in repentance.

3, This leper came to Christ *confessing true faith*. He called Jesus 'Lord'. He knew that Christ is what he claims to be – Lord and King. And he knew that Christ could do what he claimed. He worshipped the man Christ Jesus as God ('Lord, thou canst make me clean'). Jesus Christ is God. He is Lord and King. He has power sufficient to save your soul.

4. This leper came to Christ *in total submission*. '**Lord, if thou wilt, thou canst.**' He knew that the sovereign power of Christ is dispensed according to the sovereign will of Christ. He has mercy on whom he will have mercy. He ventured himself upon the sovereign mercy of Christ, saying, 'Lord, I know you have all power, do for me what you will according to your own great mercy. If he turns me away, I cannot be worse off than I am now. But he can make me whole. I must sue for mercy.'

5. This leper *obtained mercy*, and so may you! The Lord said, 'I will, be thou clean.' His healing was immediate and complete. God never has turned away one who came to Christ like this.

'Jehovah-Jireh...'

Read Genesis 22:1–14

This name, by which God revealed himself to Abraham, may be translated by a number of expressions. But however you translate it, Jehovah-Jireh expresses the idea of *the Lord seeing and being seen*. In this place we are taught that our heavenly Father sees our need; and, with the foresight of divine love, he provides us with what we need in Christ, and in that provision God himself is seen. The ram which God provided as a substitute for Isaac was typical of God's own great provision of his Son as the Substitute for sinners.

Jehovah-Jireh means, 'The Lord will *see*.' God graciously saw our need as sinners. Seeing the ruin of our race by the fall of Adam, and our great need because of that fall, God pitied us. He saw our need as transgressors of his holy law. By nature we are all sinners, children of wrath, perishing under the sentence of divine justice, and God saw our great need. In this fact there is a ray of hope. Since God sees our need, we have hope that he will provide.

Jehovah-Jireh means, 'The Lord will *provide*.' Our God provided his own Son to be a Substitute for us, graciously and freely, simply because he loved us. And the provision was gloriously effective. The ram was slain in Isaac's place, so Isaac must go free. Even so, the Son of God was slain in the place of his people, and the very justice of God demands that they go free! At the very time when we were ready to perish, God said in his law, 'Lay not thy hand upon the lad!' A Substitute was provided to satisfy our need as guilty men.

Jehova-Jireh means,' The Lord will *be seen*'. Go to Mt Calvary. There you see Abraham's prophecy fulfilled. There is God's glorious display of himself in justice and grace, in holiness and mercy, in wrath and love. Behold the revelation of God. Christ crucified is Jehovah-Jireh!

'We love him, because he first loved us'

Read 1 John 4:1-21

We may differ on many points. But in this one thing every true child of God is like every other child of God: **'We love him.'** We do not love him as we desire. We do not love him as we know we should. We do not love him as we soon shall. But we do really love him. It is not possible for a man to experience the grace of God in salvation and not love the God of all grace. It is not possible for a man to know the efficacy of Christ's blood in his own soul and not love his gracious Redeemer. It is not possible for a man to have his heart renewed by the power of the Holy Spirit and not love the Spirit of life. In spite of our many weaknesses, sins and failures, we do honestly and sincerely confess, 'Lord, thou knowest all things, thou knowest that I love thee.'

We know also that we would never have loved him if he had not loved us first. The love of God for us precedes our love for him. **'He first loved us.'** He loved us before we had any desire to be loved by him. He loved us before we sought his grace. He loved us before we had any repentance or faith. He loved us before we had any being. He loved us eternally. Does he not say, 'I have loved thee with an everlasting love, therefore with lovingkindness have I called thee'? He chose us, redeemed us and called us because he loved us.

Not only does God's love for us precede our love for God, but God's love for us is the cause of our love for him. **'We love him, because he first loved us.'** This heart of mine was so hard, this will was so stubborn, that I would never have loved the Lord, if he had not intervened to conquer me with his love. In the midst of my sin and corruption, he passed by, and behold it was 'the time of love'. He revealed his great love for me in Christ. As I beheld the crucified Christ, dying in the place of sinners, the love of God conquered this rebel's heart. Trusting Christ as my only Saviour, I am compelled to love him, because he first loved me. And now I know that whatever I am, by the grace of God, I am because he loved me. Tell me, my friend, is it not so with you?

'How can a man be just with God?'

Read Romans 3:19-31

This is the question that causes me most concern. Like other men, I am curious about the decrees of God and the events of the future. But this is the question which outweighs all others. I know that God is holy, righteous and just, and that I am a sinner. Soon I will stand before the bar of God's judgement and be weighed in the balances with his strict righteousness and justice. Woe unto the man who is found wanting in that day! How can a man be just with God?

I know this: *I cannot justify myself.* Job said, 'If I justify myself, mine own mouth shall condemn me.' It is not possible for me, (or any other man) to be justified before God by my own works. It is written: 'By the work of the law shall no flesh be justified.' Having once broken God's law, we can never make reparation.

This too I know: if ever I am justified, *it will be by the work of God alone.* The apostle Paul wrote, 'It is God that justifieth.' God can and does justify sinners. Justification is a gracious work of God, accomplished through the shed blood of Christ, his Son. The Lord Jesus Christ stood before God as the sinner's Substitute. He legally represented us before the law by the appointment of God himself. The law required perfect obedience to its precepts. Christ rendered that obedience. The law required a full payment for sin. Christ paid the awful debt. This is the only way that God could forgive sin. His law had to be fulfilled. Therefore, Jesus Christ voluntarily assumed our nature and place. Since he fulfilled the law's righteousness and its penalty, all who ever believe were 'justified freely by his grace'. Through the blood of Christ, God is both just and the Justifier of all who believe.

Yet it is equally clear that if I am justified, *I must receive that justification by faith alone.* My faith will not satisfy the law's requirements. Christ alone can do that. But as I rest in Christ and trust in the merits of his righteousness and shed blood, God declares that I am justified! 'All that believe are justified from all things.' 'We have believed in Jesus Christ, that we might be justified by the faith of Christ.'

'Christial is all!'

Read 1 Corinthians 1:17-31

Never were three words spoken which are more precious, and at the same time more profound than these three blessed words of the apostle Paul: '**Christ is all**.' Who can tell out the depth of their meaning?

Christ is *all we need*. We are sin; Christ is righteousness. We are filthiness; Christ is cleansing. We are naked; Christ is clothing. We are ignorance; Christ is wisdom. We are guilty; Christ is pardon. We are blind; Christ is healing. We are dead; Christ is life. Whatever there is that a poor, guilty sinner needs, it is found in Christ.

Christ is *all before God*. It has pleased the Father to put all the blessings of grace in his Son. Christ is the fulness of grace and glory. There is nothing that God will accept, except his Son. Christ is all God will accept for both the justification and the sanctification of his people. We must be washed in his blood, or we cannot be justified. We must be clothed in his righteousness, or we cannot be accepted before God. That righteousness which God imputed to us in justification is the righteousness of Christ alone. And the righteousness which God imparted to us in regeneration (the beginning of sanctification) is the righteousness of Christ. And the only righteousness that God will accept in the Day of Judgement is the perfect righteousness of Christ.

Christ is *all to all his people*. Unto them that believe, he is precious. He is all that we desire. If I have Christ, I have enough. Christ is all to be trusted, loved, worshipped, served and honoured. Christ is all our hope, all our joy, all our peace, all our assurance and all our comfort. Christ is all in life, all in death and all in eternity. Yes, in heaven, Christ will be all. He will be all our beauty, all our glory and all our reward.

Other refuge have I none
Hangs my helpless soul on thee;
Leave, ah, leave me not alone,
Still support and comfort me!

'The Word of God'

Read Psalm 119:1-24

Our faith rests entirely upon the Word of God. If it could ever be proved that the Bible is not the inspired, inerrant Word of God, then the gospel of Christ would be proved false. But the infidel, though he may scoff, cannot ever produce such proof. The fact that the Bible stands today shatters every argument of those sceptics who deny that the Bible is the Word of God.

This blessed book is the greatest standing miracle in the world today. Just think of this: there was never an order given to any man to plan the writing of this volume. Nor was there any concerted effort on the part of men to write it. Under the sovereign direction of the Holy Spirit, the Bible gradually developed over a period of 1600 years. Little by little, part by part, century by century, it came out in parts and fragments. It was written on two continents, in countries hundreds of miles apart. It was written in three languages — Hebrew, Aramaic and Greek. And it was written by scores of men, from every possible background variation. Yet it stands as one unified volume.

This is a book with one message. It contains one system of doctrine, one plan of salvation, one principle of conduct and one rule of faith. The one message of the Bible is that of redemption by the shed blood of Christ. Substitution is stamped upon every page. Everything in the Bible points to Christ and his substitutionary work.

There are historical statements in the Bible that could not have been known except by revelation: the account of creation, the decrees of God, the covenant of grace. And there are doctrines taught in the Bible which no human mind ever devised: the character of the triune God, the incarnation of Christ, substitutionary atonement. Add to this the perfect accuracy of the prophecies of the Bible and their evident fulfilment. I say there can be but one rational explanation for the existence of this divine book: 'All scripture is given by inspiration of God.' 'Holy men of God spake as they were moved by the Holy Spirit.' Without question, this is the Word of God!

'We know'

Read Romans 8:1-39

If Holy Scripture was a ring and the Epistle to the Romans its precious stone, chapter 8 would be the sparkling point of the radiant gem. Reading this chapter, I see several things that we who trust in the Lord Jesus Christ know.

1. We know that there is *now* no condemnation to them that are in Christ Jesus (v.1). Beloved, if we are in Christ, vitally joined to him by faith, we are free from all condemnation. Do not allow Satan to deceive you. If you are in Christ *all* your sins are under the blood! Right now, we are free!

2. We know that *all* of God's children have the Spirit of God (v. 14). 'If any man have not the Spirit of Christ, he is none of his.' The Holy Spirit is in us as the Spirit of life, adoption, comfort, guidance and prayer.

3. We know that there is *a better day coming* (v. 18). Today this earth is under the curse of sin. This world is a place of suffering, a vale of tears. But soon our Lord will create all things new. In that day, his glory will be revealed in us.

4. We know that *all* things work together for the eternal good of God's elect (v.28). All things that take place upon this earth come to pass according to God's eternal purpose for the good of his people.

5. We know that every believer is *perfectly* and *completely* saved in Christ (vv. 29-30). There is nothing lacking, nothing left undone. Christ has done all. In our Representative we are loved with a perfect love, accepted, justified, called and glorified. God saves sinners in a way that causes his Son to get the glory. He is the Firstborn among many brethren.

6. And we know that *nothing* shall ever separate us from the love of Christ (vv. 35-39). Come what may, I stand convinced, he will never cease to love his own.

How can we be so sure of these things? Because God gave his Son, we know he will with him freely give us all things. 'What shall we then say to these things?' I'll say this: 'If God be for us, who can be against us?' And I'll say this also: 'To God be the glory, great things he hath done!'

'He shall not fail'

Read Isaiah 63:1-14

This is a blessed promise concerning the person and work of the Lord Jesus Christ. It is a promise given to those who look upon him with an eye of faith. Whatever it is that the Lord Jesus has undertaken to perform will most assuredly be accomplished. He cannot fail, because he is the Son of God. 'He shall see of the travail of his soul, and shall be satisfied.'

1. Our Lord did not fail *to fulfil every promise and prophecy* of the Old Testament. Everything that was written concerning Christ was fulfilled in Jesus of Nazareth.

2. The Lord Jesus Christ did not fail *to magnify God's law* and make it honourable (v. 21.) Living upon this earth as our Representative, the God-man perfectly obeyed the law of God, weaving for us a spotless robe of righteousness.

3. Our blessed Redeemer did not fail *to make a full and complete satisfaction of divine justice* for his people. It is blasphemous to suppose that the Lord Jesus Christ tried to redeem the souls of men who perish under the wrath of God. That would mean that he failed in his work! When Christ cried, 'It is finished', the work of redemption was finished. The justice of God's law and nature was satisfied in Christ for every soul for whom he stood as Surety.

4. The Good Shepherd will not fail *to bring every sheep* given to him by his Father *into glory*. All that the Father gave him, he will seek and they will come to him. And he will present us faultless before the presence of his glory.

5. King Jesus will not fail to reign until all his enemies are put under his feet. He will not fail to establish a perfect rule of righteousness upon this earth. In this place, where the battle was fought and won, the King must reign.

I believe in the final perseverance of the Lord Jesus Christ. This is a glorious thought to comfort our souls: '**He shall not fail!**'

'That I may know him...'

Read Song of Songs 5:1-16

This was the object of Paul's life, that for which he sacrificed everything: country, kindred, honour, liberty and life itself. Notice that this was not Paul's prayer as an unconverted man, that he might know Christ and be saved. This is the desire of a saved man, one who enjoyed the full assurance that his sins were pardoned and that he was 'accepted in the Beloved'. This is the desire of a regenerate soul, '**that I may know him**'.

I am afraid that there are many very religious people who are content to live without knowing Christ. They can say with Paul, 'that I may win him and be found in him'. That they desire. But this higher aspiration has never stirred their hearts: 'that I may know him'. They are content to know the history of Christ's life, the doctrine he taught and the signs of his coming kingdom. These things are all good in their place. But the one thing needful is that we know Christ himself. This is my soul's desire. I hope that it is yours also, 'that I may know him'.

1. I want to know the glory of Christ's person, by a personal acquaintance with him.

2. I want to know the virtue of Christ's blood, by experiencing its efficacy.

3. I want to know the fellowship of Christ's sufferings by entering into the suffering of my Substitute with him.

4. I want to know the power of Christ's resurrection, by being raised by him to the newness of life.

5. I want to know the fulness of Christ's love, by experiencing and reflecting that love.

6. I want to know the peace of Christ's presence, by resting in his love, relying upon his promise and confidently trusting his faithfulness.

7. I want to know Christ himself! This is a knowledge that is given to them that believe. It is a spiritual knowledge of Christ that we desire (2 Cor. 5:16). The more we know him, the more we see how little we know him. But this I know, to know him is to love him. And soon, we shall see him as he is. Then, oh blessed thought, then, we shall know him!

'Knowing, brethren beloved, your election'

Read 1 Thessalonians 1:1-10

We do not know the mysteries of God's eternal decree. But a few things are clearly revealed in the Scriptures about election. Election is a free, sovereign, eternal, irreversible and loving act of God's abundant grace. Election is in no way contrary to the promises of God revealed in the gospel. It is promised: 'Come unto me and be ye saved all ye ends of the earth.' 'Come unto me, and I will give you rest.' 'Whosoever will, let him come and take of the water of life.' 'Believe on the Lord Jesus Christ, and thou shalt be saved.' 'If thou shalt confess with thy mouth the Lord Jesus, and believe in thine heart that God hath raised him from the dead, thou shalt be saved.' I know that the promises of God are sure and the responsibility of every man stands, election not withstanding. 'God commandeth all men to repent.' 'This is his commandment, that we believe on the name of his Son, Jesus Christ.' You must repent of your sins, believe on Christ and submit to him as Lord and Saviour. If you will not, your damnation is just. If you do, it is because God has chosen you as the object of his love before the world began.

Paul told the saints at Thessalonica that he knew their 'election of God'. But how could he know it? He tells us five things that gave clear evidence of their election. If you have experienced these things, you too were chosen in Christ before the world began.

1. God's elect have heard the gospel effectually (v.5.) They have heard the voice of God in the gospel by the power of the Holy Spirit.

2. God's elect have become followers of Christ (v.6). They imitate him in faith, in love, in patience and in spiritual joy.

3. God's elect are committed to the gospel (v.8).

4. God's elect have been converted to God (v.9). They have experienced a mighty change: a change of mind, a change of masters, a change of motives.

5. God's elect are waiting for Christ (v.10). We live not for this world, for ease, or for gain. We live in anticipation of Christ's glorious descent.

'Accepted in the beloved'

Read Colossians 2:1-15

Upon what do you rest your hope of acceptance before a holy God? Baptism? Church work? A religious experience? A moral reformation? All these things, in themselves, are vain, empty and useless. They are worse! Apart from the knowledge of Christ, they are a positive curse. If you and I trust anything, in any measure, for our total acceptance before God, other than Jesus Christ, we shall surely perish! 'Christ is become of no effect unto you, whosoever of you are justified by the law; ye are fallen from grace.'

Our text declares that 'He [God the Father] **hath made us accepted in the beloved** [God the Son].' Here is a doctrine full of consolation to our hearts. God Almighty has made all of his people accepted, perfectly and completely, in Christ! It is no marvel that we should accept Christ. But there is wonder in this – God accepts us, sinners deserving his wrath, in Christ Jesus! Beloved, there exists a positive and eternal union between Christ and his people. We are one with Christ. A rapturous thought! Bone of his bone and flesh of his flesh! 'We are members of his body, of his flesh, and of his bones.' We are one with Christ in his heart from all eternity. Our names are written beneath his in the book of God's eternal election. We are in the hands of Christ, as the Surety of our redemption and eternal glory. We are in the loins of Christ spiritually. As in Adam we sinned and died, even so in Christ we died upon the cross and rose again! And we are in his very person. By a living faith we are joined to the God-man. He lives in us and we live in him! This is the vital union of faith, enjoyed by God's elect. This is the beginning of heaven and eternal glory. Being accepted in Christ, we have become the objects of God's pleasure. As God is pleased with his Son, he is pleased with all who are in his Son. Think of this, believing soul: God is well-pleased with you for Christ's sake! 'He hath made us accepted in the Beloved.'

Thou, O Christ, art all I want,
More than all in Thee I find.

False faith

Read Matthew 7:13-27

A false faith can do many things and produce many things, which make it hard to detect. A false faith can experience deep conviction for sin like Judas. It can tremble at the Word of God like Felix. It can repent like Esau. It can obtain high office in the church like Judas, Diotrephes and Demas. A false faith can speak well of Christ: 'Never a man spake like this man.' It can experience deep religious emotions like the stony-ground hearers. It can diligently perform religious works like the Pharisees. A false faith can even preach the gospel, perform miracles, cast out demons and persevere to the end (Matt. 7:22-23). But, as I read the Word of God, I see that there are three things that a false faith can never do.

1. A false faith can never produce a heart broken over sin (Ps. 51). It can offer sacrifices to try to appease God for sin. It can do good works to try to make up for sin. It can even confess sin. But 'The sacrifices of God are a broken spirit: a broken and contrite heart, O God, thou wilt not despise.' Such brokenness and humility, because of inbred sin, a false faith cannot produce.

2. A false faith cannot rest in Christ alone as the way, the truth and the life (1 Cor. 1:30-31). True faith relies upon Christ alone for salvation. When I say that Christ alone is my Saviour, I mean that he is all my redemption and cleansing, all my justification and sanctification, all my righteousness and holiness, all my pardon and forgiveness, all my glory and desire, all my hope and reward. But a false faith must mix in human merit with the merits of Christ, free will with free grace and man's works with the work of Christ.

3. A false faith cannot and will not submit to the lordship of Christ (Matt. 6:24). We cannot perfectly submit to Christ because of our sin. We would if we could, but our sinful nature prohibits us. But all who have a true faith in the Son of God submit to Christ totally. We bow to his sovereign lordship whole-heartedly. Christ alone is our rightful Lord. He has a rightful claim upon all that we are and all that we possess. Where there is no submission in the heart, there is no faith in the heart.

'As he purposeth in his heart'

Read 2 Corinthians 8:1-24

Happy is the sight of a man who has a purpose in his heart! The man who purposes something in his heart plans for it; he makes whatever sacrifices are necessary to accomplish the purpose of his heart and he will not be turned aside from the purpose of his heart.

This was Paul's rule for Christians in their giving: 'Every man according as he purposeth in his heart, so let him give; not grudgingly, or of necessity: for God loveth a cheerful giver.' Paul tells us that we are not to compel men to give that which they would prefer to keep for themselves. The legal precept of tithing requires a man to pay his tenth to the church, whether he really wants to or not. Such a doctrine is totally contrary to the free spirit of the gospel. God's children give freely. We count it one of our highest privileges on this earth to give of our means to the work of the gospel. What a privilege it is for a redeemed sinner to provide food for a missionary's table!

Yet the believer should not be careless and haphazard in his giving. He should give according to the purpose of his heart. This means two things. First, we should give with a cheerful heart. And, second, we should plan to give. That is to say, we should plan our financial affairs so that we can give to the work of the gospel. If I have a dependable car, or a comfortable house, I ought not to trade that car for a newer model, or exchange that house for a more luxurious one, if in doing so my ability to give to the work of the gospel is hindered. It is infinitely more important for me to give of my means to the preaching of the gospel than it is for me to improve my social standing.

Are you ready to give? Am I? Let us give freely, cheerfully, abundantly and sacrificially. If we are constrained to do so, our constraint is not a legal one, but ours is a constraint of love. Knowing the love of Christ for us, we 'prove the sincerity of our love' to him by giving from a willing heart. Let us purpose in our hearts to give, for Christ's sake.

'God loveth a cheerful giver'

Read 2 Corinthians 9:1-15

There is an abundance of instruction in the New Testament about Christian giving. All of 1 Corinthians 9, 2 Corinthians 8 and 2 Corinthians 9 are taken up with this subject. But there are no commands to the people of God anywhere in the New Testament about how much we are to give, when we are to give, or where we are to give. Tithing and all systems like it are things altogether foreign to the New Testament. Like all other acts of worship, giving is an act of grace. It must be free and voluntary. But there are some plain, simple guidelines laid down in the New Testament for us to follow.

1. Christian giving must be motivated by love and gratitude towards Christ (2 Cor. 8:8-9). Love needs no law. It is a law unto itself. It is the most powerful and most generous of all motives.

2. Our gifts must arise from willing hearts (2 Cor. 8:12). If that which you give arises from a willing heart, if it is given freely and cheerfully, it is accepted of God. The Lord is not concerned with the amount of your gift, be it great or small; he looks to the motive behind it.

3. We should give to the work of the gospel in proportion to our blessings from the Lord (1 Cor. 16:2). We are expected to give generously in accordance with our own ability.

4. All of God's people should give ('everyone,' 1 Cor. 16:2; 'every man,' 2 Cor. 9:7). Men and women, rich and poor, old and young – all who are saved by the grace of God are expected to give for the support of God's church and kingdom.

5. We should be both liberal and sacrificial in our giving (2 Cor. 9:5-6). Beloved, we have not really given anything until we have taken that which we need, want and have use for and given it to the Lord (Mark 12:41-44).

6. Our gifts must be voluntary (2 Cor. 9:7).

7. We are to give as unto the Lord (Matt. 6:1-5). We give, not to be seen of men, but for the honour of Christ, hoping for nothing in return.

8. This kind of giving is well-pleasing to God (Phil. 4:18; Heb. 13:16).

'To whom we gave no place by subjection'

Read Galatians 2:1-21

In the early days of the church there were some self-appointed, free-lance preachers who came from Jerusalem to Antioch, perverting the gospel of Christ and subverting the souls of men. They were preaching the law of Moses, telling God's people that faith in Christ is not sufficient; you must also keep the law of Moses. Paul and Barnabas refused to tolerate their heresy. Paul calls these legalists 'false brethren' and 'spies'. His choice of terms was not accidental. Usually those who preach and promote the law of Moses spend a great deal of time spying on others, so that they may bolster their own claims to 'righteousness' by sitting in judgement upon others.

Paul shows us by his example that the spirit and doctrines of legalism must not be tolerated by the people of God. It matters not whether men preach the law of Moses as a basis for justification, as the measure of sanctification, as a rule of life, as a motive for Christian service, or as the grounds of reward in heaven – all preaching of law works is an intolerable evil.

Let no one confuse the issue. The issue is not godliness or ungodliness of life. The issue is not what the believer does, or how the believer lives in this world. The issue is the motive and attitude of the heart. The legalist is motivated by fear. The believer is motivated by love. The legalist hopes to be rewarded for his work. The believer hopes to honour God in his work. All law service is looked upon and performed as a matter of duty. Prayer, Bible reading, attendance at public worship and tithing always have an element of either the fear of punishment or the promise of reward, as they are performed by the legalist. The believer prays because his heart longs to commune with God, reads the Word because he wants to know God, attends worship because he desires to hear from God and gives because he loves God. The service and work of love is considered a privilege by the one who performs it. And you can be sure of this: God will never accept anything except that which is done with a willing heart (2 Cor. 8:12).

'Dost thou believe on the Son of God?'

Read 1 John 5:1-13

There is one question that is, above all others, of greatest importance. Our Lord himself asked it: '**Dost thou believe on the Son of God**?' The question is not, 'Are you religious?' Most people are. In comparison with this question, all questions concerning denominational affiliations and theological opinions are insignificant. How can I put this question to you with due solemnity? 'Dost you believe on the Son of God?' Life and death, heaven and hell, eternal bliss and eternal misery depend upon your answer. Perhaps there are some of you whose hearts are troubled by this question. You may be genuinely concerned about the state of your soul. You are wondering, 'What is it to believe on Christ?' Let me try to help you. There are three things essential to what we call saving faith.

1. Before any man can believe on Christ, he must have *a knowledge of him*. This knowledge comes through the preaching of the gospel. When the Holy Spirit applies the preached Word he makes us to know our need of Christ. He teaches us our guilt and helplessness. And he makes us to know who Christ is and what he has done. He shows us that the Son of God died in the place of sinners, satisfying divine justice, and that he has power to save sinners upon the merits of his substitutionary work.

2. There must be *an assent*, or agreement, to the testimony God has given concerning his Son. True faith is more than just agreeing with the historical facts and doctrinal truths of the gospel. But wherever there is true faith, there is an agreement in the heart with God's testimony in the gospel.

3. The sinner must *trust Christ*. Do you realize your wretched condition before God? Do you know yourself to be a sinner, helpless and undone? Do you assent to the truth of the gospel? All of this is good. But something more is required. You must cast yourself upon the arms of mercy. You must commit your soul, and all your hopes of salvation and life, to the Son of God, knowing that it is in his power to show you mercy and grant you eternal life. You must believe on Christ.'Dost thou believe on the Son of God?' God help you to believe.

Eternity

Read Matthew 16:13-28

Eternity is a subject about which the wisest man can know only a little. It is a subject which we must approach with our Bibles in our hands. Let us seek to know what is written about eternity. What does the Scripture say? Only those who recognize the sobering reality of eternity can live in a proper relationship to the things of time. Let me give you four statements which I picked up from an old writer, that will help you to live in the awareness of eternity.

1. We live in a world where all things are temporal and passing away. That man must be blind who cannot see this. Everything around us is decaying, dying and coming to an end.

2. We are all going to a world where everything is eternal. The great unseen world that lies beyond the grave is eternal. Whether it is happy or miserable, joyful or sorrowful, it will never end. The bliss of heaven is eternal and the torments of hell are eternal.

3. Our state in the unseen world of eternity depends on what we are in time. If we are the sons of God here, relying upon the merits of Christ as our only hope of salvation, we shall be the sons of God eternally, living in the glory of Christ. If we are the children of wrath here, rejecting Christ, we shall be the children of wrath in hell for ever, rejected by Christ.

4. Jesus Christ is the great Friend to whom we must turn for life and help, both for time and eternity. Jesus Christ alone can save your soul. Only his blood can wash away your sin. Only his righteousness can make you holy. Only his grace can present you faultless before the throne of glory. You must trust him now and live for ever, or you will for ever die.

Take your mind off the things of time, and think for a while about the reality of eternity. How will it be with your soul in eternity?

'As he is, so are we in this world'

Read 1 John 3:1-17

We all know that believers in this world bear a likeness to our Lord in his humiliation. As he was in this world, so are we in this world. As he was a man of sorrows and acquainted with grief, so are we. As he was the object of the world's hatred, so are we. As he was tempted by Satan, so are we. As he was despised and forsaken of men, so shall we be. As he went through many sufferings and death to glory, so must we. This is a great blessing of grace and a wondrous condescension of mercy, that we should have such a likeness to our Redeemer.

But our text does not say, 'as he *was*'. It says, 'as he *is*'. Do you behold the Son of God, our Saviour, in glory? There sits God in our nature. And though we are not yet there personally, we are there in our Representative. And being in Christ, we are like Christ. As he is the Son of God, we are the sons of God. As he is loved by God with an everlasting and unchangeable love of complacency and delight, so are we. Yes, God loves us just as he loves his well-beloved Son. As Christ is chosen of God and precious, so are we chosen and precious in his sight. Oh, blessed grace! As our Lord in heaven is perfectly righteous, so are we! He is justified and acquitted from that charge of sin, which he voluntarily took upon himself. And in him we are completely righteous. I wish that we could all grasp this truth – Christ is all our righteousness, and we are immaculately righteous in him. 'With his spotless garments on I am as holy as God's Son!' 'In him is no sin.' And, if I am in him, I am freed from, justified from and cleansed from all sin in the sight of God.

But John specifically says here that there is a likeness between the nature of God in heaven and his children upon the earth. 'God is love.' And the children of God in this world reflect this nature of their Father in heaven. The love of God is patient, kind, faithful, forgiving and sincere. And all of his children reflect this nature of love in this world, for 'As he is, so are we in this world.'

'The gospel'

Read Romans 1:1-17

The gospel is not preached until we have told men who Christ is, what he did, why he did it and where he is now. Here are five things which will always characterize the preaching of the gospel.

1. The gospel is *a message that honours God's holy law*. God would not and could not tarnish his holy law in order to forgive sin and save sinners. God is willing to be merciful, but his righteousness must be established, his holy law must be fulfilled. This is one part of our Saviour's work. He brought in an everlasting righteousness by his perfect obedience to God's law as our Representative (Jer.23:6; Rom. 1:16-17; 3:24-26).

2. The gospel is *a declaration of satisfied justice*. This is the doctrine of substitution. God satisfied the infinite demands of his own justice by the substitutionary sacrifice of his Son. Someone said, 'God cannot suffer, and man cannot satisfy; but the God-man both suffered and satisfied.' That is the gospel: Jesus Christ has fully satisfied the penalty of sin for every believer! (Gal. 3:13.)

3. The gospel of God is *a proclamation of salvation by grace alone* (Eph.2:8-9; 2 Tim. 1:9). God would have all men to know that the sinner's standing before him is altogether a matter of pure, free grace. Man gets nothing from God, and man cannot be accepted before God, except by grace. Every idea of human merit is contrary to the gospel (Gal. 5:2).

4. The gospel of Christ is *an announcement of grace freely bestowed upon men*. There are no conditions for the sinner to meet, no works for the sinner to do, no emotions for the sinner to feel, in order for him to prepare himself to believe on Christ. In preaching the gospel we freely invite all who will to believe on Christ and be saved. No sinner is excluded from the gospel except those who exclude themselves by their unbelief (Rom. 10:11-13).

5. The gospel of the grace of God *declares the accomplishment of eternal salvation*. We have no partial salvation to preach. We preach an almighty Saviour, who saves for ever (John 10:27-31).

'Doth this offend you?'

Read John 6:48-65

No man can faithfully preach the gospel of Christ without offending men. To many it is a stone of stumbling and a rock of offence. The preaching of the cross is the one means which God has ordained for the salvation of sinners. Yet, it is most offensive to the natural man. Why? The answer is not hard to find.

The gospel of the grace of God offends man's dignity, because **it addresses all men as sinners**. The gospel leaves no place for human dignity. It is the great leveller of men. All are sinners. We all by nature are nothing more than helpless, condemned sinners.

The gospel of God offends man's wisdom, because *it comes by divine revelation*. It is not possible for any man to know the gospel, unless it is revealed in his heart.

The gospel offends man's pride, because **it declares a particular and effectual redemption.** Our Lord Jesus did actually put away sin. By his mighty act of death, as our Substitute, Jesus Christ did really and completely accomplish eternal redemption for his people. There is nothing for the sinner to do, whereby he might proudly claim merit before God. You must bow to Christ, receiving all grace from him as a pure, free gift, or you must perish.

An the gospel of God's grace and glory in Christ offends man's love of self, because **it demands discipleship.** The gospel demands commitment. It demands total, unreserved surrender to the lordship of Christ. No man has saving faith in Christ who does not in his heart confess and acknowledge that Christ is Lord, submitting to his will, surrendering to his dominion, and trusting his grace. If Jesus Christ is not your Lord and King, he is not your Redeemer and Saviour.

To many the gospel is offensive. That cannot be changed. As surely as you attempt to make it pleasing to natural men, you will compromise its message and there will be no gospel in it. But to them who are the called by almighty grace, it is the power and wisdom of God.

'Why will ye die?'

Read Isaiah 1:1-20

Multitudes of every generation perish in their sins, and are lost for ever in hell, though they have been well instructed in gospel truth. Why?

Since the day that our father Adam sinned against God and plunged our race into spiritual death, bringing upon all men God's just wrath, man has tried to excuse his sin and shift the responsibility of his condemnation to someone other than himself. He arrogantly attempts to lay the blame for both his guilt and his damnation off on God. It cannot be done. If you go to hell, you will be without excuse; it will be your own responsibility. It will not be because your sins are so hideous that you could not be saved. All manner of sin may be forgiven. You will not go to hell because of God's eternal decree. Nowhere in the Bible is it written that God predestinated anyone to go to hell. It will not be because of any lack of ability in Christ, or any lack of willingness on his part to save you. Christ is both able and willing to save all who come to him by faith. And you will not go to hell because you were never given a wide, free, sincere invitation to come to Christ and be saved. Our Lord says to you, 'Come unto me, all ye that labour and are heavy laden, and I will give you rest.' He says, 'I have called, and ye refused.' No, if you go to hell the simple fact is you will go to hell because you were unwilling to come to Christ for life. As he said, 'Ye will not come to me that ye might have life.'

Try as you may to shift the blame for your lost and ruined condition, you cannot. You are lost because you will not be saved by Christ. J.C. Ryle was right when he wrote, 'The loss of man's soul is always attributed in Scripture to man's own want of will to be saved.' The axe must be laid to the root of the tree. If you are saved, it will be entirely God's fault, the result of deliberate effort on his part. If you go to hell, it will be entirely your own fault, the result of deliberate effort on your part.

'This man receiveth sinners'

Read Luke 15:1-24

Marvellous condescension! This man, who is above all other men, holy, harmless, undefiled and separate from sinners – this man receiveth sinners. This man, who is none other than God the eternal Son, before whom the angels hide their faces – this man receiveth sinners. Who can describe such love? It would be no great thing for any of us to seek after and receive sinners. They are of our own race. But that this man, the offended God, against whom the transgression has been committed, should receive such is a marvellous act of love and grace! He took upon himself the seed of Abraham. He bare the sin of many in his own body on the tree. And now he is willing to receive the vilest of the vile!

'This man receiveth sinners', not that they may remain in their sins; but he receives sinners that he might pardon their sins, justify their souls, cleanse their hearts by his purifying Word, preserve them by the indwelling of the Holy Spirit and enable them to serve him. He receives sinners that they may show forth his praise, enjoy his fellowship and worship at his throne. This man takes sinners from the dunghill and wears them as jewels in his crown. He plucks them as brands from the burning and preserves them as monuments of his mercy. How precious in the sight of Christ are those sinners for whom he shed his life's blood! The Son of God opens the golden gates of his royal heart and receives sinners right into himself. He admits the humbled, repentant sinner into a personal union with himself and makes him a member of his body, of his flesh and of his bones. There was never such a grand reception as this! This fact is still most sure today. Though the Son of God is exalted to the throne of glory, he is still receiving sinners today, just as he was when he walked the streets of Jerusalem. Say, sinner, will you flee to him?

> Come ye sinners, poor and needy,
> Weak and wounded, sick and sore;
> Jesus ready stands to save you,
> Full of pity, love and power.

Degrees of reward in heaven

Read Matthew 20:1-16

There is much talk today about degrees of reward in heaven. But the gospel of the grace of God allows no place for human merit. God is no man's debtor. That which he gives to men and does for men, both in his life and in the life to come, is the reward of pure grace, not of debt.

In order for something to claim merit before God, it must be perfect. God's infinite holiness, righteousness and justice will accept nothing less than perfection. Where is the man who has ever done anything that is perfect in the sight of God? Who among us would be so brazenly self-righteous as to desire God to judge and reward him upon the grounds of his own works? Our tears, our faith and the very best of our good works are so full of sin that, were they not washed in the blood of Christ, they would demand our eternal damnation!

Our only acceptance before God is Christ. He perfectly fulfilled every requirement of God's law as our Representative and satisfied every demand of divine justice as our Substitute. Now, being clothed in his righteousness and washed in his blood, everything that God can and will give to men is ours, because we are in Christ. 'He that spared not his own Son, but delivered him up for us all, how shall he not with him also freely give us all things?' In Christ, 'All things are yours.' When the Lord Jesus Christ presents us faultless and without blame before God, we shall be perfect, having no spot of sin or blemish of infirmity; and no good thing shall be withheld from us.

I read of no secondary joys in heaven. None of God's elect shall be placed in the back settlements of Canaan. The dying thief had no good works by which to claim anything from God. Yet he entered heaven, was accepted and rewarded by God in exactly the same way as the apostle Paul, through the merits of Christ, our Substitute, and his reward was just as full. Both the thief and the apostle have all they wanted and all that God can give: they had all of Christ!

'Our liberty'

Read Romans 14:1-23

The Lord Jesus Christ has given us true liberty. In Christ we have been freed from sin, Satan and the law. In him we are free from all religious traditions, customs and superstitions. And in Christ we are free to use every creature of God for food, happiness, comfort and satisfaction. Neither the church nor those who preach the gospel have any authority to bring God's people under bondage again, by making their own rules, dogmas and covenants for Christian conduct. I offer these suggestions with the prayer that they may help you to honour the Lord in the exercise of your liberty in Christ.

1. *Do not make the use or non-use of indifferent things a point of merit before God.* Indifferent things become idolatrous when you make the use or non-use of them a means of obtaining favour with God, a means of religious devotion, or a means of obtaining a peaceful conscience.

2. *Use all things in moderation.* The believer's principle of conduct is not total abstinence, but temperance, moderation and self-control. Eating is not wrong, but gluttony is. A glass of wine is not wrong (our Lord did provide the wine for the marriage feast of Cana), but drunkenness is wrong. Entertainment is not wrong, but revelling is. Our principle is 'Use all things wisely, abusing none.'

3. *Carefully avoid offending your brother.* I do not mean that you must submit to the self-righteous notions of men. But we must not be the cause of a brother acting contrary to his own conscience. This is what Paul means by offending the brethren. We must avoid it at all costs. My brother's conscience is more important than my personal desires.

4. *Make your use of all things subservient to the glory of God, the gospel of Christ and the welfare of the church.* In all things, make your love for Christ and his people the basis of your actions. Use your liberty in Christ for the honour of Christ, and you will not go far astray. We must avoid both licentiousness and legalism. Both are dreadful evils. God's people are called into liberty!

We belong to God

Read Psalm 100:1-5

It is true that all people belong to God, as creatures to their Creator, as property to its owner, as subjects to their ruler. All things and all people were made by God and for God and all are ruled by God's sovereign will. This is God's right as the absolute Sovereign of all his creatures (Rom. 9:15-26). But we who believe belong to God as a child belongs to its father, as a wife to her husband, as a willing bondslave to his master. Ours is an intimate, loving, family relationship with the eternal God.

We belong to God by *the sovereign purpose of his grace*. In eternity God said, 'I will be their God; and they shall be my people.' Were it not for God's electing grace, no one would ever be saved. Indeed, were it not for God's election and determination to save some, the world would never have been created. We belong to God because he chose us as his own (2 Thess. 2:13-14).

We are the Lord's by *the special purchase of his Son*. 'Ye are bought with a price,' Paul said. It is not expected that the ungodly and unbelieving should seek the honour of Christ. They were not redeemed by him. But it is most reasonable that we should willingly give ourselves to the service of our Saviour's glory. He brought us out from under the curse of the law (Gal. 3:13).

Again, we belong to our God by *the saving power of his Spirit* (Eph. 2:1-4; Psa. 110:3). We were lost, helpless, depraved and spiritually dead. But the Spirit of God came to us and called us to life. He created faith in our hearts and brought us to Christ by his sovereign, irresistible power and grace. He made us willing, voluntary bondslaves of the Lord Jesus Christ.

And we belong to God by *the solemn profession of our faith*. Believers, following their Lord in baptism, publicly declare to all the world their faith in and heart allegiance to the Lord Jesus Christ (Rom. 6:4-6). Baptism is the believer's obedient, public confession of faith. It identifies him as one who belongs to God. Since we belong to God, it is only reasonable that we should glorify God in our bodies and in our spirits, which are God's.

'Ye are not your own'

Read 1 Corinthians 6:9-20

Believer, since God chose you, redeemed you and saved you, you belong to him. By your own profession of faith, you have willingly, voluntarily given yourself up to the claims of Christ. You belong to him.

Because you belong to Christ, you have nothing to fear and everything to give you comfort. You are a child of God, an heir of God and a joint-heir with Jesus Christ (1 John 3:1; Rom. 8:17). You are not your own provider. It is a father's responsibility to provide for his children, and your heavenly Father does provide for his own (Matt. 6:31-34). You are not your own guide. It is the responsibility of the shepherd to guide his sheep, and the Lord who is your Shepherd guides his sheep through this world (Psa. 23:1-6; 37:23-24). You are not your own protector. It is the king's responsibility to protect his people, the husband's responsibility to protect his wife, and Christ who is your Husband and King protects his own with sovereign power (Isa. 43:1-5).

Because you have willingly given yourself to Christ as a voluntary bondslave, you are to be completely under his dominion (Luke 14:25-33). Being the bondslave of Christ, you must not follow your own will, serve your own interests, or lend your service to another. A bondslave has no property, no rights and no time of his own. He should have no will of his own. He has voluntarily resigned himself and all that he has to his Master.

Because you belong to God, you have no legitimate concern in this world but to glorify him. Your heart's only desire should be 'Father, glorify thy name' (John 12:28). You have no right to serve any cause in this world, except the glory of God your Saviour. Everything you are, everything you own, everything you control, every relationship of your life must be made subservient to the glory of God. Our flesh rebels against this complete subjection to God. We can never give the kind of allegiance to God that we desire in this world. But this is what we must strive after – commitment, complete consecration of our beings to the glory of our God.

'A living sacrifice'

Read Romans 12:1-21

I want to promote godliness among godly people. Let all who know the mercy of God subdue the passions of our flesh and the lusts of our hearts and avoid the moral decadence of society. 'For the grace of God that bringeth salvation hath appeared to all men, teaching us that denying ungodliness and worldly lusts, we should live soberly, righteously, and godly, in this present world' (Titus 2:11-12).

The basis of my appeal is the grace of God alone. Consecration to God is just reasonable service from those who have been saved by grace in Christ. I will not appeal to God's elect on the basis of the law. I will not hold over you the law's terror, threatening you with punishment, or try to bribe you into devotion by the promise of reward. 'We are not under the law, but under grace' (Rom. 6:15). 'Mary... sat at Jesus' feet, and heard his word' (Luke 10:39), because having been forgiven much, she loved much. Love, mercy, grace and gratitude are powerful, irresistible motivations for men and women who are saved by the grace of God. I know that such reasoning will never cause self-righteous religious people to give or do anything for God. They must be motivated by either the fear of punishment, or the promise of reward. I say again what I have said so often before: if the fear of punishment or the promise of reward will get you to do what the love of Christ does not constrain you to do, you do not yet know the love of Christ. If the law is more powerful to motivate you than the gospel of the grace of God, it is because you are yet in bondage to the law and under its curse.

Child of God, I am calling for you to 'prove the sincerity of your love' (2 Cor. 8:8). **'I beseech you therefore, ... by the mercies of God, that ye present your bodies a living sacrifice, holy, acceptable unto God, which is your reasonable service.'** 'Ye are not your own. For ye are bought with a price: therefore glorify God in your body and in your spirit, which are God's' (1 Cor. 6:19-20).

How can I live in this world for the glory of God?

Read Ephesians 4:25-5:2

This is a question of great concern for every believer. Having seen the glory of God in Christ, by the revelation of the Holy Spirit, we want to glorify God our Saviour above all things.

Most people presume that by a mere change of life-style, outward behaviour and outward appearance, they can glorify God. Therefore we see individuals and entire religious sects who dress in a peculiar manner, abstain from certain foods and beverages and isolate themselves, as much as possible, from the world. Some live in monasteries, convents and communes and even forbid marriage in an attempt to avoid evil and live in godliness. Such ascetic notions are totally contrary to the Word of God (1 Tim. 4:1-5; Matt. 15:10-20). They promote self-righteousness, but not godliness.

Yet we who believe must glorify God in our bodies and in our spirits, which are God's (1 Cor. 6:20). If I would glorify God in this world, my entire being must be consecrated to him. My body, which is the temple of God, must be used for the service of God's glory. Whatever we do with these bodies must be done as unto the Lord, for the glory of God (Col. 3:17). We must employ our bodies in the worship and service of our Master and in ministering to our Father's children. And we must endeavour to keep our bodies under the rule of Christ, not giving in to the passions of our sinful flesh (Col. 3:1-14). This is certain: I will glorify God in my body if in my spirit, in my inner self, in my heart I glorify him. 'Walk in the Spirit, and ye shall not fulfil the lust of the flesh' (Gal. 5:16). Walk before God in this world with a spirit of faith (John 6:29), adoration (Ps. 135:1-6), love (1 Cor. 13:1-13), obedience (1 Sam. 15:22-23), submission (1 Peter 5:6-7) and devotion (Luke 14:26-27), and you will live for the glory of God. This is the thing God requires of us. He says, 'My son, give me thine heart' (Prov. 23:26). If he has our hearts, he will have our bodies also and we shall glorify God in our bodies and in our spirits, which are God's.

'Sound doctrine'

Read Ephesians 4:1-16

Paul told Titus that every pastor must hold the faithful word of gospel truth firmly, as he has been taught it, so that '**he may be able by sound doctrine both to exhort and to convince the gainsayers**'. Without sound doctrine the pulpit is as useless as a broken weather-vane. Here are seven pillars of sound doctrine which are essential to the faith of the gospel. See that you hold them firmly.

1. God Almighty is absolutely sovereign in all things (Ps. 115:3). God is sovereign in creation, in providence and in salvation. He does what he will, when he will, where he will, with whom he will and he has mercy on whom he will have mercy (Rom. 9:11-23).

2. The Bible is the Word of God, by which he reveals himself to men (2 Tim. 3:16-17; Rom. 10-17). The Bible alone is inspired by God. Therefore the Bible alone is our rule of faith and practice. The only voice of authority in all matters of doctrine and spiritual instruction is the Word of God.

3. All men by nature are totally depraved (Rom. 3:10-19). Man is fallen, guilty, sinful and helpless, dead in trespasses and in sins (Rom. 5:12; Eph. 2:1-3). Unless God intervenes to save, all men will for ever perish, being justly condemned.

4. God chose and determined to save some people in eternal, electing love (2 Thess. 2:13). Without any consideration of anything except his own will, God chose some. All who were chosen of him will be saved.

5. Christ died in the place of God's elect, and accomplished their eternal redemption by his death (Heb. 9:12). Christ satisfied divine justice for his people and redeemed them from the curse of the law.

6. God the Holy Spirit saves every elect, redeemed sinner by the irresistible power of his grace (Ps. 65:4). The grace of God does not offer salvation; it brings salvation!

7. Every believer is eternally secure in Christ (John 10:27-30). Not one of Christ's sheep can ever perish. They are kept by the power of God. This is sound doctrine. This is the gospel of grace.

'The knowledge of his will'

Read Matthew 12:46-50

How can I know God's will? When two paths are set before me, both of which are morally right, or two choices are to be considered, neither of them involving sin, how can I know which is the will of God and which is not? For a believer, nothing is more important than the knowledge of God's will. We know that God's eternal will, his purpose and decree, that which he has sovereignly predestinated, must be fulfilled. It is immutable and irresistible. It must come to pass (Isa. 46:9-11). And we know that nothing comes to pass except that which was predestined to come to pass in God's eternal purpose (Rom. 11:36). Yet, it is our responsibility to seek and obey the will of God in our lives day by day (Prov. 3:5-6). There are some things you can be sure about.

It is the will of God that you trust his Son (John 5:23;1 John 3:23). This is the plainly revealed will of God. That which he commands, you are responsible to obey. Trust the blood of Christ for the satisfaction of justice on your behalf. Trust his righteousness for all acceptance with God. And trust the rule of his providence in all things.

The will of God is revealed to all who seek it and are willing to do it (Ps. 25:9;32:8). God reveals his will to those who seek it by the revelation of his Word, the inner witness of his Spirit and the acts of his providence.

When God reveals his will to you, you will know it (Ps. 86:11). You will not need the counsel of men. You will not need someone else to tell you whether God is directing you. When God, by his Word, his Spirit and his providence tells you to do something, you will know it. God never called anyone to do anything to whom he did not give the confidence and assurance of his will in the matter at hand.

When you know what the will of God is, you must do it (Gal. 1:16; Gen. 22:2, 10). If I am doing the will of God, trusting him, I have no reason to fear man, to fear hell, or to fear failure. God will protect me. God will provide my needs. And God will see the work through.

'Turned unto fables'

Read Psalm 115:1-18

Writing under divine inspiration, the apostle Paul warned Timothy that the time would come when the bulk of religious people would not endure sound doctrine. The apostasy of the religious world, Paul said, would be so great that they would seek preachers and teachers who would cater for the lusts of men rather than proclaim the gospel of the grace of God. Under the influence of these prophets of deceit, the professed church of God would be turned from the truth and turned unto fables. The time which Paul predicted has come. 'Even now are there many antichrists; whereby we know that it is the last time.' 'Many false prophets are gone out into the world,' turning men away from the truth unto fables. Here are three popular fables.

'God loves everybody.' This sounds so good to sinful men. Rebels like to hear it. If God loves me, everything is all right. God will not damn me if he loves me. Do not be so foolish as to receive this fable. God does not love everybody! He says, 'Jacob have I loved, but Esau have I hated' (Rom. 9:13). God loves his own elect, and loves them only because they are in Christ. If you are in Christ, if you believe on Christ and are made righteous by Christ, God loves you. If you are not in Christ, God is angry with you. You are an object of his wrath.

'Christ died for everybody.' Men love to hear this fable. It tells them that it is their faith, the exercise of their free will, that accomplishes redemption, that they complete the work of Christ. How man revels with pride! My friend, Christ did not die for everybody! Christ died for his own elect, for his church, his sheep (John 10:11, 15). And when he died, he obtained eternal redemption for us (Heb. 9:12; Isa. 53:8-11).

'The Holy Spirit is trying to save everybody.' You know that is not so. Can God fail to do what he tries to do? Such a thought is blasphemous. God is not trying to save everybody! God saves all his elect by his irresistible grace (Ps. 65:4). Salvation is not by man's will, but by God's will (Rom. 9:16).

'He is the Lord's anointed'

Read 1 Timothy 3:1-16

David was chosen and anointed of God to be king over Israel. But Saul, according to God's providence, was still upon the throne. Saul was a wicked man. God had rejected him. But God had not yet taken him off the throne. And David was not about to attempt an overthrow of God's providence. Painful as it may have been to endure Saul's evil deeds, David was content for Saul to reign as long as God would have him reign. He said, 'I will not stretch forth mine hand against him, seeing he is the anointed of the Lord' (v.6).

Few men have David's wisdom! Today, it is common for men to take it upon themselves to seat and unseat men in the kingdom of God. I refer specifically to the pastoral office. One of the most lamentable evils of our day is the utter disdain and contempt with which most people treat faithful gospel preachers. Such disdain and contempt we expect from the world. But I think the angels must blush when they see it in the church. True pastors are not hirelings, to be seated and unseated by men. Those who treat God's ambassadors as hired hands do so at their own peril. God will not allow any man to wrong his servants with impunity. He will reprove kings for their sakes. He says, 'Touch not mine anointed, and do my prophets no harm' (1 Chron. 16:21-22).

When a congregation seeks a pastor, it will be wise to seek carefully and patiently wait for the direction of the Holy Spirit. When a church calls a man to be its pastor, that congregation has voluntarily placed itself under the pastoral rule of that man (Heb. 13:7, 17). He is God's ambassador, God's spokesman and God's representative to that congregation. As such, he is to be treated with respect, obedience and love. He is to be esteemed very highly in love for his work's sake (1 Thess. 5:12-13). He deserves such treatment, if for no other reason, because of the God he represents and the gospel he preaches. See that you treat God's servants as the servants of the Most High God.

'Pastors according to mine heart'

Read Titus 1:1-16

God promised that he would give his church pastors according to his own heart. That means, he will give his church pastors as he sees fit and pastors who will serve the good of those people he so dearly loves. Those men God gives to his church as pastors, according to his own heart, '**shall feed you with knowledge and understanding**'. Here are three things that will characterize every God-called, Spirit-anointed, heavenly-ordained pastor.

Every true pastor is *a faithful man*. Without question, if a man is called of God to the work of the gospel ministry, he will be faithful in the work. His life and conduct will reflect his steadfastness, commitment and faithfulness to Christ. He will faithfully seek the glory of God, study and prepare to preach the Word of God, seek the welfare of God's people and preach the gospel of Christ. He will be faithful to Christ, to the Word, to the church and to his own conscience. No man should be set apart for the gospel until he has proved himself to be a faithful man (2 Tim. 2:2; 1 Cor. 4:2).

Every true, faithful servant of God is also *a fallible, sinful man*. The apostles and prophets of old were themselves only frail, fallible, sinful men. They were infallible in the writing of Holy Scripture, as they were carried along by the Holy Spirit. But they were not perfect men. Moses smote the rock in anger. Peter cursed and denied the Lord. All the apostles forsook Christ for a while. Paul and Barnabas had a terrible fight over John Mark. And you can be sure every pastor will have many faults. Those who want to find fault with any can easily do so.

Yet every true pastor is *God's ambassador, God's servant, God's messenger*. He is to be loved, cared for, respected and obeyed as God's representative in his church. I often hear people say, 'I do not follow any man.' If you follow God, you will follow that man who speaks for God. You will not err by following a faithful pastor. God commands you to do so!

The third commandment

Read Psalm 89:1-18

The name of God is profoundly sacred and God requires that all men reverence his name in heart, in action and in speech. 'Thou shalt not take the name of the Lord thy God in vain; for the Lord will not hold him guiltless that taketh his name in vain.' This is the command of God's law to all men. Though we are not motivated by the terror of the law, but by the love of Christ, I call your attention to this commandment, to remind you that the majesty and sacredness of God's name forbid all contemptuous, irreverent and needless use of his name. And certainly those to whom God has revealed himself in Christ, who know the eternal God as their heavenly Father, because of their love for him, would rather die than profane his holy name. Our hearts' desire is 'Our Father which art in heaven, hallowed be thy name!'

It is a sad commentary on our society that the name of God has become a common byword, and jokes about God, about heaven and about salvation are acceptable among 'refined' people, even in the pulpit! How often we hear men use the words 'My God!' 'O Lord!' 'Jesus!' 'God!', or some abbreviations of the name of our God, in common conversation, on television, or in song. It is so common that we think nothing of it! Father, forgive our callousness! Painful as this common blasphemy is, there is something even more grievous: I hear many of my friends, my brothers and sisters in Christ doing the same thing, taking the name of God in vain! This has got to cease! I do not care to hear people use four-letter words. I wish people would not talk in filthy language. But I would rather hear the most foul language of drunken men and have my family exposed to that than hear the blasphemous, irreverent use of God's holy name. Do not take the name of God in vain. His name is holy and reverend. Be certain that any time you use the name of God, Father, Son or Holy Spirit, it is your purpose and intention to honour him. Any other use of God's name is to take his name in vain.

Peter's fall and restoration

Read Psalm 51:1-19

Peter was a true believer, a disciple of Christ, a righteous and godly man. But in his hour of weakness he fell into grievous sin, denying his Lord and Redeemer three times. Peter was not the infallible Bishop of Rome, as the Catholics pretend. He was a fallible, sinful man, like the rest of us. Peter was tempted and he fell but he was not forsaken. The Lord graciously restored his erring child.

Like Peter, we are all fickle, frail, sinful pieces of human flesh. Saved? Yes. Redeemed? Yes. Justified? Yes. Sanctified? Yes. In Christ all these blessings are ours, and more. But none of us is without sin (1 John 1:8-10). Far from it! Sin is mixed with everything we do. There is no evil in the world we would not readily commit, were not the evil passions of our hearts restrained by the grace of our God (Matt. 15:19). Let us not be proud, presumptuous, and self-confident (1 Cor. 4:7; 10:12). Realizing our own sinfulness, we should never be severe with our brethren (Gal.6:1).

Salvation is entirely by the grace of God. Surely, this record of Peter's fall should convince all that salvation is not, in any measure whatsoever, dependent upon good works (Eph. 2:8-9). From start to finish, salvation is by grace alone. Our standing and acceptance with God are not determined by what we do, but by what Christ has done for us.

Peter also sets before us an undeniable proof that those who are saved by the grace of God can never be lost (John 10:27-29). Those who are in Christ are secure in him. We are kept and preserved by the power of God. Nothing can ever sever one of the Lord's own from him. As our Lord prayed for Peter, he prays for us, and God will not charge any with sin for whom Christ undertakes to be an Advocate (1 John 2:1-2; Rom. 4:8). None of us has reason to boast of our faithfulness. Who would dare? But we all have reason to boast of the faithfulness of God our Saviour, who will not let us perish!

Do we seek the approval of men
or the approval of God?

Read 1 Peter 2:1-25

Most of the people I meet are very concerned about the opinions which other people have about them. They want to impress men with their religious zeal and devotion. And most of their deeds of religious service, dress codes and restrictions of life are designed to impress men. They want the approval of men. They think that if they can win the approval of men they will have the approval of God. But our Lord tells us most plainly that it is not so: 'For that which is highly esteemed among men is abomination in the sight of God' (Luke 16:15). Those who seek the approval of men by their 'religious behaviour' are likely to attain the praise of men. It is not really too hard to impress men. 'Verily I say unto you, they have their reward' (Matt. 6:2).

Do not misunderstand me. It is important for believers to be blameless in their behaviour before men. 'Let your light so shine before men, that they may see your good works, and glorify your Father which is in heaven' (Matt. 5:16). But we must not be motivated by a desire to impress men and win their approval. Neither can we allow the customs and traditions of self-righteous religious people to govern our lives, bringing us into their bondage (Gal. 5:1; Col. 2:16-23). I want to honour God, my blessed Father, in my life. I want continually to honour him in thought, in word and in deed. I want to represent my Saviour faithfully before men. And I want to live in a manner that will adorn the gospel of Christ. The way to do this, I am convinced, is to walk before God and men in love, honesty, integrity and faithfulness in all things, both earthly and spiritual (Col. 3:1-3; Titus 2:5-14). But I am not nearly so much interested in men and women seeing Jesus in me as I am in knowing that Almighty God sees me in Jesus. My heart's concern is not that I may win man's approval, but rather that I may have God's approval. And God's approval is won only by faith in the Lord Jesus Christ. God approves of his Son and approves of all who are in his Son (Phil. 3:8-10).

'Remember Lot's wife!'

Read Matthew 10:16-39

Lot's wife is typical of those who profess to be followers of Christ, yet who love the world. She represents all who are convinced, but never converted; those who are persuaded, but never saved; those who flee from the wrath to come, but perish in the way. Lot's wife shows the deadly sin of loving the world. Our Lord holds her up as a beacon to warn all who care for their souls: '**Remember Lot's wife!**'

1. Remember that *Lot's wife enjoyed many great privileges*. In the days of Abraham and Lot true, saving faith was a rare thing, limited to a favoured few. There were no Bibles, no churches, no preachers and no tract societies. But Mrs Lot was among the chosen family of Abraham. Father Abraham was her uncle. Righteous Lot was her husband. She knew the covenant and promises of God. She worshipped at the same altar with Abraham. She had seen the angels of God and heard their message. Yet, in spite of all her privileges and associations, she perished!

2. Remember that *Lot's wife went some distance towards being saved*. Like Felix, she trembled. Like Agrippa, she was almost persuaded. She was aroused by the message of God's coming wrath. She fled from Sodom with her husband. She sacrificed much, leaving in Sodom two of her daughters, her sons-in-law, any grandchildren, her home, her wealth, her friends, her earthly security, everything for which she lived. She was within sight of Zoar, the place of safety. Yet she perished!

3. Remember *the sin of Lot's wife*. 'She looked back.' To us that appears only a small thing. But God looked beyond the act to her heart. Her look betrayed a heart of unbelief. Her look betrayed a heart of proud rebellion and disobedience. Her look betrayed a heart of base ingratitude for God's mercy. Her look betrayed a heart that loved the world. Her heart was in Sodom, and Sodom was in her heart.

4. Remember *the punishment that God inflicted upon Lot's wife*. 'She became a pillar of salt.' Her punishment was sudden, shameful, hopeless and eternal. Loving Sodom, with Sodom she perished. She went to hell with the world she loved!

'Not willing that any should perish'

Read 2 Peter 3:1-18

If you read the chapter carefully, you will observe that the apostle makes a clear and deliberate distinction between 'us' who believe and the 'scoffers' who believe not.

'**The Lord is not slack concerning his promise**.' Did he promise that Christ would come to judge the world and to gather his elect unto himself? Most assuredly he did. Let the wicked mock and scoff. We will comfort ourselves in the assurance that, at the appointed time, Christ will appear in his glory. Though the promise tarry, 'Wait for it; because it will surely come, it will not tarry.' 'Yet a little while, and he that shall come will come, and will not tarry.'

The Lord '**is longsuffering to us-ward**'. The promise and the longsuffering of God are to us – those who are loved, chosen, redeemed and called of God, those who believe on Christ for life everlasting. There is only one reason why God tolerates the enemies of Christ, only one reason why Christ has not yet come to judge his enemies, and it is this: God has a people in this world whom he has determined to save. He would not destroy the old world until Noah was in the ark. He would not burn Sodom until Lot was out of the city. And God Almighty, even in his strict holiness, will not send his Son to destroy this world until the last one of his chosen sheep has been brought safe into the Shepherd's fold! Indeed, 'The longsuffering of our Lord is salvation.'

Once more, it is promised that God is '**not willing that any should perish**'. To whom is this promise given? Not to Pharaoh; God killed him. Not to Korah, Dathan and Abiram; God sent them to hell. Not to Judas; God sent him to his own place. To whom then is the promise given? To us! Not one of God's elect will perish in his sin. Not one of Christ's sheep will be missing from the fold. Not one soul redeemed by Christ will be cast into hell. Why? Because God is 'not willing that any should perish, but that all should come to repentance'. And the will of God cannot be frustrated.

'The offence of the cross'

Read 1 Corinthians 1:17-31

By 'the cross', Paul did not mean the material cross. That is offensive to no one. It is a piece of jewellery. It is a universal symbol of religious sentimentalism at best, and outright idolatry at worst. Nor does he mean the mere historic fact of the cross. The fact of the crucifixion is a part of history which everyone accepts. When Paul talks about the cross, he is talking about the doctrine of the cross: substitutionary redemption, blood atonement, free justification, complete pardon in Christ. He is talking about the preaching of the cross. By the preaching of the cross I mean the proclamation of its necessity, its nature and its efficacy.

The preaching of the cross was an offence to the religious, self-righteous Jew and to the proud intellectual Greek. If Paul had been willing to allow that man had any part in the work of salvation, both the Jew and the Gentile would have accepted his doctrine. But he would not allow any space for man. He declared that salvation was altogether the work of the triune God. It is a work of the grace of God, through the mediation of Christ and by the power of the Holy Spirit. It is not a co-operative effort of God and man. It is a co-operative act of God, the Father, the Son and the Holy Spirit.

The preaching of the cross offends the pride and dignity of man. It is a vivid reminder of man's sin and hatred of God. In its profound simplicity, it offends the wisdom of man. The inventions of man's religion are declared to be vanity. It is offensive because it puts all men upon one level. Princes and paupers, moralists and harlots, scholars and drunkards are all the same in the eyes of God. All are sinners. And if any enter into glory, they must all stoop down and enter in at the door of the cross, elbow to elbow. Indeed, God is no respecter of persons.

But there are some to whom the cross is no offence. To them who are called, it is the power of God and the wisdom of God! Has God removed from your heart the offence of the cross? Do you now see its wisdom and beauty? Have you entered in by faith through the door of the cross? If so, give thanks to God alone!

'The everlasting covenant'

Read Psalm 89:19-37

We delight and take comfort in the fact that the Lord our God has established for us a covenant ordered in all things and sure. Its blessings upon the Israel of God, the church of Christ, are innumerable (Jer. 31:31-34; Heb. 8:10; 10:16-17). In our text, the apostle Paul tells us four things about the covenant of God's grace.

1. Jesus Christ is the central figure in this covenant. The covenant of grace is an eternal agreement between the three persons of the sacred Trinity for the salvation of God's elect. But at the heart and foundation of the covenant is '**our Lord Jesus, that great shepherd of the sheep**'. According to the Father's command, the great Shepherd agreed to die for his sheep and assumed the responsibility of bringing them all safe to heaven. Because of Christ's covenant engagements on our behalf, the Lord God says of his elect, 'Deliver him from going down into the pit, for I have found a ransom!' God the Father says of his Son, 'I have laid help upon one that is mighty!'

2. This covenant was sealed and ratified by the blood of Christ (Heb. 9:15-17). Having fulfilled everything agreed upon in the covenant, the Son of God sealed it with his blood. Now the covenant has the force of a will or testament. The inheritance of the crucified Christ must be given to his redeemed, believing people.

3. This is a covenant that cannot be broken. It is everlasting, and therefore immutable. All who were given to Christ were redeemed by Christ, will come to Christ and will be raised again at the last day! God promised it. He swore by his holy name that he would do it! And it will be done!

4. God has so arranged things in the covenant of grace that he will get all the glory of it. His glory he will not share with another. He must have the glory exclusively. He must have the glory eternally. Let us give him the glory now. 'Not unto us, not unto us, O Lord, but unto thy name give glory, for thy mercy, and thy truth's sake!'

Christ our Surety

Read John 6:35-45

A surety is, according to Webster, 'a person who makes himself responsible for another; one who makes himself liable for another's debts, defaults, or obligations'. This is just what our Lord Jesus Christ did in the covenant of grace. God the Father gave his elect people to Christ. He entrusted them to the care of his Son. And the Lord Jesus Christ voluntarily agreed to become responsible for their eternal welfare. By his own wilful choice, the Son of God agreed to become liable to God's holy law for the debts and obligations of his elect. He became the Surety of his people.

Therefore, in the fulness of time, he came into this world as a man, made of a woman, made under the law, to redeem them that were under the law. Our blessed Surety lived in this world as the Representative of his people, fulfilling their obligations to God's law, establishing in their stead a perfect righteousness. Then he laid down his life as their Substitute at Calvary, paying in full the debt we owed to God's holy law and justice, by reason of our sin.

And now our Surety reigns on the right hand of the Majesty on high over all flesh for the purpose of giving eternal life to all who were given to him in the covenant of grace and redeemed by him at Calvary. It is his responsibility, as the Surety, to find his sheep, save his sheep, bring his sheep home, and to present every one of his sheep faultless and blameless before the presence of the divine glory. This he will do. Our Surety cannot fail. In the last day the Lord Jesus Christ will stand before his Father and say, 'Lo, I and the children whom thou hast given me; of them which thou gavest me have I lost none.' The number of those presented in perfect holiness before the throne of God will exactly tally with the number of those given to Christ as the Surety of the covenant in eternal election. He will open the Lamb's book of life, which was written before the world began, and pointing to their names one by one, he will say, 'Those that thou gavest me I have kept, and none of them is lost.'

Three fatal errors about baptism

Read 1 Corinthians 1:14-31

There are some who flatly deny that baptism is an ordinance of the New Testament church, but their ultra-dispensationalism is so obviously contrary to the Scriptures that few people accept their doctrine. However, there are many who ignorantly receive three common, but fatal, errors about baptism. Such commonly received errors must be exposed.

1. Sacramentalism says that 'Baptism is a means of grace.' All Catholics and most Protestants teach that baptism has at least some saving efficacy. No one teaches salvation by baptism alone, but many teach that baptism is a means by which God's saving grace comes to the soul. The whole basis of infant sprinkling (it cannot rightly be called baptism) is that baptism does have some merit before God. Such doctrine is nowhere taught nor implied in the Word of God.

2. Landmarkism teaches that baptism can only be performed by the pastors of Landmark Baptist churches and that by being baptized into one of their churches a person secures for himself a higher rank, position and reward in heaven. In other words, they would have us to believe that while Christ is sufficient as our Saviour, we must earn the gifts of eternal glory by what we do. Though they would deny it, they make baptism a sacrament, 'a means of grace'. Such doctrine is fatal. Christ plus anything equals eternal damnation. Christ alone is our Saviour and our acceptance before God.

3. Ritualism simply goes through the motions of baptism as a matter of meaningless religious exercise, without any knowledge of its meaning.

In truth, baptism is the answer of a good conscience towards God. It is the believer's first act of obedience to Christ as Lord. And it is a public, symbolic confession of our faith in Christ. Baptism has no saving efficacy, but it is an essential point of the believer's obedience to Christ. Only unsaved rebels wilfully reject the commandments of the Lord. The commandment of God is 'Repent and be baptized every one of you' (Acts 2:38).

'Whosoever believeth'

Read John 1:1-14

Without question, the most profound, most mysterious and most incomprehensible thing in all the world is the gospel of Christ. Who can explain how the eternal Son of God could come to this earth in human flesh, live in perfect righteousness as our Representative before God, have our sins imputed to him, suffer and die as our Substitute in full satisfaction of infinite justice, rise from the dead in accomplishment of our justification and reign in glory as the God-man Mediator to save his people? The fact of the gospel is incomprehensibly astonishing!

Yet the message of the gospel is plain, clear and simple. It is just this: 'Believe on the Lord Jesus Christ and thou shalt be saved.' Do you ask, 'How can I be saved from my sin?' 'How can I be made righteous before God?' 'How can a sinner like me be justified in the sight of God?' There is no need for your perplexity. Paul said, 'The word is nigh thee, even in thy mouth, and in thy heart: that is the word of faith which we preach; that if thou shalt confess with thy mouth the Lord Jesus, and shalt believe in thine heart that God hath raised him from the dead, thou shalt be saved. For with the heart man believeth unto righteousness; and with the mouth confession is made unto salvation.' If you will acknowledge Christ's lordship and dominion over you, believing on him alone for the pardon of your sin and all your righteousness before God, you will be saved.

Nothing in all the world is more plain and clear than that. You do not need to figure out a way of salvation. Christ has done it all. You must simply trust him. As surely as it is true that 'The soul that sinneth it shall die', just that surely it is true that 'Whosoever shall call upon the name of the Lord shall be saved.' Not until the throne of God is overturned and the truth of God becomes a lie will it be possible for a sinner truly to believe on Christ without being saved.

The question is simply this: 'Dost thou believe on the Son of God?' If you do, you are a saved man or woman. Your sins are pardoned and you are made perfectly righteous in Christ.

'Wherefore then serveth the law?'

Read 1 Timothy 1:1-17

The law of God is holy and just and good. But it becomes a very great evil when it is perverted and used for something other than its divine purpose.

Now Paul tells us what the design and purpose of God's law is. It was never intended by God to be a means of justification or sanctification, a motive for Christian service, a rule of life for believers, or a code of moral ethics. The law of God has but one singular purpose. It exposes man's guilt and sin before God, shutting him up to faith in Christ alone for salvation. 'It was added because of transgressions, till the seed should come to whom the promise was made.' 'The law was our schoolmaster to bring us unto Christ, that we might be justified by faith.' To use the law for any other purpose is to pervert and abuse the law.

Once a man comes to Christ by faith, the law has no more claim upon him and no longer has dominion over him. The law was not made for a righteous man. The language of Holy Scripture in this matter could not be clearer or more emphatic. 'After that faith is come, we are no longer under a schoolmaster.' 'We are not under the law, but under grace.' 'Christ is the end of the law for righteousness to every one that believeth.' 'Wherefore, my brethren, ye also are become dead to the law by the body of Christ; that ye should be married to another, even to him who is raised from the dead, that we should bring forth fruit unto God.' We who are free dare not entangle ourselves again with the yoke of bondage. Our freedom has been purchased at too high a price, the precious blood of Christ. We have a higher, better, more effectual motive for our obedience, service and devotion than the law given by Moses. 'The love of Christ constraineth us!' When true love reigns in the heart there is no need for law. Love for Christ causes us to love one another. This love makes God's elect patient, kind, honest, generous and faithful. And this love is the fulfilment of the law.

'If God be for us...'

Read Isaiah 43:1-13

What a glorious thought! Is it possible? Can it be true that the eternal, omnipotent, all-wise, incomprehensible God, in the Trinity of his sacred persons, is for us? Let that once be established as a fact, both of revelation and experience, and all fear must vanish from our hearts. '**If God be for us, who can be against us**?' Who can with success oppose those for whom the Almighty is engaged?

Now here is the glorious fact of the matter concerning those who love God and are the called according to his purpose: God is for us! God is absolutely sovereign in all things. He has dominion over all the universe (Ps. 115:3; Dan. 4:34-37; Isa. 4:5-7; Prov. 21:1; Rom. 11:36).

This God is for us in *his sovereign providence* working all things together for our good (Rom. 8:28). Everything in the universe is being manipulated by God to accomplish good for his elect. The wise man said, 'There shall no evil happen unto the just' (Prov. 12:21). That is to say, Nothing shall work against God's elect. There is no limitation to the promise.

But that is not all, God is for us in *his saving purpose* (Rom.8:29-30). Notice that each verb is in the past tense. According to God's own purpose and decree, our salvation is an accomplished reality in Christ. He knew us in electing love, predestinated us to be his sons, called us his own, justified us in his purpose and glorified us in Christ. This is God's purpose for all his elect, and his purpose will be done.

Once more, God is for us in *his substitutionary provision* (v.32). In order that he might justly save us, according to his own purpose, God spared not his own Son. Everything agreed upon in the covenant of grace Christ had to endure. He was not spared the strict requirements of righteousness or the infinite wrath of justice. He was delivered up by the determinate counsel and foreknowledge of God to die as our Substitute. Now, surely, this great and merciful God, who gave his own Son for us, will freely give us all things. What then shall we fear?

'Hope in his mercy'

Read Psalm 119:49-72

The believer's hope is his confident persuasion of God's goodness and mercy in Christ. It is an expectation of all necessary good, both in time and eternity, founded upon the promises, relations and perfections of God, and upon the righteousness, shed blood and intercession of Christ. It is a combination of desire, expectation, patience and joy. By faith in our Lord Jesus Christ, we are persuaded that God is both able and willing to do us good, and we expect him to do so. This is our hope. Our circumstances may vary. Our confidence may at times diminish. Our assurance may waver. Our sense of joy may decline. But our hope never changes, for our hope is in the Lord. 'The Lord is my portion, saith my soul; therefore will I hope in him' (see Lam. 3:21-26). Here are four things which give me hope. Here are four solid, immutable pillars upon which I rest my soul continually.

1. *God's immutable mercy.* Some people trust their works; others place all confidence in their religion, but we know that 'It is of the Lord's mercies that we are not consumed.' As a guilty sinner I have no hope but in God's eternal, redemptive, immutable and daily mercies.

2. *God's unfailing love.* To those who are in Christ, 'God is love'. 'Having loved his own which were in the world, he loved them unto the end.' God's love is sure and immutable. He who so loved me that he gave his only Son to redeem me will not withhold any good thing from me. This gives me hope: 'His compassions fail not.' The eternal God will never cease to love his own!

3. *God's unchanging faithfulness.* 'Great is thy faithfulness!' This I know, God is faithful. He is faithful to his covenant and to his people. Divine faithfulness fills me with hope.

4. *God's inexhaustible goodness.* 'The Lord is good!' Surely, then, he will do good for all who seek him and wait upon him with faith, hope and patience.

'He hath made us accepted in the beloved'

Read Ephesians 1:1-14

In this text of Scripture, the apostle Paul teaches us that in Jesus Christ the people of God have been made entirely complete. God Almighty has accepted us upon the merits of Christ's righteousness and shed blood, and in his very person, as being one with him!

1. Our acceptance before God is *eternal*. There never was a time when God did not view his elect in Christ. Because God always viewed us in Christ, he always accepted us. We were in the heart of Christ from all eternity as the objects of his love and favour. We were in his hands as our Surety. Our names were written beneath his in the book of life before the world began. God chose us in Christ and in Christ we are accepted.

2. Our acceptance in Christ is *real*. We are really and truly one with the Son of God! 'We are members of his body, of his flesh, and of his bones.' Just as the race of humanity was in the loins of Adam, all the hosts of God's elect were in Christ. Before God, by God's decree, Jesus Christ is our legal, spiritual and real Representative. What that means is this: what he has done, we have done in him. When he obeyed God's law, we obeyed the law in him. When he died, we died in him. When he arose, we arose in him. When he sat down at the Father's right hand, we were made to sit together with him in heavenly places.

3. Our acceptance in Christ is *immutable*. Through our sin and unbelief, we sometimes lose the sweetness of fellowship and communion with our God. But our acceptance with God never varies! God does not accept us on the basis of anything done by us. He accepts us for Christ's sake. The only way for one of God's elect to become unaccepted is for God to reject his own Son, for we are in him! Until God rejects Christ, he cannot, and will not, reject those who are in Christ. This is our blessed security! '**He hath made us accepted in the beloved**.'

'A reasonable hope'

Read Hebrews 1:1-2:4

We all hope for eternal life and the glorious bliss of heaven. But is my hope reasonable? Peter wrote, 'Be ready always to answer every man that asketh you a reason of the hope that is in you', implying that a good hope is both reasonable and evident.

This I know: the eternal, immaculate God of heaven will never accept anything less than absolute perfection. Therefore, it is most unreasonable for me to trust myself, or anything I have done, for my acceptance with God.

My only hope is in a Substitute, one whom God will accept in my stead. God himself has provided such a Substitute for sinners like me. Jesus Christ, God's own Son, took upon himself my own nature. He lived in this world as a man for thirty-three years in perfect conformity to God's law and will, establishing perfect righteousness for sinners. Then he went to the cross, there to suffer the just penalty of God's law and justice for the sins of his people. Being both God and man, he was able to satisfy the infinite wrath of God by one great sacrifice. Dying in my place, the God-man was buried in a tomb. But on the third day after his crucifixion, my Substitute broke the walls of the grave, declaring that those people for whom he died were justified! By his resurrection, the Son of God is declared of God to be accepted as the all-sufficient Sacrifice for sin. My sins, which he bore, are all gone. My debt to God's offended justice was paid in full by the price of Immanuel's blood!

Now, it is most reasonable for me to trust him, and him alone, for my entire salvation. No other sacrifice can give my guilty conscience peace; and none other can meet the requirements of a just and holy God. God himself provided Christ as a Substitute for sinners. God laid my sins upon him. God killed him in my place. God raised him from the dead as my Representative. And God declares that all who trust him will not perish, but have eternal life. Trust him I will, I must, I do! I have no other hope. Will you trust him, too?

'He that believeth not'

Read John 3:17-36

Every sin is an infinite evil in the eyes of a holy God, and will be punished eternally in hell, no matter how small and insignificant it may appear in man's eyes. But the greatest sin in all the world is the sin of unbelief. If you go to hell it will be for this reason: you refused to believe in the Lord Jesus Christ. Hear what God says, '**He that believeth not is condemned already, because he hath not believed in the name of the only begotten Son of God**.' 'He that believeth not the Son shall not see life: but the wrath of God abideth on him.' The hottest place in hell is reserved for 'good, moral' people who refuse to believe the gospel. They hear it, and perhaps understand it mentally, but they will not believe. To persist in your unbelief is to commit an unpardonable blasphemy against the Holy Spirit.

Do not try to excuse your unbelief by blaming it on God's decree. Where is it written in the Bible that God predestinated your sinful unbelief? God's decree never shut the doors of mercy against anyone. And do not look upon your unbelief as a light thing. Once in a while, I meet with someone who talks as though he is honouring God by confessing his unbelief! If you refuse to believe the gospel, it is your own fault. And it is a hideous crime. By your unbelief, you make God a liar! You are saying that the gospel of God is a lie, the Son of God is not worthy of your trust, the Word of God is not to be believed and the witness of the Spirit is not to be received! Your unbelief exposes your proud hatred of God, your mockery of the blood of Christ and your disdain for the grace of God. There is only one reason why you are not saved, and that is that you will not come to Christ. And the only reason why you will not come is that you will not believe. You do not believe in the merit and sufficiency of Christ's blood and righteousness. And you do not believe that you need him. Else you would come to him.

Because of your unbelief God will send you to hell! And all God's creation will say, 'Amen' to your eternal damnation – yourself included! You must either turn to Christ in faith, or perish. Which will it be?

'Use not vain repetitions'

Read Matthew 6:1-15

Our Lord does not forbid the use of repetition in prayer. In fact, he teaches us that a man whose heart is heavy and burdened ought to use importunity in pleading with God (Luke 11:8-10). That which is forbidden is the use of 'vain repetition' – the use of words without meaning.

Do you find yourself, when you are praying, either in public or in private, using the same words and phrases? Asking for the same things? Saying the same things? Praying without really thinking about what you are saying? I am afraid that many people might just as well use a tape recorder as their tongues when they pray. Others use pretty words and phrases that impress men. They pray so well and in such affecting tones when they are praying in public. These are the vain repetitions our Lord warns us to avoid. Such praying is an abomination before God!

Dare I approach the Lord of heaven without sincerity, earnestness and thoughtfulness? Dare I speak to God without carefulness? Dear friends, let us take care that we do not pray out of habit, or ritual, or because it is time to pray. It would be better not to pray at all. Read the prayers of Moses, Elijah, David, Daniel and Paul. By their examples we should learn something about prayer. True prayer arises from a sense of need. It is the voice of a sincere heart crying out to the Lord. We do not know how to pray as we ought, by nature. The Spirit of God in a man's heart teaches him how to pray. He leads, guides and directs the children of God in prayer.

Pray with adoration and thanksgiving, worshipping God and giving thanks to him. Pray in faith, trusting the merits of Christ's righteousness and shed blood and resting in the promises of God. Pray with intercession, seeking God's blessing upon his people. Pray in submission, submitting your will to God's will, preferring his will to your own. And pray with sincerity, saying neither more nor less than you truly feel in your heart. Above all, seek the glory of God. When the glory of God in Christ is the motive of our prayers, we have begun to pray, but not until then.

'The putting away of sin'

Read Psalm 103:1-14

'**Now once in the end of the world hath he** [the Lord Jesus Christ] **appeared to put away sin by the sacrifice of himself**' (Heb. 9:26). It was for sinful men like us that the great Redeemer appeared. Once, in the end of the world, when the fulness of time was come, the Son of God appeared at the appointed place to put sin out of existence. Jesus Christ came into the world for this express purpose, to redeem hopelessly sinful men. He came into the world to give a real deliverance from sin by putting it away. He came to establish peace between man and God; for when sin is gone peace is lawful. Jesus Christ did not come into the world to make sin a harmless mistake. He did not come to give you a covering for your sin. He did not come to help you forget your sin. The Son of God came into this world to put away sin by the sacrifice of himself.

Sin is an infinitely evil thing. Sin is an attack upon the very throne of God. It is an offence against God's holiness, the transgression of God's law and the rebellion of the heart against God's sovereignty. Sin is the monstrous attempt of depraved man to rape God and rob him of his dignity and glory as God! Sin is man's denial of God's right to be God!

It is a very hard thing to put away sin. All the Jewish sacrifices of the Old Testament, costly and numerous as they were, could not put away sin. All the religious zeal and devotion of the scribes and Pharisees could not put away sin. Not even repentance, faith and a holy life can put away sin. Even if you and I were to suffer the wrath of God in hell for ever, we could not put away one sin. But the Lord Jesus Christ has put away sin! By his one all-sufficient, infinitely meritorious sacrifice at Calvary, the Son of God has put away all the sins of all his people for ever! He did not put our sins away into hiding, or in reserve, to bring them out at another time. The blood of Christ has put sin out of existence for his people! In the sight of God's law, so far as his holiness and justice are concerned, the man or woman who trusts Christ has no sin!

Three common errors about sanctification

Read Romans 7:14-25

Even those who are well instructed in the gospel doctrines of election, redemption, justification and regeneration commonly embrace seriously erroneous views of sanctification. They teach that salvation is altogether by grace, and they realize that sanctification is an essential part of salvation, but they insist that sanctification is partly a work of God and partly a work of man. Such mixing of grace and works in this aspect of salvation leads many to embrace a perverted doctrine of sanctification.

Pentecostalism teaches that sanctification is a second work of grace, whereby the believer is made totally free from sin, and the old nature of sin is eradicated from his being. Such a proud doctrine is directly contrary to the plain statement of Holy Scripture: 'If we say that we have no sin, we deceive ourselves and the truth us not in us' (1 John 1:8). And the notion of 'sinless perfection' is contrary to the experience of every believer. Believers confess their sin. They do not hide it. Honesty compels us to acknowledge that, though we are no longer under the dominion of sin, we do have a continual struggle with sin. Sin is mixed with everything we think or do. Any man who says he is without sin is a liar.

The self-righteous legalist makes sanctification nothing more than outward, legal morality. He thinks that sanctification is accomplished by his separation from the world, his obedience to religious customs and traditions and his abstinence from the use of things he considers evil. 'Touch not, taste not, handle not' is his creed.

And among most of those whom we recognize as orthodox, evangelical Christians, sanctification is thought to be the progressive increase of the believer's 'personal holiness'. We are told that the children of God attain higher degrees of holiness by their own works in sanctification, until at last they are ripe for heaven, and that sanctification buds forth into ultimate glorification. Usually, this 'progressive sanctification' is made to be the basis of the believer's assurance on earth and the basis of his eternal reward in heaven.

'We are sanctified'

Read Colossians 2:1-10

I hear men talk of progressive sanctification. I am told that God's people grow in holiness and righteousness. Some men will even dare to assert, 'I am holier than thou.' They think that their good works, their piety, their devotion, their prayers, their meditations and their Bible reading since they professed faith in Christ make them more holy, inwardly and outwardly, before God. But it is all a self-righteous delusion. God says of all such pretenders of piety, 'These are a smoke in my nose, a fire that burneth all the day.' It is true, God's elect grow in the grace and knowledge of our Lord Jesus Christ. We grow in faith, devotion, submission and even obedience to Christ. But never in all the Word of God do I read of a man who trusted Christ claiming to grow in holiness, purity, or sanctification before God. In fact, the very opposite is true. When Isaiah saw the Lord, he said, 'Woe is me! for I am undone; because I am a man of unclean lips.' When Job had grown the most in grace and had seen the most of God's glory, he cried, 'Behold, I am vile!' When David had the greatest assurance of God's pardoning grace, he had also the greatest awareness of his own sin. He said, 'I acknowledge my transgressions: and my sin is ever before me.' When Paul had faithfully preached the gospel for many years he said, 'I know that in me (that is, in my flesh) dwelleth no good thing.' When Paul was about to lay down his life in martyrdom, when he reached a far higher degree of faithfulness and dedication than anyone I know, he did not call himself the holiest of all saints, he called himself the chief of all sinners.

Where do you find sanctification? I can tell you where all of God's saints find it – Christ is our sanctification. He is all my righteousness, all my redemption, all my sanctification and all my holiness before God. Sanctification is not by the works of the flesh any more than justification is. Sanctification is the work of God's sovereign grace whereby he has separated us to be holy in Christ by election, declared us to be holy in Christ by redemption, and made us to be holy in Christ by regeneration.

'Ye are sanctified'

Read 1 John 3:1-10

C.H. Spurgeon made this statement, with which I fully agree, about the doctrine of progressive sanctification: 'I do not admire the term "progressive sanctification", for it is unwarranted by Scripture; but it is certain that the Christian does grow in grace, and though his conflict may be as severe in the last day of his life as in the first moment of conversion, yet he does advance in grace, and all his imperfections and his conflicts within cannot prove that he has not made progress.'

A believer does not gradually become less sinful and more holy in the sight of God. Can there be degrees of righteousness and holiness in the sight of God? The very term 'holiness' implies perfection. Anything less than absolute perfection is not holiness, but sin.

The only holiness any fallen man can have is that holiness which God gives to all believers in Christ, and it is perfect holiness. God's elect were sanctified in eternal election, when we were set apart for God and declared to be holy in God's eternal purpose. In time we were actually perfected and made holy in the eyes of God's law and justice, by the righteousness and shed blood of Christ as our Substitute. When Christ died at Calvary he 'perfected for ever them that were sanctified', those who were set apart by God for himself in election. Perfect holiness was legally imputed to God's elect by the obedience of Christ. Then, in divine regeneration, a perfectly holy nature has been imparted to all who are born of the Spirit. To be born again is to have the divine nature implanted in us, so that we are partakers of the divine nature. This is sanctification. It is not progressive, but perfect and complete, in Christ.

While we live in this world we grow in grace and in the knowledge of Christ. We grow in faith and in love and in hope. But we do not grow in holiness before God. Christ is our only holiness before God. So long as we live in this world our old nature will continue to be nothing but sinful flesh. It never gets sanctified.

'Righteousness and sanctification'

Read Colossians 1:9-23

I hear men talk of becoming less and less sinful and progressively holier from day to day. I hear men talk about their 'progressive sanctification' a great deal. But the more they boast of their progressive holiness, the more harsh, judgemental and mean-spirited they become towards their 'lesser brethren'. Their doctrine is this: 'God's children,' they say, 'grow in righteousness and personal holiness until they are ripe for heaven.' They actually teach that glorification is the end result of their own progressive attainments in 'personal holiness'. If their doctrine is true, if it is possible for men gradually to become less sinful and more holy, then it is possible for men, by diligence, self-denial and mortification of the flesh, eventually to attain sinless perfection in this life.

Such doctrine, of course, is contrary to Holy Scripture (1 John 1:8, 10). Any man who says that he is without sin, even for a fleeting second, is deceived, the truth is not in him and he makes God a liar. And honesty compels me to acknowledge that this doctrine of 'progressive sanctification' is totally contrary to my own experience. I have, I believe, over the past nineteen years, grown in grace. My love for, faith in and commitment to Christ have grown, increased and matured by the grace of God. But my sin has not diminished. My outward acts of sin are more restricted and controlled than before, but the inward evil of my flesh has not lessened. If anything, it is worse now than ever. With aching heart, I confess my sin. Though I am redeemed, justified and sanctified in Christ, I am still a man in the flesh, and my flesh is full of sin. By painful experience, I have learned that 'I am carnal, sold under sin... For I know that in me (that is, in my flesh) dwelleth no good thing.' Christ alone is my redemption. Christ alone is my righteousness. Christ alone is my acceptance with God. And Christ alone is my sanctification.

'Cities of refuge'

Read Numbers 35:11-33

When the children of Israel were settled in the land of Canaan, God ordained that six cities of refuge be set aside, to which a man might flee for security, if he had unintentionally killed another man. These cities of refuge were located strategically throughout the land, so that any one of them could easily be reached within a day's journey from any place in the land of Canaan. If the guilty man could get into the gates of the city before the avenger of blood caught him, he would be secure. These cities of refuge together form a picture of the Lord Jesus Christ. They typically represent him to whom we have 'fled for refuge to lay hold upon the hope set before us' (Heb. 6:18).

We are informed by the ancient Jewish rabbis that, at least once every year, the magistrates of each city were responsible to survey the road to their city, making certain that the road was clear of all debris and easily passable. There must be no obstacles in the way that would hinder any who might flee to the cities of refuge. The magistrates would send out work crews to remove all large rocks and fallen trees from the road, taking the greatest possible care to remove every stumbling-block. Any low places in the road would be filled. Any high places would be levelled. All along the road they placed markers with the word 'refuge' written in bold letters. When the fugitive came to a cross-roads, he needed not hesitate for a moment. Seeing that blessed word, 'refuge', he kept on his breathless pace with relentless determination until he reached the place of merciful safety. Once he entered the gates of the city, he was secure.

The Lord Jesus Christ is the refuge for sinners. All who come to him are saved from the wrath of God. The way to Christ is plainly revealed: 'Believe on the Lord Jesus Christ, and thou shalt be saved.' And Christ, by his righteousness and blood, has removed every obstacle that might keep the sinner who seeks him from finding him. He even sends his Spirit to reveal the way, lead us in the way and bring us safely to our souls' refuge.

'Cities of refuge'

Read Joshua 20:1-9

The six cities of refuge which Joshua appointed in the land of Canaan were types of our Lord Jesus Christ. Even their names represent him.

Kedesh means '*holy*'. Christ is the holy one, both as God and as man. Being the holy God-man, he is abundantly qualified to be our Mediator, Saviour and Redeemer. Christ is made of God unto us righteousness and holiness, justification and sanctification (Ps. 16:10; Heb. 7:26; 1 Cor. 1:30).

Shechem means '*the shoulder*'. Christ carried the enormous load of our sin upon the cross and put it away (Isa. 53:6.) The government of the world in general and of his church in particular is upon his shoulder (Isa. 9:6). And in conversion, he finds his lost sheep, lays it upon his shoulder and carries it home (Luke 15:4).

Hebron means '*fellowship*'. 'Truly our fellowship is with the Father and with his Son Jesus Christ' (1 John 1:3). In Christ we have access to and fellowship with the eternal God, and shall have uninterrupted communion with him in heaven's eternal glory (1 Cor. 1:9; Eph. 2:18; John 17:24).

Bezer means '*a fortified place*'. 'I will say of the Lord, he is my refuge and my fortress: my God; in him will I trust' (Ps. 91:2). 'The name of the Lord is a strong tower: the righteous runneth into it, and is safe' (Prov. 18:10). Christ is the fortress and defence of his people, the stronghold in which the prisoners of hope are secured.

Ramoth means '*exalted*'. Christ is our exalted Saviour. 'God hath highly exalted him' (Phil. 2:9). Christ is the one by whom we have been exalted from our low estate to sit among princes and to inherit the throne of glory (Eph. 2:4-7). And Christ is the one we exalt, honour and magnify (Rev. 5:9-10).

Golan means '*revealed*', or '*manifested*'. Christ is God manifest in the flesh (1 Tim. 3:16). He is the one revealed to us, to whom we are called and by whom we are saved (Gal. 1:15-16). In Christ the glory of God is revealed (2 Cor. 4:6). And that revelation of the glory of God in the face of Jesus Christ is salvation.

'Fled for refuge'

Read Psalm 91:1-16

The manslayer in Israel had to flee to one of the cities of refuge which God had appointed. If he had fled to any other city for refuge, he would have found no mercy. The avenger of blood would find him and slay him. If he would be saved, he must flee to the refuge God had appointed. Even so, all who would be saved by the grace of God must flee by faith to the refuge God has appointed, and that refuge is Christ. 'Neither is there salvation in any other: for there is none other name under heaven given among men, whereby we must be saved' (Acts 4:12). The only refuge for our souls is the Lord Jesus Christ. Both for salvation and for the consolation of our souls in any time of trouble, we must flee to Christ alone. Christ is our refuge, not the church. Christ is our refuge, not our works.

Salvation is obtained only by fleeing to Christ. There was no place of mercy, peace, safety and rest for the manslayer until he ran through the gates into one of those cities of refuge. It was not enough that he knew where the city was located, how large the city was, what provisions were in the city and how to get to the city. If he would be saved he must enter the city.

Once he entered the city four things happened: (1) He declared his cause, confessing his offence. (2) He came under the protection of the city. (3) He received a complete acquittal of all guilt. (4) He was cleansed from all guilt, representatively, when the high priest died. None of these benefits were his until he entered the city. But once he entered, all were his, and his soul was peaceful.

In exactly the same way, when the guilty sinner flees to Christ for refuge, he declares his cause: 'I am a sinner in need of mercy' (1 John 1:9). He comes under the protection of Christ (John 10:27-28). He receives a complete acquittal, full justification, being absolved from all guilt (Rom. 3:24). And he is cleansed from all sin by the blood of Christ, who died as his Representative (Heb. 9:14). Having fled to Christ for refuge, we are safe and secure in him.

'Believe on the Lord Jesus Christ, and thou shalt be saved'

Read 1 John 5:1-13

Salvation is obtained by faith alone. It is not obtained by faith and baptism, faith and obedience, faith and experience, or even faith and faithfulness. Salvation is obtained by faith alone, faith in the Lord Jesus Christ. It is true, faith is obedient. Faith is confessed in baptism. Faith does bring both feelings and experience and cause faithfulness. But these things come as the result of salvation and life in Christ. They are not the cause (Eph. 2:8-10).

What is this faith? The Amplified Version gives a helpful translation of this verse: 'Believe in and on the Lord Jesus Christ, that is give yourself up to him, take yourself out of your own keeping and entrust yourself to his keeping, and you will be saved.' Believing on Christ is not 'a bare historical faith, as only to believe that he was the Son of God, and the Messiah, and that he was come in the flesh, and had suffered, and died, and rose again, and was now in heaven at the right hand of God, and would come again to judge the quick and the dead, for there may be such a faith and no salvation' (John Gill). Paul's commandment, 'Believe on the Lord Jesus Christ', requires us to look to Christ alone for salvation and life, to rely upon Christ, trusting him and committing the care of our immortal souls to him, and to expect peace, pardon, righteousness and eternal life from him. To believe on Christ is to trust him, venture everything upon him, commit everything to him and receive him. Faith is leaving our souls in the hands of Christ.

This faith in Christ is the commandment of God (1 John 3:23). I see no reason why I should be allowed to believe, to trust Christ and be saved by him. But God commands me to do so. Therefore I do believe. Without anything to commend myself to God, I trust Christ. Live or die, sink or swim, I trust him. And doing what God himself has commanded me to do, I cannot perish! The sure result of faith is eternal salvation. 'Believe on the Lord Jesus Christ, and thou shalt be saved.' You cannot believe Christ and perish!

'Believing in God with all his house'

Read Philemon 1-25

In the first part of his book *The Pilgrim's Progress*, John Bunyan describes Christian as a lonely pilgrim, travelling his road to the Celestial City all alone. Along the way, he met some friends, like Faithful and Hopeful, and he was happy to have their company. But he was still a lonely pilgrim. Neither his wife nor his children walked in the path of faith. In the second part of the book, Bunyan gives us a happier portrait of the pilgrim. Christiana joins her husband, Christian, and their children are also walking in the way. Pilgrim, with his family by his side, along with a great many friends, all are travelling as a convoy to the heavenly kingdom.

What a delightful picture! Sometimes godly men and women have to go to heaven alone. Grace does not run in blood lines. Election separates many from their nearest kinsmen. Often the example, the prayers and the admonitions of a believer have no influence over those who are dearest to him. And the believer has to walk in the path of faith, leaving his family behind. Many a Lot has had to flee from his perishing wife. Many a David has been required to mourn over his doomed Absalom. And many an Abraham has prayed without success for his beloved Ishmael. Grace does not run in blood lines. Faith is not an heirloom, passed on from father to son by the will of the father. Salvation is not a birthright. Yet, it is often true, thank God, it is very often true, that the God of Abraham becomes the God of Sarah, then the God of Isaac and then the God of Jacob. God very often saves one and then uses him as an instrument to draw the rest to himself. As Spurgeon put it, 'He calls an individual and then uses him to be a sort of spiritual decoy to bring the rest of the family into the gospel net.' Sometimes God passes by entire families and none are saved. Sometimes God is gracious to one or two in the household. And sometimes whole families are enclosed within the circle of electing love, redeemed by the blood of Christ and called by the efficacious grace of the Holy Spirit. Nothing could be more blessed to a man than to be the father of a family devoted to Christ.

'Oh that Ishmael might live before thee!'

Read 1 Chronicles 29:1-19

We must leave our families, husbands, wives, mothers, fathers, sons and daughters in the hands of God. If they are saved, like all other sinners, they must be saved by the sovereign will and pleasure of God, by his free grace in Christ. Our children, like all others, are children of wrath, deserving God's just punishment for their sins. If God saves our families, we will serve him with gladness. And if God does not save our families, we will still go on serving him with gladness. Even with regard to our beloved families we must, like Eli, say, 'It is the Lord: let him do what seemeth him good' (1 Sam. 3:18). We dare not rebel against the sovereign purpose of our God.

However, we must make certain that none in our households perish through any neglect or carelessness of our own. It is a tragic fact that Lot's family perished due in great measure to the fact that Lot gave too much attention to their material happiness and far too little attention to their spiritual, eternal welfare. Eli's sons were slain under the wrath of God, because Eli was a slothful father who refused to exercise loving discipline in his family (1 Sam. 3:13).

There is nothing selfish about exercising special care for your own family and earnestly seeking your own family's salvation. In God's providence, your family is the first, primary sphere of your responsibility. It is not wrong, but most natural and proper, that your desire for the salvation of others should, first of all, be towards your own family. Those who live under your roof have special claims upon your care. God has not reversed the laws of nature. He has sanctified them by the rule of his grace. It is only right that Abraham should pray for Ishmael, that Hannah should pray for Samuel and that David should pray for Solomon. It is only right that Andrew should first find his brother Simon and bring him to the Saviour, and that Eunice should teach her son Timothy the way of salvation and life in Christ. Let every believer resolve, by the grace of God, to do whatever can be done to bring his or her family into the kingdom of heaven.

'All his house'

Read Acts 16:25-40

In Acts 16 the Holy Spirit directs our attention to the Philippian jailor and 'all his house'. He gives us seven instructive pictures of that family.

1. The jailor and all his house *were lost and perishing*. This man and his family lived in the prison compound at Philippi, in darkness and ignorance as children of wrath (Eph. 2:11-12). But they were elect, chosen of God and precious. And the time of mercy had come.

2. God saw to it that the jailor and all his house *heard the gospel*. The Lord arranged an earthquake to open the door for the gospel to be preached to this jailor at midnight. Having heard the gospel himself, the jailor called his family together so that they might hear and be saved.

3. The jailor and all his house *believed on Christ*. Each one heard the gospel of redeeming love and saving grace. Each one believed. And each one was saved.

4. The jailor and all his house *confessed Christ in baptism*. All who were baptized were believers, and all who believed were baptized. Immediately upon their profession of faith, they confessed Christ, being buried with him in the watery grave.

5. The jailor and all his house *served Christ*. Believing and being baptized, each one seems to have said, 'What can I do for Christ?' And they did what was at hand: they served the needs of God's messengers. They washed their wounds, fed them and entertained them willingly at a most unaccommodating time.

6. The jailor and all his house *rejoiced in the Lord*. Faith in Christ caused them to rejoice. They were forgiven, justified, accepted in Christ and heirs of eternal life. Why should they not rejoice?

7. Though it is not written in the text, it is clearly revealed that the jailor and all his house *are now in glory*. There, seated before the throne of the Lamb are the jailor, his wife, all his children and all his servants. What a delightful picture! I cannot help asking myself this question: 'Will all my house be there with me?' Will yours? May God be so gracious to you and to me.

'Your children'

Read Ephesians 5:21 - 6:9

God only knows who his elect are. If our sons and daughters are numbered among them they will be saved. Not one of God's chosen ones will perish. Christ will have those whom he has redeemed. In God's time he will call his own from death to life by the power of the Holy Spirit. If some of our children are not chosen of God, they will not be saved. They will not believe. And those who will not believe deserve to perish. But it is our responsibility to do what we can to bring our families into the family of God. I offer these words of instruction to you who believe, to you who are interested in the immortal souls of your sons and daughters.

1. If you want your family to be saved, *see to it that you worship God with your family*. If you do not see to it that your children hear the gospel, it is because you do not care for their souls. If you neglected to feed your children, it would be reasonable to assume that you cared nothing for their bodies. And if you do not provide them with the gospel of Christ, both by private instruction and by bringing them to hear the Word preached, it is obvious that you do not care for their souls. You can do nothing that is more positively harmful to your family than to rob them of the ministry of the Word.

2. If you care for the souls of your children you will *exercise loving discipline in your home*. Eli was a believer. He showed his wicked sons the way of faith and life in Christ. He taught them the gospel. He taught them right from wrong. And he prayed for them. But he was a miserable failure as a father, because he exercised no discipline over them. 'He restrained them not!' God told him plainly that the cause of his sons' death was his lack of discipline as a father.

3. If you want your children to follow Christ, *let them see that you follow Christ*. By all means see to it that your sons and daughters regularly attend the ministry of the gospel. See to it that you pray for them and discipline them. But if your religion is all lip service, they will soon detect your hypocrisy. Set before them an example of love for, faith in and devotion to the Lord Jesus Christ.

'The Holy Scriptures'

Read 2 Peter 1:10-21

The Bible is the Word of God, inspired, infallible, without error. That is not a debatable point of theology. It is a fact, plainly revealed, which all Christians rejoice to acknowledge. Those who deny the inerrancy of Holy Scripture are not Christians. They are infidels. The Bible was not written and compiled by the will of man: 'But holy men of God spake as they were moved by the Holy Ghost' (2 Peter 1:21). The Bible was written by supernatural inspiration. It reveals supernatural things. It can only be understood by supernatural illumination (1 Cor. 2:9-14). To the natural man the Word of God is mysterious, unexplainable and confusing. To the man who is taught of God it is wonderfully simple and comforting. When blessed of God to the hearts of those who read it and hear it preached, the Bible has a marvellous power to transform the lives of men. It is 'quick, and powerful, and sharper than any two-edged sword, piercing even to the dividing asunder of soul and spirit, and of the joints and marrow, and is a discerner of the thoughts and intents of the heart' (Heb. 4:12). As it has power to transform the lives of men, the Bible has power to comfort and encourage the hearts of men. There is no source of comfort for the troubled heart like the Word of God, no source of strength and encouragement for the despondent soul like the promises of Holy Scripture. That blessed volume is the Word of God. I have proved it to be time and again in my own heart. For me, that is stronger proof than all the arguments of learned apologists and philosophical critics. I have seen and felt the power of Holy Scripture in my own life and in the lives of others. The Holy Scriptures, being the Word of God, win our reverence, claim our faith and demand our obedience in all things. And 'these are written, that ye might believe that Jesus is the Christ, the Son of God; and that believing ye might have life through his name' (John 20:31). The Bible was not written to be a textbook on science, history, morality, or even theology, though, where it speaks of these things, it is infallible. The Word of God was written to reveal the Lord Jesus Christ and redemption by him.

'For the transgression of my people was he stricken'

Read Isaiah 53:1-12

Without question these words teach us that the Lord Jesus Christ died for and redeemed a particular people. It gives me no particular pleasure to tell people that there are some in this world for whom Christ did not die, but I must insist upon it. If I told you that Christ died for all men alike, in an effort to redeem all men, the implication of my doctrine would be that salvation is determined not by what Christ has done for men, but by what men do for themselves. And that is totally contrary to the plainest statements of Holy Scripture (Rom. 9:16). It does give me great pleasure to tell sinners, as the Word of God plainly asserts, that Christ Jesus died for some perishing sinners, and all of those for whom he died will be saved by the merits of his sin-atoning sacrifice.

The Word of God plainly teaches that our Lord Jesus Christ died as a Substitute in the place of some of Adam's fallen race, but not all. Christ himself said, 'I am the good Shepherd: the good Shepherd giveth his life for the sheep... I lay down my life for the sheep.' Then he turned to some who were in the crowd, and said, 'Ye are not of my sheep' (John 10:11, 15, 26).

Christ died to make propitiation for our sins, to satisfy the justice of God for his people, so that God might be just and the justifier of all who believe (Rom. 3:24-26). Because God is just, we know that he cannot punish sin twice, once in the sinner's Substitute and again in the sinner himself. If God punished my sin in Christ, he cannot punish sin in me too. That would not be just and equitable. Belief in God's justice and righteousness will not allow us to accept the notion that Christ died for any who ultimately perish under the wrath of God. That would be a travesty of justice. There would be a holiday in hell; Satan and the demons would rejoice and mock the Son of God for ever, if it should ever come to pass that one for whom Christ died and whom he tried to save perished in spite of his redemptive work. The fiends of hell will never have such a holiday. Every soul for whom Christ died will be with him in glory. He will see to it!

'To him give all the prophets witness'

Read John 5:30-47

The Bible is a book with one message and purpose. The message of the Bible is redemption by the blood of the Lord Jesus Christ and its purpose is the salvation of sinners for the glory of God.

This is the thing I want you to see: the singular purpose of Holy Scripture is to reveal the Lord Jesus Christ. The Bible was written to show us our blessed Saviour. This fact was beautifully illustrated by our Lord himself when he came into the synagogue at Nazareth. He opened the book of God and read to the people from the prophecy of Isaiah. Then he closed the book, laid it down and, as the people waited to hear his sermon, he said, 'This day is this scripture fulfilled in your ears' (Luke 4:18-21). Sitting before them, God in human flesh, our Saviour said, 'I am the one of whom the prophet spoke!'

The risen Christ met two of his disciples on the Emmaus road and walked with them. As they talked together, he opened the Scriptures to them and caused them to understand that all the Scriptures spoke of him (Luke 24:27, 44-47). When Philip the evangelist met the Ethiopian eunuch, the eunuch was reading from Isaiah 53. Beginning at that place, Philip 'preached unto him Jesus' (Acts 8:35). When Peter stood up and preached to the Gentiles at Caesarea, he said, 'To him [the Lord Jesus Christ] give all the prophets witness, that through his name whosoever believeth in him shall receive remission of sins' (Acts 10:43). When Paul came to Thessalonica, 'As his manner was, [he] went in unto them [in the synagogue], and three sabbath days reasoned with them out of the scriptures, opening and alleging that Christ must needs have suffered, and risen again from the dead; and that Jesus, whom I preach unto you, is Christ' (Acts 17:2-3). In the book of Hebrews, when Christ came into the world, we are told that he said, 'Lo, I come (in the volume of the book it is written of me,) to do thy will, O God' (Heb. 10:7).

Jesus Christ and him crucified is the sum and substance of Holy Scripture.

'Having obtained eternal redemption for us'

Read Galatians 3:1-14

The apostle Paul tells us that when the Lord Jesus Christ appeared in heaven with his own blood, offering to God the Father the merits of his sin-atoning sacrifice as the sinner's Substitute, he '**obtained eternal redemption**'. His one sacrifice for sin was gloriously effectual. When our Saviour cried, 'It is finished', he fully accomplished the redemption of his people. The death of Christ effectually secured and guaranteed the eternal salvation of all God's elect. Those sinners whom he represented, for whom he died, will never be condemned.

1. I know that all for whom Christ died will be saved, because they are completely forgiven of all sin. 'We have redemption through his blood, the forgiveness of sins, according to the riches of his grace' (Eph. 1:6). God charged our sins to Christ, Christ nailed them to the cross and his blood washed them away (Col. 1:13-15).

2. Those for whom Christ shed his blood must be saved, because they are completely freed from the curse of the law (Gal. 3:13; Rom. 8:1). When Christ was made to be sin for us, he was made a curse for us. When he died under the curse of the law for us he removed our sins. Removing our sins, he removed us from the curse. Where there is no sin there can be no curse.

3. All God's elect will be saved, because they have been completely justified by the death of Christ. Justification is received by faith, but it was fully accomplished at Calvary. Christ was 'delivered for our offences, and raised again for our justification' (Rom. 4:25). To be justified is to be cleared of all charges, to be just as if I had never sinned. No charge will be laid against God's elect, because God has fully justified us in Christ (Rom. 8:33).

4. And all who were crucified with Christ will be with Christ in heaven, because they are already in heaven representatively. When Christ died as our Substitute, we died in him. And when he arose and ascended back into heaven as our Representative before God, we arose and ascended into heaven with him (Eph. 2:4-5). Blessed be God, the finished work of Christ was the full, effectual accomplishment of redemption for all his elect!

'The Lord is my Shepherd'

Read John 10:1-16

One of the most beautiful and most frequently used pictures of Christ in the Scriptures is that of a shepherd. A shepherd is one who tends sheep. He serves sheep. He knows his sheep. He leads them, feeds them, protects them and nurses them. The shepherd leads his sheep out in the morning, tends them through the day and puts them in the fold at night. What could be more blessed than the realization that 'The Lord is my Shepherd'? Our Saviour is not a hireling shepherd, who cares not for the sheep. He is an owner-shepherd, one who both owns and cares for the sheep.

Throughout the Word of God, Christ is presented to us as a Shepherd. He is Jehovah's Shepherd, the one who was smitten by the sword of divine justice, so that his sheep might go free and be saved (Zech. 13:7-9). Christ is the Good Shepherd, who willingly, voluntarily laid down his life for his sheep (John 10:11). We deserved to die, but Christ took our place. He died in our room and in our stead, as our Substitute. He willingly took our sins upon himself, endured the penalty of the law which should have fallen upon us and paid all the debt we owed. Christ is the great Shepherd, who rose from the dead in triumph and victory (Heb. 13:20). Christ is the Shepherd and Bishop of our souls, who saves us and preserves us unto life everlasting (1 Peter 2:25). Christ Jesus is the Shepherd of the sheep, who gathers his little lambs in his arms and carries them in his bosom (Isa. 40:11). Our Lord is the Covenant Shepherd of his people, under whose care we have peace (Ezek. 34:22-25). And Christ is the Chief Shepherd, who soon will appear the second time without sin unto salvation (1 Peter 5:4).

What a blessed, delightful picture! Christ is our Shepherd! And we who believe are his sheep. We belong to him! We are his by covenant agreement (John 6:39), by lawful purchase (1 Peter 1:18) and by our own voluntary consent (Gal. 3:26). Rejoice in this: Christ knows us by intimate, eternal love! Sheep of God, snuggle up in the arms of your Shepherd today, and be at peace.

The parable of the lost sheep

Read John 10:17-30

This parable is recorded to illustrate one thing: it shows us the deep, self-sacrificing love of the Lord Jesus Christ for perishing sinners. It opens the very heart of the eternal God and shows us how delightful it is to God to save sinners, because 'He delighteth in mercy' (Micah 7:18).

In this parable our Lord mentions three groups of sheep: the one hundred, the ninety and nine and the one lost sheep.

1. *The one hundred* represent all mankind in this world. All the sons of Adam, both the righteous and the wicked, belong to the Lord Jesus Christ as his creatures. All were made by him and all belong to him. And all people belong to Christ, our Mediator and King. Whether willingly or unwillingly, all are his servants, under his sovereign dominion. God the Father has given Christ power, dominion and authority over all flesh, so that he might give eternal life to all his elect (John 17:2).

2. *The ninety and nine* represent the self-righteous Pharisees of this world. In their own eyes they are righteous and just and need no repentance. They feel no need of a Saviour. They do not want mercy and grace. So they are left to perish in the wilderness of their own ignorance. To them the Lord says, 'The Son of man is come to seek and to save that which was lost' (Matt. 18:11). 'They that are whole [in their own opinion] need not a physican, but they that are sick. I came not to call the righteous, but sinners to repentance' (Luke 5:31-32).

3. *The one lost sheep* represents all of God's elect in this world, lost and ruined in sin. Christ, our Good Shepherd, is totally consumed with seeking and saving his lost sheep. He seeks his sheep until he finds it. And when he finds his sheep, he lays it upon his shoulders and carries it safely home. In his incarnation the Shepherd came after his lost sheep. In his life he continually sought his sheep. In his death he laid the sheep upon his shoulders. In his resurrection he bore the sheep on its way. And in his ascension be brought it home rejoicing. Not one of the Shepherd's sheep will perish. They are his responsibility. He must, and he will bring all his lost sheep safely home rejoicing.

'I give unto them eternal life and they shall never perish'

Read 2 Timothy 1:1-12

Here is *a divine gift*: '**I give unto them eternal life**.' There was nothing in our hearts or conduct which caused God to bestow eternal life upon us (Jer. 31:3) and there is nothing in the believer's heart or conduct which can cause the Lord to take away his gift of life (Isa. 54:10). It is contrary to the nature of God to take away those gifts which he has freely bestowed upon his people (Rom. 11:29). Knowing that eternal life is entirely the free gift of God, in no way earned by or dependent upon man, we are persuaded that those to whom eternal life is given are eternally secure in Christ (Eccles. 3:14). Eternal life must, of necessity, be eternal.

Here is *a divine promise*: '**And they shall never perish**.' Our Lord here makes a blanket promise. It takes into consideration all times, circumstances, contingencies, events and possibilities. What if they are babes and their faith is weak? 'They shall never perish!' What if they are young men and their passions are strong? 'They shall never perish!' What if they are old men and their vision grows dim? 'They shall never perish!' What if they are tempted? 'They shall never perish!' What if all hell breaks loose against them? 'They shall never perish!' What if they fall? 'They shall never perish!' What if they sin? 'They shall never perish!' What if they sin again? 'They shall never perish!' This promise takes in all the flock. Not one of Christ's sheep will ever perish, no, not even one! This is not the distinctive privilege of a few. It is the common mercy of all. If you are a believer, if you trust the Lord Jesus Christ as Lord and Saviour, if you have received eternal life from him, you will never perish! Christ himself has promised it.

Here is *a divine security*: '**Neither shall any man pluck them out of my hand**.' We are preserved in the heart of our Saviour's eternal love and we are preserved in the hand of his omnipotent grace. 'All thy saints are in thy hands.' We are in the hands of God our Saviour, always in his hands. What a blessed place to be!

'He will reprove the world of sin'

Read John 16:1-14

When God the Holy Spirit comes to a man's heart in saving power and grace, this is the first thing he does: he reproves, convinces and convicts the sinner that he is a sinner, deserving eternal damnation. Where there is no conviction by the Holy Spirit of sin, there is no saving faith in Christ. The Spirit of God so thoroughly convinces a man of his sinfulness that he gladly takes his place with the publican and cries, 'God be merciful to me; I am the sinner.'

He convinces us of the *fact* of sin. We have sinned against God. In our father Adam we rebelled against God, we were born with hearts of rebellion and sin and we have chosen the path of rebellion against God. We are all sinners by nature, sinners at heart, sinners by choice and sinners by deed.

The Holy Spirit convinces us of the *fault* of sin. Our sin is much more than an act of evil against man. Sin is an affront to God. It is an attack upon the throne of God. It is a denial of God's right to be God. Sin is is a monstrous attempt to rape God, to rob him of his dignity and glory as God. 'Against thee, thee only have I sinned, and done this evil in thy sight.'

In conviction, the Holy Spirit convinces us of the *folly* of sin. It is the most foolish thing in the world that a man should sin against God. Sin is utter madness. What fool will dare to stand against the Almighty?

God the Holy Spirit convinces us of the *filth* of sin. He shows us that sin has made us loathsome and obnoxious in the sight of God. It has rendered both me and all that I do unacceptable to a holy God.

The Spirit of God convinces us of the *fountain* of sin. Sin arises from our own evil hearts. Sin is not so much what we do as it is what we are. Because man's heart is a fountain of evil, it brings forth nothing but corruption, vileness and sin.

And the Holy Spirit convinces us of the *fruit* of sin. 'The wages of sin is death.' The just reward of my sin is eternal damnation. But, blessed be God, he also convinces us of the *foregiveness* of sin in Christ.

'By grace are ye saved'

Read Ephesians 2:1-10

The entire work of salvation, all that is involved in bringing a sinner from the dungheap of fallen humanity into the eternal glory of heaven, is accomplished by the free and sovereign grace of God. 'Works' is a dirty word among believers. And 'merits' is a foreign word to God's church, not found in our vocabulary. From the foundation stone to the top stone, we cry nothing else but 'Grace, grace unto it.'

Language could not be clearer. Paul tells us that if any man is saved it is altogether by grace. It is written in the Word of God: 'God hath saved us and called us with an holy calling, not according to our works, but according to his own purpose and grace, which was given us in Christ Jesus before the world began.' In Ephesians 1 Paul ascribes our salvation entirely to the three persons of the sacred Trinity.

God the Father planned and purposed our salvation. He chose us in Christ in eternal election. He predestinated us to sonship in eternal love. He made us accepted in the Beloved by his eternal decree. Salvation originated in the mind of God. He devised a plan whereby he could be just and yet justify the ungodly: he would do it by a divine substitution. He gave his only Son to be our Substitute. And he accepted the sacrifice of Christ for us.

Our salvation was purchased and accomplished by *God the Son*. Through his blood he paid our debt, satisfying the claims of the law against us. And that precious blood of Christ did actually wash our sins away, accomplishing eternal redemption for us. Then, in the fulness of time, *God the Holy Spirit* effectually applied that salvation to our hearts. He caused us to hear the gospel and receive it by faith. He sealed all the blessings of grace to our hearts. And he preserves us unto the day when Christ will claim his purchased possession.

Why has God chosen to save sinners in this way? 'That no flesh should glory in his presence.' And he has done it 'according to the good pleasure of his will, to the praise of the glory of his grace!'

'He brought him to Jesus'

Read John 1:35-51

Yes, salvation is all of grace. It is the Good Shepherd who goes out to seek his sheep. He finds them, and he brings them home. But according to his infinite wisdom and condescending grace, it is our Lord's good pleasure to employ men in this heavenly work. Andrew was present when John said, 'Behold the Lamb of God!' And Andrew beheld him. Immediately Andrew went and found Simon and told him, 'We have found the Christ.' '**And he brought him to Jesus**.' Andrew could not give Simon faith. He could not show him Christ's glory. He could not save him. But there was something he could do: he could tell Simon what he had seen. He could tell Simon about Christ. And he could bring Simon to the place where he might meet Christ for himself. You know the result of Andrew's effort. Simon was converted and he became the mighty spokesman of the early church.

Andrew never preached like Peter did. But had it not been for Andrew's witness to his brother, Peter would never have preached either. Maybe you can't preach. But you can be an Andrew. Go and tell men what you have experienced; tell them about the Christ of God. Then bring them with you to the place where they are most likely to meet Christ for themselves. Bring others with you to the house of God to hear a man preach the gospel of Christ.

I cannot believe that a man has tasted the honey of the gospel if he is content to eat it all by himself. Free grace compels a man to be generous. We do not want to feast on the riches of Christ by ourselves. We want to bring others to our Lord that they may enjoy his riches with us. You have a tremendous opportunity before you. How many people do you know who are perishing for a lack of knowledge? You have at your disposal tracts, articles, tapes and your own experience by which you can share the knowledge of Christ and his gospel. Who knows? Maybe God will be pleased to use you to bring another sinner like yourself to a saving knowledge of Christ.

What a glorious prospect! Let it inspire you to begin the work today.

'We are members of his body'

Read John 15:1-17

Child of God, can you begin to imagine what this text teaches? There is a living, loving and lasting union between the Lord Jesus Christ and all his people. It is beyond imagination, but it is true – we are one with our Redeemer! What does this imply?

Certainly, it implies *a similarity of nature* between Christ and his church. By the incarnation our Lord assumed our nature. He is God the eternal Son. But he is also a real man. As a man, he lived in perfect righteousness, died as our Substitute, arose from the grave and reigns in glory. Ever rejoice in the eternal deity of Christ, but never forget that your Saviour is a real man. And by the new birth, the Son of God has given us his nature. We are 'partakers of the divine nature'. Christ bears our nature in heaven and we bear his nature upon the earth.

The text also implies *an intimate relationship*. We are wed to the God-man. We cannot understand this relationship, but we can enjoy it. Christ espoused us to be his bride before the world began. He redeemed us for himself. He prepared our wedding garments. He allured us into the wilderness and there won our hearts by his all-prevailing love. My God, my Maker, my Redeemer, my Saviour, my King is also my Husband. 'Let him kiss me with the kisses of his mouth; his love is better than wine.'

Again, the text implies *a mysterious origin*. As Eve was taken from the side of Adam, the church was born from the bleeding side of Christ, the second Adam. He died that we might live.

These words also imply *a loving possession*. We belong to Christ. 'Ye are not your own, ye are bought with a price.' For many years we were in the arms of another. But all the while we belonged to him who loved us, chose us and redeemed us.

Once more, our text implies *a vital union*. 'We are members of his body.' Those words imply much more than unity. They imply identity. We are one with Christ! He must have us. The Head cannot be complete without his body. The King must have his subjects. The Shepherd must have his sheep. This is a vital union. Christ must have his redeemed ones. And we must have him.

'He commanded us to preach'

Read Acts 1:1-11

Recently, I read an article in a religious periodical which suggested that one of the greatest problems in our churches is that we spend too much time preaching. What nonsense!

Our Lord's last great command was this: 'Go ye into all the world, and preach the gospel.' This was Paul's dying charge to Timothy: 'Preach the Word.' And preaching was the one business of the great apostle's life. He wrote, 'Woe is unto me, if I preach not the gospel.' God never called anyone to discuss the gospel, to debate the gospel, or to refine the gospel. But he does call men, whom he has gifted and qualified for the work, to preach the gospel. And he sends them forth into the world for that one purpose. And he gives but one reason for doing so: 'It pleased God by the foolishness of preaching to save them that believe.'

Beloved, this is the one business of God's servants. And it is not only the primary purpose for our assemblies, it is the only purpose. The local church is to be a sounding-board for the gospel of Christ, nothing more and nothing less. Not all of God's saints are gifted for preaching, but they all are engaged in the work. By their love, their prayers and their generosity, they hold up the hands of God's servants.

I say this is the one purpose of the church with good reason: preaching is the means of salvation. 'Faith cometh by hearing, and hearing by the Word of God.' Preaching is the means of edification. God gives his church pastors according to his own heart, 'for the perfecting of the saints, for the work of the ministry, for the edifying of the body of Christ'. And preaching is the means of sanctification. 'Sanctify them through thy truth: thy word is truth.'

Well is it written: 'How beautiful [greatly desired] are the feet of them that preach the gospel of peace, and bring glad tidings of good things!' God save us from those who would turn aside his church from this great work. Let us press on, as the Lord enables us, preaching the gospel to every creature.

'Let not your hearts be troubled'

Read Isaiah 40:12-31

Sometimes I get weary and despondent. It appears that my labours in the gospel are vain. My preaching often falls upon deaf ears. The outward, visible results of our ministry are disappointing. Part of this despondency arises from sinful pride. The other part has its roots in sinful unbelief. These feelings of despondency are contrary to the gospel of the grace of God, dishonouring to Christ our Lord and damaging to the testimony of the gospel. Our Lord knew that as long as we were in this world, being weak and sinful men, we would be terribly prone to anxiety, self-pity and feelings of emptiness and uselessness. Therefore he gave us this gentle word of comfort: 'Let not your hearts be troubled: ye believe in God, believe also in me.'

Beloved, in spite of the way things often appear, you and I have every reason to be optimistic, encouraged, hopeful and confident regarding the work of the gospel. Our Saviour, that one for whose honour we labour and whose will we seek to obey, sits upon the throne of universal dominion. He is the sovereign Lord and King of all things and he reigns in the serenity of total control. The gospel which we preach is his gospel. And it will not return to him void.

Our God and King is performing his will. Sometimes it does not appear, in our eyes, to be so, but God is doing, and will do, all his pleasure. He is governing all things according to his will. I do not know what the Lord's purpose for me in this life is. But of this I am certain, God himself has sent me forth as his messenger in this generation, and whatever he intends to do with me for his glory, he will do it! I know also that God has a people in this world whom he is determined to save and God will save all his people. I do not know what God's purpose and plan is for our generation, but I do know that in the end two things will ultimately be accomplished: all of God's elect will be saved and Jesus Christ the Lord will be glorified. And whatever the Lord is pleased to do in the meantime will be best for me and best for all his people. We have no reason for despair, but every reason for expectation (1 Cor. 15:58).

'The Most High ruleth!'

Read Isaiah 45:5-25

It requires only a casual reading of Holy Scripture to see that the God of the Bible is vastly different from the god of modern religion (e.g. Ps. 115:3; 135:6; Dan. 4:35; Isa. 46:9-10; Rom. 9:15-16; 11:33-36; 1 Tim. 6:15). The modern idea of God which prevails most widely, even among those who profess to believe the Bible, is that of a miserable failure. The god of twentieth-century religion is a helpless, effeminate being who commands the respect of no truly thoughtful man. He is helpless, frustrated and defeated. The god being preached from the average pulpit is an object of pity rather than reverence. To say (as most do) that God the Father has purposed the salvation of all men, that God the Son died with the express intention of redeeming the whole human race and that God the Holy Spirit is now trying to win the whole world to Christ, when it is evident that the great majority of our fellow men are dying in sin and passing into a hopeless eternity, is to say that God the Father is disappointed, that God the Son is dissatisfied and that God the Holy Spirit is defeated. I have stated the issue in plain terms, but such must be the conclusions of modern theology. To argue that God is trying his best to save all mankind, but that the majority of men will not let him save them, is to insist that the Creator is impotent and that the will of the creature is omnipotent. Such theology is not only slightly off the mark, it is degrading to God and blasphemous!

The one true and living God is an absolute and universal Sovereign. His purpose cannot be frustrated. His power cannot be defeated. His will cannot be resisted. Anything, or anyone, that can successfully frustrate God's purpose, defeat his power and resist his will by virtue of his supremacy would become God. This is what modern religion is attempting to do: it is attempting to do what Adam tried to do in the Garden of Eden – namely, to bring God down off his throne and exalt man to the place of Godhood. But, blessed be God, it will never happen. It is still true: '**The Most High ruleth**.' His purpose will be done. His glory will be manifest in all his creation.

'Christ died for us'

Read Psalm 22:1-15

The Word of God sets forth many precious truths which we love to study and proclaim. Yet all the blessed doctrines of Holy Scripture may be summed up in one doctrine: substitution. The very first doctrine of the Bible, *creation*, can only be properly understood if we realize that all things were created by our Substitute. The doctrine of God's *providence* is a wonderful and precious doctrine. And what is providence but the upholding of all things by the word of the power of our Substitute? We believe the grand old doctrines of *eternal election* and *sovereign predestination* and we are not bashful to proclaim them. But election is in the person of our Substitute. We are predestinated to be conformed to the image of the only-begotten Son of God, our Substitute. How we glory in the doctrine of the *atonement*! But if there were no substitute, no mediator between God and man, if there was no one who could satisfy both the needs of fallen man and the justice of a holy God, there would be no atonement. The doctrine of *glorification* causes our hearts to rejoice in the glorious expectation of the sons of God, but we could have no hope of future glory if there were no substitute into whose likeness we must be made.

The one theme of the Bible is substitution. Everything in the Bible either promises it, typifies it, or proclaims it. Every ritual of the Old Testament, every garment of the priesthood, every sacrifice, every article of furniture in the tabernacle, the tabernacle itself, all the laws of Israel, the temple, the temple service and the prophets of God all have but one message, and they all proclaim it clearly: 'God commendeth his love toward us in that, while we were yet sinners, Christ died for us.' This was the message which God the Holy Spirit caused to flow from the pens and from the mouths of every inspired prophet and apostle. And if God is pleased to bless his church in our day, it will be through the proclamation of this message: 'He hath made him to be sin for us, who knew no sin, that we might be made the righteousness of God in him.'

'Who is even at the right hand of God'

Read Psalm 22:16-31

Because the Lord Jesus Christ humbled himself and became obedient unto death, even the death of the cross, in order to redeem, pardon and justify God's elect, he has been exalted to the throne of universal dominion at the right hand of God. Today the God-man reigns in sovereign serenity over all things. The purpose of his mediatorial reign is that he might give eternal life unto as many as the Father gave into his hands, as the Surety of the covenant, before the world began. Nothing can be more comforting to the believer's heart than the fact of Christ's exaltation and lordship. This is the basis of our assurance and confidence before God.

The *exaltation* of Christ assures me that my sin is gone. By way of divine imputation, our sins were laid upon Christ. He bore our sins in his own body on the tree. In his body our sins were nailed to the cross. Because he bore our sins, he died and was buried. Now the fact that he is risen and exalted to the throne of heaven is proof positive that our sins are all taken away. In the book of God's law and justice not one sin is recorded against any believer!

The *lordship* of Christ assures me that all things work together for my everlasting good. In the covenant of grace the Lord Jesus Christ voluntarily assumed the responsibility for my eternal welfare, as my Surety. Now he has authority and power over all flesh and he governs all things with a sovereign and omnipotent hand to secure nothing but good for them who are the called according to his purpose.

The *sovereign majesty* of the Lord Jesus Christ assures me that all of God's elect are safe. Not one of that vast multitude given to Christ in the covenant of grace and redeemed by him at Calvary will ever perish. The primary purpose of his glorious reign as Mediator and King is 'that he should give eternal life unto as many as thou hast given him'. Every believer is safe and secure, because our Head is exalted to the throne of heaven and where the Head is his members must also be.

'In him is no sin'

Read Psalm 103:1-12

The Lord Jesus Christ was manifested to take away our sins and in Christ there is no sin. Though he was made to be sin for us, our Lord had no sin of his own. 'He knew no sin, neither was any guile found in his mouth.' 'He was holy, harmless, undefiled, and separate from sinners.' In order for him to be a suitable sacrifice for sin, it was necessary that our Saviour be without sin. The sinner's Substitute must himself be innocent, righteous and holy.

Yet in order to redeem us from our sins and to justify us before God, the Son of God had to be made sin for us. By a legal transfer and imputation, the Son of God was made to be sin for us. Our sin and our guilt were imputed to the Lord Jesus Christ and God's holy law exacted from him the just penalty of our sins. 'He hath made him to be sin for us, who knew no sin, that we might be made the righteousness of God in him.' 'Christ hath redeemed us from the curse of the law, being made a curse for us: for it is written, cursed is every one that hangeth on a tree.'

And having taken our sins upon himself, suffering for us the just penalty of our sins, our glorious Mediator in heaven once again has no sin. That one who sits in heaven and makes intercession for us has no sin. We know and are assured that because he is perfect. He is holy. He has no sin. This is the basis of our assurance and confidence with God. We have a perfect Substitute and sacrifice whom the Father will accept.

But this text is speaking of those who are in Christ. He is telling us that in Christ *we* have no sin. In ourselves we are sinners. The old nature of sin is with us and will be with us so long as we are in this world. Anyone who denies this is a liar and makes God a liar. But before God, in the sight of God, those who are in Christ by a living faith have no sin. 'He was manifested to take away our sins.' And he has done it! '**And in him is no sin.**' The all-seeing eye of God's holy law sees no sin in the believer, because the believer has no sin.

'Many are called'

Read Matthew 22:1-14

Here our Lord is talking about the general call of the gospel which goes out to all men every time the gospel is preached. There is an inward, divine call which is given by the Holy Spirit to all of God's elect. This call of the Holy Spirit is always effectual and irresistible. By almighty, irresistible power the Spirit of God draws all of the elect to Christ. This call is given only to God's elect, it always produces faith in Christ and it always results in salvation (Ps. 65:4; Rom. 8:28-30; 1 Cor. 1:21-24; 2 Tim. 1:9). There are many examples of this effectual irresistible call in the Scriptures (Matt. 4:18-22; Luke 19:5). But this is not the call mentioned in our text.

In this parable, our Lord is speaking of that call which goes forth in the earnest proclamation of the gospel. This call is *universal and unconditional.* We are ambassadors of Christ, sent to offer men terms of peace with God. The King himself has sent us to call his enemies to total, unconditional surrender. We have no authority to change his terms. It is surrender or die! This call is *given by divine authority.* Those who are truly sent of God speak to men in God's stead! Because this call is given by divine authority, it is *most urgent.* God will not trifle with those who trifle with the gospel freely preached to perishing men by his servants (Prov. 1:23-33). And this call which we issue to sinners in Christ's name is most *sincere and gracious.* If you will hear his voice and harden not your heart, God will save you.

Someone may say, 'But, if only God's elect will be saved, why preach the gospel to every creature? Why call upon all men? Why invite all?' We preach the gospel to all men, because God has commanded it. The ground of our responsibility is not the decree of God, but the command of God. God has chosen to save his elect by the foolishness of preaching. We have no way of knowing who God's elect are until they believe, so we preach indiscriminately to all. When I have preached the gospel to all men, I am free from the blood of all men, and those who believe not are left without excuse. If they had believed, they would have been saved.

'Few are chosen'

Read Luke 14:7-24

The vast majority of those to whom the gospel is preached will not believe it. Some flatly reject it. Some pay no attention to it. Some, in order to soothe their consciences, pretend to believe it and join the church. And multitudes substitute a religious form for faith in Christ, the waters of baptism for the blood of Christ and their own works for the righteousness of Christ (Matt. 7:13-14). '**For many are called, but few are chosen**.'

Blessed be God, he has chosen some! There are some in this world God has chosen to save and they will all, sooner or later, believe on Christ. The rest have been left to themselves. God has done them no injustice. He simply lets them have their own way. He does not violate their will. He does not force them to do what they choose not to do. He does not give them what they do not want. Pity the man God leaves alone! That man will never believe on Christ and be saved (John 10:16,26; Acts 13:46-48).

There is no question about it at all, God has an elect people in this world, a people whom he is determined to save, saying, 'I will be their God, and they shall be my people.' (See John 15:16; Rom. 9:11-13; Eph. 1:3-6; 1 Thess. 1:4; 2 Thess. 2:13.) These are the people for whom we labour. We are seeking the Lord's sheep. We preach the gospel for the elect's sake. Can you rejoice in electing love? How we ought to rejoice that our names are written in heaven, written in the book of life before the foundation of the world! (Luke 10:20, cf Rev. 13:8; 16:8.)

'Few are chosen.' Are you among this favoured company? Are you one of God's elect? If you do truly rest your soul upon Christ alone, trusting his righteousness as your only righteousness and his blood as your only atonement, clinging to him as your only hope and acceptance before God, rejoice! You would never have such faith had God not chosen you in Christ before the world began (John 6:37-40). Saving faith is the result of eternal, electing grace (Phil. 1:29).

'Who gave himself for our sins'

Read Psalm 40:1-17

Our Lord died as a vicarious sacrifice in the place of God's elect, his sheep, all who believe. Had he died in the place of every man in the world and borne all their sins, every man would be saved. But, in as much as all men are not saved, one of two conclusions must be drawn. Either Christ failed in his efforts to redeem some of those whom he represented, which is blasphemy; or he actually died as the Substitute only of those who are in fact redeemed and saved by him, which is the truth of Scripture. 'For the transgression of my people was he stricken', saith the Lord.

And our Lord's once-for-all sacrifice for sin was an effectual atonement. That is to say, he did actually put away the sins of his people, redeem us from the curse of the law and secure our everlasting salvation by his death and resurrection in our place. He did not make the pardon of sin, redemption and salvation possibilities for all men; he actually accomplished those things for some men. 'Christ hath redeemed us from the curse of the law.' 'By his own blood he entered in once into the holy place, having obtained eternal redemption for us.' He has 'put away sin by the sacrifice of himself'. The believer's faith does not give merit to the blood of Christ and make it effectual. The blood of Christ gives merit to the believer's faith and makes it effectual.

If Christ died only for a specific people, how can I know that he bore my sin and died for me? I know that Christ died for sinners and I know that I am a sinner. I know that he died for every sinner who believes on him and that all who believe on him will be saved, because God said so. Now as a guilty sinner I do with all my heart trust the Lord Jesus Christ as my only and all-sufficient Saviour. Since I trust him, I know that he died for me. Will you trust him too? If you can, then he died for you!

'How shall they believe in him of whom they have not heard?'

Read Amos 8:1-13

A few months ago, I listened very carefully to one of America's most well-known fundamentalist preachers. On his nationwide television broadcast he was talking about his 'salvation experience', and this is what he said: 'When I got saved, I did not know anything at all about the Bible, I could not quote one verse of Scripture, and I did not know anything at all about the lordship of Christ; I simply believed that there was somebody in heaven who loved me and would forgive me of my sins.' His testimony, I am sure, was true to his experience. It reflects the essence of 'easy-believism' and 'decisionism'.

But in the text quoted above, and in the whole context of Romans chapter 10, Paul tells us that true faith and true salvation come as the result of knowledge. Do not misunderstand me, I do not suggest that you must become a theologian to be saved, or that you can obtain salvation by your own mental powers, but I do say that where there is no knowledge of the gospel there is no true saving faith.

It is not enough simply to believe; you must believe what God reveals in his Word. In order to believe on Christ, you must know something about Christ. You must know who he is. He is the God-man, the Lord of glory. Salvation begins with a knowledge of Christ's lordship. Everywhere in the New Testament men and women sought mercy from the hands of the Lord and called upon the name of the Lord Jesus Christ. It is not possible for me to trust Christ as the all-sufficient Saviour of my everlasting soul until I know who he is, the Lord Jesus Christ. And you must know what the Lord Jesus Christ has done. Being both God and man, by his one great sacrifice, through the shedding of his blood unto death, the Lord Jesus Christ has put away all the sins of all who trust him, and now the risen exalted Christ reigns in heaven to save sinners. This saving knowledge that produces faith comes by divine revelation through the preaching of the gospel. Anyone who is totally ignorant of the gospel cannot believe the gospel.

'I am sick of love'

Read Song of Songs 2:1-16

The Lord Jesus Christ has been most gracious to me. He has brought me into his church and family and made me to be one of his own. He has made me, at various times, to sit down in blessed fellowship with him, feasting upon the rich and blessed truths of the gospel. His banner over me is love. My heart rejoices in his eternal, special, electing, immutable love for my soul. But now my soul is weary. A heavenly love-sickness has come over me, because my blessed Lord and Redeemer, the great Lover of my soul, does not openly and clearly manifest himself as he has in days gone by.

'I am sick of love,' because *I long for his presence*. I know that Christ is always present with his church. Wherever two or three gather in his name, he is in their midst. But I long for him to make his presence known. My heart and soul yearn for a fresh and constant sense of his love. When he reveals himself all is well. When he hides his face, everything seems empty and vain.

'I am sick of love,' because *I long for his return*. The thought fills my soul with gladness that one day the Lord Jesus Christ will return to this earth. In that blessed day, the knowledge of the Lord will cover the earth as the waters cover the sea. Oh, may it please the King to return in his glory very soon! We long for him.

'I am sick of love,' because *I long to be with him*. Is it not reasonable for the Lord's people to long to be with him where he is? To be with him is to be free from sin. To be with him is to enter into rest. To be with him is to come into the glorious liberty of the sons of God. I will be content to remain here, so long as he sees fit. But my heart has already departed. 'I am sick of love.'

While I am here, I can be content, if he will give me the comfort of his grace. 'Stay with me flagons, comfort me with apples.' Though at times the Lord is pleased to withdraw his manifest presence, he has left behind the wine of his grace and the fruits of his labours to sustain my heart. These are the pillows of my soul. I rejoice in them. Yet I long for my well-Beloved.

'I have found a ransom!'

Read Job 33:13-33

This is God's 'Eureka!' In the person of his Son, the Lord Jesus Christ, he found a ransom for his chosen people. By the substitutionary sacrifice of his own well-beloved Son in the place of his people, the Lord God found a way to punish sin to the satisfaction of his divine justice and to be gracious in saving every believer. By this one mighty, all-sufficient, sin-atoning ransom, he would be perfectly just while at the same time justifying every believer.

This ransom was the invention of divine wisdom. Only the infinite mind of the eternal God could or would have devised such a gracious and just plan to save fallen man. Truly the cross of Christ displays most gloriously the manifold wisdom of God.

This ransom was the gift of divine love. 'For God so loved the world that he gave his only begotten Son, that whosoever believeth in him should not perish, but have everlasting life.' 'God commendeth his love toward us, in that while we were yet sinners, Christ died for us.' 'Herein is love, not that we loved God, but that he loved us, and sent his Son to be the propitiation for our sins.' The price of our ransom is the precious blood of Christ. Justice could demand no more and love could give no more than the precious blood of Christ.

This ransom has been fully paid. Just before he breathed out his spirit, our Lord cried triumphantly, 'It is finished!' Those words simply mean, 'The ransom is paid, redemption is complete.' By his mighty atoning sacrifice, our Lord Jesus Christ has satisfied the law of God, honoured the justice of God, brought in everlasting righteousness and put away all the sins of all who will ever trust him. God neither requires, nor will he accept, anything from the sinner to complete the work. Christ has done it all!

And this ransom is gloriously effectual. Every soul that was purchased from the hands of divine justice by the blood of Christ must be saved by divine power. The very justice of God demands it. In the fulness of time the Lord will 'deliver him from going down to the pit', saying, **'I have found a ransom**!'

'That faith of our father Abraham'

Read Romans 4:1-16

1. The faith of Abraham *leaves home at God's command* (Gen. 12:1-4). God called Abraham out of his idolatrous, unbelieving family. If he believed God, he had to forsake his family. He had to forsake their religion, their customs, their principles, their wealth and their company. God said, 'Get thee out... So Abram departed.' God's call to Abraham was most gracious, but most demanding. It involved total surrender to the sovereign Lord.

2. The faith of Abraham *denies self* (Gen. 13:5-9, 14-15). In giving Lot his way and his choice, Abraham found God's will and walked in God's way. True faith waits on God. Abraham did not seek after the goods of this world, but the glory of his God (Rom. 12:10; Phil. 2:2-7).

3. The faith of Abraham *looks to the Lord alone for all things* (Gen. 14:17-23). 'The just shall live by faith.' As Abraham refused to receive anything from the wicked king of Sodom, faith refuses to live by the principles of the world. God's people live upon faith (Matt. 6:23-34; Mark 4:18-19; 1 Tim. 6:6-10).

4. The faith of Abraham *denies and excludes works* (Gen 21:8-14). It was no easy thing for Abraham to throw Ishmael and Hagar out of his house. But God commanded it and it must be done. Ishmael represented the works of the flesh. Isaac represented the promise of God. Ishmael stood for the works of the law. Isaac stood for the grace of God. The two could not dwell together. Works and grace cannot be mixed. True faith says, 'Good-bye' to all fleshly works and clings to Christ alone.

5. The faith of Abraham *lays the most precious possession on the altar and rests in the Lord* (Gen. 22:1-14). God graciously taught Abraham the gospel of substitution, and thereby revealed the glory of his grace to him. And Abraham, in true faith towards God, submitted everything to the will of God. Because he believed God, he took his most precious possession, his son Isaac whom he dearly loved, and sacrificed him upon the altar to the Lord. When the trial was over, Abraham knew the Lord to be Jehovah-Jireh, 'the Lord who provides'.

'Faith cometh by hearing'

Read John 3:1-18

The Lord our God is absolutely sovereign. He saves his people altogether by grace, without any works of their own. No one believes or preaches that any more fully than I do. But there are some who conclude that since salvation is of the Lord, it is not necessary for men to hear the gospel, repent of sin and believe on Christ. Such reasoning is just as heretical as Arminianism. Our doctrine must rest upon the plain statements of Holy Scripture, not upon human logic and reason. Here are three facts, plainly revealed in the Word of God.

1. *No one will ever be saved who does not hear the gospel.* God could have chosen to send angels to reveal his grace, or he could have chosen to take his people to heaven upon the merits of Christ's righteousness and shed blood, without ever sending a preacher to them. But he did not. In his infinite and wise sovereignty, God determined to make the preaching of the gospel an essential instrument in the salvation of his elect.

2. *No one will ever be saved who does not repent of his sin.* Our Lord said, 'Except ye repent ye shall all likewise perish.' It is not possible for a man to enter into heaven who does not enter by the gate of repentance. Christ himself said so! Repentance is a change of mind, a change of masters and a change of motives. Men may argue and debate the subject, but the Word of God is unchanged. You have but two alternatives: you must either 'repent or perish'!

3. *No one will ever be saved who does not believe on the Lord Jesus Christ.* It is written: 'He that believeth on the Son hath everlasting life: and he that believeth not the Son shall not see life; but the wrath of God abideth on him.' Faith is indispensable to salvation. Faith in Christ is the sure token and evidence of God's electing grace. Whoever believes is elect. Whoever dies in unbelief is not elect. God's purpose of grace includes all the means as well as the ultimate end of eternal salvation.

Mark it down. Those who are chosen of God and redeemed by Christ will hear the gospel, repent of sin and believe on Christ.

'My times are in thy hand'

Read Psalm 37:1-25

'**My times**'. They change and vary from day to day, but they change only in accordance with his unchanging love. They vary, but only according to the purpose of him in whom there is no variableness or shadow of turning. 'My times', that is to say, my ups and my downs, my health and my sickness, my prosperity and my adversity, my wealth and my poverty, my happiness and my sorrow – all of these are in the hands of my Lord and Redeemer, who arranges and appoints the length of my days and the darkness of my nights according to his wise and holy will. My times of refreshing and my times of depressing are in the hands of my God and Saviour and I am glad that it is so.

'My times' – all of them, in the beginning of life, in the course of life and in the end of life, '**are in thy hand**'. The close of my life is no more at the disposal of fate, or chance, or Satan than the beginning of my life. My life will not close until the hand of my Father's love closes it. I shall not die before my time and I shall not be forgotten and left on the stage of time too long. I want you to get the sense of this: not only are we in the hand of the Lord, but everything that surrounds us is in his hand. All the people, things and events which make up the environment of our existence are in the hand of our God. Child of God, this should bring comfort and joy to your heart. We dwell in the palm of God's hand! We are absolutely at his disposal. And everything that concerns us is arranged by his hand.

May the Lord graciously enable us to enter into the peaceful realization of his good providence! 'Cast all your care upon him, for he careth for you.' It is written: 'Thou wilt keep him in perfect peace, whose mind is stayed on thee: because he trusteth in thee. Trust ye in the Lord for ever: for in the Lord Jehovah is everlasting strength.'

> Rock of Ages, cleft for me,
> Let me hide myself in thee!

'Comfort of the Scriptures'

Read Psalm 119:1-24

I rejoice in every aspect of divine revelation. Everything that I have read in the Bible and been taught by the Holy Spirit is delightful to my heart. Every doctrinal truth and every principle of Holy Scripture is wilfully accepted and submitted to by faith. Yet there are some truths which yield special comfort to my soul. Here are three blessed, soul-comforting truths of the gospel.

1. *The Lord our God is absolutely sovereign.* In creation, in providence and in salvation, God has his way and accomplishes his will. Nothing ever comes to pass in God's creation except that which my heavenly Father has purposed. He says, 'I am God, and there is none else; I am God, and there is none like me, declaring the end from the beginning, and from ancient times the things that are not yet done, saying, My counsel shall stand, and I will do all my pleasure' (Isa. 46:9-10). My heart can safely trust a sovereign God. The God of heaven is a God who does what he will, has mercy on whom he will and graciously accomplishes the eternal salvation of his covenant people by his own right arm.

2. *Redemption is accomplished by the finished work of Christ, the sinner's Substitute.* When our Lord Jesus Christ cried, 'It is finished!' redemption's work was done. Nothing is left to be completed by us. Peace, pardon, justification, reconciliation, the forgiveness of sin, acceptance with God were all perfectly accomplished for God's people at Calvary. He did not leave so much as one thread for us to sew into the robe of righteousness, by which we are clothed. He did not leave so much as one ounce of suffering for us to pay to the offended justice of God. He did it all! Accomplished redemption is good news for hell-bound sinners!

3. *'Whosoever shall call upon the name of the Lord shall be saved.'* There are no exceptions, no qualifications, no limitations. The invitation is as free as the salvation it proclaims. Anyone in the whole wide world who will call upon Christ as Lord will be saved, even you, even me! It is true, we will not call upon him until he calls us. But the fact that I call upon Christ the Lord in faith is proof positive that he has chosen me and redeemed me. Will you call upon him too?

'We are ambassadors for Christ'

Read Matthew 10:27-42

It is true, preachers are just men. Like all other men, they sin, they make mistakes, they are subject to error and they are apt to offend people sooner or later. But if a man is truly a gospel preacher, called and sent of God, he has upon him a divine authority. He is God's spokesman to men! This authority does not make the Lord's servant proud and tyrannical, rather it causes him to tremble with reverence. And this fact will cause wise men to listen attentively and obediently to that man who comes with a message from God.

If God ever speaks to you it will be through a preacher. The days are over in which God spoke to men by angels, or in dreams. Paul said, 'Faith cometh by hearing, and hearing by the word of God... and how shall they hear without a preacher?' If the Lord sends one of his servants your way, you would be wise to hear him every time you have opportunity. God might have something to say to you.

The greatest blessing God can ever bestow upon a people is to send them a faithful gospel preacher. 'How beautiful upon the mountains are the feet of him that bringeth good tidings, that publisheth peace; that bringeth good tidings of good, that publisheth salvation, that saith unto Zion, Thy God reigneth!' The preacher may or may not be learned, eloquent, polite, or handsome, but if he is God's messenger it will be your greatest earthly blessing to have him in your midst and your greatest curse in this world to lose him.

Whatever you do to the King's ambassador is done to the King himself. To hear him is to hear the King. To obey him is to obey the King. To honour him is to honour the King. To reject him is to reject the King.

God's people will esteem God's servants very highly in love for their work's sake. Any man who brings you a message from God, who labours in the study of the Word that he may feed your soul with the precious truths of the gospel ought, for that reason, to be loved and honoured by you. You should promote him, support him, defend him, love him, obey him and follow him.

'Can these bones live?'

Read Ezekiel 33:1-11

Death is a terrible picture of our natural condition before God, but it is by no means an exaggeration. The whole world lies before us as a valley of dry bones, according to Ezekiel's vision; and if ever these dry bones are to live, it will not be through some innate energy in the bones themselves, or through the influence of the most zealous prophet. Education cannot develop life out of death. Persuasion cannot excite a dead man to life. And reason cannot instil life in a corpse. The arm of the Lord must be revealed, or the case is beyond hope. Let men do all they can: weep, plead, preach and prophesy – all will be vain. Unless the Lord himself breathes life, the dry bones cannot live.

No, Ezekiel could not make the dry bones live, but he could prophesy to them. God commanded him to do so and God gave him the ability to do so. Therefore Ezekiel was responsible to prophesy unto the dry bones. Spurgeon said, 'We cannot turn the dry bones into living men, but we can prophesy upon them, and, blessed be God, we can also prophesy to the four winds, and by our means the dead may live.' Even so, we cannot give dead sinners life. Eternal life and faith in Christ are gifts of divine grace created in the hearts of men by the sovereign power of God. But there are some things we can and must do for the souls of men. We can preach the gospel of Christ unto men. We can make known the way of life unto men. We can instruct men in gospel truth. And that which we can do, we must do. 'Necessity is laid upon me; yea, woe is unto me, if I preach not the gospel.' If I know that a man is perishing under the wrath of God and I know the way of eternal life by faith in the blood and righteousness of Christ, and if God gives me the ability and the opportunity to preach the gospel to that perishing sinner, it becomes my responsibility to do it. I preach the gospel because I love Christ, I love his gospel and I love the souls of men. I do it willingly and cheerfully. Yet I am under constraint to fulfil my responsibility. God says, 'His blood will I require at thine hand!'

'Fret not'

Read Matthew 6:19-24

We all have to deal with depression. You and I are not alone in our troubles. All of God's people face the same troubles, heartaches, pains and sorrows that you face. And at times we all become emotionally, mentally and spiritually depressed. The only difference is that some are able to cope with depression, while others feed it. Like you, I sometimes have fits of morbid depression. But I have found that there are some things which always help me to overcome my sinful depression. Yes, I said, 'sinful'. Depression is both a foolish and sinful thing. When you get to the essence of it, you are sure to find that it amounts to nothing but pride and self-pity. Here are some things which help me to overcome this evil.

1. *The Word of God* is a source of great consolation and encouragement. The next time you feel depression coming, take your Bible down and read it. Meditate upon the promises of God, the redemption of Christ, the grace of God upon you, the providence of God for you and the home awaiting you.

2. *Personal worship, communion and fellowship with Christ* will soon drive away your dark depression. Go to the Lord in prayer. Pour out your soul to him. Worship and praise him in private. Spend much time with the Man of sorrows, and your sorrows will soon become very insignificant.

3. *The fellowship of God's people* does much to defeat depression. Usually, when you are greatly depressed, you want to be alone. Nothing could be worse for you than that. Seek out some child of God and chat with him about God's abundant mercy in Christ, not about your mutual woes! And be sure that you meet together with God's elect in the house of worship. Many suffer with depression far longer than they need, simply because they neglect the assembly of the saints and the ministry of the Word.

4. *Cast all your care upon the Lord* – he does care for you! His shoulders are broad enough and strong enough to carry your load. There is no need for you to carry it. Faith in Christ is the best cure for every form of depression.

'He delighteth in mercy'

Read Micah 7:1-20

This statement from God's prophet should raise a universal shout of 'Hallelujah' from the fallen sons of Adam. The God whom we have offended, the God whom we have blasphemed, the God whose law we have broken delights in mercy!

Wisdom and power, justice and truth, holiness and infinity are all attributes of God. I am sure he delights in them all. But here one attribute, as singled out by inspiration, gives delight to the eternal God – mercy! God delights to show mercy. It is both pleasant and essential to his being. He can no more cease to be merciful than he can cease to be just and holy.

This mercy which God delights to show unto men is in Christ. Read Micah's prophecy again. In the midst of great trial, Micah's heart was fixed upon Christ. As he anticipated the coming of Christ, he was comforted with this precious truth: '**He delighteth in mercy**!' Micah looked for the mercy of God in Christ. And, if you hope to find mercy, you must seek it in Christ. Since Jesus Christ has suffered and died in the place of sinners, satisfying God's holy law and justice, God is both able and willing to be merciful to sinners! That is the good news of the gospel.

There is only one way to obtain this mercy. You must come to Christ by faith. Bow down at his feet, acknowledging his sovereign lordship. Confess your sin. Sue for mercy, saying, 'God be merciful to me, a sinner.' And believe his Word. 'He that believeth and is baptized shall be saved.'

Depth of mercy, can there be
Mercy still reserved for me?
Can my God his wrath forbear,
Me the chief of sinners spare?

Indeed he can and will for Christ's sake, because, 'he delighteth in mercy'.

'It shall be for ever'

Read John 17:1-26

We know that every true believer's salvation is safe and secure in Christ, because the work of grace which God has begun he will carry on to perfection. The apostle Paul assures us of this: 'Being confident of this very thing, that he which hath begun a good work in you will perform it until the day of Jesus Christ' (Phil. 1:6). It will never be said of our God that he began a work which he was not able to complete. Every man considers it his shame to undertake a work, and be compelled to give it up before completion, because he lacked the ability, the skill, the wisdom, the power, or the dedication necessary to get the job done. But it is not possible for the Lord God to be confronted with such shame. He has never known failure and he never will. He began with us in eternal election. Though thousands of years rolled by, his purpose never changed. According to his wise and holy will, in the fulness of time, he redeemed us by the substitutionary atonement of his own Son. And though we went astray from him as soon as we were born and spent our days and nights in rebellion, yet he stood by his purpose of grace. He graciously preserved us until the time appointed when he would save us. Then, at the appointed time, in the time of his love, he gave us life in Christ. Since that day, our sins have been many. Our faithfulness at best has been feeble. Our service has been insignificant. But he who called us has been faithful. He has kept us by the power of his grace. He has never failed us yet; and he never will. He will not give up that work to which he has been faithful for so long. Our God will perform that which he has begun, until he brings us safe into eternal glory. He is willing to complete his work in us. He is wise enough to complete his work in us. And he is powerful enough to complete his work in us. Many ask, 'Can a saved man ever be lost?' I reply, 'Not until God ceases to be God!'

I know that if God has saved me, and if God has saved you, by his matchless grace: '**It shall be for ever!**'

'The Lord our Righteousness'

Read Isaiah 1:1-19

Beloved, we sustained a great loss by the Fall in this matter of righteousness. We suffered the loss of a righteous nature and the loss of all legal righteousness in the sight of God. Man sinned; he was therefore no longer innocent of the transgression. Man did not keep the commandment; he was therefore guilty of the sin of omission. In that which he committed, and in that which he omitted, man's original character of uprightness was completely wrecked. Jesus Christ came to undo the mischief of the Fall for his people.

Christ Jesus, by his one sacrifice, has satisfied the penalty of sin in his flesh. 'He, his own self, bare our sins in his own body on the tree.' But it is not enough for us to be pardoned. It is required of man that he keep the whole law. God requires of man a perfect obedience. He must continue in all things written in the book of the law to do them. Man must have a perfect righteousness, or God will not accept him. Man must have a perfect obedience, or God will not reward him. God cannot accept anything less than perfection.

How is this necessity supplied? There is no righteousness in us. Even the work of the Holy Spirit in sanctification is imperfect in this life. If we would be righteous, we must have the righteousness of another. Christ alone is our righteousness. We are accepted in the Beloved. The righteousness by which the saints are clothed, through which we are accepted and with which we are made meet to inherit eternal life, is the work of Christ. The perfect life of Christ as our Representative constitutes the righteousness of his people. By his death Christ washed away our sins. His life covers us from head to foot. His death was his sacrifice to God. His life is his gift to man, by which we satisfied the demands of the law. In his life, Christ rendered a perfect obedience to the law as our Representative. In his death, he satisfied the claims of the law as our Substitute. Christ is '**the Lord our Righteousness**'.

Who should be baptized?

Read Romans 6:1-23

After Philip had plainly preached the gospel to the Ethiopian eunuch, they came to a place having a large body of water and the eunuch desired that Philip would baptize him. Upon the eunuch's request, Philip set before him one essential prerequisite for baptism: '**If thou believest with all thine heart thou mayest.**'

This issue has great importance in our day. There are many brethren who soundly believe the gospel of God's free grace, who are doing a great harm by the practice of infant baptism. They preach nothing but free grace in their pulpits, but they turn around and 'baptize' a baby. Regardless of what the theologians say, in the minds of those who sit in the pews such a ritual must have some merit before God. If baptism has no merit and no saving efficacy, why would anyone baptize an infant? And if you do not baptize infants, there is no need to pervert baptism into sprinkling. Infant baptism and sprinkling are merely popish furniture in the house of Protestantism, which should have been cast out with indulgences.

Your baptism is very important. By it you either profess the gospel of Christ or you pervert the gospel of Christ. Only by immersion can you properly confess the gospel in this ordinance. Baptism is the answer of a good conscience towards God. Let us see to it, then, that our baptism is in accordance with the Scriptures.

According to the New Testament, there is but one thing essential to baptism. The person being baptized must have a personal heart faith in Jesus Christ. The essence of baptism is not in the person or church performing it, but in the heart obedience of the person being baptized. You must have a personal faith in the person, work and power of Jesus Christ, the Son of God. To be baptized without faith in Christ is as dangerous as partaking of the Lord's Table without faith. In both cases the unbeliever fails to discern the Lord's body. If the Holy Spirit enables you to trust Christ alone for your complete salvation, you should be baptized, publicly 'calling on the name of the Lord'.

'The time is short'

Read Ephesians 5:1-21

We are living in a world where all things are temporary. Everything here is perishing. And we are going to a world where all things are eternal. If we are wise we shall live in this world of time with our hearts fixed on eternity. And when we look at all things in this world with an eye to eternity there is one striking fact that we cannot avoid.

The time of your *life* is short. 'What is your life? It is even a vapour that appeareth for a little time, and then vanisheth away.' 'My days are swifter than a weaver's shuttle.' My friend, your days are numbered. Soon you will have taken your last breath. Be warned! The time for *salvation* is short. Today is the day of salvation. This is the accepted time. Today you must come to Christ, laying hold of his righteousness and shed blood as the only grounds of your acceptance before God. For you who are the children of God, the time for *service* is short. 'The hour cometh when no man can work.' Let us give ourselves to the service of our Redeemer while the time remains. And, blessed be God, the time for *suffering* is short. Let us not faint, nor grow weary, 'For our light affliction which is but for a moment, worketh for us a far more exceeding and eternal weight of glory; while we look not at the things which are seen, but at the things which are not seen: for the things which are seen are temporal; but the things which are not seen are eternal.'

Since the time is short, we must be detached from the things of this world. We must hold the dearest objects of this life with a loose hand and cling only to Christ. Take your dearest earthly possessions – your money, your lands, your friends, your family – and place this brand upon them – perishing! Christ alone and the riches of his grace are eternal.

What then must we do with the time that we have? We must redeem the time. Buy up every opportunity to worship and serve Christ. Buy up every opportunity to point men and women to Christ, the Way, the Truth and the Life. Much time is gone already, the days are evil and the time that remains is short. Therefore I say, redeem the time.

'His name shall be called Wonderful'

Read Psalm 111:1-10

Never was there a name so wonderful as the name of our Saviour. He is the Lord Jesus Christ. The Lord – our Master, our King, our Sovereign, our God. Jesus – our Saviour, our Redeemer, our Deliverer. Christ – Anointed One. He was anointed by God as the Prophet, Priest and King of his people. This is the one whom the Father deemed able to save us and worthy of all glory. He is wonderful in the estimation of the Father, of the heavenly angels and of all his people.

1. He is wonderful in his *covenant*. In covenant mercy, the Son of God agreed to become our Saviour and to accomplish for us a perfect salvation.

2. He is wonderful in his *compassion*. Behold how he loves us! He has loved us with an eternal, sovereign, distinguishing, personal, perfect and infinite love.

3. He is wonderul in his *condescension*. In a gigantic step downwards, he took upon himself our nature. Poverty, pain and persecution followed the Man of sorrows all his days. As great as the humiliation of the incarnation was, it was nothing in comparison with that humiliation he endured upon the cross as our Substitute! He bore shame, scourging, scoffing and spitting for us. At last he was made to be sin for us! Being slain in our place, he was buried in a borrowed tomb.

4. He is wonderful in his *crowning*. After three days in the grave, the Son of God came forth triumphant over the grave. Forty days later he ascended to the throne of glory as our Mediator King. The God-man is crowned with glory and honour, never to be humbled again. All the universe is under his sovereign rule.

5. He is wonderful in his *care*. The Son of God rules all people and all events, working all things together for the good of his people. The Lord of glory is our Protector, Provider and Preserver.

6. He is wonderful in his *coming*. 'Behold, he cometh!' Yes, he is coming again! He is coming now! Soon the Son of God, our Saviour, will again be upon the earth. All things will be put under his feet!

A cheerful motive for cheerful giving

Read 2 Corinthians 8:1-15

Nowhere do I find in the New Testament that Christian men are commanded to tithe. Such a commandment would be contrary to the gospel of grace and the spirit of the new covenant. Legal commandments are good enough for children of bondage, like Ishmael. But the children of promise are motivated from a better principle. For them it is enough to say, 'Ye know the grace of our Lord Jesus Christ.' We do not divide out our tenth, like religious misers. We give ourselves and all that we have to Christ. Cheerfully we give all that we can for the cause of Christ and the support of the gospel ministry. Why? Because we know his grace.

   '**Though he was rich, yet for your sakes he became poor.**' Brethren, the wealth of God, the treasures of the infinite, the riches of eternity are the possession of our blessed Saviour. From the highest throne of glory to the lowest pit in hell, Jesus owns it all. It is true Christ is the lowly man of Nazareth. But he is more. He is the eternal God, possessing all the riches of divine wisdom, power and glory.

   Yet he became poor (Phil. 2:5-8). The eternal Son of God took manhood into union with himself. The God of glory robed himself in human flesh. Behold the depths of his poverty at Calvary! He was betrayed, mocked and beaten. He was crucified. God made his Son to be sin for us! There he was robbed of all the joy of heaven and the comfort of his Father's presence. His dying bed was a malefactor's cross. His resting place was a borrowed tomb. What was the reason for such humiliation?

   'That ye through his poverty might be rich.' What riches are ours through the mediation of Christ! In him we have all and abound. The riches of grace and redemption, time and eternity are ours. Do men who know such grace need the threat of the law to make them tithe? No! The love of Christ constrains us. And in everything grace produces more than the law. Let us then give cheerfully and bountifully.

'The man after God's own heart'

Read 2 Samuel 12:1-24

God, who 'looketh on the heart', looked on David's heart and declared, 'I have found David the son of Jesse, a man after mine own heart' (Acts 13:22). When I read that statement of our God about his servant David, my heart cries, 'Father, give me that kind of heart.' But a question immediately arises: 'When the Lord looked upon David's heart, what did he see?'

He saw *a broken and contrite heart* (Ps. 51:1-17). David's heart was broken, not because he had been caught in his sin, but because he had committed the sin. It was brought down with contrition not only because of what he had done, but also because of what he was. He saw his sin in the light of God's holiness and in the light of God's mercy in blood redemption through Christ, and his heart was broken before the Lord.

The Lord saw in David *a believing heart* (Ps. 31:5, 14). David believed God, and it was imputed to him for righteousness. He trusted God for the forgiveness of sin through a Substitute (Ps. 32:1-5; 130:1-8). He trusted God's rule of all things in providence, declaring, 'My times are in thy hand', and 'What time I am afraid, I will trust in thee.' And David confidently trusted the Lord's immutable faithfulness. He said, 'When my father and my mother forsake me, then the Lord will take me up.'

When God looked upon David's heart, he saw *a heart of submission* to the will and the rule of his Lord, This is beautifully exemplified in the death of his son (2 Sam. 12:20). Every believing heart is a submissive heart. There are no exceptions. Submission to God's providence is not a prayerless, effortless, lazy, indifferent fatalism. It is bowing to the will of God with willingness and confidence.

As the Lord looked upon David, he saw a man with *a loving and devoted heart* (Ps. 116:1). His heart was full of love, devotion, adoration and praise to God. He loved all that God is and all that God had done. He was devoted to the Word, the will, the worship and the work of God. And David's heart was full of love to men as well. Who was ever more loving, kind and generous to men than David was to Mephibosheth?

'Faithful men'

Read 1 Timothy 3:1-16

There are but two offices in the New Testament church: *elders* and *deacons*.

The word '*elders*' refers to those who are the spiritual leaders and teachers of the congregation. The pastor of a church is the presiding elder, or overseer of the congregation. Where there is need for more than one elder in a large assembly, those elders who serve with the pastor must serve in submission to him, as his assistants in the ministry. While it is evident that in the New Testament most of the churches, if not all of them, had more than one elder, it is also evident that only one elder stood as the overseer and spiritual ruler of the congregation. It is not possible for a church to have peace and harmony under the government of a board of elders, or a board of deacons. There can only be one captain on a ship. And there can only be one overseer in a congregation. The spiritual overseer of the church is God's messenger in that congregation, the pastor. He is not a dictator, lording over God's people. But a faithful pastor must rule the church of God. He rules the house of God just as a husband rules his household. He rules with love, tenderness and understanding. But he rules firmly for the glory of God and the welfare of God's people (1 Tim. 3:5; Heb. 13:7,17).

Deacons are those men whose responsibility it is to take care of the physical, financial affairs of the congregation. They are to be spiritual men, willing to serve their pastor and church for the glory of Christ. Deacons are to relieve their pastor of all mundane affairs, so that he can give himself exclusively to the ministry of the Word (Acts 6:2-4). The service of a deacon is most honourable and helpful. Faithful deacons take care of the church property, visit the sick, care for the needy and see to it that the needs of the pastor and his family are met. By relieving their pastor of all these cares, the deacons enable him to give his time and attention to study, prayer and the preaching of the gospel of Christ. There are few men so spiritually minded that they are willing to serve as faithful deacons for the gospel's sake.

'Without Christ!'

Read Ephesians 2:8-22

'Without Christ!' A more miserable condition cannot be conceived! It is bad enough to be without money, without health, without a home, or without friends. But it is far worse to be without Christ! No tongue can tell the depth of wretchedness and misery that lie in those two words. There is no poverty like this, no need like this, Yet this is the condition that we were all in, when God laid hold of us by his mighty grace: '**At that time ye were without Christ**.'

When must we say that a person is without Christ? To be sure, all men are without Christ by nature. Sin has separated us from God. A man is without Christ when he has no knowledge of who Christ is, what he has done and where he is now. The purpose of preaching the gospel is to inform men of the person and work of Christ. Yet it is not enough simply to know the historical facts concerning the person and work of Christ. You may know all that is to be known about Christ and still be without Christ. A man is without Christ when he has no heart faith in Christ.

What does it mean to be without Christ? Paul points out four solemn deprivals of the soul without Christ. Without Christ you are '**aliens from the commonwealth of Israel**', separated from the people of God. Without Christ, you are '**strangers from the covenants of promise**'. All the promises of God are in Christ Jesus, yea and amen. The covenant promises of forgiveness, guidance, protection and providence are for those who are in Christ. Without Christ you have no promise from God, except that of judgement. Without Christ, you have '**no hope**'. There is no hope of redemption, no hope of righteousness, no hope of acceptance with God, no hope of mercy, no hope of heaven. Without Christ, you are **without God**, perishing without the knowledge of God. Without Christ, you are among the lost, ruined, condemned sons of Adam in the world.

How can you be in Christ? You must be born again in Christ. You must be in Christ by faith. As soon as you trust Christ, you are in Christ.

'Accepted in the beloved'

Read Colossians 2:1-15

The believer's acceptance before God is in Christ and only in Christ. God never has accepted, and he never will accept, any man, or anything done by any man, except in Christ and upon the merits of his righteousness and shed blood. And all who believe in Christ always have been, and always will be, accepted in Christ, our Substitute. We were accepted in Christ in eternity, before the world was, before we were created, before we had done any good or evil, before we fell in our father Adam.

Our acceptance before God in Christ is an *eternal* acceptance. Though we sinned in Adam, though we came forth from our mothers' wombs speaking lies, though we stubbornly rebelled against the Lord our God for many, many years, we were still 'accepted in the beloved'.

Our acceptance with God in Christ is an *immutable* acceptance. Since we first came to Christ in faith and repentance, our lives have been a constant struggle with sin. Everything that we are and everything that we do is marred by sin. But still God declares that we are 'accepted in the beloved'.

Our acceptance before God in Christ is an *absolute, perfect and unconditional acceptance*. I wish that every child of God could enter into the sweetness, the comfort and the joy of what I am saying. Our acceptance before God is altogether in Christ. It is altogether a matter of pure, free, sovereign grace. Therefore it never changes. Our acceptance with God is in no way whatsoever dependent upon what we do. We are not more pleasing and acceptable to God when we do good, and we are not less pleasing and acceptable to God when we do evil. Our acceptance is *in Christ!* It depends not upon what we do, but upon what he has done.

I know that the legalist will say, 'That's antinomianism; it will give men a licence to sin!' But the children of God will find this matter of our acceptance in Christ a source of great comfort, a cause for great joy and a motive to love Christ and seek his glory. If God's children are comforted, I rejoice.

'If the trumpet give an uncertain sound'

Read Galatians 1:1-16

This religious generation in which we are living has been tricked, deceived and lied to by their leaders. The time has come for the servants of God to speak in plain English and tell men the truth. '**If the trumpet give an uncertain sound, who shall prepare himself to battle**?' If the gospel is to be preached and understood by men, these three questions must be answered.

What happened in the garden? Was man totally ruined by the Fall, or was he just partially handicapped? The Scripture says, 'In Adam all died.' The sin of Adam brought about the total ruin and spiritual death of our race, so that the natural man has no ability or desire to bring himself back into fellowship with God.

What happened at Calvary? Did Christ, by his substitutionary sacrifice and atonement, make redemption a possibility, or did he actually accomplish the redemption of his people? The Scripture says that he 'obtained eternal redemption for us'. He did not just make it possible for sin to be put away, but he 'put away sin by the sacrifice of himself'.

How is salvation accomplished? Is it the gift of God, or is it of man? The Scripture says, 'Salvation is of the Lord.' Is salvation by works, or by grace? The Scripture says, 'By grace ye are saved.' Is eternal life an offer of grace, or an operation of grace; an invitation, or a gift? The Scripture says, 'The gift of God is eternal life.' Is the gospel a generous proposal, or a proclamation? Is it good advice, or good news? It is the proclamation of good news: 'It is finished!' Is salvation by choice, or by revelation? It is a revelation: 'Flesh and blood hath not revealed it unto thee, but my Father which is in heaven.' 'When it pleased God... he called me by his grace to reveal his Son in me.' Is salvation the result of man's will, or the result of God's will; is it accomplished by God's choice or by man's choice? The Scripture says, 'It is not of him that willeth, nor of him that runneth, but of God that showeth mercy.' Are repentance and faith moral persuasions, accomplished by the gifted preacher, or are they holy dispositions created in the heart by God Almighty? The Scripture says these are gifts of God (Rom. 2:4; Eph. 2:8).

'We are bound to give thanks'

Read Psalm 92:1-15

Can you rejoice in electing love? Paul did. He said, 'Blessed be the God and Father of our Lord Jesus Christ, who hath blessed us with all spiritual blessings in heavenly places in Christ: according as he hath chosen us in him before the foundation of the world' (Eph. 1:3-4). 'We are bound to give thanks always to God for you, brethren beloved of the Lord, because God hath from the beginning chosen you to salvation, through sanctification of the Spirit and belief of the truth' (2 Thess. 2:13).

Can you rejoice in electing love? Peter did. He said, 'Ye are a chosen generation, a royal priesthood, an holy nation, a peculiar people; that ye should show forth the praises of him who hath called you out of darkness into his marvellous light.' 'Elect according to the foreknowledge of God the Father' (1 Peter 2:9; 1:2).

Can you rejoice in electing love? David did. He leaped and danced before the ark of God, because God had chosen him above Saul. He said, 'Although my house be not so with God; yet he hath made with me an everlasting covenant, ordered in all things and sure: for this is all my salvation and all my desire' (2 Sam. 23:5).

Can you rejoice in electing love? Our Lord did. On the night before his crucifixion he taught his disciples the doctrine of election in very plain and clear terms, in order to comfort and encourage their hearts. He said, 'Ye have not chosen me, but I have chosen you, and ordained you, that ye should go and bring forth fruit, and that your fruit should remain: that whatsoever ye shall ask of my Father in my name, he may give it you' (John 15:16). Yes, the Lord Jesus Christ gave thanks and rejoiced before God the Father for his gracious election of our souls to eternal salvation. He said, 'I thank thee, O Father, Lord of heaven and earth, because thou hast hid these things from the wise and prudent, and hast revealed them unto babes. Even so, Father, for so it seemed good in thy sight' (Matt. 11:25-26).

Surely, every true believer should be filled with praise and joy towards God when he hears the good news of God's electing love.

'Who is he that condemneth?'

Read Romans 8:28-39

For some people the answer to that question is not hard to find. Hear the Word of God: 'He that believeth not is condemned already, because he hath not believed on the name of the only begotten Son of God... He that believeth not shall not see life; but the wrath of God abideth on him.' You are condemned already because of your sin. You must be pardoned, or for ever die! Awake now and flee to Christ! He alone can pardon you and free you from condemnation.

There are many who would condemn the true believer if they could. God's people often meet with their enemies in this world and those wicked men would delight to sentence us to condemnation. Satan, that arch-enemy of our souls, would condemn us, it if were in his power. Sometimes our own consciences condemn us. But, blessed be God, 'If our heart condemn us, God is greater than our heart, and knoweth all things!'

God alone has the power to condemn us, but he will not. He has declared that he will never condemn any who trust in his Son. He who has the power of condemnation is our Saviour. He knows that we are so perfectly justified that we cannot be condemned.

We raise the bold challenge: '**Who is he that condemneth**?' With confident joy we reply, 'Nobody can condemn us!' With unshaken faith we declare, 'There is therefore now no condemnation to them which are in Christ Jesus.' Does anyone ask, 'What is the grounds of this confidence?' Paul states it plainly: 'It is Christ that died, yea rather, that is risen again, who is even at the right hand of the Father, who also maketh intercession for us.'

1. Christ died as our Substitute; we cannot die.
2. Christ has risen for our justification; we are justified.
3. Christ is seated at the right hand of God; the work of our redemption is finished and accepted.
4. Christ makes intercession for us; he must prevail, we must be saved.

'Will ye also go away'

Read John 6:35-71

This is a question which I frequently ask myself.

When any turn from Zion's way,
(Alas, that numbers do!)
Methinks I hear my Saviour say,
'Wilt thou forsake me too?'

And now I put this question to you. Do not put it off as insignificant and meaningless. There are three very important lessons for us to learn from this event in the ministry of our Lord.
1. Many who seem to be the disciples of Christ go back and walk no more with him (v. 66). Throughout the history of the church, there have been many who seemed to be true and sincere Christians, who finally fell away and perished. For various reasons, such people make a profession of faith and join the church. But after a while, they are offended at the Word and they leave us. Why? 'Because they were not of us.' They had no true saving union with Christ. This is a painful, but necessary thing. When we see others fall away, we are made to realize that we stand only by the grace of God.
2. The Lord Jesus Christ takes very great care to protect his true disciples from falling away. Our Lord puts this question to us, not because of any ignorance (he knows what is in the heart of men) but because of his great love to his own. At the first sign of decay from our first love, he knocks at our hearts with this question: 'Will ye also go away?' Thus he would keep us to himself with the cords of love. 'Have I not loved you, redeemed you, chosen you, called you and sanctified you? Will you now forsake me?' And by this our Lord teaches us that all of his disciples follow him with a willing heart.
3. The true believer realizes that he has none to turn to but Christ. 'Lord, to whom shall we go?' Brethren, we must cling to Christ. Christ alone satisfies our hearts. He is our God, our Saviour, our life, our hope. Relying upon his grace, we say, 'No, we cannot go away. We must have Christ.'

The believer's great concern

Read 1 Corinthians 9:15-27

Once one of our Lord's disciples said unto him, 'Lord, teach us to pray.' In answer to that request, our Saviour gave us an example of prayer which instructs us in those things which ought to be of greatest concern in the life of every believer. In Luke 11:2, Christ identifies those things which should be uppermost in the hearts and minds of God's elect at all times.

'**Our Father which art in heaven, hallowed be thy name**.' Brethren, it should be our soul's desire to seek the honour of our God in all things. God's name stands for himself and we who know the glorious excellency and majesty of God should seek to extol and magnify the name of God. It is the preacher's pleasant duty to exalt the name of God in his message, and it is the heart's desire of every true believer to magnify his God in his attitude and conduct in all things. Beloved, let this be the principle by which our lives are governed – that God's name may be reverenced and honoured in our lives.

'**Thy kingdom come**.' We do not live unto ourselves. We live upon this earth for the glory of God and for the increase of his kingdom. We should spend out our lives for the conversion of sinners to Christ. Our Lord was consumed with this zeal, even unto death. Surely we should love the souls of men enough to carry to them the message of salvation by Christ. We know that there is a kingdom of men which Christ purchased at Calvary. Let us seek to bring those men to the Saviour by the preaching of the gospel.

'**Thy will be done**.' We recognize that God's sovereign purpose will be accomplished, Yet it is possible for us to miss the will of God in a given area. In order to know his will, we must seek his face, his wisdom, his guidance and his strength. I do not want to miss the will of God. How pleasant it is to walk with God — seeking his honour, seeking his kingdom, seeking his will. Is this your great concern?

'He is precious!'

Read Psalm 73:1-28

This is not some far-fetched, fanatical notion. It is a fact. God the Holy Spirit has caused it to be written in the volume of inspiration as the truth of God. It is confirmed by the history of the church from Abel to Malachi, from John the Baptist to John the beloved. It is confirmed by those martyrs who suffered imprisonment and death from Stephen to Polycarp, from Latimer and Ridley to Bunyan. The blood of God's saints cries out from the ground, from the dungeons of Rome and from the torture chambers of the pope's Inquisition: 'Christ is precious.' And it is confirmed by the experience of all who truly believe. From their inmost soul, God's elect all agree: 'He is precious.' This is faith's estimation of Christ.

When we think of our Saviour's glorious person, we say, 'He is precious.' He is the God-man. Jesus Christ is himself God Almighty, the eternal son of the eternal Father. The brightness of the Father's glory and the express image of his person is Christ. And he is man, the perfect man, 'holy harmless, undefiled, and separate from sinners'. He is precious in himself, intrinsically precious. He is the rose of Sharon, the lily of the valley, the fairest among ten thousand. He is altogether lovely. Who can compare with this glorious person? He is precious.

And when I recall what he has done for my soul, I am overwhelmed with his love and grace. Beholding Christ as my redeeming Substitute, my heart is constrained to say, 'He is precious.' In love he chose us and became our Surety in the covenant of grace. He lived upon the earth, in conformity to the law of God, to accomplish our righteousness. And he died in our stead upon the cursed tree, putting away all our sin. For us, he arose and assumed the throne of universal dominion. Behold, your crucified, risen, exalted, reigning Redeemer and know this: 'He is precious!'

Is Christ precious to you? If he is you are a true believer. If he is not, you do not have the faith of God's elect.

'There is forgiveness with thee'

Read Psalm 38:1-21

Here is the good news of the gospel: sinners though we are, deserving of God's eternal wrath, we may yet obtain the forgiveness of sins! Though the God of heaven is glorious in holiness, righteousness, justice and truth, he delights to show mercy. It is the glory of God to forgive sinners!

This matter of forgiveness is an absolute certainty. David does not speak with hesitation. He says, 'There is forgiveness.' I know that God forgives sin, because it is his nature to do so. I know that God forgives sin, because all the prophets and ceremonial sacrifices of the Old Testament proclaimed that he would. I know that God forgives sin, because he sent his Son into this world to die, the just for the unjust, that we might receive the remission of sins. I know that there is forgiveness with God, because he proclaims it in the gospel. And I know that the God of heaven forgives sin, because he has forgiven my sin!

Not only is the forgiveness of sin certain, it is also a matter of strict justice. God, in his holiness, truth and justice, cannot simply, arbitrarily pronounce the sinner forgiven. His law must be satisfied. 'The soul that sinneth, it shall die!' Therefore the Son of God took upon himself human flesh. Living in perfect obedience to the law of God, Christ accomplished for us that perfect righteousness which God required of man. The law was obeyed by our legal Representative. Still our sins had to be paid for. So our loving Redeemer voluntarily gave himself up into the hands of the law, to suffer and die as our Substitute. Having endured the utmost extremity of God's infinite wrath and justice, Christ declared, 'It is finished!' He made an end of sin. He brought in an everlasting righteousness. He obtained eternal redemption for us! Now God in justice cannot charge those for whom Christ died with sin. He is faithful and just to forgive us.

And, blessed be God, this forgiveness is entirely free. Faith cannot put away sin. Only Christ can do that. But faith receives the forgiveness of sin, trusting the merits of Christ alone. Believe on Christ this day and receive the forgiveness of sins.

'By the grace of God I am what I am'

Read Psalm 80:1-19

Paul knew nothing of human merit. He knew that he did not even deserve to be considered by God. He had been before a blasphemer, a persecutor and injurious. 'But', he wrote, 'I obtained mercy... and the grace of our Lord Jesus Christ was exceeding abundant.' For the apostle Paul there was no confession more suitable to his own experience than this: '**By the grace of God I am what I am.**' And it is equally appropriate to each one of us who have experienced the grace of God.

1. This is *our doctrinal confession*: 'By the grace of God I am what I am.' If you are saved you do not owe your salvation to anything you have done. And for those of you who are not converted, if ever you are to be saved, it will not be because of any goodness in you. We must deny our own merits, or we cannot have the merits of Christ. The source of God's goodness to us lies altogether in his sovereign mercy. Everything in salvation was accomplished for us and in us by Christ alone. He chose us, redeemed us, justified us and called us. And it is Christ alone who preserves us unto eternal glory.

2. This is *our constant experience*: 'By the grace of God I am what I am.' Being made to know something of the depravity of our own hearts, we do with weeping eyes testify that we are what we are by the grace of God. When we feel the power of lusts within us, or temptations from without, when we see others whom we esteemed highly for their profession fall and turn from the faith, when we have ourselves been restored to fellowship with Christ after a fall and when we are made to rejoice in the fulness of God's blessings in Christ, we rejoice to say, 'By the grace of God I am what I am.'

3. This is *our grateful acknowledgement*. We realize that the only distinction between us and all other men is the distinguishing grace of God. As you read the black catalogue of human sin, do not forget these words: 'And such were some of you.' But now, by the grace of God, we are washed, justified and sanctified. Realizing what we were, we rejoice to say, 'By the grace of God I am what I am.'

The doctrine of grace

Read Romans 9:1-18

God 'hath saved us, and called us with an holy calling, not according to our works, but according to his own purpose and grace, which was given us in Christ Jesus before the world began'. It may seem strange to some, but Paul's method of establishing Timothy in confidence and boldness was not to assure him of the rewards of the faithful, or the morality of suffering for a noble cause. Instead, in order to excite Timothy to boldness and to keep him constant in the faith, Paul instructs him in the great doctrine that the grace of God reigns in the salvation of sinners. Many suggest that the doctrines of grace will kill a church, destroying evangelistic zeal and the motive for personal holiness. Paul was not of this opinion. When he was concerned for the future life and ministry of his beloved friend, Timothy, he felt that the surest way to secure his faithfulness was to instruct him in the doctrine of God's free and sovereign grace.

We should never doubt the power and usefulness of truth. Usually men look upon doctrinal truth as nothing more than unpractical theory. We sometimes think that legal precepts are more effective than gospel truth to produce obedience in the saints. I am persuaded that the very root and vital energy of practical holiness is the truth of the gospel. To teach people the truth that God has revealed in his Son is the surest way of leading them to obedience and perseverance in love, faith and holiness.

In this verse we are plainly taught that salvation is of the Lord. Human merit has nothing to do with it! God chose us in Christ, redeemed us in Christ, regenerated us and called us in Christ. And the grace that we now enjoy was given to us according to his own gloriously sovereign purpose in Christ before the world began. There is no doctrine more practical than this. It strips away human pride. It gives a sure ground of confidence and assurance to our faith. It most highly exalts and honours the name, person and work of Christ. This doctrine alone gives hope to sinners and encourages evangelism.

'What think ye of Christ?'

Read Matthew 22:15-46

Most people go to hell asking questions about religious matters. One of Satan's most deceptive snares, whereby the souls of men are blinded to the glory of Christ, is religious curiosity. The Herodians asked, 'Is it lawful to give tribute unto Caesar?' The Sadducees were curious about the resurrection body. The Pharisees asked, 'Which is the great commandment in the law?' The point is this: most people avoid dealing with the real soul-searching issues of the gospel by giving themselves up to vain questions about religion. Religious people are still asking the same questions as the Herodians, Sadducees and Pharisees. Who will be the greatest in heaven? What kind of body will we have in the resurrection? Who are the guests at the marriage feasts? What does the law say? And they are, like their predecessors, going to hell, because they miss the one issue which is of eternal consequence: '**What think ye of Christ**?'

We must have a *biblical* answer to that question. We think that Jesus Christ is the perfect and eternal God. We think he is the perfect representative man. He came to this earth with a mission to accomplish. He came here to save his people. The God-man was born at Bethlehem to die at Calvary. We think that Jesus Christ actually accomplished the redemption of his people, through his one sacrifice for sin. We think, according to the Scriptures, that he now sits upon the throne of glory as the sovereign Lord of all things. To think anything less than this of Christ is to think contrary to God's revelation.

But our text speaks of more than mere doctrinal knowledge. We must have an *experimental* answer to this question. How do you think of Christ? Those who are truly born again have been taught of God and learned to think properly of Christ. We think that Christ alone is precious. Christ is our only hope of acceptance with God. We think of Christ with all confidence, expectation and desire. He is all. Christ is all to be trusted, all to be loved, all to be preached, all to be hoped for. He is all in earth and all in heaven, all in time and all in eternity.

Who is the God of the Bible?

Read Psalm 135:1-21

'**Our God is in the heavens: he hath done whatsoever he hath pleased.**' My friend, the God of the Bible is an absolute sovereign, and anything less than an absolute Sovereign is not God. This is the one characteristic of God which men rebel against universally. Therefore we must insist upon it continually. God can do what he pleases. What has it pleased God to do?

1. It pleased God *to make us his people* (1 Sam. 12:22; Eph.1:4). The Lord did not have to make us his people and he did not need us. But it pleased the Lord to make us his own – by covenant election, by special adoption, by sovereign regeneration and by faith in Christ. If we are God's people, it is only because it pleased God to make us such.

2. It pleased God *that all fulness dwell in Christ* (Col. 1:18-19). God the Father resolved in eternity to reveal himself unto men by Christ, the Mediator. And every revelation that God makes to men is in Christ. All the promises, blessings and mercies of God are in Christ. Jesus Christ is the fulness of divine grace and is the fulness of divine glory. He is the glory of creation, being the firstborn of every creature. He is the glory of the church, for he is the Head of the body. And he is the glory of eternity, for in heaven we shall see his face.

3. It pleased God *to bruise Christ in the place of sinners* (Isa. 53:10). It was foretold in Genesis 3:15 that Satan would bruise the Saviour's heel. But here it is God, the Father, bruising his Son for us. Like grain is bruised and crushed under the millstone, Jesus Christ was bruised in body and crushed in soul, when he was made to be sin for us. And it pleased God to bruise him! What was God's pleasure? It was not the suffering of his Son that pleased him, but the result of that suffering. By bruising Christ in our place, his people are redeemed!

4. It pleased God *to reveal his Son in us* (Gal. 1:15-16). In the fulness of time, God reveals his Son in all of those for whom he was bruised. This is God's effectual call. When Christ is revealed in a man, faith is begotten in him.

'Naaman the Syrian'

Read 2 Kings 5:1-19

'**Many lepers were in Israel in the time of Eliseus the prophet; and none of them was cleansed, saving Naaman the Syrian.**' The cleansing of Naaman was a famous story of the Old Testament Scriptures, with which the Jews of our Lord's day were very familiar. But when our Lord recalled it to their attention, 'they were filled with wrath'. Those men understood perfectly well what Christ was saying and they greatly resented it. That which our Lord was teaching is just as violently opposed by modern religious people as it was by the Jews. But for those who are taught of the Spirit, this is a most delightful and comforting doctrine: salvation is accomplished by the sovereign prerogative of God. This little story plainly sets forth God's method of grace.

The sovereignty of God's grace was clearly displayed in the cleansing of Naaman. It is evident that Naaman was the object of sovereign grace, because he was the most unlikely candidate for mercy. Naaman was a heathen, Gentile idolater. He was a sworn enemy of Israel, the people of God. Besides, Naaman lived a long way from the prophet's home. Yet the grace of God passed by many lepers in Israel. Going far afield, it found this Syrian soldier. Blessed be God, he still operates in this same sovereign manner! Those whom men consider the least likely candidates for mercy are the objects of God's free grace. Many others were passed by, more noble, more excellent than he, but God chose Naaman.

But mark this also: the grace of God always operates in a definite manner. God has not only ordained who will be saved. He has ordained the method by which they will be saved as well. First, Naaman had to hear the good news that healing was possible. Whenever God intends to save a sinner, he will send someone to tell him the gospel. It may be a little Hebrew maid, or it may be an old man. But always, 'Faith cometh by hearing.' For another thing, it was imperative for Naaman to heed the message and obey the command. Even so, men must hear the gospel and in humble faith wash in the blood of Christ.

A simple but forcible contrast

Read Ephesians 4:17–5:2

'Hatred stirreth up strifes: but love covereth all sins.' Hatred is the selfish principle of an unregenerate man. It may be varnished by religion and smoothed by hypocrisy, but it is a subterranean storm, continually stirring up mischief and evil. Hatred creates or keeps alive carnal strifes. It causes coldness. It creates disharmony. It stirs up 'envyings and evil surmisings'. Hatred carps at the least infirmity in others and aggravates the least fault. Hatred resents the most trifling offence. It is provoked by the least imaginary wrong. 'An ungodly man diggeth up evil.' Such strifes are kindled to the great dishonour of God. They mar the beauty of the gospel. Let us resist this evil of the old man by watchfulness and prayer 'and grieve not the Holy Spirit of God'.

Love is the fruit of the Spirit. It covers a multitude of evils. Let us study 1 Corinthians 13 in all its detail, and make it the pattern for our lives. Let this be the mirror of our hearts and the standard of our profession. Love covers, overlooks, speedily forgives and forgets. Love invents reasons to avoid strife. Love puts the best possible construction on doubtful matters. Love seeks unity and agreement. Love does not rigidly examine a brother's failures. It will not deliberately expose a brother's faults. It refuses to uncover the sins of another.

To refrain from gross slander, while leaving room for needless and unkind doubt, is not covering sin. Nor is the 'seven-times forgiveness' the true standard of love. Love, like its divine Author, covers all sins. Who among us does not need the full extent of this covering? What is our brother's evil against us, compared with our sin against God? Can we hesitate to blot out our brother's few pounds, who look for a covering for our debt of ten million pounds to God? Let us imitate Christ's spirit of forbearing, forgiving, self-sacrificing love: 'Even as Christ forgave you, so also do ye.' 'And above all things have fervent charity among yourselves: for charity shall cover a multitude of sins.'

'Don't ever forget'

Read Ezekiel 16:1-14, 60-63

'**Hearken unto me, ye that follow after righteousness, ye that seek the Lord: look unto the rock whence ye are hewn, and to the hole of the pit whence ye are digged.**' Believer, I say, don't forget what you are by nature, and what you were when God called you to life in Christ. Though God has so freely forgiven us of our sins that they will never be remembered against us any more for ever, the prophet here teaches us that we must not forget them, lest we forget what the Lord has done for us by his loving grace.

Let us always remember who we were, where we were, and what we were when God saved us by his grace. We were ourselves the fallen sons of Adam, rebels before God. We were lost and ruined in this perishing world. Like Ezekiel's deserted infant, we were helpless, polluted and perishing. We were dead in trespasses and sins. Physically, we were alive, alive to our lusts, alive to the world, alive to Satan, alive to sin. But spiritually, we were dead, dead to righteousness, dead to truth, dead to Christ, dead to God. In a word, by nature, we were sinners. Sinners by birth, sinners by choice, sinners in heart, sinners in practice, sinners against God, sinners against men, we were nothing but perishing, hell-deserving sinners.

Remember also your merciful Deliverer. We could never deliver ourselves. No man or angel could deliver us. But the God-man, Jesus Christ, has delivered us. There came the Deliverer out of Zion, and he turned away all our transgressions. He delivered us from the curse of the law by his sacrifice of blood in our place. And he delivered us from the powerful bondage of sin by his sovereign power in regeneration. Blessed be God, he did not leave us to our own free will. 'But God', in loving, merciful, sovereign and saving power intervened in our lives. He stopped us in our mad race towards hell and arrested us by his grace! 'By grace ye are saved!'

Now, child of God, don't ever forget: 'Salvation is of the Lord.' To the triune God alone we ascribe all honour, majesty, praise and dominion.

'Walk in the Spirit'

Read Galatians 5:16–6:10

Paul tells us that if we walk in the Spirit we shall not fulfil the lust of the flesh. And he makes it plain that he is not telling us that we should be seeking some sort of a 'deeper life experience'. Walking in the Spirit, according to the apostle Paul, is the most practical thing in the world. To walk in the Spirit is to be motivated in life by the Spirit of adoption, faith and love, rather than by legal fear. 'If ye be led by the Spirit, ye are not under the law' (Gal. 5:18). Just as an intoxicated man is under the control of wine, the child of God is to be under the control of the Holy Spirit (Eph. 5:18). If you and I are led by the Spirit of Christ and under his influence, there are three things which will mark our lives. These are not the works of the flesh. They are not things produced by us. Rather, they are the fruit of the Holy Spirit.

1. *Joy in our own hearts.* 'Speaking to yourselves in psalms and hymns and spiritual songs, singing and making melody in your heart to the Lord' (Eph. 5:19). Being united to Christ by faith, through the operation of the Spirit of God, the children of God have joy. We rejoice in the Lord. We rejoice in what he has done for us. And we rejoice in what he is doing in the world around us. Our songs of praise are but outward expressions of inward joy.

2. *Thanksgiving towards God.* 'Giving thanks always for all things unto God and the Father in the name of our Lord Jesus Christ' (Eph. 5:20). Those who are born of God live by faith and not by sight. This faith, which is the fruit of the Spirit, gives us confidence in God's power, providence and promises. We therefore give thanks for all things, knowing that God has promised and will accomplish nothing but good for them who are in Christ.

3. *Humiliation before our fellow man.* 'Submitting yourselves one to another in the fear of God' (Eph. 5:21). The true believer is one who has learned submission. He submits to Christ as King. And that submission makes him submissive towards others. He does not demand his 'human rights'. Rather, he submits his rights to the rights of others. 'This I say, brethren, walk in the Spirit, and ye shall not fulfil the lusts of the flesh.'

'The heavenly calling'

Read Hosea 2:1-23

This heavenly calling, of which all of God's elect are partakers, is that sovereign and gracious work of the Holy Spirit which brings men to life and faith in Jesus Christ. This is the effectual and irresistible operation of God the Holy Spirit. When we talk about the Holy Spirit's effectual call, we are not saying that God saves sinners against their will. We simply mean that when the Holy Spirit is sent on an errand of mercy into a man's heart, he never fails to bring that man to Christ. He so changes the sinner's nature that he is perfectly willing to receive Christ as Lord and Saviour.

1. There is a heavenly calling which is always effectual, bringing men to salvation and life. To be sure there is a true and sincere call which goes forth in the preaching of the gospel which men resist. 'Many are called, but few are chosen.' But there is a heavenly calling which always brings salvation. 'Whom he called, them he also justified.' 'Thy people shall be willing in the day of thy power.' 'Blessed is the man whom thou choosest, and causest to approach unto thee.' It is this calling which distinguishes the believer from the unbeliever. To the unbelieving Jew, Christ crucified is a stumbling-block. To the unbelieving Greek, he is foolishness. 'But unto them which are called,' Christ is 'the power of God and the wisdom of God'.

2. This heavenly and effectual call is necessary for the salvation of men. It is necessary because of man's nature. By nature man has neither the will nor the ability to come to Christ for salvation (John 5:40; 6:44). If God the Holy Spirit does not effectually call a man to Christ, he never will nor can come. It is necessary because of the purpose of God. We are 'called according to his purpose'. God has determined to save his elect. But they cannot be saved without his omnipotent call. It is also necessary because of the purchase of Christ. If the Holy Spirit did not call to life those whom Christ has purchased, the Son of God would be robbed of the satisfaction of his soul.

'Shall come to me'

Read Psalm 110:1-7

No man by nature will ever, of his own accord, come to Christ and be saved. He has neither the will nor the ability, in himself, to do so. If language means anything, this is an evident truth of Holy Scripture. 'Ye will not come to me that ye might have life.' 'No man can come to me, except the Father which hath sent me draw him.' Yet many do come, so many that in the last day our Lord shall have gathered around him a great multitude which no man can number, even ten thousand times ten thousand. When will sinners, who will not and cannot of themselves do so, come to Christ and be saved? The answer is found in Psalm 110:3: 'Thy people shall be willing in the day of thy power, in the beauties of holiness from the womb of the morning: thou hast the dew of thy youth.'

In this world, among the fallen mass of humanity, there is a people who belong to the Lord Jesus Christ – 'thy people'. They were chosen by him in eternal election, given to him as their Surety in the covenant of grace and redeemed by him at the cross of Calvary. They are his people. Every one of them will willingly come to him in the day of his power. There is a day appointed by God for each of his elect, a day when he will draw them to Christ by the invincible power of irresistible grace. There comes a time when the Good Shepherd must and will seek his lost sheep and effectually bring each of them into his fold. Like the millions of dew drops of the morning, all who were chosen and redeemed by Christ will be brought forth into life in the morning of his grace. Mysteriously, divinely, the multitudes of Christ's people will be made willing and will come to him for life.

'To him shall men come'

Read Isaiah 11:1-16

Can we be sure that Christ will see of the travail of his soul with satisfaction? Can we be sure that all of God's elect will come to Christ and be saved? Indeed we can! It is written of our Lord: 'Thou hast the dew of thy youth.' King Jesus does not grow old. His purpose does not change. His vision is not dimmed. His power has not diminished. He is God over all and blessed for ever. Like himself, his grace is immutable. He will not fail! He will have his redeemed ones. When all is done, when all the Lord's enemies are in hell, when all his decrees have been accomplished, Christ will stand before the Father with all the hosts of his people to present them before the presence of his glory, saying, 'Lo, I and the children thou hast given me.'

It is not possible that the Son of God could fail in his work of redemption. 'By his own blood he entered in once into the holy place, having obtained eternal redemption for us.' 'He shall see of the travail of his soul, and shall be satisfied.' We believe, according to Scripture, that our Lord died as a Substitute for sinners, that he fully satisfied the law of God in our place and finished the work of redemption. And every soul for whom the Son of God suffered and died will be with him in glory. He did not make us redeemable, reconcilable and pardonable. He redeemed, reconciled and pardoned his people!

'The axe is laid unto the root'

Read Jeremiah 5:30–6:17

The Word of God nowhere suggests, as many blasphemously assert, that Christ died trying to save those who finally perish in hell. It is time we laid the axe to the root of the tree. I solemnly lay these seven charges against the doctrine of universal redemption and against all who preach that doctrine.

1. Universal redemption would make the blood of Christ of none effect. It says that the blood of Christ did not actually accomplish and secure anything, but only made certain things possible.

2. Universal redemption would destroy the love of God. It makes God's love meaningless and changeable. Does God at one time love a man enough to slay his own Son for him and at another time hate that man enough to send him to hell?

3. Universal redemption would destroy the justice of God. Where is the justice of God if he can punish the same offence twice, once in Christ and again in the soul for whom Christ died?

4. Universal redemption would destroy the wisdom of God. What wisdom can there be in God devising a plan to save every person in the world, when he knew that in the end that plan would fail?

5. Universal redemption would rob God of his glory in saving sinners. If, after all, it is my faith rather than Christ's blood that redeems my soul, why should I give him the praise?

6. Universal redemption would make the death of Christ a vain thing. If one soul perishes for whom Christ died, to that extent he died in vain.

7. Universal redemption would provide a sinner with no motive to love and serve Christ. If he loved me no more than he loved Judas, why should I love him any more than Judas did? Why should I serve him?

'Behold, he cometh!'

Read 1 Thessalonians 4:1-18

John began his letter to the seven churches of Asia with a benediction of grace: 'Grace be unto you.' Then his loving heart arose to grateful adoration. He adored Christ because of who he is and what he has done. Our blessed Saviour is 'the faithful witness, and the first-begotten from the dead, and the Prince of the kings of the earth'. And he has done marvellous things for us. He loved us. He redeemed us. And he has made us kings and priests to God. The Son of God takes such stuff as he finds in the dunghill of fallen humanity and makes for himself kings and priests unto God! And now John's adoration arises to expectation: 'Behold, he cometh!' Like John, our reverence should be deepened and our adoration increased by the conviction of the speediness of Christ's glorious advent: the Lord Jesus Christ, the King of Heaven, is coming in all the glory and majesty of his eternal Godhead, to the delight of his people and the dismay of his enemies.

1. King Jesus is coming! The second coming is an absolute certainty. It is not a matter of speculation or debate. As surely as he came to die, he will come to reign. That very one who died at Calvary will come again to reign upon the earth. Who shall prevent him? His heart is with his bride and he will surely come to her. Notice John puts it in the present tense: 'He is coming.' Every event of providence is a footstep of the King in his descent. He is coming and soon he will appear!

2. King Jesus is coming in majestic glory. Once he came in humiliation. In humiliation he died. But he will never be humbled again. When Christ comes, he will ride upon the clouds of glory and it is no secret matter. 'Every eye shall see him.' All the redeemed shall see him. All his enemies shall see him.

3. King Jesus is coming in triumphant judgement. At that glorious day, the Son of God will gather all his redeemed unto himself. And he will ease himself of all his adversaries. And he shall reign for ever. Hallelujah! 'Even so. Amen.'

'Salvation in three stages'

Read Ephesians 1:1-19

God **'delivered us from so great a death, and doth deliver: in whom we trust that he will yet deliver us'**. The word 'salvation' is the all-inclusive word of the gospel. It includes everything that is required to bring a sinful soul into the glorious and eternal union of life with Christ in heaven. Paul's deliverance from physical death gives us an illustration of spiritual salvation in three stages. It is a mistake to view salvation in only one aspect as being the whole. The Primitive Baptists err in making the decree of God alone salvation. The fundamentalists err in making the new birth alone salvation. If we would view it rightly, we must look upon salvation from start to finish as the work of God, recalling the past, observing the present and anticipating the future.

1. *We have been saved* (2 Tim. 1:9). In one sense of the word, our salvation is eternal. God's elect have always been viewed by him in Christ, 'accepted in the beloved'. In the decree of God we were eternally called, justified and glorified. To be sure, all of God's elect were redeemed, justified and sanctified at Calvary. Redemption was not only an act of mercy. It was a legal transfer. Our sins were imputed to Christ and his righteousness was imputed to us. And we were saved by the new birth. Repentance and faith are as necessary for salvation as election and redemption. All who were chosen and redeemed will in God's time be born again. They will all repent and believe the gospel. At Calvary, Christ saved us from the penalty of sin. In the new birth he saved us from the dominion of sin.

2. *We are now being saved* (Phil. 1:6, 2:13). While we are upon the earth, the Holy Spirit is performing within us that work of sanctification which will result in glorification.

3. *We trust that we shall yet be saved* (Rom. 8:23; 13:11). Not until we are brought before the throne of God in perfect holiness and purity, in body and soul, will our salvation be complete. But complete it will be. God will not fail in his work. The future is as sure as the past.

'When ye come together in the church'

Read Psalm 91:1-16

Every Sunday people gather in public assemblies all around the world and they have been doing so for many years. But what is the purpose of our public gathering as a church? One obvious answer to that question is that God has commanded it. We must not forsake the assembling of ourselves together. But that is only a very minor reason for God's true children as they gather together. It is true that we love the fellowship of the saints and that we need this fellowship for our own spiritual growth. But this is not the primary reason for our public assembly.

Whether we gather on Sunday morning, Sunday night or Wednesday night, the purpose of our public assembly is that we may worship God, Father, Son and Holy Spirit.

> Brethren, we have met to worship,
> And adore the Lord our God.

As often as we come together, let us celebrate the praises of our covenant God. In our singing, our praying, our preaching and our hearing, it should be our goal to praise our triune God for his grace and glory. For another thing, when we come together, we should come seeking a message from God. Our hearts long to hear the Lord speaking to us through the Word. We want a message from Christ to comfort and challenge, assure and search, abase and uplift, wound and heal our hearts. And when we come together as a church, let us come to be instructed by God. Beloved, we need to be constantly taught of God. We need to be taught our weakness and sin. We need to be taught Christ's love and grace, his ability to redeem, his willingness to forgive, his power to save, his promises to comfort, his strength to preserve and his merits to glorify.

As often as we gather in our public assembly of worship, may it please our God to fill our hearts with praise to him for his covenant grace, his redeeming love, his sanctifying presence and his saving fulness.

A searching question and a satisfying answer

Read 1 John 2:12-29

Our Lord had pressed upon his hearers the great truths of the gospel. He told them plainly that he was God the eternal Son. He taught them man's complete spiritual depravity and inability. He explained to them the fact that salvation is altogether by God's sovereign grace. And he insisted that no man is born again except that man who is joined to Christ by a living and vital union of faith. But those men who followed Christ only for material gain, or out of a religious curiosity, or because they had eaten the miraculously produced loaves, were offended at his doctrine. And 'from that time many of his disciples went back, and walked no more with him'.

Then our Lord turned to the twelve and asked this searching question: **'Will ye also go away?'** Now I put the question to you. Many have gone away. It is likely that many more will yet do so. I fear that some who appear to be devoted today might become offended because of the gospel tomorrow and go back, go back to the world's way. Will you?

But this I know, those who are truly born again, those who have experienced the grace of God, been redeemed by the blood of Christ and been called to life by the Holy Spirit cannot go away. Those who truly know Christ can never leave him. We know our desperate need of him. Therefore God's elect return with this satisfying answer: **'Lord, to whom shall we go?'** Sometimes we are tempted and the world tugs hard at our hearts. But we know that no one can satisfy our need and our heart's desire but Christ. Christ alone has the words of eternal life. He is the life itself and the way to life. We believe and are sure that Jesus of Nazareth is that Christ whom God has sent. He is God's anointed Prophet, Priest and King. He is the promised Redeemer. He is the Son of the living God. The law cannot help us. The world cannot satisfy us. We must cling to Christ. He is all.

'Christ hath made us free'

Read Galatians 4:8-31

It is common today for preachers to say that the law is the believer's rule of life. Very few people would tell us that the law is a means of justification. But many insist upon bringing the children of God back under the yoke of bondage for sanctification.

The apostle Paul says that such reasoning is foolish! 'Having begun in the Spirit, are ye now made perfect by the flesh?' He states the fact very plainly: 'Ye are not under the law, but under grace.' 'Christ is the end of the law for righteousness to every one that believeth.' We have been made free, for ever free, by the Son of God, and we are free indeed! **'Stand fast therefore in the liberty wherewith Christ hath made us free, and be not entangled again with the yoke of bondage.'**

Not only is it unwise, it is a sinful practice, contrary to the faith of the gospel, for a believer to make the law a basis for his life before God. Our acceptance before God is entirely the work of Christ. He is all our righteousness, both in justification and in sanctification. If you do anything, whether it be circumcision, the keeping of the sabbath, or even purity of conduct, in order to be accepted by God, you are fallen from grace! And Christ shall profit you nothing!

In Jesus Christ, by virtue of his representative obedience and substitutionary death, we are free from the law. We have no curse from the law, no covenant with the law, no condemnation by the law and no commitment to the law. Does that mean that we are lawless? Can we now sin without fear? Perish the thought! We live by the commandment of God. 'And this is his commandment, that we should believe on the name of his Son Jesus Christ, and love one another, as he gave us commandment.' We trust Christ alone for our entire acceptance before God. And we walk before our brethren in love. These are 'those things that are pleasing in his sight'.

Why should we support missionaries?

Read 1 Corinthians 9:1-18

Many answers are given to that question in the Word of God. But the apostle here gives four excellent reasons for doing so. Having commended Gaius for his good work in this regard, John encourages him to continue with these reasons.

1. It is a work pleasing to God. John told Gaius that when one of God's servants came through town, not only was he to care for him while he was there, but he was to **'bring'** him **'forward'** on his journey. That is to say, he was to provide such things as the preacher needed to carry on his mission. This is a **'godly sort'** of work. The margin reads, 'worthy of God'. It is a work with which God is pleased. God delights to see those who love Christ showing their love by generosity towards his servants.

2. We should do it **'for his name's sake'**. There is one thing that compels the true servant of God to take his wife and children to a far-off place to preach the gospel, leaving relatives and friends behind. He has a burning jealousy for the name of Christ. He preaches the gospel so that men everywhere may bow down, trust and worship at the name of Christ (Rom. 1:1, 5). Our Lord is so highly honoured by the service of such men that he says that what we do for them, we do for him (Matt. 10:40-42).

3. They have no other means of support. **'They went forth taking nothing of the Gentiles.'** Our Lord expressly forbids his servants to beg for support, especially from the unbeliever (Matt. 10:5-10; Luke 10:1-7). And Paul condemned those pretentious servants of Christ who merely peddled the gospel (2 Cor. 2:17; 1 Thess. 2:5-9). You can mark this down: if God is in a work, God will support it through the generosity of his people. And no servant of God should have to provide a piece of bread for himself. The people of God ought to take care of him.

4. What is more, by our loving and generous support of God's servants we become **'fellow-helpers to the truth'**. When we supply a man's needs so that he can preach the gospel, we become allies with him in the work! What a privilege!

Grace – both sure and free

Read Isaiah 55:1-13

'All that the Father giveth me shall come to me; and him that cometh to me I will in no wise cast out.' Here our Lord teaches us the twin truths of divine sovereignty and human responsibility. These two truths are not enemies; they are friends. We do not have to choose one or the other. Both are true. Any man who believes either, as it is taught in the Scriptures, must believe the other.

God has a people whom he will save. As surely as the Bible is true, God has a people whom he has chosen and who are redeemed by the blood of Christ. All of these must and will, in due time, be brought to Christ in true faith, by the sovereign will and power of God. God's purpose will never be thwarted. His will cannot be overturned. His grace will not be frustrated. And it is equally true that whosoever comes to Christ by faith will have eternal life. The Son of God himself says that he will not refuse any sinner who comes to him in true faith! Jesus Christ is both able and willing to save to the uttermost all that come to the Father by him. If you go to hell, you will have no one to blame but yourself. You have been invited to Christ. God himself invites you. But you would not come! Nothing but your sinful will keeps you from him!

To all who come to Christ, having been given to him in eternal election and by irresistible grace, this promise is given: 'I will in no wise cast [them] out.' Here is the security of God's elect! Jesus Christ says, 'I will never, no never, under any circumstances, for any reason, at any time, under any pretence, cast out of my arms, my love, my power, my favour or my grace any sinner who comes to me!' More secure is no one ever than the loved ones of the Saviour. The Good Shepherd keeps his own sheep. He will not lose one of them!

Without question, God's grace in Christ is both certain and free. Will you come to Christ and receive grace from the hands of the sovereign Lord? Or will you perish in your proud unbelief?

'All things are yours'

Read 1 Samuel 30:1-6, 17-25

We rejoice in the fact that all the blessings of the covenant are sealed to us by the redeeming blood of Christ. Since God has reconciled us to himself, while we were yet enemies, through the sacrifice of his Son, we are confident that he will freely give us all things in Christ.

This promise gives us confidence in our pilgrimage here upon the earth. And it fills our hearts with joyful anticipation with regard to heaven. Children of God, this is our promise for all of eternity: 'All things are yours.' I read of no secondary joys in heaven. There are no back settlements in the heavenly Canaan. There are no second-class citizens in the heavenly Jerusalem. Whoever invented the doctrine of degrees in heaven knew nothing of free grace. All the saints shall see the Saviour's face. What more can any child of God desire?

Heaven, in all its fulness, is altogether the reward of grace, and not of debt. All the people of God are loved with the same love, perfectly. There are no degrees in God's perfect love. They were all chosen in Christ at the same time and elected to the same glory. All the blessings of the covenant were given to us in Christ Jesus before the world began. All the promises of God in Christ Jesus are 'Yea' and 'Amen' to all the elect. We are all redeemed with the same price, the precious blood of Christ. And by that blood, the Lord has blotted out all our transgressions, iniquities and sins, so that he has promised never to remember them against us any more for ever. In Christ we are all perfectly justified and made righteous. We are made the very righteousness of God in him. And we are all the sons of God by eternal adoption and faith in Christ. All the saints of God are made kings and priests unto the Lord. Child of God, our only grounds of acceptance before God is Christ. We shall be like him, without spot or wrinkle, perfect in righteousness and glory. Can there be any degrees in perfect glory? Certainly not! This is the promise given to those who believe, both for time and eternity: 'All things are yours!'

'According to the foreknowledge of God'

Read Deuteronomy 7:1-14

Many try to avoid the biblical doctrine of election and the sovereignty of God's electing grace by telling us that election was based upon God's eternal knowledge that some sinners would, of their own free will, repent and believe on Christ. But such doctrine is contrary to the plain statements of Holy Scripture (Deut. 7:7-9; Jer. 31:3; Rom. 9:11-18); and it makes God's electing grace dependent upon foreseen merit in the sinner, attributing salvation to the works of man rather than the grace of God. If the word 'foreknowledge' does not mean 'foreseen repentance and faith in men', what does it mean?

Divine foreknowledge certainly includes *the omniscience of God*. God, knowing all things, had a thorough knowledge of all his elect and all that would concern them from eternity. He knew the depths of sin and rebellion, disobedience and ungodliness, guilt and depravity into which we would fall before he called us by his grace. Nevertheless, he set his heart upon us and chose us (Jer. 1:5).

The foreknowledge of God is nothing less than *divine foreordination*. In 1 Peter 1:20 the very same word is translated 'foreordained'. Omniscience, the fact that God knows all things, is an attribute of God, essential to his being. But foreknowledge is a voluntary, deliberate act of God, an eternal act of his grace. God knows all things that come to pass before they come to pass, because he sovereignly predestinated and sovereignly controls all things (Isa. 46:9-11; Rom. 11:36).

Primarily, the word 'foreknowledge' signifies *the everlasting love of God the Father for his own elect*. 'Whom he did foreknow, he also did predestinate to be conformed to the image of his Son' (Rom. 8:29). In this sense God knew some, but not others (Matt. 7:23). Foreknowledge is God's eternal love and unalterable delight in his elect, as he viewed us in his dear Son.

Election is not a dry, arbitrary choice of some to eternal life. Election is God's eternal, determinate choice of his people, based upon his loving knowledge and approval of each and all of them in Christ Jesus before the world was.

'All things are of God'

Read Genesis 1:1-31

'All things,' past, present and future; 'all things,' in heaven, earth and hell; 'all things,' regarding angels, men and devils; 'all things,' good, bad, or indifferent – **'all things are of God'.** This is high doctrine. This is gospel doctrine. This is soul-cheering, heart-comforting doctrine to those who know God. To the degree that we are able to receive this blessed truth of Holy Scripture that 'All things are of God', our hearts will be at peace, resigned to the will of God, submissive to the hand of God, confident of the providence of God and content in all things.

All things are of God in *creation*. God made heaven, earth and hell and all that they contain: 'In the beginning God created the heaven and the earth' (Gen. 1:1). This world did not just evolve out of nothing, by some unexplainable explosion in space. God Almighty created all things by the word of his power through his Son, the Lord Jesus Christ. 'In the beginning was the Word, and the Word was with God, and the Word was God. The same was in the beginning with God. All things were made by him; and without him was not anything made that was made' (John 1:1-3). Jesus Christ our God is the sovereign Creator and Sustainer of all things. 'By him were all things created, that are in heaven, and that are in earth, visible and invisible, whether they be thrones, or dominions, or principalities, or powers: all things were created by him and for him: and he is before all things, and by him all things consist' (Col. 1:16-17). To embrace evolution in any form is to deny God altogether and depart from the faith of Christ. 'Through faith [belief of God's revelation] we understand that the worlds were framed by the word of God, so that the things which are seen were not made of things which do appear' (Heb. 11:3).

'All things are of God'

Read Isaiah 45:5-13; Romans 11:33-36

All things in *providence* are of God. 'We know that all things work together for good to them that love God, to them who are the called according to his purpose' (Rom. 8:28). 'For of him, and through him, and to him, are all things: to whom be glory for ever' (Rom. 11:36). Every event of providence is ordered and ruled according to the sovereign will of our God. The thoughts of men and the actions of men, good and bad, angels and demons, the path of every grain of dust on a windy day and the path of the whirlwind – everything in this universe is absolutely under the control and direction of God's sovereign providence. Nothing happens by accident. Our great God, in his sovereign majesty, rules everything with as much ease as if there were nothing to rule. With undisturbed serenity, God rules! Beacuse God rules all things, we know that all things will be so ruled of God as to bring about the spiritual and eternal good of all who trust him and all things will be to the praise of his glory, 'According to the purpose of him who worketh all things after the counsel of his own will' (Eph. 1:11). Because God is totally, absolutely, universally sovereign in providence, we know that his purpose will be accomplished and his promises will all be fulfilled. Anything less than a totally sovereign God cannot be confidently trusted.

All things are of God in *salvation*. 'Salvation is of the Lord' (Jonah 2:9). 'By grace are ye saved through faith; and that not of yourselves: it is the gift of God' (Eph. 2:8). 'Of him are ye in Christ Jesus, who of God is made unto us wisdom, and righteousness, and sanctification, and redemption: that, according as it is written, He that glorieth, let him glory in the Lord' (1 Cor. 1:30-31). Election, redemption, regeneration, sanctification, preservation, resurrection and glorification are works of God alone. God gave us life. God gave us faith. God gave us a new heart and a new will by revealing Christ in us. And we 'are kept by the power of God' (1 Peter 1:5). We worship and trust and love the one true and living God, who is sovereign in creation, sovereign in providence and sovereign in salvation.

'I have redeemed thee'

Read Isaiah 52:13-53:12

Here are four words which set forth and help to define that blessed work of the Lord Jesus Christ by which our souls were redeemed and our eternal glory secured.

Sovereignty. Our Lord's act of redemption was an act of divine sovereignty. 'He laid down his life for us.' There was nothing in us which compelled him, or moved him, to redeem us. He voluntarily laid down his life for us because it was the free and sovereign pleasure of his love to do so. Christ, the sovereign God, determined that he would die, how he would die, where he would die, when he would die, who his murderers would be, for whom he would die and what the results of his death would be.

Success. Because our Redeemer is the eternal, sovereign Son of God, we are assured that his death and his redemptive work for the atonement of sin are a success and not a failure. The prophecy has been fulfilled: 'He shall not fail.' In stating that the Lord Jesus Christ is a successful Saviour, I am simply proclaiming that which must be a self-evident truth: whatever the Lord Jesus Christ intended to accomplish at Calvary has been done. He is God! His purpose and will in redemption must, of a certainty, be fulfilled (Isa. 46:9-10).

Substitution. The Lord Jesus Christ died as a Substitute for a particular people. And those people for whom Christ stood as a Substitute at Calvary, bearing their sins and enduring the wrath of God in their place, will never perish. They are redeemed! (2 Cor. 5:21.)

Satisfaction. Our blessed Saviour's one, substitutionary sacrifice for our sins has completely and perfectly satisfied the wrath and justice of God against us. His sacrifice was infinitely meritorious, so that every sinner who believes on Christ is freely justified and fully pardoned. Through the propitiatory sacrifice of the Lord Jesus Christ, by which the law and justice of God are satisfied, God is both just and the justifier of all who believe (Rom. 3:24-26). 'There is therefore now no condemnation to them which are in Christ Jesus!'

'How that Christ died'

Read John 10:1-18

The one vital issue of the gospel is this: **'How that Christ died for our sins according to the scriptures'** (1 Cor. 15:3). The gospel is not a declaration of God's love, which all men delight in. Neither is it a mere statement of the fact that Christ died upon the cross, which all men can understand. The gospel reveals the justice of God and the effectual satisfaction of that justice in the sinner's Substitute, the Lord Jesus Christ. Everyone knows that Christ died on the cross, but few know *how* he died.

How did the Son of God come to die the painful, shameful, ignominious death of the cross? Isaiah tells us that 'It pleased the Lord to bruise him.' Christ died according to the eternal purpose and decree of God. Because he and his Father loved us, the Son of God voluntarily laid down his life for us, according to the will of God (John 10:11, 17, 18; Heb. 10:5-14; 1 John 3:16; Acts 2:23).

Why did the Lord of Glory endure such a death for sinners? When Christ died as the sinner's Substitute, God made him to be sin and made his soul an offering for sin (2 Cor. 5:21; Isa. 53:10). In order for God to save his elect people, whom he loved with an everlasting love, justice had to be satisfied. And there was no way for justice to be satisfied without the substitutionary death of the incarnate God in our place (Rom. 3:24-26).

What are the results of our Lord's sin-atoning sacrifice? Isaiah tells us that there are three things which are the sure results of Christ's substitutionary death (Isa. 53:10). First, 'He shall see his seed'. He shall see all his seed, justified, sanctified and glorified. 'He shall not fail' (Isa. 42:4). 'He shall see of the travail of his soul, and shall be satisfied' (Isa. 53:11). In other words, all of those for whom he died shall live for ever with him in glory. Second, 'He shall prolong his days.' That is to say, though he died for our sins, he lives in glory to make intercession for his redeemed ones. Third, 'The pleasure of the Lord shall prosper in his hand.' That is to say, he must rule all things as the God-man, our Substitute in glory, to accomplish God's eternal purpose of grace.

'He saved us'

Read Jonah 2:1-10

How can a sinner be saved? Push aside all that you have heard preachers say about salvation, open the book of God and you will find that in order for you to be saved you must be the object of three essential acts of divine grace.

You must have a complete *redemption* from the curse of God's holy law. Your sin must be punished. Your guilt must be removed. The law and justice of God, that demand your eternal damnation, must be satisfied. Your only hope of redemption is the shed blood of Christ, the sinner's Substitute. The gospel of the grace of God declares that this redemption was accomplished by Christ, when he died at Calvary, for all who believe (Rom. 3:24-26; 2 Cor. 5:21; Gal. 3:10-13; Heb. 9:12).

You must also have a perfect *righteousness*, such as the holy, righteous God of heaven will accept. A holy God requires holiness. He requires perfect, flawless righteousness. Sinful men, such as we are, cannot produce such righteousness. But the Lord Jesus Christ, the God-man, has produced righteousness in the earth by his life of obedience to God. And his righteousness is of infinite merit before God. Without this perfect righteousness, you can never be accepted by God (Heb. 12:14). It is this perfect righteousness of Christ which God imputes to all who believe.

And you must be regenerated by the grace and power of God. *Regeneration*, the new birth, is not something you do. It is something God does for you and in you. Regeneration is a creation of spiritual life in a man (2 Cor. 5:17). It is a resurrection from spiritual death (Eph. 2:1-4). If God the Holy Spirit comes to you and gives you life by the power of his grace, you will live. You will repent of your sin. You will believe on Christ. You will bow to Christ. You will follow Christ. God's saving grace is sovereign, effectual and irresistible.

'We know'

Read Psalm 107:1-31

'We'. Paul is talking about those who are born again by almighty grace, those who are redeemed by Christ, regenerated by the Holy Spirit and live by faith in the hope of eternal glory. **'We know'.** Being taught by the Holy Spirit of God who dwells in our hearts and gives us understanding in Holy Scripture, we have an intuitive and confident knowledge of God's good providence. This is what we know: **'that all things'**, both good and bad, prosperous and adverse, pleasant and painful, **'work together'** – the many things that exist and the many things that happen in our lives are not independent and isolated. They are so many gears in the machinery of divine providence, all working together. Being under divine control and ordered by divine arrangement, all the affairs, events, creatures and men in the universe are being manipulated by our heavenly Father, so that 'all things work together **for good**'. Though any event of life, singled out and standing alone, may seem terribly evil, when it is viewed as one spoke in the great wheel of divine providence, we see that it is truly good. It may be a physical evil, but it is working for spiritual good. It may be a temporal evil, but it will surely bring eternal good. To whom is this great promise made? **'To them that love God'.** If there is in my heart a genuine love for God as he is revealed in Holy Scripture, he created that love, because he loves me. 'We love him, because he first loved us.' If I love him, it is evidence that he loves me and will do me good, nothing but good. **'To them who are the called'.** Those who love God are those who have been singled out from eternity as the objects of his grace and separated unto him by the irresistible call of the Holy Spirit. This is that effectual call of God the Holy Spirit which gives life to dead sinners and creates in their hearts faith and love towards God. If you are one of the called ones, this promise is to you. The promise is sure, because it is **'according to his purpose'**. Rejoice! 'All things work together for good' because God in eternity purposed to do us good, and he rules the universe 'according to his purpose'.

'Contentment'

Read Philippians 4:1-13

Here are five things which, if God the Holy Spirit is pleased to establish them in our hearts, will surely give every believer contentment.

1. *The purpose of God.* All things that have ever come to pass in this world, both great and small, both prosperous and adverse, both pleasing and painful, both good and evil, come to pass according to God's eternal, immutable, unalterable purpose. Learn this in your heart, and you will learn to be content. 'For of him, and through him, and to him are all things: to whom be glory for ever' (Rom. 11:36).

2. *The providence of God.* Everything in heaven, earth and hell is sovereignly ruled, governed and manipulated by God in infinite wisdom, according to his own holy purpose for the eternal, spiritual good of his people. Nothing in this universe breathes or moves without God's decree and God's direction. 'We know that all things work together for good to them that love God, to them who are the called according to his purpose' (Rom. 8:28).

3. *The power of God.* Our God is almighty. He has purposed us good and he has the power to accomplish his purpose. He cannot be frustrated or defeated. 'He doeth according to his will in the army of heaven, and among the inhabitants of the earth: and none can stay his hand, or say unto him, What doest thou?' He is God. You can safely trust him.

4. *The presence of God.* 'Let your conversation be without covetousness; and be content with such things as ye have: for he hath said, I will never leave thee, nor forsake thee' (Heb. 13:5). Can you get a sense of this fact? If you are one of God's believing children, the omnipotent, eternal God is with you! Surely, the presence of God with you should give your heart contentment at all times.

5. *The promises of God.* Open the book of God's promises, and find a rich source of contentment for your soul. To you who are in Christ Jesus, all the promises, those exceedingly great and precious promises of God, are 'yea' and 'Amen' (2 Cor. 1:20).

Praise inspired by election

Read 2 Thessalonians 2:1-17

Multitudes are perishing, being deceived by the strong delusion of Arminianism, free-willism, easy-believism and decisionism. God has sent 'them strong delusion, that they should believe a lie: that they all might be damned who believed not the truth, but had pleasure in unrighteousness. But we are bound to give thanks always to God for you, brethren beloved of the Lord, because God hath from the beginning chosen you to salvation' (2 Thess. 2:11-13). Yes, my friend, we also would be damned in false religion had it not been for God's eternal election of us to salvation by the Lord Jesus Christ. Had God left us to the choice of our sinful free will, we would be eternally lost. This fact humbles us before God and inspires our hearts to sing his praise with David of old, saying, 'Blessed is the man whom thou choosest, and causest to approach unto thee, that he may dwell in thy courts: we shall be satisfied with the goodness of thy house, even of thy holy temple' (Ps. 65:4). Here are three reasons for which every believer should continually offer praise and thanksgiving to God.

1. *We were chosen* by God in eternal love. Before the world was made the eternal God set his heart upon us. He loves us with an everlasting love. In his great love, God chose us and determined to save us by the substitutionary sacrifice of his own dear Son, the Lord Jesus Christ. 'Blessed is the man whom thou choosest,' O Lord.

2. *We have been called* by divine, irresistible grace. At the time appointed God sent his Spirit to us, revealing Christ in the gospel, and gently, tenderly, effectually, irresistibly caused us to come to him in faith. Aren't you thankful God would not let you perish in unbelief? 'Blessed is the man whom thou causest to approach unto thee.'

3. *We shall be satisfied* with the goodness of God's house. We are satisfied with all the needs of our souls here by the goodness of God's grace and providence. And we shall be satisfied with all the goodness of God in eternal glory (Ps. 17:15).

Absolute forgiveness

Read Hebrews 10:1-17

By his one great sacrifice for sin, the Lord Jesus Christ has for ever removed all sin from all his people. He bore our sins in his own body on the tree. He was made to be sin for us. The Lord Jesus Christ, our great Substitute, took the shame, the guilt and the curse of our sin upon himself, and died under the penalty of God's law and justice for us. Pouring out his life's blood unto death, he 'obtained eternal redemption for us'. 'Christ hath redeemed us from the curse of the law, being made a curse for us: for it is written, Cursed is everyone that hangeth on a tree.'

Because God has transferred sin from his people to his Son and punished sin in his Son to the full extent of his own infinite justice, he freely forgives us of all sin. *God's forgiveness of our sin is an act of divine justice.* Grace devised the plan of redemption and provided Christ as the all-sufficient Substitute for sinners. But justice, being satisfied by the sacrifice of Christ, cannot exact any penalty whatsoever from those sinners for whom Christ died. God is faithful to his own covenant, faithful to his own law and faithful to his own righteous character. Therefore he must in justice forgive all the sin of all the people for whom Christ died. It is written: 'He is faithful and just to forgive us our sins.'

God's forgiveness of sin is a complete, absolute forgiveness. He will never charge any believer with any sin. Though we sin a thousand times a day, as we all do, God will not charge his people with sin. Though David commits adultery and murder, God will not charge David with sin. Though Peter denies Christ with an oath, God will not charge Peter with sin. Though you and I commit the most hideous offences, God will not charge us with sin, if we are in Christ. No matter what sin we may commit, God will not charge it against us! Our standing and acceptance with God are not in ourselves but in Christ our Substitute, who put away our sin. No wonder David exclaimed, 'Blesed is the man to whom the Lord will not impute sin!' (Rom. 4:8.)

'I was made a minister'

Read Jeremiah 1:1-19

In these verses, we have one of Paul's many descriptions of the work of the ministry. Paul recognized the great responsibility that was laid upon his shoulders as the servant of God and he wanted the churches to know something of this work, so that they might properly pray for those who were called to it.

The work of the ministry is the greatest work under heaven. It requires all of a man, and more. It is too great for a man. 'Who is sufficient for these things?' is the constant cry of those who labour in the gospel. Now I want you to be aware of the great magnitude of this work. I want you to see three things that Paul shows us concerning the ministry.

1. Every true minister is *under God's authority* (v.7). If there is anything that this generation needs to learn about the ministry it is that God alone makes a minister, and God's ministers are under divine authority. No man, no seminary and no group of men can make a minister. This is 'the gift of the grace of God ... by the effectual working of his power'. God alone can qualify a man for this work. And he is under the authority of God alone.

2. Every true minister is *endowed with a gracious attitude* (v. 8). Paul thought very little of himself. He had great views of Christ, which caused him to have a low estimation of himself. He had a high estimation of his brethren. These two things always go together, a humble opinion of one's self and a high opinion of our brethren. Paul thought very highly of his work. To him preaching was the most blessed work on earth. And Paul had the highest possible thoughts of his subject: 'That I should preach the unsearchable riches of Christ.'

3. Every true minister is *motivated by a glorious ambition* (v. 9). Paul had one glorious all-absorbing desire. He wanted to make Christ known unto all men. He wanted to declare unto all men the mysteries of the gospel: eternal election, substitutionary redemption, full justification, union with Christ.

May it please God to give his church more men with divine authority, humbled attitudes and this glorious ambition.

'I have no pleasure in the death of the wicked'

Read Ezekiel 18:20-32

'As I live, saith the Lord God, I have no pleasure in the death of the wicked: but that the wicked turn from his way and live: turn ye, turn ye from your evil ways; for why will ye die, O house of Israel?' Do you see it? God has sworn that he has no pleasure in the death of the wicked. It is true God will, God must punish sin. His law, his justice and his righteousness demand it. But God's law, justice and righteousness can never find pleasure or satisfaction in the eternal death of the ungodly. Indeed, if all the race of Adam were to suffer the eternal fires of hell, God's righteous justice could never find pleasure and satisfaction. Man, who is but a finite creature, can never satisfy the claims of infinite justice. If this were possible, the fires of hell must some day burn out. But infinite justice demands an infinite satisfacion. Hell must therefore be eternal! God's justice can never be satisfied in the death of the wicked. He has no pleasure in the death of him that dieth.

But God does have pleasure in the death of the sinner's Substitute, Jesus Christ. Being the infinite God, our Lord Jesus Christ was able to satisfy all the claims of infinite justice. Being the sinless man, he was able to stand in our room and bear the fulness of God's wrath for us. In his incarnation, his birth, his life and his death, the Lord God beholds Christ as the Substitute of his people and says, 'This is my beloved Son, in whom I am well pleased.' In the death of the God-man, God's law, justice and righteousness have pleasure and satisfaction. Therefore there is no possibility of one soul for whom Christ died perishing in hell. The law has no claim against a believing sinner!

It is God's pleasure, for Christ's sake, to be merciful. He gives life to perishing sinners and forgives all our sins for Christ's sake. So, then, why will ye die? Turn now and seek the Lord, cry out for his mercy and trust his Son. Only in Christ does God have any pleasure. Lay hold of God's Beloved now.

'They are not all Israel, which are of Israel'

Read Philippians 3:3-21

Among those who make a profession of religion there have always been debates as to who are the true church and people of God. Some Baptists, the Roman Catholics, the Campbellites and many others profess to be the true church, the true people of God. Such people make the external observations of religion the basis of their claim. Like the Pharisees, they pride themselves on their outward and strict adherence to the ceremonies of religion. And they exclude everyone from the body of Christ who does not conform to their particular standards of religion. But those who are God's true children can never be satisfied with the mere outward form of religion. They delight in the privileges of public worship, but they must have more. They feel the necessity of that vital power, life and heart of Christianity. In Philippians 3:3, the apostle Paul gives us a threefold description of those who are the true people of God: 'For we are the circumcision, which worship God in spirit, and rejoice in Christ Jesus, and have no confidence in the flesh.'

1. They worship God in the spirit. True worship is the exercise of faith, love and praise towards God, through the merits and mediation of Christ. It is spiritual. God's people worship him in their hearts by the power of the Holy Spirit. Our outward acts of devotion are only a reflection of our inner life in Christ.

2. They rejoice in Christ Jesus. Those who have a true apprehension of themselves realize that there is nothing in them to boast of or rejoice in. We make Christ alone our glory and boast. We rejoice in Christ's wisdom, his righteousness, his redemption, his strength and the riches of his grace. To them that believe Christ is all. 'He that glorieth, let him glory in the Lord.'

3. They have no confidence in the flesh. The true people of God place no confidence in themselves, nor in anything they have done, either moral or religious. Christ alone is the confidence of the true believer before God. We trust him for our justification, our sanctification and our eternal glory. He alone is our hope in life, in death and in the judgement.

'The soul that sinneth, it shall die'

Read Genesis 18:16-33; 19:27

There is nothing in all the Bible more clear than this fact. I know that God Almighty will punish sin – he must! The righteousness, holiness, truth, faithfulness, immutability and justice of God demand that he punish sin. The infinitely holy and just God of heaven must demand an infinite satisfaction for sin. Hell is a real place, a place of eternal, unlimited, unalterable woe for both body and soul, a place where God punishes sin relentlessly. If you die in your rebellion and unbelief, hell will be your eternal portion. God will be perfectly just in sending every rebel to hell.

There are certain emotions which arise in my heart when I think of men suffering for ever in hell. When I look upon the torments of the damned, I bow in *submission to the will of God* (1 Sam. 3:18; Lev. 10:3). I know God is just and righteous. No one will be found in hell but those who have well earned it. A sight of the damned in hell fills my heart with *gratitude for the grace of God* (Eph. 2:4-5; Gal. 1:15). I deserve to go to hell. I did everything in my power to secure my place among the damned. But God intervened to save me! Considering the misery of those who are eternally lost, a deep feeling of *humility* comes upon my soul (2 Sam. 9:8). Who am I that God should have mercy upon me? I am but a brand plucked from the burning. And a sense of *solemn fear* takes hold of me, when I think of the multitudes in hell, who perished with a false peace. I fear, lest, after all, I should come to that awful place of torment. I fear religious deception, hypocrisy and self-righteousness. I fear missing Christ.

There are certain facts that grip my soul as I think of the torments of the damned. Sin is an infinitely evil thing. Hell itself is not sufficient punishment for sin. The Lord God is infinitely and inflexibly just. He will not pass by sin. God Almighty is willing to save sinners (Ezek. 33:11). No man would ever go to hell, were it not for his own wilful unbelief! And I find comfort here: all of God's elect have been effectually and fully redeemed from the pit of destruction by the blood of Christ (Job. 33:24).

'I ... glory ... in the cross'

Read Matthew 27:27-56

With the apostle Paul, I have made it my solemn determination 'not to know anything among you, save Jesus Christ, and him crucified'. I say, **'God forbid that I should glory, save in the cross of our Lord Jesus Christ.'** To glory in the cross is to trust the crucified Christ alone as my Saviour. To glory in the cross is to live by the cross and for the cross. And to glory in the cross is to proclaim it boldly and constantly. That which is in the eyes of men most offensive and most repugnant, I take to be my glory. The cross of Christ is my one message. I glory in that message with good reason.

1. The cross of Christ is *a covenant respected*. Before the world began God the Father, the Son and the Holy Spirit chose a people and agreed to save them upon the condition that a suitable ransom would be found, a ransom that could fully satisfy divine justice. That ransom was found in the voluntary agreement of the Lord Jesus Christ to assume our nature and die in our stead at Calvary.

2. The cross of Christ is *a conquest realized*. Our Lord did not die at Calvary as the helpless victim of circumstances. He laid down his life as a mighty, conquering King. As he was bringing the death-blow to his enemies and ours he cried, 'It is finished!' And by his mighty act of redemption he obtained a mighty conquest. He crushed the serpent's head, breaking the power of the old dragon's usurped dominion. He took the sword of justice and swallowed it up in his own heart. He took the enormous load of our sin and made an end of it, establishing everlasting righteousness for us. All of this Christ did for us in our stead. He obtained the victory as our Substitute.

3. The cross of Christ is a *compassion revealed*. Our Lord Jesus Christ, the Son of God, took our sins upon himself and died in our place upon the cursed tree, because of his great love for us: 'Hereby perceive we the love of God, because he laid down his life for us!' My heart is constrained by the love of Christ to glory in the cross. I cannot do otherwise.

'Ye must be born again'

Read Revelation 20:1-15

1. Unless a man is born again, he cannot understand anything spiritual. 'Verily, verily, I say unto thee, Except a man be born again, he cannot see the kingdom of God' (John 3:3). The natural man is totally void of all spiritual understanding. You may be a logical, rational, reasonable and well-educated man, but with regard to the things of God the unregenerate man is as ignorant and foolish as a madman (Rom. 8:5; 1 Cor. 2:14). Until men are born again by the Spirit of God, divine sovereignty, human depravity, electing love, substitutionary redemption, effectual grace and persevering faith cannot be appreciated. Men rebel against these things, simply because they have no heart to understand and receive them.

2. Unless you are born again by almighty grace, you can never enter into the kingdom of God. 'Verily, verily, I say unto thee, Except a man be born of water and of the Spirit, he cannot enter into the kingdom of God' (John 3:5). You can reform your life without the new birth. You can quit swearing, smoking, drinking, running around and quit any outward vice without being born again. You can be baptized without the new birth. You can join a church, be zealous in religion, teach a Bible class, serve as a deacon or elder, you can even preach with great success without being born again. But unless you are born again, you can never enter into the kingdom of God. Unless you are born again, you will never be a part of the church and family of God, you will never have eternal life, you will never enter into the worship and fellowship of God's saints and you will never be admitted into the glory and bliss of God's presence in heaven (Rev. 21:27). Only new creatures will enter the New Jerusalem. Only heaven-born citizens will possess the bliss of heaven.

3. 'Ye must be born again', because by nature you are a fallen, depraved, sinful child of human flesh: 'That which is born of the flesh is flesh' (John 3:6). All flesh is defiled, corrupt, sinful and condemned. All flesh must die! Unless you are born of the Spirit, you will die in your sins and your flesh will be justly damned for ever!

'Love one another'

Read John 13:18–38

Men look upon many things as evidences of divine grace in the heart. Most of those 'evidences' which men look upon and applaud are so many forms of self-righteousness. They are things seen of men, pleasing to men and honoured by men, but they are an abomination to God (Luke 16:15).

But our Lord Jesus Christ has plainly told us that there is one distinguishing characteristic by which all true believers may be identified. 'By this shall all men know that ye are my disciples, if ye have love one to another.' If I have in my heart a true love for the people of God, then I am one of God's elect. If love is absent from my heart, grace is also absent from my heart. Just in case any do not know how to measure true love, Paul gives us a clear description in 1 Corinthians 13:4–7.

Love is longsuffering. It is patient with the weaknesses, infirmities and offences of others. Love is not sharp, bitter, quick-tempered and malicious, but kind. Love is not proud and selfish. It does not envy others, promote itself and behave rashly. Love is not self-seeking. Love is not easily provoked. True love for someone will prevent me from being easily offended by him and will cause me to forgive him quickly. Love thinks no evil. Love always looks for and thinks the best of its object. It looks for reasons to think good and not evil. Love does not harbour suspicion and jealousy and resentment. Love patiently bears all things in its object. If I love someone I will bear, without anger or hurt feelings, almost anything from him, because I trust him and believe the best concerning him.

All anger, wrath, malice, suspicion and gossip are contrary to that love which characterizes God's elect. They spring from the old man, from the heart of sinful flesh. We must repent of such things and turn from them. It is my constant prayer that the Lord God will teach me to love my brethren and teach me to show them true love for Christ's sake.

'The Lord be magnified'

Read John 12:1–28

'Let all those that seek thee rejoice and be glad in thee: let such as love thy salvation say continually, The Lord be magnified.' This must be our one desire, our one goal, our one ambition. Let us join our Redeemer in this prayer: 'Father, glorify thy name.' In this psalm we have a prayer of our Lord Jesus Christ. Having done the Father's will and put away our sins, the Lord Jesus Christ prays that all of God's children would follow his example and say continually, 'The Lord be magnified.'

1. Who can use this saying? This is distinctly the language of men and women who have been saved by the grace of God. Notice how they are described. They seek the Lord. Feeling their need of him, they seek him by faith in Christ. We seek the mercy of God in Christ for pardon, righteousness, fellowship, honour, glory and immortality. Seeking God in Christ, the believer finds salvation and life. God's children rejoice in him. We rejoice in who he is and what he has done and what he is doing for us. Now, being saved by the power of God, all of God's elect love his salvation. We love the gospel of substitution. We love him who is our Substitute. Once more, the psalm characterizes God's children as those who seek his glory. They say continually, 'The Lord be magnified.'

2. What do we mean by this saying? It means that we desire the honour of God in all things. We want to magnify God in the thoughts of our hearts and in our actions and attitudes before men. The paramount desire of our souls is that our God and Saviour be magnified. Let every redeemed sinner say continually, 'The Lord be magnified.'

3. Why should we say this? No one is worthy of honour, glory and majesty but Christ our God. He loved us. He redeemed us. He preserves us. He will bring us to glory. And we use this saying with confidence, because we know that the Lord will be magnified.

'Buy the truth, and sell it not'

Read Proverbs 4:1–19

Like wise merchants, we must secure the genuine article – the truth; not something that resembles the truth, not a part of the truth, but the truth. It is not enough to gaze at the truth, admire the truth and talk about the truth. We must buy it. The truth which we must buy is the gospel of God's free grace in Christ. This is the truth which we bind around our necks and is written upon the tables of our hearts.

Far too many take a fair bid for the truth, but are unwilling to pay its price. Herod heard the truth, but he bought it not, loving pleasure more. The rich young ruler made a bid for the truth, but bought it not, loving riches more. Agrippa was convinced of the truth, but bought it not, loving fame and popularity more.

But there are some who are so convinced of the value of the truth that they consider nothing too valuable to give for it. Moses gave up all the 'treasures of Egypt' that he might buy the truth. Paul gave up his Jewish privileges and high reputation that he might buy the truth. The Hebrews 'took joyfully the spoiling of their goods' that they might buy the truth. The martyrs 'loved not their lives unto death' that they might buy the truth.

You who believe have bought the truth of redemption by Christ alone. You consider it more valuable than life itself. You have bought it without money and without price, by the simple obedience of faith in Christ. But you would gladly give all things for it. My admonition to you is this: 'Sell it not.'

Many who appear to have bought the truth do sell it. And they sell their own souls with it. And 'What shall it profit a man, if he gain the whole world, and lose his own soul?' To all outward appearance, Lot's wife, Esau, Judas and Demas had the truth. They had it in name, in profession and in outward conduct. But they sold it for nought. Their apostasy clearly proved that they had never received the love of the truth. With them it was only a speculative notion. It was never grafted into their hearts. Settle this question: do you know the truth? Is it written upon your heart by divine power? See to it, my friend, that you 'buy the truth, and sell it not'.

'God so loved the world!'

Read John 3:1–16

Far too many of God's children miss the blessed message of this text by trying to fit it into their theological system. The Calvinist strives earnestly to make the text read, 'God so loved his elect.' The Arminian tries to make it teach universal redemption, suggesting (contrary to Scripture) that there is no such thing as electing love and distinguishing grace. If we can put aside the prejudices of our theological systems and read this verse as poor sinners in need of divine mercy, we will find much to comfort our hearts and encourage our faith. Here our Lord plainly declares God's revelation of his infinite love to perishing sinners.

'God so loved the world.' He did not have to love the world. There was nothing in the world which merited or constrained his love. He did not need to love the world. But it was eternally the pleasure of God to set his heart upon the fallen sons of Adam in sovereign infinite love! The word 'world', as it is used here does not refer to extent of God's love, but to the character and condition of the people whom God loved, 'The whole world lieth in wickedness.' Men who had broken God's law, who by their own wilful sin had rebelled against God's authority, men who were depraved, helpless, dead, perishing sinners, are the objects of God's love!

'That he gave his only begotten Son.' Our misery was so great that none could deliver us but the eternal Son of God. God's love was so great that he withheld not the Son of his love. At Mt Calvary God gave his Son to die in the place of sinners whom he loved. He gave his Son over to the hands of inflexible justice, to satisfy the claims of justice against our sins, so that we might not die.

'That whosoever believeth in him should not perish, but have everlasting life.' We deserve to die. We were all perishing under the wrath of God. But, by divine revelation, we have seen the Son of God dying as our Substitute. Believing that his blood and righteousness alone can satisfy God's holiness and justice, we have cast ourselves upon Christ. And now we live!

God's Word – our rule

Read Isaiah 8:1–22

The only King in Zion is Christ, God's anointed King. The only Head of the church is Christ, God's exalted Head. The only Lawgiver in Israel is Christ, God's appointed Prophet. And the only voice of authority in the church of Christ is the Word of God, the Holy Scriptures. If ever you prosper under the blessings of God, you must learn this lesson. The church of the New Testament is not a democracy where 'every man does that which is right in his own eyes'. It is a kingdom under the dominion of the sovereign Christ. Therefore I urge you to put away your customs, traditions, by-laws and opinions, and bow down in reverent submission to the Holy Scriptures. Be no longer satisfied with a form of godliness, built upon religious tradition, but void of power. Seek, rather, to submit to the Word of God, seek the power of God and seek the presence of Christ. Let me give you these reasons for submitting all things to the Word of God.

1. The Scriptures alone are given by divine inspiration. In every word and phrase, 'holy men of old spake as they were moved by the Spirit of God'.

2. The Scriptures alone reveal the way of salvation and life through faith in Christ. It is only through the declaration of God's Word that sinners are brought to salvation, trusting the merits of God's Son, our Substitute.

3. The Scriptures alone are authoritative and profitable. Our doctrine must arise from the plain statements of Scripture. All righteous reproof, correction and instruction come from the faithful exposition of the Word of God.

Let us examine ourselves and our churches by the Word of God. There should be nothing in the church today that was not established in the church by our Lord and his apostles. Any addition is a subtraction. The law of church government, according to the Scriptures, is love and trust. The business of the church is the preaching of the gospel and the purpose of the church is the glory of Christ.

'Worthy is the Lamb!'

Read Revelation 4:10–5:14

If there is one thing that I want to impress upon the hearts of men and women, it is that Christ alone is worthy of honour, worship, praise, love, trust and glory. I read it in God's book, I hear it in the preaching of the gospel and I have experienced it in my soul: **'Worthy is the Lamb!'** The apostle Paul said, 'This man was counted worthy of more glory.' The angels are not worthy, but Christ is. No man is worthy, but Christ is. The church is not worthy, but Christ is. The preacher is not worthy, but Christ is. In heaven, all the saints and angels unite in this glorious eternal song: 'Worthy is the Lamb!'

Christ is worthy of all honour, because he is the divine Creator (Rev. 4:11). In heaven everyone delights to worship Jesus Christ as God. And if ever a man gets to glory, he will have to worship Jesus Christ upon the earth as God the eternal Son, the Creator of all things. He created the world in the beginning by infinite power. He creates men anew by sovereign power. And he creates all the events of providence according to his own wise decree. In the end, all things will prove to be for his pleasure, his honour and his glory (Prov. 16:4).

Christ is worthy of all worship, because he is our merciful Redeemer (Rev. 5:9–10). God counted him worthy to be the Substitute, Surety and Redeemer of his people, committing the salvation of our souls into his hands as 'the Lamb slain from the foundation of the world'. His righteousness is worthy to clothe us. His sufferings are worthy to make us clean. His power is worthy to preserve us. His love is worthy to win our hearts. Christ proved himself worthy. As the Lion of Judah he prevailed with God. As the Lamb of God, he redeemed us to God, making us a generation of priests and kings. And now, with our hearts, we say Christ is worthy! He is worthy of our faith, obedience, love and worship!

Christ is worthy of eternal praise, because he is God's exalted King (Rev. 5:11–14). As God's exalted King every creature of God, in heaven, in the earth, and under the earth will say, 'Worthy is the Lamb that was slain!'

'A priest upon his throne'

Read Acts 5:29–42

'This man, after he had offered one sacrifice for sins for ever, sat down on the right hand of God' (Heb. 10:12). The prophet Zechariah realized more truth concerning the mediatorial offices of the Lord Jesus Christ than do the majority of our modern 'theologians'. He knew that our Lord could not be an effectual Priest unless he was also a sovereign King. Therefore he spoke of him accomplishing his work and being exalted as **'a priest upon his throne'** (Zech. 6:13). Here the apostle Paul plainly shows us that Zechariah's prophecy was accomplished. Both the prophets of the Old Testament and the apostles of the New teach us that Christ's ability as our Saviour is vitally linked with his power as God's exalted King. Here the apostle assures us that Christ is indeed able to save unto the uttermost them that come unto God by him, with two blessed facts of the gospel.

1. The Lord Jesus Christ has put away sin by his one atoning sacrifice. 'This man', this divinely mysterious person, in all of his glorious Godhood and perfect manhood, has put away sin by one all-sufficient sacrifice. Our High Priest has accomplished what the priests of Israel and all the 'priests' of Rome could never accomplish. He took away sin! There is but one atoning High Priest. There was but one sacrifice for sin, and that sacrifice was offered only once.

2. Having perfectly accomplished our redemption, the Lord Jesus Christ was exalted to the throne of glory. The Priest sits upon his throne. Having power over all flesh, he gives eternal life, repentance and remission of sins to as many as the Father gave him. Our Surety sat down for ever in heaven. Jesus Christ stood in the sinner's place. The guilt of all his elect was imputed to him. God accounted him to be a sinner. As such, he could not enter heaven until he had washed that sin away in his own blood. Until those sins of his people were gone, our High Priest could not sit down in the holy place. But, blessed be his name, our Surety is freed from sin and so are we.

Glorious redemption

Read John 19:8–30

'Mercy and truth are met together; righteousness and peace have kissed each other.' Modern theologians seem to be bent upon making a mockery out of our Redeemer's sacrifice. They have made a substitute for substitution. Their doctrine appears to be that Jesus Christ did something or other which, somehow or other, was in some way or other connected with man's salvation. But David had a better vision of Christ's redeeming work. Looking through the types and shadows of the law, he saw the coming Lamb of God and sang of glorious redemption. He saw that the coming Redeemer King would be God's propitiatory sacrifice, showing his favour to his people. Before it ever took place, he declared the deliverance of the chosen seed.

Looking upon the merits of his coming Redeemer, David sang of the full forgiveness of sin: 'Thou hast forgiven the iniquity of thy people, thou has covered all their sin. Selah. Thou hast taken away all thy wrath: thou has turned thyself from the fierceness of thine anger.' Then he prophesied of the coming of Christ, declaring that his appearance would be the revelation of divine glory.

Never was the glory of God more fully revealed than in the substitutionary sacrifice of Immanuel at Mt Calvary. At the cross, David foresaw all the glorious attributes of God embracing one another to accomplish man's redemption. At the cross, God's love shines forth in undiminished glory, and his justice appears in blazing wrath! In putting away our sins by the sacrifice of his Son, God is as merciful as if he had never punished sin. And he is as true as if he had fulfilled every threat to the sinner. In mercy, God sent his Son to die in our place. In his love and pity he redeemed us. In truth, he fulfilled every threat of his holy law in the person of our Substitute. As a merciful God, he pitied us, but as a holy God, he could not but hate our transgressions; as a God of truth, he could not but fulfil his own threatening; as a God of justice, he must avenge himself for the offence against him. He gave Christ as a God of mercy and required satisfaction as a God of justice.

The effectual preacher

Read Luke 4:14–32

'The Lord hath anointed me to preach good tidings.' These words prophetically describe one great work of the Lord Jesus Christ: he was to come as a preacher. Not only is the eternal Son of God the author of the gospel and the subject of the gospel, he is the only effectual preacher of the gospel. He is 'the messenger of the covenant'. Through his incarnation and death, he created the gospel and it is he who effectually preaches the gospel.

Christ proclaimed the gospel through the prophets of the Old Testament, in anticipation of his atoning sacrifice. They were his mouthpieces. It was he who went and preached to Noah's disobedient generation, when the longsuffering of God waited while the ark was being prepared. When those holy men of old 'prophesied of the grace that should come', it was 'the Spirit of Christ within them' testifying 'beforehand the sufferings of Christ, and the glory that should follow'.

During his life upon the earth, our Lord proclaimed the gospel of the kingdom of God, of the love of the heavenly Father for his wayward child and of God's anointed King. It was Christ who condescended 'to seek and save that which was lost'. He went to the publicans and sinners, the dregs of society, and proclaimed God's redeeming mercy. Christ himself brought the good news of salvation to the Samaritans.

After his resurrection, it was Christ who commanded his disciples in all ages to proclaim the gospel to every creature, promising the power of his presence. It was Christ who poured out his Spirit on the Day of Pentecost, through the merits of his death and resurrection. It was Christ who preached the gospel to Saul of Tarsus. And every true preacher today speaks in Christ's name. Rather, Christ preaches through him as his ambassador. Every true gospel preacher can say with Paul, 'We pray you in Christ's stead, be ye reconciled to God.'

We preach, but Christ alone preaches effectually. He created the gospel, is the theme of the gospel, and in truth he is the one and only preacher of the gospel. He applies the gospel irresistibly by the Holy Spirit. When Christ preaches, salvation comes.

'Ephraim is joined to idols: let him alone'

Read Romans 11:22–36

More solemn words than these were never spoken. Prophet after prophet had been sent to Ephraim. Moses, Elijah, Elisha, all testified God's message to Ephraim. They were warned against their sin of idolatry and of God's sure judgement. But they would not hear. They despised God's servant and his message because at heart, they despised God. Finally, the Lord said to his prophet, 'Ephraim is joined to idols; let him alone.'

Exactly the same thing happened to the nation of Israel. They had the law and oracles of God, the prophets and the priesthood. Finally, God's own Son came among them. But they despised all. As Ephraim was glued in heart to his idols, Israel was joined to her rituals and traditions, and our Lord said, 'Let them alone: they be blind leaders of the blind' (Matt. 15:14). Judicially, God gave Ephraim and Israel up in reprobation. I fear that such judgement might come upon some of my own generation.

Perhaps you think that this does not take place with individuals. You have always heard that God is at the beck and call of the sinner. Read what God says in Proverbs 1:23–33. My friend, you must hear God when he speaks to you by the gospel, and hearken to his voice. I say, according to the Scriptures, if men continually harden themselves against the Word of God, they do but seal up their own reprobation. The day will come when, like Esau, you will seek repentance, but God will not grant it. You will call for mercy, but God will not show mercy. Continued rebellion against God's warnings of wrath, both by his servants and providence, continued disobedience to conscience, continued rejection of the tender wooings of the gospel are the things that bring about this awful curse: 'Let him alone!'

Once such condemnation is passed upon your soul, nothing will move your heart. The sermons of the preacher only serve to harden you. Conscience no longer speaks. Your destruction is sure! Therefore, I urge you, harden not your heart. Receive not the grace of God in vain.

'The fruits of Christ's death'

Read Psalm 68:17–35

'Verily, verily, I say unto you, except a corn of wheat fall into the ground and die, it abideth alone: but if it die, it bringeth forth much fruit.' Our Lord Jesus Christ is that 'grain of wheat' fallen into the ground. But as such he brings forth much fruit. It is not possible that his death could be in vain. Behold the abundance of fruit brought forth by the death of Christ.

1. Through the death of Christ the wrath of God was appeased for us (Rom. 3:25–26). It was not possible that God could accept us without the satisfaction of his justice for our sins. Now our Substitute has fully appeased that justice upon the cross. Justice cannot fall upon us, for it has fallen on our Surety.

2. The death of Christ silenced the law (Gal. 3:13). The law of God has no curse, no condemnation, no accusation against the believer. The curse of the law, being executed upon our Surety, can never speak against us.

3. If God is appeased and the law is cancelled, the removal of our guilt must necessarily follow (Eph. 1:7). In the court of heaven, we were declared innocent when the Son of God died for us. When the Holy Spirit gives us faith to trust the merits of Christ, he takes away the guilt of our own consciences.

4. Another fruit of our Saviour's death was the conquest of Satan (John 12:31). Sons of God, rejoice, the tempter's power is broken! The serpent's head is crushed! The accuser of our brethren is cast out! The strong man is bound, and his house spoiled!

5. Perfect sanctification is also a fruit of Christ's death (Titus 2:14; Eph. 5:25). Sanctification does not come by legal obedience. It is accomplished by the daily application of the Saviour's blood to our hearts. We are sure that it will be one day perfected in us (in heaven), because Christ died to secure it.

6. Heaven is the sure and final home of all those for whom Christ died (Rom. 5:17; 6:8; 8:23). Jesus Christ not only redeemed our souls, he redeemed our bodies as well. And he will not lose that which he purchased at so dear a price. He will bring all his ransomed ones home to glory!

'Eternal redemption'

Read Isaiah 54:1–17

'By his own blood he entered in once into the holy place, having obtained eternal redemption.' The death of Jesus Christ in the place of sinners was much more than a mere hopeful act on his part. Our Saviour did not die to make redemption a possibility for all of Adam's race. He died as the Substitute and Surety of his people and obtained eternal redemption for us. I want to share with you four blessed truths about our redemption by Christ.

1. Redemption by Christ was appointed by God in eternity. This was an act of loving sovereignty. God was not in any way obliged to redeem fallen sinners. And he had nothing to gain by doing so. Yet, by divine statute, our Lord was set up in eternity as 'the Lamb slain from the foundation of the world'. And, in the fulness of time, he was 'delivered by the determinate counsel and foreknowledge of God'. Before the world began, God gave his Son to die for the objects of his love. Christ agreed to bear our sins in his own body upon the tree.

2. Jesus Christ accomplished our redemption at Calvary. We have, by faith, been to Calvary and beheld the Son of God dying in our place. We hear the expiring Immanuel cry, 'It is finished!' And we know the great transaction is done. At that time our sins were put away; our souls were pardoned. Nothing could be added to it and nothing taken from it. It is the work of the God-man, and it is for ever.

3. God Almighty accepted our redemption by the blood of Christ. The resurrection of Christ and his ascension into heaven are proof positive that God has accepted the finished work of his Son as our Redeemer and accepted us in him. The exalted God-man declares that justice is satisfied and God is reconciled to all who are represented in him.

4. This redemption by Christ is effectually applied by the Holy Spirit. He graciously sprinkles our hearts with the blood of Christ and reconciles us to God. By faith we receive justification and the forgiveness of sin.

Christ our mighty Saviour

Read Isaiah 41:1–20

'He is able also to save them to the uttermost that come unto God by him, seeing he ever liveth to make intercession for them.' The one message of the Bible is salvation by the substitutionary work of Christ. Everywhere in the book of God we are told that men are perishing and all of Adam's fallen race are in desperate need of salvation. In many places we are taught that Christ Jesus is willing to save sinners. In this verse we read that he is able to save!

Here is one characteristic of God's elect: they all come to God by faith in Christ. If you will not come to God, trusting Christ alone, you cannot be saved. If you do come, with a true heart of faith, you cannot perish. This coming to God is a spiritual act. You do not come to God by walking the aisle of a church. It is an act of the heart, an act of faith. You must come to God through his appointed Mediator, Jesus Christ.

Moreover, the apostle assures us that all who come to God by faith in Christ will be perfectly saved. Christ Jesus is able to save sinners of the deepest dye. And mark this, my friend, he saves us to the uttermost! In spite of all our past sins, our present corruptions and Satan's temptations, Christ Jesus saves us to the uttermost. Though death, judgement and eternity lay before us, we are confident, for Christ saves to the uttermost. Let others speak, if they will, of degrees of salvation, we believe in a perfect salvation. Christ has set out to make his people perfect; and he will accomplish his purpose. This is the secret of our security. We fall, perhaps, seven times in a day, but Jesus Christ saves to the uttermost.

Now, child of God, here is the ability of our Saviour: 'Seeing he ever liveth to make intercession for them.' That very one who died to put away our sin sits as a priestly King upon the throne of glory, and pleads for our salvation. He pleads his perfect righteousness as our Representative and satisfying death as our Substitute, and God will not allow one of those for whom his Son pleads to perish.

Husbands and wives

Read 1 Corinthians 11:1–15

Today there is a great emphasis upon what is called freedom and liberation. Everyone wants to have his rights. Another way of phrasing it would be that everyone wants to have his way. Perhaps a word in season is needed. The spirit of this generation is contrary to the spirit of Christ. The worldling asserts his rights. The believer submits to the rights of others. The one place where the truthfulness or hypocrisy of our faith will be known is in the home.

It is the privilege and responsibility of a Christian wife to submit to her own husband. **'Wives, submit yourselves unto your own husbands, as unto the Lord.'** Wife, God has graciously given you a husband to love you and provide for you. He has given you a head, to whom you should delightfully submit. I trust that your husband loves Christ and his gospel. If so, I know that he loves you. He seeks only your good. Is it not reasonable that you should submit to him? His position is not that of a tyrant! But he is as much your head as Christ is the Head of the church. See to it then that you reverence and obey your husband, 'even as Sara obeyed Abraham calling him lord'. You may mark it down, any woman who is not in subjection to her husband is not in subjection to Christ.

Now, husband, if you desire the reverence and obedience of your wife, you must win it, just as Christ has won your reverence and obedience. Husbands must love their wives into subjection. **'Husbands, love your wives, even as Christ also loved the church, and gave himself for it.'** It is true, you must assume your position as the head of your home. But if you would have your wife to reverence you in her heart, you must win that reverence. You must love her, provide for her, protect her and tenderly nourish and cherish her. Give yourself for her good, even as Christ gave himself for your eternal good. It is not commanded that you should be willing to die for her, though that may be included. But you must give yourself for her.

It is easy for a woman to reverence a man who loves her and it is easy for a man to love a woman who reverences him.

Blessed forgiveness

Read Psalm 32:1–11

'**If we confess our sins, he is faithful and just to forgive us our sins, and to cleanse us from all unrighteousness.**' Any one sin, of the slightest degree, is enough to exclude us for ever from the presence of God in heaven and to drag us down into hell. But if we are united to Christ by faith we have no sin before God! When David realized this glorious grace, he exclaimed, 'Blessed is the man to whom the Lord will not impute sin!' How can we enjoy this blessed forgiveness?

John tells us that we must confess our sin – our repentance, faith and confession of sin do not accomplish our forgiveness. That cannot be. The judicial ground of our forgiveness is the shed blood of Christ alone! But until a man confesses his sin, he cannot receive the forgiveness accomplished at Calvary. Our hearts must be reconciled to God and that reconciliation is begun in confession. Our confession must be made in humble sincerity towards God, with faith in Christ's atoning sacrifice. You cannot mention every offence, but you dare not hide one. Confess that you are vile by nature, wicked in practice and evil in heart. Lie down as low as you can at the footstool of mercy. 'He that covereth his sins shall not prosper: but whoso confesseth and forsaketh them shall have mercy.'

God's forgiveness of such sinners is both faithful and just. God has promised to forgive repenting, believing sinners for Christ's sake. And he is faithful to his Word. But he can only forgive us in a way consistent with his justice. In holy justice God slew his Son as our Substitute. With that one sacrifice, justice is fully satisfied. And now, upon the ground of the finished work of Christ, the justice of God pleads as strongly as his mercy for our forgiveness!

Our forgiveness is complete! If we confess our sins, trusting the blood of Christ alone for cleansing, God will not impute iniquity to us. This is blessed forgiveness.

'Behold, a sower went forth to sow'

Read Matthew 13:1–23

The man who preaches the gospel is compared to a farmer who sows his fields with seed. We preach the gospel earnestly to all men, broadcasting the precious seed. But only when the gospel is received 'in an honest and good heart' does it bring forth fruit. In this parable of the sower our Lord tells us three things about all true believers:

1. The true believer *receives the Word in an honest and good heart*. No man's heart is honest by nature. It must be made honest by the grace of God. This is one of the first acts of divine grace in a man's soul: his heart is renewed, and made to see things in their true light (Ezek. 36:26; John 3:19–21). We see who God is, what sin is and what we are.

A good heart is a broken and contrite heart. In order for soil to be good and ready to receive seed, it must be broken by the plough. Even so, a good heart is one that has been broken by God the Holy Spirit. Until the heart is broken, it is unfit to receive the seed of the gospel. It must be broken by the conviction of sin, the severity of the law, the sight of a crucified Christ and the knowledge of divine love.

A good heart is one that has been made tender and soft. There the seed takes deep and permanent root.

2. The true believer not only receives the word, *he keeps it*. The gospel is kept in the heart of faith. Our Lord holds us and we go on holding him. True faith is persevering faith. True grace is enduring grace. When God prepares the heart and sows the seed, the plant cannot die (Heb. 3:6; 10:23, 38, 39).

3. The true believer *brings forth fruit*. He does not produce fruit, but brings it forth. The fruit is the produce of the Spirit of God. The fruit has not yet come to perfection, but it is real. Mark my words, there is no such thing as a fruitless believer. They all repent. They all believe. They all obey (John 15:5, 6, 16). They bring forth heart fruit (Gal. 5:22–23). They bring forth lip fruit (Heb. 13:15). And they bring forth life fruit (Rom. 6:14-16).

Life from the dead

Read John 11:25–44

What is the new birth? It is nothing less than a resurrection from the dead! Three blessed truths are set forth in this text, in which the children of God can read their experience.

1. You *were dead.* Spiritual death, like physical death, may be more manifest in one than it is in another. For example, Jairus' daughter looked almost as though she were still alive, but she was, in reality, just as dead as Lazarus who had been in the grave for four days. Many around us are morally upright, honest and good in the eyes of men, but spiritually they are just as dead as the harlot, the drunk and the blasphemer. All men are by nature dead in trespasses and sins. We died in our father, Adam. We are legally dead, born under the sentence of the law. Some are less corrupt than others. But all are utterly destitute of spiritual life. Sin brings forth death and death, sooner or later, brings forth corruption. The natural man's corrupt heart corrupts his entire being. And being dead, we were utterly helpless and impotent.

2. But here is the marvellous intervention of divine grace: you *have been quickened.* God has, by almighty power, given you life from the dead! This is the new birth. It is not a decision of man's free will. It is not a co-operative effort on the part of God and man together. It is a resurrection to life, accomplished by the life-giving voice of the Son of God! (John 5:21, 24, 25.) God Almighty sovereignly interposes his love, grace and mercy to give life to dead sinners!

3. Now, children of God, you *are alive!* We were dead, but now we are alive. And we owe it all to the manifold grace of our triune God. Dwell no longer in the graveyard of sin. No longer be held in bondage by the fear of the law. Speak to God as a living child to his living Father. Are we alive? Then we are one with Christ! Let us, as living men who were dead, live to love and glorify our Saviour.

How does a sinner meet the doctrine of election?

Read Ephesians 1:1–14

Election is a doctrine plainly taught in the Bible. It is not possible for a man to read the Word of God and, with a sincere conscience, deny that election is true. Nor can a man, familiar with the Scriptures, in honesty deny that God's election of his people in Christ is both personal and particular, eternal and immutable. We therefore preach this blessed truth of God without apology or hesitation.

But Satan and the ministers of Satan turn the truth of God into a lie. In dealing with men, I have on occasion met poor souls who desperately felt their need of Christ and his righteousness. But they stumbled over the doctrine of election, thinking, 'If I am not elect, I cannot believe; and I have no reason to suppose that I am elect. Therefore, I dare not trust Christ and confess him.' Who are you, and who am I, to suppose that we can thus know the mind of God?

In our text a poor, sinful, idolatrous Gentile came to Christ in desperate need of mercy. The Lord confronted her with the doctrine of sovereign election: 'I am not sent but unto the lost sheep of the house of Israel.' But this poor soul knew that she could not obtain the mercy she desired from anyone except the Lord Jesus Christ, so she pressed her case before him. If she did not find mercy here, she would never find mercy. What could she lose by throwing herself upon him?

Do you feel the burden of sin pressing you down? Is your case so great, your misery so vexing that you know no one can help you but Christ? Like Job resolve to wait for him to show mercy, saying, 'Though he slay me, yet will I trust him.' Like Jacob cry, 'I will not let thee go except thou bless me.'

This is great faith. And it will always obtain the blessing. The question is not 'Am I elect?' It is 'Do I believe?' Feeling your great need of Christ and believing that he is able to show mercy, you will have mercy – election notwithstanding. Then, having obtained mercy, look back to God's electing love, and say, 'Blessed be God.'

'Lest the cross of Christ should be made of none effect'

Read Galatians 2:1–21

Whenever believers come to consider any doctrine, we should always ask three questions:'Is this doctrine plainly stated in the Word of God? Does this doctrine glorify God? Will this doctrine give man room and cause to boast before God?' You can be sure of this: any doctrine taught in the Word of God will both glorify God and remove all ground of boasting from man. God has determined 'that no flesh should glory in his presence ... That according as it is written, He that glorieth, let him glory in the Lord' (1 Cor. 1:29–31).

On that basis alone, the theory of universal redemption, the doctrine which says Christ died for and made an atonement for the sins of all men, as much so for those who perish under the wrath of God as for those who are saved, must be rejected as heresy. This doctrine makes the cross of Christ of none effect and declares that the determining factor in man's salvation is not the work of Christ but rather the free will of man! Such a doctrine as this must be exposed and denounced for what it is, the most hideous doctrine that has ever been perpetrated in the world. It is more harmful to the souls of men than any other. It treads under foot the Son of God, counts the blood of the covenant a useless thing and does despite to the Spirit of grace.

I know that I am using strong language, but where the souls of men and the glory of God are at stake there is no room for pretty words and accommodating speech. Either the Lord Jesus Christ effectually accomplished the redemption of those people for whom he died, or he failed in his work! If a building contractor makes a bid and agrees to build a specifically designed building within a certain amount of time for a specified price, but only gets the building 90% complete, he is a failure. The part that he did may look beautiful, but if someone else has to finish the job, the original contractor is a failure. He must hang his head in shameful reproach and forfeit all honour and reward. My friend, the Lord Jesus Christ is no failure! 'He shall see of the travail of his soul, and shall be satisfied' (Isa. 53:11).

Can a saved person ever be lost?

Read Psalm 89:1–37

Can a saved person ever be lost? Our Lord Jesus Christ emphatically answers that question for us. Listen to what he says in John 10:27–30: **'My sheep hear my voice, and I know them, and they follow me: and I give unto them eternal life; and they shall never perish, neither shall any man pluck them out of my hand. My Father which gave them me, is greater than all; and no man is able to pluck them out of my Father's hand. I and my Father are one.'** Our Lord himself has spoken it, and it is true – not one of his own will ever perish! Any person who is truly saved, born again by almighty grace, a true believer in the Lord Jesus Christ, is eternally secure in the hands of Christ.

To be sure, there are many who make a profession of faith in Christ, reform their lives and to all outward appearance seem to be saved people that do fall from grace and perish. But the apostle John tells us that those who fall away, forsake the gospel and perish in their sins were never truly saved. He says in 1 John 2:19, 'They went out from us, but they were not of us: for if they had been of us, they would no doubt have continued with us: but they went out, that they might be made manifest that they were not all of us.' Any man who leaves Christ never truly knew Christ.

I readily grant that if our salvation were in any measure dependent upon us, we would most certainly be lost and without hope. But salvation is entirely the work of God's grace and power in Christ. And since it is the work of God, it cannot be destroyed. Solomon said, 'I know that whatsoever God doeth, it shall be done for ever; nothing can be put to it, nor anything taken from it: and God doeth it, that men may fear before him' (Eccles. 3:14). Paul said, 'He which hath begun a good work in you will perform it until the day of Jesus Christ' (Phil. 1:6).

'They shall not depart from me'

Read Isaiah 43:1–13

Are you one of the Lord's sheep? Are you a true believer? Have you heard the Saviour's voice calling you to himself? Has he given you eternal life? Do you follow him in true faith? If so, you are one of his chosen, redeemed, saved sheep. You have eternal life. And you will never perish. There are many things to give us comfort and confidence regarding the security of our salvation in Christ. The purpose of God secures the salvation of all his elect. He said, 'I will be their God, and they shall be my people.' If one of the chosen number could be lost, God's eternal purpose would be overturned. The promise of God demands our security in Christ. He said, 'I will never leave thee, nor forsake thee.' The blood of Christ requires the eternal salvation of all his redeemed ones. He said, 'I am come that they might have life, and that they might have it more abundantly. I am the Good Shepherd: the Good Shepherd giveth his life for the sheep.' But if even one of those sheep for which he died, which he purchased with his own blood, perishes at last, then his blood would be shed in vain and that cannot be! The satisfaction of Christ demands that all his people be preserved unto eternal glory. If one of those for whom he suffered and died were to perish at last, he could not be satisfied. His cross would be discovered a miscarriage. But that cannot be. It is written: 'He shall see of the travail of his soul, and shall be satisfied.' The work of the Holy Spirit secures the everlasting preservation of every true believer. We are 'sealed (or preserved) with that Holy Spirit of promise, which is the earnest of our inheritance until the redemption of the purchased possession, unto the praise of his glory.'

This is our assurance and security in Christ. We do not in any way trust in ourselves. But we do trust the Lord our God. The faithfulness of God, the blood of Christ, the intercession of Christ and the power of the Holy Spirit assure us that none of Christ's sheep will ever perish.

'The atonement'

Read Mark 15:6–39

There is much confusion in our day about the redemptive work of our Lord Jesus Christ. There are many who teach that Christ actually redeemed some of those who are finally lost in hell! I have heard preachers make some shocking statements about the redemptive work of Christ. I heard one man say that 'Christ died just as much for Judas as he did for Paul.' Another one blasphemously declared that 'The blood of Christ will be fuel for the flames of hell.' The popular idea of redemption is that though Christ has died to satisfy the wrath and justice of God against sin, and though he has paid the lawful price for the redemption of sinners, some of those who were redeemed by Christ will, after all, be required to suffer for their sins. If such a notion is accepted, then it must be concluded that the justice of God has fallen to the ground, the God of heaven has ceased to be just. If my debt has been paid by Christ, God cannot in justice demand payment from me.

> Payment God cannot twice demand,
> First at my bleeding Surety's hand,
> Then again at mine!

If so much as one soul for whom Christ shed his blood at Calvary perishes in hell, then the justice of God is destroyed. And if Christ died to redeem some men who are not ultimately saved, then he can never see of the travail of his soul and be satisfied, as the Scriptures declare he will. How can he be satisfied while some of those for whom he died are in hell? Once more, if even one sinner for whom Christ shed his blood in death perishes in hell, then it must be concluded that the blood of Christ was shed in vain. Such blasphemous absurdities as these cannot be tolerated by a believing heart. They rob Christ of his redemptive glory, rob God of his justice and rob sinners of all real hope.

'The atonement'

Read Luke 23:32–47

Because there is much confusion about the redemptive work of the Lord Jesus Christ, I want to be very plain and clear. The Bible nowhere teaches, nor does it anywhere imply that our Lord Jesus Christ died to redeem and save every person in the world. I hold it to be an authoritative doctrine, consistent with all common sense and most plainly revealed in Holy Scripture, that whatever Christ has redeemed, Christ will have. This simple foundation truth must be well established in our hearts: whatever the Lord Jesus Christ has redeemed he must have. Otherwise his redemptive work at Calvary would be a failure.

It is repugnant to reason and contrary to the plainest statements of Holy Scripture to assert that Christ has died to purchase what he will never possess. It is nothing less than blasphemy to declare, as many do, that the intention of our Saviour's death can be frustrated. I am sure that all who weigh the matter and honestly consider it, must see that the intention of Christ in his death must be fulfilled and that the design of God, whatever that may be, must be carried out. I believe that the efficacy of Christ's atonement is just as great as God meant that it should be, and that what Christ has redeemed is precisely what he meant to redeem and exactly what the Father had decreed he should redeem. Therefore I cannot, for one moment, give any credence whatever to that doctrine which tells us that all men are redeemed. The Lord Jesus Christ did not die to redeem those men and women who ultimately perish in hell!

Our Lord declares that he is 'the Good Shepherd: the Good Shepherd giveth his life for the sheep'. He did not give his life for those who are not his sheep. It is written: 'He shall see of the travail of his soul, and shall be satisfied.' That is to say, all of those for whom he suffered and whom he died to redeem will be with him in glory. Not one of his redeemed ones will perish.

'A broken spirit'

Read Job 40:1–5; 42:1–6

I am convinced that no man has ever experienced the grace of God in salvation until his heart is thoroughly broken before a holy God as he has revealed himself in the Lord Jesus Christ. If ever a man finds out who he is, who God is, who the Lord Jesus Christ is and what he has done for sinners – if a man ever really learns these things, he will be a broken man. When Job stood in the presence of his three miserable friends, he vindicated himself and even cursed his day. He said, 'Why did I not perish from the womb? Why did I not give up the ghost when I came out of the belly?' But when he stood in the presence of God, he was a broken man and he spoke as a broken man. He saw himself in all the hideousness of his sin and he saw God in all the holiness of his majesty. Then he said, 'Behold, I am vile.' 'I have heard of thee by the hearing of the ear: but now mine eye seeth thee. Wherefore I abhor myself, and repent in dust and ashes' (Job 40:4; 42:5–6). There is no pride and egotism here, no haughtiness, no self-vindication. Once Job had seen the Lord, he was broken. He loathed himself and blamed himself. Once Job had seen the Lord, he honoured God and vindicated him. The truly broken heart will always vindicate God, no matter the cost.

This brokenness can only be produced in our stubbornly sinful hearts by a saving revelation of Christ in our hearts. Brokenness is found at the cross. The Lord God declares that when he pours upon the hearts of his elect the Spirit of grace, then 'They shall look upon me whom they have pierced, and they shall mourn for him, as one mourneth for his only son, and shall be in bitterness for him, as one that is in bitterness for his firstborn' (Zech. 12:10). Have you been to the cross? Have you had the crucified Christ revealed in your heart? Has your heart been broken by the knowledge of the Lord? O Lord, evermore break our hearts before thee! Amen.

'That I may know him'

Read Ephesians 3:1–21

A true spiritual knowledge of Christ will be a *personal* knowledge. I cannot know Christ through another person's acquaintance with him. No, I must know him myself. I must know him by my own heart's personal experience.

It will be an *intelligent* knowledge. I must know him, not by visions and dreams, but as the Word reveals him. I must know his natures, divine and human. I must know his offices, his attributes, his works, his shame and his glory. I must meditate upon him until I 'comprehend with all saints what is the breadth, and length, and depth, and height; and ... know the love of Christ, which passeth knowledge' (Eph. 3:18–19).

It will be an *affectionate* knowledge of him. Indeed, if I know Christ at all, I must love him. An ounce of heart knowledge is worth a ton of head learning.

Our knowledge of Christ will be a *satisfying* knowledge. When I know my Saviour, my mind will be full to the brim, I shall feel that I have that for which my soul pants.

At the same time, it will be an *exciting* knowledge. The more I know of my Beloved, the more I shall want to know of him. The more I have, the more I shall want. Like the miser's money, my treasure in Christ will make me covet more of him.

To conclude, the knowledge of the Lord Jesus Christ will be a most *happy* knowledge. It is so elevating that it will carry me up above my trials and doubts and sorrows. Such knowledge will cause me to rise up above my earthly cares. It will cover me with the immortality of the ever-living Saviour. It will strengthen me with his eternal joy. Come, my soul, let me count everything but loss for the excellency of the knowledge of Christ Jesus my Lord.

'His great love'

Read 1 John 4:1–21

Everyone talks about the love of God. We all know those scriptures that tell us 'God is love' (1 John 4:8). 'God so loved the world that he gave his only begotten Son, that whosoever believeth in him should not perish, but have everlasting life' (John 3:16). 'God commendeth his love toward us, in that, while we were yet sinners, Christ died for us' (Rom. 5:8). 'Hereby perceive we the love of God, because he laid down his life for us' (1 John 3:16). Love is not a fickle, sentimental passion in God, like it is with us. It is not an emotion of his heart, but an attribute of his nature. 'God is love!' Love is an essential part of God's character. I rejoice to declare to men that the God of heaven is love. He is a God who delights to show love, mercy and grace to men. In the sacrificial death of the Lord Jesus Christ at Calvary, as the sinner's Substitute, the infinite, magnanimous love of God for his people is most clearly revealed. John wrote, 'In this was manifested the love of God toward us, because that God sent his only begotten Son into the world, that we might live through him. Herein is love, not that we loved God, but that he loved us, and sent his Son to be the propitiation for our sins' (1 John 4:9–10). God's love towards us is free, sovereign and gracious. We did not love him, but he loved us. Our love for God is preceded by and caused by his love for us. 'We love him, because he first loved us' (1 John 4:19). God so loved us that he willingly sacrificed the Lord Jesus Christ, his own well-beloved Son, to satisfy his own justice in our place and redeem us. Who can comprehend, or explain, the love of God for us?

> Could we with ink the oceans fill,
> And were the skies of parchment made,
> Were every stalk on earth a quill,
> And every man a scribe by trade:
> To write the love of God above
> Would drain the oceans dry,
> Nor could the scroll contain the whole,
> Though stretched from sky to sky!

'What manner of love'

Read John 15:1–17

I cannot begin to explain the love of God. But I do want to share with you four facts about the love of God revealed in Holy Scripture.

1. The love of God is *without beginning*. There never was a time when God began to love his people. Like God himself, his love for us is eternal. He says, 'Yea, I have loved thee with an everlasting love' (Jer. 31:3). In eternal love he chose his own elect in Christ, before the world was. In love, he predestinated us unto the adoption of children in Christ. Those whom God loves today he has loved always and will love always.

2. The love of God is *without measure*. It would be far easier to measure the waters of the ocean in a tea cup than to measure the love of God in our puny brains and hearts. Paul tells us that the height and depth and length and breadth of the love of God in Christ pass all knowledge.

3. The love of God is *without change*. God's love is perfect. It never changes. He does not love today and hate tomorrow. Our love to him varies from day to day, but his love towards us knows no variation. If you are truly one of his own, there is nothing you can do that will cause him to cease loving you, or even to love you less. This immutable, unchanging love is a love such as we might expect from our God.

4. The love of God is *without end*. He will never cease to cherish his own. Children of God, take comfort in this word of grace today: 'God is love.' The love of God for us is without beginning, without measure, without change and without end.

'No condemnation'

Read Romans 8:1–31

Come, my soul, meditate on this. God declares that you are entirely free from condemnation. Believing in the Lord Jesus Christ, you are actually and effectually cleared from all guilt. Your prison doors are opened. You no longer wear the chains of a slave. You are delivered now from the bondage of the law. Free! Free! Free! Thank God, I am free at last! Free from the law! Free from sin! Free from death! Free from judgement! The Saviour's blood has procured your full discharge. Now you have a right to approach your Father's throne. There are no flames of vengeance to frighten you now. There is no fiery sword of judgement to threaten you now. Justice cannot strike the innocent. Once you were unable to see the Father's face, but now you see it clearly. Once you could not speak to him, but now you come before his throne and speak to him in prayer with the boldness of a son. Once the fear of hell was upon you, but now you no longer fear the dreadful pit. How can there be any punishment for the guiltless? He who believes is not condemned and cannot be punished.

And more, all of those privileges that you might have enjoyed if you had never sinned are now yours, because you are justified. All the blessings which you would have had if you had kept the law, and many more, are now yours, because Christ has kept the law in your place. All the love and acceptance that perfect obedience could have obtained from God belong to you, because Christ was perfectly obedient in your behalf. God has imputed the merits of his own Son to your account, that you might be exceedingly rich through him, who for your sake became exceedingly poor.

Oh, what grace the Lord has bestowed upon his people in Christ! What a great debt of love and gratitude believing souls owe to the Son of God! Let these words of grace comfort your soul and cheer your heart today: 'There is therefore now no condemnation to them which are in Christ Jesus.'

'Earthen vessels'

Read Romans 7:1–25

We must all face the fact that flesh is flesh. Though all who believe are saved by the grace of God, washed in the blood and clothed in the righteousness of Christ, so long as we are in this world, we are just earthen vessels. When Paul talks about that salvation which brings into our hearts 'the light of the knowledge of the glory of God in the face of Jesus Christ', he reminds us that **'We have this treasure in earthen vessels, that the excellency of the power may be of God, and not of us'** (2 Cor. 4:6-7).

The more we think of the utter weakness of our flesh, the more thankful we are that our security and preservation in Christ are not dependent upon our own weak nature, but upon God's constant power and sustaining grace. We are so feeble that if the matter were left in our hands, we should all fall and perish very soon. Many cannot endure the teachings of Holy Scripture regarding this matter of our security and preservation in Christ, because it makes the whole of salvation a work of divine grace, from beginning to end. It allows no room for human merit and works.

We do not pretend to live above sin. Sin is a sadly common fact of life. You will never find one of those men who lived and walked with God in the Bible bragging about his righteousness or his perfection. In fact, they all struggled with sin in their flesh. All of God's people are like Paul. We have two natures within us, two principles struggling for supremacy: the one is good, the other evil; the one is righteousness, the other sin; the one is spirit, the other flesh. If we could avoid it, we would never sin. We abhor our sin as an infinitely evil thing! We long for the day when we shall be totally free from sin. But, for now, we have the treasure of God's saving grace in these earthen vessels, so that the excellency, the greatness, the power and the glory of our salvation may be attributed to God and not to us.

'My grace is sufficient'

Read Psalm 73:1–28

The believer is like a man climbing up a hill. Occasionally he slips down, but his face is always set towards the summit. The unregenerate man is always going down, because his face is set in that direction. The believer is like a man on a ship. He may slip and fall many times on the deck, but he never jumps overboard. Our judgements may at times be wrong, like those of the bewitched Galatians (3:1). Our affections may cool like those of the church at Ephesus (Rev. 2:4). Grace may at times seem to be lost to a child of God, but it never is really lost. The people of God, like the church in the Song of Solomon, may become slothful and negligent, but their hearts awake (5:2). The sun is sometimes eclipsed, but it regains its splendour. The trees lose all their fruit and leaves in the winter, but they have fresh buds in the spring. Israel may flee before her enemies at times, but she enters the land of promise triumphantly when her journey is over. So too, the true believer falls many times, but the Lord raises him up and he will finally enter into heaven triumphantly, through the blood, the righteousness and the grace of Christ. It is utterly unthinkable that one of God's elect should fail to enter into eternal glory. Like Jonah, we all may, at times, flee from the will of God, but grace will pursue us, preserve us and cause our hearts to return to him who loved us and gave himself for us.

I am like you, a man struggling with sin. At times my sinful thoughts and my sinful deeds almost cause me to despair. But I am reminded by the gospel and by the Spirit of God that his grace is sufficient, even for me. My salvation and my acceptance with God are not in myself, but in my Substitute. Like you, I am just an earthen vessel, but Christ is the Lord our Righteousness. He is all my salvation, all my desire and all assurance. I hang all my hope upon him. Do you?

'A broken heart'

Read Matthew 5:1–12

A broken heart, a contrite spirit and a subdued will are rare things in our day. This is the day of human rights, human dignity and human sovereignty. Self-esteem, self-worth and self-promotion are the cry of the day. All men are demanding what they call 'their rights'. Every man does that which is right in his own eyes. All men by nature are exceedingly proud, selfish people. Preachers today, knowing man's natural pride, have capitalized upon it. They have developed a flesh-pleasing theology of pride. Our forefathers exalted the dignity, the majesty and the supremacy of the eternal God. But the smooth-tongued prophets of deceit in our day have set themselves to exalt the dignity, majesty and supremacy of man. It seems that religion today is dedicated, not to the honour of God, but to the honour of man. Its purpose is to make man feel good about himself. Therefore we hear little about brokenness of heart, contrition of the soul and the subduing of man's will.

Of this one thing you may be sure: 'The sacrifices of God are [still] a broken spirit: a broken and a contrite heart, O God, thou wilt not despise' (Ps. 51: 17). The Lord God declares, 'To this man will I look, even to him that is poor and of a contrite spirit, and trembleth at my word' (Isa. 66:2). I am convinced that God will have broken material with which to build his kingdom. Sooner or later, the Lord God will bring us to nothingness before his presence, or we shall never experience his salvation. God's people, all of God's people, are a broken people.

That person who is saved by the grace of God has seen himself and his sin in the light of the crucified Christ and his heart is broken by what he sees (Zech. 12:10). Such a person takes sides with God against himself (Ps. 51:4). Justifying God in his own condemnation, he is justified by God and freed from all condemnation.

'God so loved the world'

Read Romans 1:17–2:4

You know John 3:16 by memory. You learned it as a small child. It was probably the first text of Holy Scripture that you can remember hearing: **'For God so loved the world, that he gave his only begotten Son, that whosoever believeth in him should not perish, but have everlasting life.'** Everyone knows those words by memory, but do you know the meaning of those precious words? I am afraid that very few people do.

'God so loved the world.' Our Lord does not tell us how much God loved the world. He leaves it for our hearts to consider reverently. He simply says, 'so', 'God *so* loved'. God would have us not only to believe in the reality of his love, but also to admire the greatness and magnitude of his love. The love of God, like God himself, is infinite.

The word 'world' describes the character of those men and women who are the objects of God's infinite love. Our Lord is not telling us that God loves every person in the world. We know that is not true, because God himself said that he hated Esau. The word 'world' refers to mankind in general, in all its corruption and misery. Our Lord is not talking about the extent of God's love. He is describing the character of those who are loved by God. God loves fallen, guilty, depraved sinners, scattered throughout the whole world. 'The whole world lieth in wickedness.' God is no respecter of persons. He does not love the Jews only, but Gentiles also. He does not love white men only, but black men also. His elect are found among men of every nation, kindred, tribe and tongue throughout the whole world. God might have poured out the vials of his wrath upon us, as he did upon the angels that fell. But no, he spared us! 'For God so loved the world!' Justice demanded our punishment. Holiness required the extermination of our race. But that must not be. 'For God so loved the world.' Let all men give praise to the eternal God. Were it not for his love, we should all be in hell.

'He gave his only begotten Son'

Read Romans 3:9–31

'God so loved the world that he gave his only begotten son.' In the eternal purpose of his love God gave his Son to be the sinner's Substitute and appointed him to make a sacrificial atonement for sin. Then, 'In the fulness of time God sent forth his Son, made of a woman, made under the law, to redeem them that were under the law.' At the appointed time Christ came to do that work which he and his Father had agreed upon in eternity. He is Immanuel, God in our nature, God come to save. Having lived in perfect righteousness as a man, perfectly fulfilling the law of God for his people, as our Representative, 'In due time Christ died for the ungodly.' He was made to be sin for us, that we might be made the righteousness of God in him. God gave his Son into the hands of his own law and justice, to make satisfaction for sin. God gave his Son up to die the cursed death of the cross, so that those sinners whom he loves with an everlasting love might never die. Here is the infinite magnitude of God's love for us: 'He gave his only begotten Son'!

  'That whosoever believeth in him should not perish, but have everlasting life.' What does John 3:16 tell us? It tells us that God loves sinners. It tells us that Christ died to redeem sinners. It tells us that God saves sinners. And it tells us that any sinner in all the world who believes on the Lord Jesus Christ will be saved by him. Christ did not die to give life to any who refuse to believe on him. But he did die for, and he does give life, eternal life, to every sinner who believes on him. Are you a sinner? Do you trust the Lord Jesus Christ? If you do, this day you have eternal life in him. And you will never perish. 'For God sent not his Son into the world to condemn the world; but that the world through him might be saved.' 'He that believeth on him is not condemned' (John 3:17–18).

'The gospel'

Read Romans 1:1–16

The gospel is not the mere historical fact that Jesus Christ, the Son of God, died at Calvary 2,000 years ago, was buried in the tomb of Joseph and rose again the third day. James tells us that the devils believe that and tremble. The gospel is the plain and biblical declaration of how Christ died for our sins according to the Scriptures (1 Corinthians 15:3).

How did Christ die? What did Christ accomplish in his death? What do the Scriptures teach us about the death of our Lord Jesus Christ?

First, the Lord Jesus Christ *voluntarily* laid down his life for us: 'I am the good shepherd: the good shepherd giveth his life for the sheep' (John 10:11). 'I lay down my life, that I might take it again. No man taketh it from me, but I lay it down of myself. I have power to lay it down, and I have power to take it again' (John 10:17–18). Our Lord did not die as the helpless victim of circumstances. He was born at Bethlehem for the express purpose of laying down his life at Calvary in the place of his people. Secondly, the Son of God died *vicariously* in the place of his people. That is to say, he died as a real Substitute in the place of God's elect: 'He hath made him to be sin for us, ... that we might be made the righteousness of God in him' (2 Corinthians 5:21). 'For the transgression of my people was he stricken' (Isaiah 53:8). Christ did not die for every person in the world, hoping to save everybody. The Bible nowhere says that he did. Christ died for every sinner in the world who believes on him and his death secured their faith in him. He died as a Substitute for God's elect.

Thirdly, the Lord Jesus Christ died *victoriously*, accomplishing the redemption of his people. He did not try to redeem; he did redeem. He did not make it possible for all men to be redeemed; he actually 'obtained eternal redemption for us' (Heb. 9:12). He did not make it possible for sin to be put away; he 'put away sin by the sacrifice of himself' (Heb. 9:26). When he cried, 'It is finished' redemption's work was done. All the people of God were justified and pardoned by his victorious death. His atoning sacrifice was a real atonement for sin.

'Train up a child'

Read 1 Samuel 2:1–21

If you would train your children well, you must train them in the way they *should* go, not in the way they *would* go. Our sons and daughters are born with a decided bias towards evil. If we let them choose their way, they are sure to choose wrong (Prov. 22:15; 29:15). If we would be wise, we must not leave a child to the guidance of his own will.

Train your children with love, patience and tenderness. I do not mean that you should spoil your children. But I do mean that you should let them know that you love them. Love is the secret to proper training. Nothing will compensate for the absence of love and tenderness. Anger and harshness will frighten a child, but they will not persuade the child that you are right. If your children see you often out of temper, they will soon cease to respect you.

Train your children to be industrious and responsible in life. Life is not all fun and games. Children need to be taught responsibility, the earlier the better.

Train your children with loving, but firm discipline. Determine to make your child obey you. It may cost you much trouble and cost him many tears, but it will be best for the child (Prov. 13:24; 19:18; 22:15; 23:13–14; 29:15–17; Heb. 12:5–11). Be firm and earnest in disciplining your children. Do not punish them rashly, or in anger. Do not use abusive words with them. Such things only create hostility. A loving, but firm use of the rod is essential to the proper training or children.

Again, train your children with a primary concern for their souls. If you love your children, think of their souls. In every step you take regarding them, in every plan you make for them, and in every decision you make which concerns them, ask yourself one question: 'How will this affect my child's soul?'

Once more, train your children with the firm persuasion that much depends on you. You cannot convert your children. But you are the one who moulds your children's character. And you do it, for better or for worse, in their earliest years.

'By his grace'

Read Psalm 106:1–12, 43–48

Our salvation is not according to our merits in its commence-
ment, in its continuance, or in its consummation. 'For by grace
are ye saved through faith; and that not of yourselves: it is the gift
of God: not of works, lest any man should boast.'

The sovereign love and unmerited grace of God are the cause
of our salvation. Since his love and grace are unchangeable, their
effect must be unchangeable. That is to say, God constantly
communicates his love and grace to every believer. Once his love
is revealed and his grace bestowed upon the heart, he never takes
them away: 'For the gifts and calling of God are without
repentance.' God was not moved to bestow his grace upon us by
anything which he saw meritorious or attractive in us. And the
absence of everything good in us will not cause God to withdraw
the grace he has bestowed. When he first bestowed grace upon
us, the Lord knew that we were totally depraved and sinful. He
knew that we were full of evil and void of good. And though,
since our conversion, we have all been guilty of ingratitude,
unfaithfulness and sin of every kind, these things do not provoke
the Lord our God to change his mind and withdraw his
sustaining grace. He knew what we would be before he saved us.
He chastens us because of our sin, like the loving Father he is, but
he never withdraws his love. If he had not intended, from the
beginning, to bear with our sin in longsuffering and patience and
to forgive our sin for Christ's sake, he would never have saved us
and called us in the first place.

This is what I am saying: the cause of our salvation is entirely in
God. His electing love, redeeming grace and saving power were
given to us by an act of his sovereign goodness, without any
consideration of what we were or might become. There was
nothing in us to attract his grace. And there is nothing in any true
believer's heart or conduct which can ever cause the Lord our
God to alter his purpose of grace and withdraw his love from us.

'The Lord reigneth!'

Read Psalm 93:1–5; 97:1–12

I worship the one true and living God; I worship the God who is sovereign. I worship that God who reveals himself in the pages of Holy Scripture. Who is your God? Do you worship the true and living God or do you worship some religious idol that men call god? He who is God is totally sovereign in all things!

What do we mean when we declare that God is sovereign? Why, we mean that God is God. We mean that God is in control, ruling and governing all things exactly according to his own eternal intention. To declare that God is sovereign is to declare he is almighty, the possessor of all power in heaven and earth, so that none can defeat his counsels, thwart his purpose, or resist his will (Ps. 115:3). To say that God is sovereign is to declare that he is 'the governor among the nations' (Ps. 22:28). He raises up kings and kingdoms, overturns kings and kingdoms and determines the course and destiny of all things as it pleases him. To declare that God is sovereign is to declare that he is the 'only potentate, the King of kings, and Lord of lords' (1 Tim. 6:15). This, my friend, is the God of the Bible. This is the one true and living God of heaven and earth.

I bow to a sovereign God. I dare not argue with him, dispute his claims, or try to bargain with him. I bow before his throne as the undisputed, sovereign King of the universe. I worship a sovereign God. I dare not think of him lightly or take his name in vain. I trust my soul into the hands of a sovereign God. I hope in the mercy of a sovereign God. My God is God. Is he your God?

'A god that cannot save'

Read Isaiah 45:20 – 46:13

Anyone who reads the Bible, with the slightest bit of interest, must see that the god of modern religion does not even faintly resemble that God who reveals himself in Holy Scripture. The god of this generation is moved by sentiment, emotion and impulse. The God of heaven acts according to justice and the principles of holiness and righteousness. 'Justice and judgement are the habitation of thy throne' (Ps. 89:14). The god of this generation has a will, a purpose and a desire, but his will is defeated both by men and Satan. He desires, but he cannot accomplish his desire. He wills, but he cannot perform his will. He purposes, but he cannot do what he has purposed. The God of the Bible works all things according to the counsel of his own will and purpose. This is what God says about himself: 'I am God, and there is none else; I am God, and there is none like me, declaring the end from the beginning, and from ancient times the things that are not yet done, saying, My counsel shall stand, and I will do all my pleasure' (Isa. 46:9–10). Today's Jesus offers eternal life to as many as will let him save them. The Christ of the Bible gives eternal life to as many as the Father has given him (John 17:2). Today's god has a wonderful plan for your life, if you will just fulfil the necessary requirements. The one true and living God works in you both to will and to do according to his good pleasure (Phil. 2:13; Rom. 8:28). The god of modern-day fundamentalism has provided a remedy for sin, and it will work if only the sinner will co-operate with God. The living God has provided a perfect righteousness and an effectual atonement for all of his elect through the righteous obedience and substitutionary death of his Son at Calvary (Heb. 10:11–14).

This is what I am saying: the god of modern religion is a puny pigmy. He is an idol. The God of the Bible is great and glorious. He is the only true God.

'Acquaint now thyself with God'

Read Daniel 4:1–37

Who is God? All true saving faith must begin with a real, spiritual heart knowledge of the one true and living God. Our Lord Jesus Christ said, 'This is life eternal, that they might know thee the only true God, and Jesus Christ, whom thou hast sent' (John 17:3). It is not possible for a person to be saved until he knows God as he has revealed himself in Holy Scripture. If you are interested in your own soul, it would be most wise to consider this question: who is God? And the only place where you can find the answer to that question is in Holy Scripture.

On one occasion Martin Luther, the great German Reformer, said to Erasmus, 'Your thoughts of God are too human.' It was a very solemn accusation, but it was true. Our Lord said to the religious leaders of his day, 'Ye neither know me, nor my Father' (John 8:19). And I lay this charge against the preachers and religious leaders of our day: they do not know the God of the Bible. Their thoughts of God are too human. This is the charge which God himself brings against this religious generation: 'Thou thoughtest that I was altogether such an one as thyself' (Ps. 50:21).

I am not interested in knowing the god of this day, the god who is popular in the religious world. I want to know the one true and living God, the God of Abraham, Isaac and Jacob. 'My soul panteth for the living God,' the God and Father of our Lord Jesus Christ. The god of this day no more resembles the one true and living God than a flickering candle resembles the glory of the noonday sun. The god with whom most men are familiar is a weak, pathetic, frustrated and defeated figment of man's imagination. He was born and came forth from the hearts of evil men.

'I will do all my pleasure'

Read Romans 9:10–26

The God of heaven is infinitely, totally and absolutely sovereign. It is written, 'Our God is in the heavens: he hath done whatsoever he hath pleased' (Ps. 115:3). 'Whatsoever the Lord pleased, that did he in heaven, and in earth, in the seas, and in all deep places' (Ps. 135:6).

My friends, there is no possible alternative between a sovereign, omnipotent, supreme God, who does what he will, when he will, with whom he will and in the way he will, and no god at all. You cannot have a frustrated, defeated god. If there is any power that can resist him, change him, or defeat him, he is not god. Either God is sovereign, supreme and almighty, or there is no god. A god who has to give an account of what he thinks, what he purposes, or what he does is no god at all. Therefore it must be concluded, the god of modern, religious fundamentalism is no god at all. He is the idolatrous figment of man's imagination. Those who preach this weak, defeated, frustrated god are false prophets. And those who worship him are lost. Their religion is idolatry. Someone said, 'A god whose will can be successfully resisted, a god whose designs can be defeated or frustrated, a god whose purpose or counsel depends in any way on the help or co-operation of any creature, has no claim to deity. Instead of being an object of your worship, he merits nothing but your contempt.'

I worship God on the throne. I believe and trust God on the throne. I preach God on the throne. The Lord our God is totally sovereign. He is sovereign in creation, sovereign in providence and sovereign in salvation. He says, 'I will have mercy on whom I will have mercy, and I will have compassion on whom I will have compassion. So then it is not of him that willeth, nor of him that runneth, but of God that showeth mercy' (Rom. 9:15–16).

'The Lord is great ... above all gods!'

Read Psalm 115:1–18

Most people today do not know who God is. The modern idea that religious people have about God is that he is an old man, sitting in a rocking chair somewhere above the earth, weak, frustrated and defeated, because he is not able to accomplish his purposes. The preachers and religious leaders of our day have persuaded this generation that God is good but not powerful, God is gracious but not great, God is merciful but not majestic. The god of the twentieth century has a purpose, he has a will, he has a plan, but his hands are tied. Man, they say, will not let God have his way. Satan, they tell us, has God's creation in chaos. Such a god as this is not worthy of worship, trust, reverence and submission. Such a god as this merits nothing but man's contempt. Such a god as this is no god at all. He is but the idolatrous figment of man's depraved imagination.

My God is not at all like that. My God is worthy of worship. My God merits my trust, confidence, reverence and submission. You see, my God truly is God. He is the God of the Bible. The God whom I worship, trust and serve is an absolute sovereign. When I say that God is sovereign, I am simply saying that God does what he will, when he will, with whom he will, in the way he will. He does not ask anyone's permission to act. He simply does as he pleases. And he does not stand before anyone in judgement to give an account of his actions. He is God, 'who liveth for ever, whose dominion is an everlasting dominion, and his kingdom is from generation to generation: and all the inhabitants of the earth are reputed as nothing: and he doeth according to his will in the army of heaven, and among the inhabitants of the earth: and none can stay his hand, or say unto him, what doest thou?' This is 'the King of heaven, all whose works are truth, and his ways judgement: and those that walk in pride he is able to abase' (Dan. 4:34,35,37). My friend, either God is absolutely, totally, universally sovereign, or he is not God.

'A God ... that is profitable for nothing'

Read Isaiah 44:1–28

Did you ever notice what a great difference there is between the God who is revealed in the Bible and the god that is being preached today? The God of the prophets and apostles is not even similar to the god of today's preachers. The modern conception of God, which is prevalent today, even among those who profess to believe the Bible, is a miserable misconception and a terrible perversion of the truth. The god of the twentieth century is a helpless, effeminate creature, who commands the respect of no truly thoughtful man. The god of this age is nothing more than an emotional, sentimental, sympathetic being without any real power. The god who is preached in most pulpits, even in the most conservative churches, is an object to be pitied, not a God to be worshipped.

Arthur Pink stated the issue very plainly: 'To say that God the Father has purposed the salvation of all mankind, that God the Son died with the express intention of saving the whole human race and that God the Holy Spirit is now seeking to win the world to Christ, when, as a matter of common observation, it is apparent that the great majority of our fellow men are dying in sin, and passing into a hopeless eternity is to say that God the Father is disappointed, that God the Son is dissatisfied, and that God the Holy Spirit is defeated.'

I am stating the issue very plainly, but there is no escaping this conclusion. Let me be perfectly understood. To say that God is trying his best to save all men, but that the majority of men will not let God save them is to say that the will of God is impotent and that the will of man is omnipotent. That is nothing short of blasphemy! Many try to remove the difficulty by throwing the blame on Satan but that doesn't work either. If Satan is defeating the purpose of God, then Satan is almighty and God is no longer supreme. That too is blasphemy!

'I have purposed it, I will also do it'

Read 1 Kings 18:21–40

To declare, as many do, that God's plan has been frustrated by the entrance of sin into the world is to dethrone God. Some would have us to believe that God was taken by surprise when Adam sinned in the garden and that he is now trying to remedy and correct this unforeseen calamity in his creation. Such a notion is degrading to the character of God. It brings the Most High God down to the level of erring mortals. We are told that man is a free moral agent, that he is the determiner of his own destiny and that he has the power to resist God and hold the Almighty in check. Such a blasphemous notion would strip God of his attribute of omnipotence. Men would have us to believe that man has burst the bounds originally set by God and that God is now a spectator, more or less without power over the sin and suffering brought into the world by the fall of Adam. But such doctrine is in direct contradiction of Holy Scripture. It is written in the Word of God: 'Surely the wrath of man shall praise thee: the remainder of wrath shalt thou restrain' (Ps. 76:10). To put it very plainly, to deny the sovereignty of God in all things is either to make God what you want him to be, which is idolatry, or it is to enter upon a path which, if logically followed, must bring you to atheism.

My friend, the sovereignty of the God of the Bible is absolute, irresistible and infinite. In declaring God's sovereignty, I am simply affirming his right as God to govern this universe, which he has created for his own glory, just as he pleases. He is the Potter; we are the clay. We have no more power over God than clay has over the potter. God moulds the clay of Adam's race into whatever form he chooses. From the lump of fallen humanity, he makes one vessel unto honour and another into dishonour. This is his right. He is God. He is under no law, rule, or power beyond his own sovereign will and holy nature. He is God.

'I will have compassion on whom I will'

Read Matthew 11:2–27

God loves some men and he hates others. God does not love everyone in the world. He is sovereign in the exercise of his love. He said, 'Jacob have I loved, but Esau have I hated' (Rom. 9:13). This, I know, is a difficult truth for men to receive. It is impossible for you to rejoice in it, unless God gives you a heart to do so. When I say that God is sovereign in the exercise of his love, I simply mean that God loves whom he chooses to love and he does not love those whom he chooses not to love. God does not love Satan. There is nothing in the old serpent to love. There is nothing in him to attract God's love. And there is nothing in God compelling him to love that which is evil. Nor is there anything in all the fallen sons of Adam to attract God's love. We are all by nature 'children of wrath'. There is nothing to compel God's love towards us. If there is nothing in any member of the human race to attract God's love and yet he does love some men, then the cause of love must be found in God himself. I love my wife because she is lovely. She possesses those qualities and attributes of a woman which cause me to love her. I love her because she is who and what she is. Not so with God's love towards us. He loves us because he would love us. He loves us in spite of who and what we are. The cause of God's love towards his own elect is his own sovereign choice, determination and pleasure. God is sovereign in the exercise of his love.

In the final analysis, the exercise of God's love must be traced back to his own sovereign pleasure. Otherwise he would love by rule. If he loved by rule, then he is obliged to love. And if he is obliged to do something by some force outside himself, he is not God. Some people are shocked to hear me say that God does not love the entire human race. But their shock reveals an ignorance of Holy Scripture. 'As it is written, Jacob have I loved, but Esau have I hated.' If God loved Jacob and hated Esau, and that before they were born, before they had done anything, either good or evil, then the reason for his love is not in them, but in God.

'I have loved you, saith the Lord'

Read Isaiah 49:1–26

In Ephesians 1:3–5, we see a clear picture of God exercising his love sovereignly. 'Blessed be the God and Father of our Lord Jesus Christ, who hath blessed us with all spiritual blessings in heavenly places in Christ: according as he hath chosen us in him before the foundation of the world, that we should be holy and without blame before him in love: having predestinated us unto the adoption of children by Jesus Christ to himself, according to the good pleasure of his will.' It was in love that God the Father predestinated his chosen ones unto the adoption of children by Jesus Christ to himself, 'according' – according to what? According to some good thing he saw in them? According to some decision they would make? According to some foreseen merit of their own? No. According to what he foresaw they would become? No. Listen to the carefully worded answer of the Holy Spirit. God chose his own elect and predestinated us, 'according to the good pleasure of his will'.

God loves his own elect personally, with an everlasting love. He says, 'Yea, I have loved thee with an everlasting love: therefore with lovingkindness have I drawn thee' (Jer. 31:3). God's love for his own elect, like God himself, is immutable. It never changes. Those whom God loves will never become the objects of his anger, wrath and vengeance. God's love for his own elect is persevering. He loved us before we fell in Adam and after we fell. He loved us before Christ came to redeem us. He loved us throughout the days of our rebellion and unbelief. He loved us when we hated him. He loved us before we were regenerated by the power of his Spirit and made to love him. And though we sin against him continually, he loves his own still. He will never cease to cherish his own. Are you one of those whom God loves with an everlasting love? If so, you should rejoice in God's sovereign exercise of his love towards you.

'It is God that justifieth'

Read Romans 5:1–21

1. Every believer is eternally justified in the purpose of God. Paul, speaking of God's eternal decree in predestination, declares that all of God's elect were justified in his eternal purpose of grace: 'Whom he did predestinate, them he also called: and whom he called, them he also justified: and whom he justified, them he also glorified.' From eternity God looked upon his Son as our Substitute, and as he looks upon us in his Son, we are, and always have been, righteous in his sight. Thomas Goodwin said, 'We may say of all spiritual blessings in Christ, what is said of Christ, that 'His goings forth are from everlasting.' In Christ we are blessed with all spiritual blessings. As we are blessed with all others, so with this also, that we were justified then in Christ!'

2. All of God's elect were justified at Calvary. Having lived in perfect obedience to the law of God as our Representative, establishing a perfect righteousness for us, the Lord Jesus Christ suffered and died as our Substitute at Calvary, satisfying the penalty of God's law and justice against us. In the person of our Substitute, we have satisfied the law's requirements and its penalty. And now God, in perfect consistency with his justice and holiness, declares that we are forgiven of all sin and justified: 'Being justified freely by his grace through the redemption that is in Christ Jesus.'

3. Every believer receives justification by faith in Christ. Christ justified us by his great sin-atoning sacrifice and all who believe on Christ as Lord and Saviour receive all the many benefits of his finished work, one of which is justification. It is written that our Lord Jesus Christ 'was delivered for our offences, and was raised again for our justification. Therefore being justified, by faith we have peace with God through our Lord Jesus Christ.' Faith does not cause God to justify us. The obedience of Christ has done that for us. But faith, resting upon Christ alone as Saviour, obtains peace with God, even the peace of perfect and complete justification.

'My church'

Read Psalm 102:1–28

What is the church? The church is not a material building. The church is not a particular denomination of believers. The church is not a particular, individual congregation of believers. And the church is not a combination of all the various churches and denominations of the world. The church of our Lord Jesus Christ is made up of all true believers throughout all ages, both in heaven and upon the earth. It includes all who have repented of sin and fled to Christ by faith and been made new creatures in him by the grace of God. All who are truly saved by the grace of God, washed in the blood of Christ, clothed in the righteousness of Christ and born again by the power of the Holy Spirit are in the church of our Lord Jesus Christ. This is the body of Christ. This is the bride of Christ. This is the whole family of God, whose names are written in heaven. The members of this church all come to the throne of grace. They all worship with one heart. They are all children of the same Father, members of the same family and heirs of the same promises. This is the church that is in Christ and the church in which Christ dwells. This is what Paul says, concerning all true believers and the one true church of our Lord Jesus Christ: 'Ye are come unto Mount Sion, and unto the city of the living God, the heavenly Jerusalem, and to an innumerable company of angels, to the general assembly and church of the firstborn, which are written in heaven, and to God the Judge of all, and to the spirits of just men made perfect, and to Jesus the Mediator of the new covenant' (Heb. 12:22–24).

This is the church which Christ loved, the church he came to save, the church he purchased with his own blood, the church of which he is the Head, the church for which he rules and governs all things. This is the church which the Lord Jesus Christ shall present before his Father in glory. 'Christ loved the church, and gave himself for it; that he might sanctify and cleanse it with the washing of water by the word, that he might present it to himself a glorious church, not having spot, or wrinkle, or any such thing; but that it should be holy and without blemish' (Eph. 5:25–27).

What happened at Calvary?

Read Mark 15:1–39

Certainly it is not possible for me to state in a few brief lines all that took place when Jesus Christ suffered in our stead at Mount Calvary. But our Lord does tell us plainly that three things definitely occured as the result of his death.

1. The cross of Christ was the judgement of the world. The world was judged for sin. The world was proved to be guilty and sinful. The world was found guilty of hating God. When the pure, holy and spotless Son of God came to the earth, the men of this world crucified the Lord of glory with wicked hands.

2. By his death upon the cross, our Lord spoiled Satan of his universal monarchy. The first Adam, by eating the fruit of the forbidden tree, was cast out of paradise. The second Adam, by dying upon the cursed tree, cast Satan out of his place of usurped dominion. By virtue of his death and resurrection, the Lord Jesus Christ has crushed the serpent's head. He no longer has power to accuse us, neither does he have power against us.

3. By his death upon the cross, Jesus Christ has become the centre of attraction and the object of faith for perishing sinners. The boundaries of God's kingdom have been enlarged to include Gentiles as well as Jews. Now the crucified, risen, exalted Christ draws sinners from the four corners of the earth, through the preaching of the gospel. He draws sinners who could not come and who would not come to himself. He draws them lovingly and tenderly. And, blessed be his name, he draws them effectually. It is the crucified Christ who conquers the hearts and wills of men. The terrors of the law will alarm you. The fear of hell will torment your mind. But, if ever you get sight of the Son of God dying in your stead, he will break your heart and conquer your will.

'I die daily'

Read 2 Corinthians 4:17 – 5:10

As a believer, a man redeemed by the blood of Christ, saved, forgiven and justified by the grace of God, I purposefully endeavour to live in the habit of dying. I want to be able to say with Paul, **'I die daily.'** Daily we must put down the passions of life in this world and die to it. A man who is dead to the world cannot be greatly charmed by it. My friend, you would be wise to hold everything in this world with a loose hand. Once a pastor was visiting one of the old men in his congregation. They were sitting in the man's garden. He had a large estate, a fine home and a good piece of property. His wife, his children and his grandchildren were all present. And the old man said to his pastor, 'These are the things that make it hard to die.' Indeed, they are! But all of these things are perishing. We must hold them very loosely. Child of God, you must be ready, at a moment's notice, to turn loose of anything in this world. For your soul's sake, for your happiness and peace, I urge you not to build your nest in any of the trees of this world. They will all be cut down and cast into the fire.

I try to live in this world like a traveller, staying in a motel. I am only spending a few days and a few nights in this place. So the things here should not greatly disturb me. What does the price of tea in China matter to us? What does the price of a loaf of bread or a gallon of petrol matter to a man who lives in the prospect of eternity?

And I try to live each day as though I knew it would be my last. This is the day the Lord has given me. I have no promise of tomorrow. I must press as much work and service for the honour of Christ into this day as I possibly can. 'The time is short.' George Whitefield said, 'I try to keep all my affairs so arranged that, if I were to die at any time, they would be no trouble to those who come after me.' I am not suggesting that we live irresponsibly or neglectfully. But I am saying this: we must be ready to die at any time. We must be united to Christ by faith. We must live for the honour and glory of Christ. We must not live for this world.

'Your election of God'

Read 1 Thessalonians 1:1–10

What does the Bible teach about election? Any honest man who reads the Bible must recognize that the Word of God does teach the doctrine of divine election and that this doctrine is a prominent theme of the New Testament. You may not understand it, you may not be able to explain it, but you cannot deny that our Lord and his apostles taught election. You know it and I know it. But what is election? What does the Bible teach about election? These are the questions we must seek to understand.

Divine election is God's eternal choice of his people. It is God's eternal and gracious purpose to save all who in time are saved. Election is that eternal act of God's grace by which he separated and distinguished you who are saved, and all who ever will be saved, from the rest of mankind, saying, 'I will be their God and they shall be my people.' If you are saved, you know that your salvation is God's work. True, you do believe on Christ, but God enabled you to believe and caused you to believe. God has distinguished you from the rest of mankind. He has done something for you which he has not done for other men. Now all I am saying is this: election is God's eternal purpose to save you.

Listen to the Scriptures. Our Lord said, 'Ye have not chosen me, but I have chosen you' (John 15:16). Luke tells us that when Paul and Barnabas preached the gospel, 'As many as were ordained to eternal life believed' (Acts 13:48). Paul tells us that every blessing of grace comes to us from God the Father, through the merits of the Lord Jesus Christ: 'According as he hath chosen us in him before the foundation of the world, that we should be holy and without blame before him in love: having predestinated us unto the adoption of children by Jesus Christ to himself, according to the good pleasure of his will' (Eph. 1:4–5). It is written that 'God hath saved us and called us with an holy calling, not according to our works, but according to his own purpose and grace, which was given us in Christ Jesus before the world began' (2 Tim. 1:9).

'The purpose of God according to election'

Read 2 Timothy 1:1–18

Here are six things which the Word of God teaches about divine election. If you search the Scriptures, you will find that these six things are true.

1. God's election of his people is *sovereign and eternal* (Rom. 9:11–23). God chooses whom he will, and none can call him into account. Is it not right for God to do with his own what he will? Election is God's sovereign, eternal purpose to save a specific people.

2. Divine election is *an act of God's free grace* (Rom. 9:16). I know that God did not choose us arbitrarily. He had some wise and holy reason for doing so. But I know also that the reason does not lie in us. God chose us not because we were either good or evil, but simply because he would. 'Even so Father: for so it seemed good in thy sight' (Matt. 11:26). We can say no more.

3. God's purpose of election is also *irreversible* (Isa. 46:9–11). 'The gifts and calling of God are without repentance' (Rom. 11:29). Election is God's unchangeable purpose of love. Having chosen his people, he will never go back on his word that is gone out of his mouth. The purpose of God in election is immutable. He is of one mind and who can turn him?

4. Divine election is *effectual* (Rom. 8:29–30). Every soul chosen by God in eternity was redeemed by Christ at Calvary and will be regenerated by the Holy Spirit at God's appointed time. In due time all of God's elect will believe on Christ and be brought to eternal glory. Not one of the elect will perish.

5. God's purpose of grace in election is *personal* (Jer. 1:5; 31:3). God calls his own children by name. He chose us, not as an indiscernible mass, but individually and personally. Yet he chose all his elect at once.

6. God's eternal purpose of election is *in Christ* (Eph. 1:4). Christ was chosen as the Head of an elect race, and we were chosen in him. God loved us eternally in Christ.

'The election hath obtained it'

Read Psalm 33:1–22

When Paul wrote to the Thessalonian believers he said, 'We are bound to give thanks alway to God for you, brethren beloved of the Lord, because God hath from the beginning chosen you to salvation through sanctification of the Spirit and belief of the truth' (2 Thess. 2:13).

We know that the doctrine of divine, sovereign, eternal election is not contrary to all the promises of the gospel. You know the promises: 'Come unto me, all ye that labour and are heavy laden, and I will give you rest.' 'Whosoever shall call upon the name of the Lord shall be saved.' 'He is able to save unto the uttermost them that come unto God by him.' 'He that believeth and is baptized shall be saved.' 'Him that cometh unto me, I will in no wise cast out.' 'Believe on the Lord Jesus Christ, and thou shalt be saved.' Election does not restrict the gospel invitation. It simply guarantees the fact that some will receive it. Election does not limit the promises of the gospel. It simply secures a people to enjoy those promises. The gospel of the grace of God says that any man in all the world who comes to Christ in faith will be saved. And the gospel also declares that there are some who most assuredly will come to Christ, because God has chosen them in eternal election.

And divine election is in no way contrary to the plain statements of Holy Scripture about man's responsibility. What does God require of you? 'This is the work of God, that ye believe on him whom he hath sent' (John 6:29). You cannot believe, unless God the Holy Spirit creates faith in you and causes you to believe. Yet it is your responsibility to believe. You must repent. You must believe the gospel. You must trust Christ. You cannot save yourself. The Son of God alone can save you. But there are some things you can do. You can pray. You can read the Bible. You can go to hear God's servant preach the gospel. You can confess your sin. You can seek the Lord. You can sue for mercy, crying, 'God be merciful to me, a sinner.' If you do seek the Lord with a sincere, believing heart, it is because he has chosen you and caused you to believe.

'Faith in Christ'

Read John 1:1–18

True faith is something more than learning doctrine. Doctrine is important. It is essential. No man can be well-grounded without sound doctrine. It is not possible for a man to receive Christ and reject his doctrine. But many rejoice in the doctrine of Christ who do not have faith in Christ. True faith is much more than personal morality. The Pharisee was rigidly moral in his outward conduct (Luke 18:11–12), but he did not have the faith of God's elect. True faith will make a man honest. It will produce a heart that seeks after holiness and true godliness. But many who are personally moral have no faith in Christ. True faith is something far beyond mere lip service to Christ. It is one thing to profess Christ, and another thing to possess Christ. It is one thing to talk about faith and another thing to live by faith. It is one thing to call Jesus 'Lord' with your lips and something else altogether to submit to Lord Jesus Christ in your heart (Matt. 15:8–9). True faith is something more than all the endless activities, ceremonies, rituals and programmes of religion.

The opinion of modern religion is that faith produces a life of health, wealth, happiness and prosperity. But the faith of God's elect, that faith which brings salvation, is a faith that brings about a living union with the living Redeemer! Faith does more than walk down an aisle and accept Jesus as a Saviour from hell. Saving faith does more than give God one day in seven in which to act pious and religious. Saving faith does more than set aside ten per cent of my income for the work of the Lord. Faith does more than quit a few outward habits, while breeding inward contempt, rebellion and malice. True saving faith, the faith of God's elect, is the complete trust and confidence of the heart upon Christ for acceptance with God. It involves total submission and unreserved commitment to the Lord Jesus Christ.

This faith is a gift of God. It is not mentally accepting a creed, or believing certain facts about the Lord Jesus Christ. It is an inward disposition and active principle of the heart created in us by the sovereign power and irresistible grace of God the Holy Spirit (Eph. 2:8–9; Col. 2:12; John 1:12–13).

'The love of God'

Read Hosea 3:1–3; 14:1–9

Children of God, rejoice in and give thanks for the love of God in Christ. None of us deserves to be loved by God. There is nothing in us by nature, either actually or potentially, that could have caused God to love us. He is holy; we are evil. He is pure; we are defiled. He is righteous; we are sinful. He is the glorious God of heaven; we are the filthy worms of the earth. Yet the infinite, eternal God loved us! He loved us freely! There is no cause to be found for the love of God for us except in himself. He says, 'I will have compassion on whom I will have compassion.'

The love of God for our souls is sovereign. I cannot explain the sovereignty of God's love for his own elect, but I can rejoice in his love. He did not love Esau or Judas, but he did love Jacob and John. He did not choose to love many of my friends and companions or many of my own kinsmen, but blessed be his name, he did choose to love me! I was more undeserving of his love than all the others combined; nevertheless he loved me. Shall I not rejoice in his love?

The love of God for his own elect is eternal. His love for us, like himself, is without beginning. The Lord God loves us with an everlasting love. Before angel loved angel, before man loved man, before either angels or men were created, Jehovah loved us, and said, 'I will be their God, and they shall be my people.'

The proof of God's love for us is in the sacrifice of his own Son, the Lord Jesus Christ, to save us. 'God commendeth his love toward us, in that, while we were yet sinners, Christ died for us' (Rom. 5:8). God so greatly loved us that, though the price of our redemption must be the blood of his own Son, he willingly made the sacrifice!

And God's love for his own is an immutable love. It changes not. The Lord God will never cease to cherish his own. His love will never come to an end. It can never be exhausted. It never even diminishes or becomes cold. God loves us perfectly and without end. No, not even our many sins affect his love. 'Behold, what manner of love the Father hath bestowed upon us!'

'Your Father knoweth'

Read Luke 12:13–34

Why do we worry so much? I know that we all live with a great deal of stress. We have families to feed, children to clothe, train and educate and bills to pay. These are all things about which we are and should be concerned. I do not suggest that we should be careless and irresponsible. That would be contrary to the gospel of Christ. But I do say that we should not worry. Our concern for these things should not make us anxious, fretful and irritable.

Worrying is a fruitless, futile exercise. What did you ever get by worrying, except headaches and ulcers? We only worry about those things that are beyond our control. We worry about things that happened yesterday. We worry about what might happen tomorrow. We worry about what other people may say, or think, or do. We never worry about things that we can control. It is a futile, pointless thing to worry. Not one of us has ever accomplished a single thing by all of our worrying combined.

But what is more important, worrying is a very evil thing that dishonours our God. I speak to you who are believers, to you who seek the glory of God. Our worrying is sinful. It reveals a lack of faith. When I worry about something, it reveals that I do not trust the wisdom and goodness of God's providence. I only worry when I am discontent and dissatisfied with what God is doing for me, or because I do not truly trust him to do what is best. In other words, to worry is to murmur against the Lord my God!

Let us understand the words of our Lord and stop worrying. He is telling us that there is no need for any believer ever to worry. Our heavenly Father will provide for us everything that is needful and protect us from everything that is harmful. Let us not concern ourselves about the affairs of this world, but only about those things that concern the kingdom of God and his righteousness. He is saying, 'Don't worry.' Trust the Lord, 'Casting all your care upon him; for he careth for you' (1 Peter 5:7).

Saved by grace

Read Psalm 34:1–22

One of the great texts on salvation by the grace of God is Ephesians 2:8–10. The apostle Paul, writing under divine inspiration, says, 'For by grace are ye saved through faith; and that not of yourselves: it is the gift of God: not of works, lest any man should boast. For we are his workmanship, created in Christ Jesus unto good works, which God hath before ordained that we should walk in them.' In these three verses of Scripture Paul tells us how God saves sinners, why he saves sinners the way he does and what the sure result of God's saving grace is.

How does God save sinners? **'By grace are ye saved through faith.'** Salvation, from start to finish, is the work of God's free grace in Christ. Grace planned the way of salvation by the substitutionary sacrifice of the Lord Jesus Christ. Grace chose those who would be saved in eternal election. Grace brought the Lord Jesus Christ down from heaven to die in our place at Calvary. Grace calls sinners to Christ by irresistible power. Grace gives us life. Grace preserves us in life. And grace will present us holy and without blame before the presence of his glory in heaven. All the many blessings of grace in salvation come to all of God's elect 'through faith'. Faith is not our saviour. Christ alone is the Saviour of his people. But faith in Christ is essential to salvation. Each of God's elect look to Christ in faith and receive salvation from him. Faith is the channel through which salvation comes. **'And that not of yourselves: it is the gift of God.'** Paul is telling us that grace is the gift of God, salvation is the gift of God and faith is the gift of God. None of these things are to be attributed to us. We believe according to the working of God's mighty power within us. Faith is not the work of the sinner. It is the work of God in the sinner.

Saved by grace

Read Psalm 56:1 – 57:11

Why does God save sinners by grace alone, apart from any works performed by us? It is God's purpose 'that no flesh should glory in his presence ... He that glorieth, let him glory in the Lord.' Therefore Paul emphasizes this point, that salvation is **'not of works, lest any man should boast'.** If there was anything which the sinner could do that would contribute anything towards his salvation, then at least a part of the glory of salvation must be attributed to man. God will not allow that. He will not share his glory with another. Salvation is by grace alone, without works. Salvation is not the work of man; neither is it a co-operative work of God and man together, God doing his part and man doing his part. Salvation is the work of God and the work of God alone. **'We are his workmanship.'** God has created us new creatures in Christ Jesus by the mighty power of his sovereign grace. Let all proud, foolish thoughts of self-salvation by the works of the flesh be for ever put out of your heart and mind. 'Not unto us, O Lord, not unto us, but unto thy name give glory, for thy mercy, and for thy truth's sake.' We will praise the God of heaven for his great grace, because he has saved us and not we ourselves.

What is the sure result of God's saving grace? **'We are his workmanship, created in Christ Jesus unto good works, which God hath before ordained that we should walk in them.'** Good works will not save anyone. But you may be sure of this: whenever the grace of God comes, bringing salvation to the heart, good works will follow. When grace reigns in the heart it produces good works. The good works which grace produces are the works of faith and love, righteousness and peace, patience and goodness.

Salvation is accomplished by the grace of God, without works. Salvation is given through faith in Christ. And salvation produces good works.

Why did Christ have to die?

Read Hebrews 9:1–28

When our Lord spoke of his death, he said, **'As Moses lifted up the serpent in the wilderness, even so must the Son of man be lifted up.'** Why? Why must he die?

It will not suffice to say, 'God loves us so greatly that he wants us to live with him for ever in heaven.' My wife lives with me in my home. I love her so much that I want her to live with me in my home for ever. But I have not died for her. Why did Jesus have to die? The answer to that question is vital. Learn the answer to that question and you will learn the gospel.

The apostle Paul gives us the answer to that question. Being inspired by God the Holy Spirit, Paul wrote this answer: the Lord Jesus Christ died upon the cross, so that God 'might be just, and the justifier of him which believeth in Jesus'. You see, we are guilty sinners. God is holy, righteous, just and true. And a perfectly holy and just God could never save, justify and accept any sinner until atonement is made for his sin. A holy God must punish sin. Before the sinner can go free, God's holy, infinite wrath and justice against the guilty sinner must be satisfied. The Lord Jesus Christ died upon the cross to satisfy God's infinite wrath and justice against the sins of his elect, so that God in perfect justice might justify the ungodly. This is the gospel. This is the doctrine of Holy Scripture. The Lord Jesus Christ, the incarnate God-man, is that one 'whom God hath set forth to be a propitiation [a satisfactory sacrifice] through faith in his blood, to declare his righteousness for the remission of sins that are past, through the forbearance of God; to declare, I say, at this time his righteousness: that he might be just and the justifier of him which believeth in Jesus' (Rom. 3:25–26). The Lord Jesus Christ died upon the cross to make an all-sufficient, satsifactory sacrifice for sin. 'Now once in the end of the world hath he appeared to put away sin by the sacrifice of himself' (Heb. 9:26).

'Salvation is of the Lord!'

Read Genesis 3:1–21

To say that salvation is of the Lord is to say that salvation is in no way dependent upon or determined by man's works and man's will.

Salvation is not the work of man, nor is it a co-operative effort between God and man, God doing his part and man doing his part. Salvation is the work of God alone. It is altogether the work of his grace. Human works and human merit do not even enter into the picture. It is all of grace – not grace plus baptism, not grace plus church membership, not grace plus works. Grace alone accomplishes salvation. Grace plus anything ceases to be grace. 'If by grace, then it is no more of works: otherwise grace is no more grace. But if it be of works, then is it no more grace: otherwise work is no more work' (Rom. 11:6). Man's works can never merit salvation.

And it is not man's will that determines who will be saved. Your salvation is not dependent upon your sinful will; it is dependent upon God's sovereign will. God alone determines whom he will save. He does not even consult, or ask the opinion of man. You are subject to God's will. God is not subject to your will. He says, 'I will have mercy on whom I will have mercy, and I will have compassion on whom I will have compassion. So then it is not of him that willeth, nor of him that runneth, but of God that showeth mercy' (Rom. 9:15–16). If God has determined to save you by his matchless grace in Christ, you will be saved. He will give you a new heart, a new nature and a new will. You will delightfully come to Christ in true faith in the day of his gracious, saving power. If God has not determined to save you, if he does not send his Spirit to quicken you, give you faith and bring you to Christ, you will never come to Christ, because you will never desire him. My friend, **'Salvation is of the Lord.'** He can be gracious to you, or he can pass you by. He can save you, or he can damn you. It is entirely up to him. You have no claim upon God and you have no control over him.

'My doctrine'

Read Exodus 20:1–21

Here are three vital truths revealed in the Word of God. I say that these truths are vital, because those who are in error concerning these three truths have not yet learned the gospel.

1. God will by no means clear the guilty. He said that he would not in Exodus 34:7. 'The soul that sinneth, it shall die' (Ezek. 18:20). There is no means whereby a holy, righteous, just and true God can clear guilty men and women. God demands holiness, absolute perfection. Any deviation, in thought, word, or deed, from perfect holiness God will not accept. A holy God must punish sin. A just God cannot clear the guilty. God will not clear the guilty upon the basis of their repentance. God will not clear the guilty upon the basis of their faith. God will not clear the guilty upon the basis of their sacrifices. God will not clear the guilty upon the basis of their moral reformation. Be sure you know and understand this truth. A holy God cannot and will not clear the guilty.

2. Now be sure that you understand this also: you are guilty (Rom. 3:10–12,19,23; 5:12,18,19). Every son of Adam, by nature, is guilty before God. You are guilty. You are guilty of Adam's sin. You are guilty of inward sin. You are guilty of outward sin. Judgement is passed. God declares that you are guilty. God will by no means clear the guilty; and you are guilty.

3. Yet there is hope, because God has found a way to make the guilty not guilty. Through the substitutionary sacrifice of the Lord Jesus Christ, God's own Son, in the place of sinners upon the cross, God makes the guilty not guilty. God made his Son to be sin for all who believe on him, imputing our sins to his Son. And God made every believer to be righteous, innocent, not guilty, imputing the righteousness of his Son to us. 'He hath made him to be sin for us, who knew no sin; that we might be made the righteousness of God in him' (2 Cor. 5:21). This is the vital truth of the gospel.

'To die is gain'

Read Psalm 23:1 – 24:10

Children of God, don't be afraid of death and don't weep for those who have died in the Lord. For us, **'to die is gain'**.

Death will bring us into the presence of many friends. Death takes the wife from the husband, the child from its mother, the father from his family, but we cheer ourselves with the prospect of a glorious reunion (1 Thess. 4:13–18). It is true, above all else, we shall see Christ and be with him, but it is also promised that we shall sit down with Abraham, Isaac and Jacob. Yes, we shall know one another in heaven.

Death will bring an answer to our prayers. How often have you prayed that you might be delivered from your trials, temptations and troubles? We shall be delivered from them then. 'God shall wipe away all tears from our eyes.' How often have you prayed that you might be freed from sin? When this body is in the grave, 'There shall be no more sin.' Many, many times you have prayed that you might be more like Christ, in love, in purity, in conduct. When we have laid aside this robe of flesh, we shall awake in his likeness. We shall be like him, for we shall see him as he is.

But most of all, 'To be absent from the body is to be present with the Lord.' This is our chief concern. This is our noblest ambition. This is the happiness and glory of heaven. This is heaven! We shall be with Christ, for ever with the Lord! 'There cannot be heaven without Christ. He is the sum total of bliss; the fountain from which heaven flows, the element of which heaven is composed. Christ is heaven and heaven is Christ ... Just to be with Christ is all the heaven a believer wants. The angels may be there or not, as they will, and the golden crowns and harps present or absent, as may be, but if I am to be where Jesus is, I will find angels in his eyes, and crowns in every lock of his hair; to me the golden streets shall be my fellowship with him, and the harpings of the harpers shall be the sound of his voice. Only to be near him, to be with him – this is all I want' (C.H. Spurgeon). This is heaven: 'To die is gain!'

'Thou hast hid these things from the wise and prudent, and hast revealed them unto babes'

Read Psalm 147:1–20

This fact is demonstrated in the Scriptures over and over again. Only those who are wilfully ignorant will miss it. God hides the gospel from some men and reveals it to others, according to his own good pleasure and his own sovereign will. God revealed the gospel to Abel, but Cain was blind to it. God told Noah and his family the message of his grace, but all the rest of the world was lost in ignorance. God spoke graciously and revealed himself to Abraham, but the gospel was hidden from all the other men of Ur. God revealed his grace to Lot and sent the messengers of mercy to Lot, but all the other families of Sodom perished in ignorance. God told Moses, Aaron and the children of Israel how to be saved on the night of destruction in Egypt, but he gave Pharaoh and the Egyptians no message of mercy.

How many there are today in the church of Christ who can attest to this fact from their own experience! God sends his servants to some cities and countries to establish a gospel witness; others he leaves without light. He calls one member of a family; the others he leaves in darkness. He called you and gave you life in Christ, but many of your friends and companions are yet in the bondage of death and sin. What made the difference? Surely it was not because you were better than they were. In all likelihood, you were the worst of the crowd. The difference is just this: 'He hath mercy on whom he will have mercy.' 'Oh the depth of the riches both of the wisdom and knowledge of God! How unsearchable are his judgements, and his ways past finding out!' (Rom. 11:33.)

There is a people in this world who have been purchased and redeemed by the blood of the Lord Jesus Christ. In the time of his grace and love, God the Holy Spirit will come to those very people, the elect of God, the redeemed ones of Christ, with irresistible power and he will reveal the gospel in their hearts, causing them to believe on Christ. All others will be left to perish in their chosen ignorance.

'Who verily was foreordained'

Read Psalm 22:1–31

God sovereignly ruled the whole affair of his Son's death upon the cross. The death of Christ did not take God by surprise. He planned it in eternity and he was in control of the whole affair. If men had done what they wanted to do, they would have stoned Christ to death on several occasions. But they were not allowed to exercise their will until the time appointed by the Father. If Satan could have had his way, he would have killed Christ in the garden of Gethsemane, but God's Son must die upon the cross of Calvary, according to God's unalterable purpose.

It is true, those wicked men – the Jews, the Gentiles, Pilate and the Roman soldiers – did exactly what their wicked hearts wanted to do. They stripped him because they wanted to strip him. They beat him because they wanted to beat him. They lied about him because they wanted to lie about him. They nailed him to a tree, hung him up and laughed as they watched him die, because that is what man's wicked free will wanted to do. They spat in his face and plucked out his beard because they hated the Son of God.

But God was in control all the while, secretly ruling the actions of those evil men, so that they did exactly what God from eternity ordained must be done. They did neither more nor less than what God had decreed. Peter told the Jews that Christ, 'being delivered by the determinate counsel and foreknowledge of God, ye have taken, and by wicked hands have crucified and slain' (Acts 2:23).'Though they found no cause of death in him, yet desired they Pilate that he should be slain. And when they had fulfilled all that was written of him, they took him down from the tree, and laid him in a sepulchre' (Acts 13:28–29). All that our Lord Jesus Christ suffered in his crucifixion and death, he suffered because 'it pleased the Lord to bruise him; he hath put him to grief' (Isa. 53:10). God sovereignly determined that Christ would die, for whom he would die, when he would die, where he would die and all that he would suffer in his death.

'The salvation of the righteous is of the Lord'

Read Exodus 15:1–19

Salvation is not something that sinners do for God. Salvation is something that God does for sinners. Salvation is not a co-operative effort of God and man, in which God does his part and man does his part. 'Salvation is of the Lord!' It is entirely the work of God's free, sovereign, irresistible grace in the Lord Jesus Christ. And the thing we must come to understand is this: the God who saves is sovereign in the exercise of his saving power. No part of a sinner's salvation is to be ascribed to the works, the merit, or the will of the sinner. From start to finish, from beginning to end, salvation is the work of God's free, sovereign, irresistible grace in Christ. Election is by grace. Redemption is by grace. Regeneration is by grace. Justification is by grace. Preservation is by grace. Sanctification is by grace. Glorification is by grace. And in the whole work of salvation, God is sovereign in the exercise of his grace and his saving power towards sinful men.

God sovereignly selects the people whom he will save. It is a self-evident fact that God does not save all men. Some people do perish. Some people do go to hell. That being true, it is also a self-evident fact that it never was God's intention, purpose, or desire to save all men. The Word of God is very clear in this matter. From eternity of old, before the world began, God chose to save some of Adam's fallen race and determined to save them, passing by the rest, refusing to show them mercy, according to his own wise and holy will. He predestinated some to eternal life, but not all. Did he not say so? 'Ye have not chosen me, but I have chosen you' (John 15:16). 'Few are chosen' (Matt. 22:14). God has blessed us with every spiritual blessing in Christ 'according as he hath chosen us in him before the foundation of the world' (Eph. 1:4). In sovereign, eternal election God chose the people whom he would save.

'The salvation of the righteous is of the Lord'

Read Exodus 15:20–27

God sovereignly seeks those whom he has chosen. The sinner is not seeking after God. 'There is none that understandeth, there is none that seeketh after God' (Rom. 3:11). God seeks the sinner whom he loved with an everlasting love and determined to save. In all the works of providence God is seeking his own. He so arranges things that the sinner whom he intends to save is brought to the place where God will be gracious to him. He sends a preacher to preach the gospel of his grace to that sinner. And he sends forth his Spirit in sovereign, irresistible power and grace to give that sinner life and faith in Christ and fetch his chosen ones to himself. The Lord God is not seeking to save all men. He seeks his own elect. The Good Shepherd seeks his own sheep. And he always finds them. What does the Scripture say? He seeks his sheep 'until he find it'. And when he finds his sheep, he always brings it home.

God sovereignly saves his own elect. Did you know that the Word of God never talks about God 'trying' to do anything? God does not try to rule the world; he rules the world. God does not try to redeem; he has redeemed. God does not try to put away sin; he has put away sin. God does not try to justify; he justifies. God does not try to save; God saves. Every person who was chosen of God in eternity, every person who was redeemed by Christ at Calvary, every person who is called by the effectual, irresistible grace of God the Holy Spirit will be saved, without exception. This is what God says: 'I will have mercy on whom I will have mercy, and I will have compassion on whom I will have compassion. So then it is not of him that willeth, nor of him that runneth, but of God that showeth mercy' (Rom. 9:15–16). O Lord God, we rejoice to know and to declare that 'Thy people shall be willing in the day of thy power' (Ps. 110:3). 'Blessed is the man whom thou choosest and causest to approach unto thee' (Ps. 65:4). 'It is the Spirit that quickeneth; the flesh profiteth nothing' (John 6:63).

'He doeth according to his will'

Read Isaiah 40:10–31

A god who has no power over men and Satan could never be trusted to fulfil any promises. If God has no power to accomplish his will, perform his designs and fulfil his purposes, regardless of wicked men and Satan, if God cannot rule the wills of men, the actions of men and the power of Satan, we can never trust him to fulfil any of his promises. Paul said, 'We know that all things work together for good to them that love God, to them who are the called, according to his purpose.' But how do we know that? How can we possibly know that God will accomplish his purpose and make all things work together for the eternal good of God's elect, if he does not sovereignly rule all things, both bad and good? Surely Satan would not allow God to accomplish his purpose, if he had any power to resist it. Surely wicked men would never permit God to acomplish his will, if they had any power to prevent it. We can only trust a sovereign God to fulfil his promises. Only a sovereign God, who rules and governs all things with absolute control, could honestly promise those who trust him that everything, small and great, bad and good, will ultimately accomplish their eternal spiritual good and his own glory.

Now answer this question: is your God a trustworthy Sovereign in whom you safely trust, or is your god only a puny pigmy that has no power? I know this, the one true and living God, the God of the Bible, the God whom I trust with my immortal soul, the God to whom I look for the fulfilling of every promise he has made, is a God who is absolutely sovereign. He rules this universe with the ease of omnipotent power. All things, both great and small, breathe and move, live and die, according to his wise degree. All things are under his control. All things accomplish his will. If I did not believe such a God as this, I would be honest and confess myself an atheist. I prefer atheism, a complete denial of God's existence, to the alternative of making God helpless, and robbing him of his eternal glory as the sovereign God of heaven and earth.

'Them also I must bring'

Read Isaiah 45:20–25

The *purpose* of God demands the salvation of all his elect. God has purposed to save some men, those whom he has chosen. If one of them should perish, God's purpose would be defeated, his grace would be frustrated and he would cease to be God.

The *purchase* of Christ demands the salvation of every sinner for whom he died. The Lord Jesus Christ poured out his life's blood unto death upon the cross to purchase his sheep, to satisfy the claims of justice against his sheep. Now if so much as one of those sheep, whom Christ purchased with his blood, were to perish, then the blood of Christ would be shed in vain and the blood of the cross would be a useless thing.

The *promise* of God the Father to his Son and of God the Son to his Father in the covenant of grace demands the eternal salvation of some men. God the Father promised his Son that, as the reward of his life of righteousness and substitutionary death of atonement in the place of his people, he would give him a seed and generation to serve him. God said to his Son, 'Ask of me, and I shall give thee the heathen for thine inheritance' (Ps. 2:8). Therefore our Lord spoke with confidence and said, 'All that the Father giveth me shall come to me' (John 6:37). God has given him power over all flesh for this specific purpose, 'That he should give eternal life to as many as thou hast given him' (John 17:2). And the Lord Jesus Christ promised God his Father that in the last day he would present all his chosen people before the presence of his glory, perfect, holy and without blemish, saying, 'Behold I and the children which God hath given me' (Heb. 2:13). You see then, there are some sinners in this world, the elect of God, who must be saved. If even one of them were to perish, the promise of God would fall to the ground, be broken and become a lie.

What about you? Do you hear his voice? Do you follow him in faith? If so, you must be with him in glory. You must never perish.

'Them which are called'

Read 1 Corinthians 1:9–31

Did you know that God calls some sinners to life and faith in Christ, and does not call others? Most people think that God calls all men, that God seeks all men and that God is trying to save all men. But nothing of the kind is taught in the Word of God. God calls some and passes by others. He gives light to some and leaves others in darkness. 'He hath mercy on whom he will have mercy.' When God intends to save a sinner, he calls that sinner with a personal, particular and distinguishing call. This is clearly the teaching of Holy Scripture.

You have read what the Scripture says about the Good Shepherd: 'He calleth his own sheep by name, and leadeth them out' (John 10:3). He does not call everyone. 'He calleth *his own sheep*.' They are his own sheep because God the Father gave them to him, entrusting them to his care, in the covenant of grace, in eternal election, before the world began. They are his own sheep because he died for them. 'The Good Shepherd giveth his life for the sheep' (John 10:11). The Lord Jesus Christ did not die for all men. He died for his sheep. He purchased them with his own precious blood. Justice held us in bondage, condemned, but Christ paid the price that justice demanded, suffering our condemnation and bought us. We are his property.

'He calleth his own sheep *by name*.' That is to say, 'He does not call all men in a general way, leaving it to man to decide who will and who will not come. Rather, he calls those sheep who were given to him and purchased by him. He calls them personally, one by one.'

And this divine call distinguishes the sheep of Christ from all other men, because, when he calls his sheep, 'He leadeth them out and they follow him'. This is how we know who God's elect are. The Shepherd calls them, they hear his voice and they follow him. Those who are not called by him, those who do not hear his voice, those who do not follow him are not among the number of his chosen, elect sheep. But those who are 'the called' are saved. God's call is always effectual. It always results in salvation.

'He calleth his own sheep by name'

Read John 10:1–28

There are many examples of this divine call in the Word of God. You who are saved will bear me witness that it was a personal call which brought you to Christ. It was some sermon, anointed of God, which led you to feel that you were, without question, the person for whom the sermon was intended. Perhaps the text was 'Thou, God, seest me.' And the preacher laid such particular stress on the word 'me', that you thought God's eye was fixed particularly on you. Before the sermon was finished, you could almost see God opening the books to condemn you. Your heart whispered, 'Can any hide himself in the secret places that I shall not see him? saith the Lord.' You may have been seated in a packed auditorium, but you had a solemn conviction that God spoke directly to you by the voice of his servant.

God does not call his people in masses, but one by one. God does not call his people in general, but in particular. God's call is personal, particular and distinguishing. You know that this is the doctrine of the Bible. There were many crowding the Jericho road, but our Lord came to a certain place and said to a certain man, 'Zacchaeus, make haste and come down.' 'Jesus saith unto her, Mary; and she turned and said unto him, Master.' Jesus saw Peter and John fishing by the lake, and he said unto them, 'Follow me.' And they followed him. He saw Matthew sitting at the receipt of custom and he said unto him, 'Arise, and follow me.' And Matthew arose and followed him.

When the Holy Spirit comes home to a man, God's arrows do more than merely graze his helmet, or make some little scratch upon his armour, they penetrate between the joints and harness, entering the marrow of his soul and the deep recesses of his heart. Have you received this personal, particular, distinguishing call of divine grace? Arise, then and come to Christ, saying,

> Let me at the throne of mercy
> Find a sweet relief,
> Kneeling there in deep contrition,
> Help my unbelief.

'Today, if ye will hear his voice'

Read Luke 19:1–10

Our Lord said to Zacchaeus, 'Zacchaeus, make haste, and come down; for today I must abide at thy house' (Luke 19:5). Every word is important; but I call your attention particulary to these two words of that text: '**haste**' and '**today**'. God's call is urgent. It demands an immediate response. Sinners sit under the ministry of the Word year after year, hearing God's servant faithfully and earnestly preach the gospel, urging them to repent and believe on Christ, but they reply, 'Tomorrow, perhaps.' Tears may run down their cheeks, but they are wiped away. Some good feelings and good desires appear, but like the morning dew they quickly disappear before the sun of temptation. The sinner may say, 'I solemnly vow from this day forth to become a reformed man. After I have once more indulged in my darling sin, I will renounce my lusts, and decide for God.' You see, he has only heard the preacher's voice. The preacher's voice can never reach your heart and that is where the problem lies. The sign-post on the road to hell reads, 'Tomorrow'.

But God's call is not for tomorrow. It is written, 'Today if ye will hear his voice, harden not your hearts: as in the provocation, when your fathers tempted me.' God's grace always comes with urgent dispatch. If God draws you, you will run after him. If God calls you, you will come, immediately, without delay. Tomorrow is not written in the almanac of time. Tomorrow is in Satan's calendar, but nowhere else. Tomorrow is a rock upon which many a man has wrecked his soul. Tomorrow is the fool's cup which he thinks is at the end of the rainbow, but it is a cup which none have ever found. Tomorrow is a dream. Tomorrow is a delusion. Tomorrow you will lift up your eyes in hell, being tormented in its flame. The ticking of the clock says, 'Today'. The pulse of your body whispers, 'Today.' I hear my heart speak as it beats within me and it says, 'Today'. Everything cries, 'Today'. And the Holy Spirit, in union with these things, says, 'Today if ye will hear his voice, harden not your hearts.'

'Come unto me'

Read 2 Corinthians 5:11 – 6:2

Reader, are you inclined now, by the grace and power of God, to seek Christ? Is there a prayer arising in your heart now? Are you saying, 'Now, or never! I must be saved now'? If you are, I hope it is the effectual call of our Lord, for if he calls, you will make haste and come to him. May God give you grace to come to Christ without delay.

Come to Christ just as you are. In all your sin and degradation, in all your filth and corruption, come to Christ. Do not try to clean up your life and then come. Come to Christ and he will clean up your life. Do not try to repent and then come. Come to Christ and he will give you repentance. Do not try to overcome your sinful heart and then come. Come to Christ and he will conquer your sin.

> Just as I am, without one plea,
> But that thy blood was shed for me,
> And that thou bidst me come to thee,
> O Lamb of God, I come.

Come to Christ, bowing to him as your rightful sovereign Lord. That leper had the right spirit and attitude. He fell down before the Lord in reverent submission, saying, 'Lord, if thou wilt, thou canst make me whole.' You do the same. Confess your sin. Confess that you rightly deserve to die for ever in hell. And say, 'But, Lord, if you will, you can save me through the blood and righteousness of your dear Son.'

Come to Christ in simple faith. Trust his righteousness for all your righteousness before God. Trust his blood for all your cleansing. Just fall flat down on the merits of Christ, trusting him alone for your eternal salvation. God give you grace to come to Christ this very day.

'Come down'

Read Matthew 15:21–28

Anyone who experiences the grace of God in salvation will be brought down in the dust of humiliation before the throne of his sovereign mercy. Before God exalts a man, he abases him. Before God clothes any sinner with the garments of Christ's righteousness, he strips the sinner of the filthy rags of his own righteousness. Take the case of Zacchaeus again. 'When Jesus came to the place, he looked up and saw him, and said unto him, Zacchaeus, make haste and come down; for today I must abide at thy house' (Luke 19:5). When God calls the sinner to Christ, he always says, '**Come down**'. The way of salvation is a downward path. You must come down.

God's call is a humbling call. Many a time the preacher calls men to Christ with a call which makes them proud, exalts them in their own esteem and leads them to think, 'I can come to God when I like. I do not need the influence of God the Holy Spirit. It is not God's call that is the thing that determines whether or not I shall be saved, but my own free will.' Today sinners are being called to go up and not to come down. But God always humbles the sinner. One of the first steps you must take is to go down from your own good works. That is a gigantic step down, far too humbling for most, but it must be taken.

Some stand upon their own self-sufficiency. But Christ says, 'Come down. You must come down from your own good works and come down from your own self-sufficiency.' That is another great step downward, but it must be taken. Down, my friend, you must come down. Come down from all your hope in yourself and in what you do. Come down until you see that you are utterly without strength, until you are utterly lost, until you see that you are nothing and can do nothing. Come down until the waters of God's wrath swell around you and you are made to see that you justly deserve to die. Come down until you are made to see your utter wickedness, vileness, corruption and filthiness. You must come down, down to the feet of Christ. The place of mercy is in the dust. Come down!

'I must abide at thy house'

Read Isaiah 6:1–8

It was not 'Zacchaeus, come down, because I hope you will let me abide at your house.' It was not 'Zacchaeus, come down, because God loves you and has a wonderful plan for your life, if you will only give me permission to abide at your house.' No. Our Saviour said, 'Zacchaeus, make haste, and come down; for today I *must* abide at thy house.' He knew the strong, irresistible necessity of God's purpose of grace. He said, 'must', because Zacchaeus must be saved. Just as much as man must die, just as much as the sun must give light, just so must every blood-bought sinner be saved. **Today I must abide at thy house.'** When the Lord comes to a sinner with this 'must' of mercy, what a time it is for the sinner then! At other times, we resist his grace, and say, 'Shall I let him in?' But this time, he says, 'I must come in,' and there is no resistance at all. There was no knocking at the door. Grace knocked the door of our hearts open and broke it down bolt and bar and mercy entered in. Christ said, 'I must save, I shall come in, I will be gracious to whom I will be gracious.'

My friend, if the Lord Jesus Christ ever comes to you in the power of his Spirit and says, 'I must abide at thy house,' there will be no resistance in you. You will gladly receive him. If God says, 'must', the sinner cannot and will not say, 'no'. God's will must prevail. Man's will must bow. Let God say, 'must', and it must be done.

The sinner runs away from Christ, but Christ pursues him and overcomes him. If our hearts be shut hard against him, he puts his hand in at the door. If we refuse to arise and open to him, he opens the door and says, 'I must come in.' In his own well-determined hour of mercy, the Lord Jesus Christ enters into the hearts of those whom he has chosen and redeemed and dwells there for ever. He says, 'Today I must abide at thy house,' and so it must be!

'He made haste and came down'

Read John 6:37–45; Romans 8:28–39

That call of God the Holy Spirit by which sinners are irresistibly drawn to the Lord Jesus Christ is always effectual. Preachers preach and plead and urge sinners to come to Christ and trust him, with no effect. Be they ever so learned, eloquent and clever, preachers can never change the hearts of men. But when God the Holy Spirit calls sinners to Christ by the gospel, he effectually changes their hearts by the sovereign power of his grace. One clear example of this effectual call is that wretched publican to whom our Lord was so gracious, Zacchaeus.

As soon as our Lord said to him, 'Zacchaeus, make haste, and come down; for today I must abide at thy house,' Zacchaeus 'made haste and came down' (Luke 19:5–6). The call of grace changed Zacchaeus for ever. His heart became generous. His home was opened. His table was spread. His conscience was purged. His soul was filled with the joy of grace. The Lord Jesus became Zacchaeus' Master and Zacchaeus willingly surrendered himself and all that he possessed to the claims of Christ. He said, 'Behold, Lord, the half of my goods I give to the poor; and if I have taken anything from any man by false accusation, I restore him fourfold.' Though grace had infinitely enriched Zacchaeus' heart and soul, it greatly reduced his bank account. It may do the same to you. Though Zacchaeus could never have done any good works which God would accept for his salvation, once he was saved by the grace of God, grace brought forth good works from him.

This is one means by which God's elect are known. If any man is truly saved, if he is called of God with the call of effectual grace, that call produces good works.

Saving faith always produces good works

Read Ephesians 2:1–10

What are those good works which grace always produces?

Zacchaeus believed Christ. He believed Christ's claims as Lord and received him as such. The first result of the Holy Spirit's call is *faith in Christ*. Faith is not produced by the preacher. Faith is not produced by the sinner. Faith in Christ is a supernatural work, produced in the hearts of men by the Holy Spirit in effectual calling. It is the gift of God. It is the operation of God in a man's heart that causes him to believe. We believe by the working of his mighty power. The saving, effectual call of the Spirit always produces faith in Christ.

Zacchaeus surrendered himself to Christ as Lord. The effectual call of the Holy Spirit causes proud sinners to bow in humiliation before Christ as Lord and King. Where there is no knowledge of Christ's lordship, there is no knowledge of his saviourhood. Where there is no *surrender to Christ the Lord*, there is no faith in Christ the Saviour. Where there is no submission to Christ, there is no salvation by Christ.

Zacchaeus became a gracious man. Before he was a selfish, self-centred, self-seeking publican. He robbed widows and orphans to increase his riches. He walked over the poor to make gain for himself. But no more! Grace entered his heart and made him gracious. As it was with Zacchaeus, so it is with all who are born again by the Spirit of God. *Grace makes men gracious*. Grace produces love, love brings forth generosity and generosity shows itself by acts of benevolence, hospitality and kindness.

Has the gracious call of God had such an effect upon you? If so, then it may be said of you as it was of Zacchaeus: 'This day is salvation come to this house forsomuch as he also is a son of Abraham [one of the chosen seed]. For the Son of man is come to seek and to save that which was lost' (Luke 19:9–10).

God of heaven, send forth your Spirit with mighty, sovereign, irresistible, effectual power this day, to call dead sinners to life and faith in your Son, the Lord Jesus Christ.

'I have redeemed thee'

Read Romans 5:1–21

There are some people among whom I am glad to be numbered, though they may be a despised few, who believe the Bible doctrine of particular, effectual redemption. We believe that the blood of Christ is of infinite value, but that the intention of Christ in his death never was the salvation of all men. Without question, if Christ had intended to save all men by his death, if that had been the object and purpose of his atonement, all men would be saved; but that never was his purpose. We believe, according to the Scriptures, that the intention of Christ's atonement and the effects of his atonement are the same. It was our Lord's intention to redeem his own elect by the shedding of his blood, and by the shedding of his blood all of God's elect have been redeemed. This is clearly the doctrine of the Bible. The Lord Jesus Christ voluntarily laid down his life for the redemption of a particular people and by his death at Calvary the Son of God effectually accomplished the redemption of those people. All that our Lord Jesus Christ intended to do he has done!

1. Christ has redeemed all of God's elect from the curse of the law: 'Christ hath redeemed us from the curse of the law, being made a curse for us: for it is written, cursed is every one that hangeth on a tree' (Gal. 3:13).

2. Christ has put away the sins of his people: 'Now once in the end of the world hath he appeared to put away sin by the sacrifice of himself' (Heb. 9:26).

3. Christ has purchased for himself a people: 'Ye know that ye were not redeemed with corruptible things, as silver and gold, from your vain conversation received by tradition from your fathers; but with the precious blood of Christ, as of a lamb without blemish and without spot: who verily was foreordained before the foundation of the world' (1 Peter 1:18–19).

4. Our Lord Jesus Christ has perfected for ever those who are sanctified, or set apart in eternal election as the special, chosen objects of God's love and grace: 'For by one offering he hath perfected for ever them that are sanctified' (Heb. 10:14).

'The redemption that is in Christ Jesus'

Read Hebrews 10:1–22

Our redemption was purposed by God in eternity. Both the sacrifice of Christ and the results of that sacrifice were purposed by God before the foundation of the world. From all eternity God looked upon his Son as 'the Lamb slain from the foundation of the world'; and he looked upon his chosen people in Christ as men and women redeemed, justified, reconciled and accepted in him. In the mind and purpose of God the work of redemption was finished before the worlds were made (1 Peter 1:18–20; 2 Tim. 1:9).

The redemption of God's elect was actually accomplished by the death of Christ at Calvary. When our Saviour cried, 'It is finished!', the work was done. We were redeemed. The prophet Daniel described Christ as the Messiah, the Prince, that one who must come 'to finish the transgression, and to make an end of sins, and to make reconciliation for iniquity, and to bring in an everlasting righteousness' (Dan. 9:24). Either Christ has actually accomplished these things for his covenant people, or he is not that Messiah of whom Daniel spoke. He has finished the transgression of his people by dying for it. He has made an end of sins by putting them away. He has reconciled us to God by satisfying the claims of God's offended justice against us. And he has brought in an everlasting righteousness by his perfect obedience to the law as our Representative.

It is this redemption, purposed by God in eternity and accomplished by Christ at Calvary, which the Holy Spirit applies to the hearts of sinners in regeneration, creating faith in Christ (2 Cor. 4:6; Heb. 9:14). If you believe on the Lord Jesus Christ this day, God's distinguishing grace towards you in redemption is the cause of your faith. If you believe, God purposed to redeem you in eternity. If you believe, the Lord Jesus Christ died for you and purchased you at Calvary. With his own precious blood he redeemed you particularly. With his own precious blood he redeemed you effectually. How you ought to love him! How you ought to praise him! How you ought to give yourself to him! He loved you and gave himself for you!

'Who his own self bare our sins'

Read Leviticus 1:1–17

Because he was made to be sin, the Lord Jesus Christ bore the consequence of our sin. Christ answered for our sins at the bar of God's justice. He paid the full penalty of the law for our sins. When justice came to punish sin and found it upon Christ, it arrested him and bruised him so sorely that he sweat blood through the pores of his body. Justice took Immanuel, like a malefactor, off to the hall of judgement. There was none to declare his innocence, or plead for his release. He was brutally beaten and given over to the Roman soldiers. He was publicly stripped, abused, mocked, derided and spat upon. They took him out to the hill of doom and nailed him to the cross. They lifted him up, hanging between heaven and earth, and watched him die. Thus, Christ 'his own self bare our sins in his own body on the tree'. Because he bore our sins, the sword of God's justice was drawn against him and the cup of wrath was poured out upon him. He took the place of the guilty, became guilty and bore the penalty of guilt that we deserve. The Son of God was crushed to death beneath the wheel of divine justice!

Now since the Lord Jesus Christ has borne our sins and satisfied the claims of divine justice against sin for us, we do not bear them. God laid our sins upon his Son and exacted sin's penalty from him. God charged his Son with our sins. Justice will not allow God to charge sin to his people. God transferred our sins to his Son. He will not transfer them back to us again. God punished his Son for our sins. He will never punish us for sin. Justice will not allow the same crime to be punished twice. Righteousness will not allow the same debt to be paid twice. The law, the justice and the righteousness of God punished all my sin in Christ my Surety and will never punish me. 'Blessed is the man to whom the Lord will not impute sin' (Rom 4:8). God will never impute sin to those for whom Christ died. He will never charge a believing soul with sin; because Christ bore our sins away!

'With the mouth confession is made unto salvation'

Read Romans 10:1–17

Our Lord said, 'Out of the abundance of the heart the mouth speaketh' (Matt. 12:34). That which a man knows, he can explain. That which a man believes, he can tell. That which a man has experienced, he can put into words. If you cannot tell anyone what you believe and why you believe it, it is very likely that you do not really believe. There are multitudes who say, 'I believe in Jesus Christ.' Almost everyone does. The devils in hell believe in Christ, but they do not know him. They are not saved. And most people who say they believe in Jesus Christ are like the devils – they are not saved. There are very few people in the church or out of it who can tell you anything about the Lord Jesus Christ. They cannot answer the most simple, basic, elementary questions about the person and work of Christ: 'Who is he? What did he do? Why did he do it? Where is he now? What is he doing there?' There is a reason for man's ignorance in these matters. He simply does not know Christ. You cannot tell what you do not know any more than you can come back from where you have not been. If you know Christ, you can and will confess Christ. That which a man has experienced in his heart, he can and will confess with his mouth.

A faith that I cannot explain is no faith at all. Peter says, 'Sanctify the Lord God in your hearts: and be ready always to give answer to every man that asketh you a reason of the hope that is in you with meekness and fear' (1 Peter 3:15). A hope that I cannot explain is a false hope. A salvation that I cannot confess with my mouth, according to the Word of God, is no salvation at all. I do not say that a man must have great learning and knowledge in order to be saved. I do not say that a person must be a good speaker to be a child of God. But I do say that a person who has a good hope of salvation in Christ must be able to tell what his hope is. Where in the New Testament do you ever find that men were called Christians who knew nothing about Christianity?

'With the mouth confession is made unto salvation'

Read 2 Timothy 1:1–18

Our confession of Christ must be according to the Word of God. I have no reason to believe that I am a child of God unless I can open the Bible and show you why, and upon what basis, I have such a hope.

This is what I am saying: if you are a child of God, you can tell how you came to be a child of God (1 John 3:1–3). If you are redeemed, you can explain how you were redeemed (Gal. 3:13). If you are justified, you can declare how God can be just and yet justify the ungodly (Rom. 3:24–26). If you have faith in Christ, you can explain what faith in Christ is (John 3:14–15). If you have experienced the grace of God in salvation, you can explain how it is that God saves sinners by his almighty, free grace in Christ (Eph. 2:8–9; 2 Tim. 1:9).

If I am saved, if I am a child of God, I must be able to confess and declare my faith to you, and I will. I want to tell you three things which I know, three things which I have experienced, three things which I believe, according to the Word of God.

1. I believe that all men were ruined by the fall of our father Adam. Adam was the federal head and representative of our race before God. When he sinned, we sinned. When he fell, we fell. When he died, we died. 'Wherefore, as by one man sin entered into the world, and death by sin; and so death passed upon all men, for that all have sinned' (Rom. 5:12).

2. I believe in redemption by the blood of Christ. The Lord Jesus Christ, the Son of God, bore our sins in his own body on the cross, suffering the just penalty of sin as our Substitute, and obtained eternal redemption for all God's elect, by his sin-atoning sacrifice (Isa. 53:10–11; 2 Cor. 5:21).

3. I believe in regeneration by the irresistible power and grace of the Holy Spirit. In the time of God's appointment the Holy Spirit sovereignly gives eternal life to God's elect, producing faith in them (Ps. 65:4; John 3:8).

'Who hath blessed us'

Read Psalm 135:1–21

Know this: all of God's people are blessed of God. You may be poor, you may have no material possessions to call your own, you may be sickly, in constant bodily pain and ready to die, but if you are in Christ, if you are a child of God, you are blessed, blessed of God with all spiritual blessings in Christ Jesus.

> When upon life's billows you are tempest tossed,
> When you are discouraged, thinking all is lost,
> Count your many blessings, name them one by one,
> And it will suprise you what the Lord has done.

Children of God, we are blessed!

We are blessed according to the purpose of God. 'God hath saved us and called us with an holy calling, not according to our works, but according to his own purpose and grace, which was given us in Christ Jesus before the world began' (2 Tim. 1:9). 'Blessed be the God and Father of our Lord Jesus Christ, who hath blessed us with all spiritual blessings in heavenly places in Christ Jesus' (Eph. 1:3).

All the blessings of God's grace and glory, for time and eternity, were freely given to all believers by God's eternal electing love: 'According as he hath chosen us in him before the foundation of the world, that we should be holy and without blame before him: in love having predestinated us unto the adoption of children by Jesus Christ to himself, according to the good pleasure of his will' (Eph. 1:4–5). God in his eternal purpose gave us and guaranteed the accomplishment of all these blessings in his people: adoption, justification, acceptance, redemption, forgiveness, regeneration and all the fulness of eternal glory. Do you see how blessed you are? What more could anyone desire? And all of this God has done for us 'to the praise of the glory of his grace' (Eph. 1:6).

'Who hath blessed us'

Read Psalm 136:1–26

We are blessed by the providence of God. To all true believers, all who are chosen of God, redeemed by Christ and called by the Holy Spirit, it is promised that all things, both the evil that darkens our days and the good that lights our way, work together for our spiritual and eternal good. Child of God, our heavenly Father has promised us good and nothing but good, for time and eternity. He has promised that nothing will ever happen except that which will have a good effect upon his own. 'There shall no evil happen to the just' (Prov. 12:21). Yes, we do experience things which seem to the eye of flesh to be evil, things which cause us pain, heartache and sorrow. But God will see to it that these things, and all things, work together for our good. God is as good as his word and faith takes God at his word. By our own experience, by the Word of God and by the inner witness of the Spirit, 'We know that all things work together for good to them that love God, to them who are the called according to his purpose' (Rom. 8:28). It is not true that all things will just happen to turn out for good. But it is true that all things work together, according to God's wisdom, purpose and power, for the good of his elect. And soon we shall see that it has been true.

> In heaven's eternal light we'll see,
> All things worked out for good.

And we shall be blessed in the presence of God. When our life's journey is over, we shall stand before God perfectly holy and perfectly righteous, being washed in the blood of Christ and robed in his righteousness. Through the imputed righteousness of Christ, God has 'made us meet to be partakers of the inheritance of the saints in light' (Col. 1:12). All the blessings of eternal glory which were promised to us in the covenant of grace, earned for us by the righteousness of Christ, purchased for us by the blood of Christ and claimed for us by the ascension of Christ into heaven will be ours in real possession. Not one of God's children will lack any portion of the heavenly inheritance. In Christ we are worthy of all and we shall have all. We are blessed indeed!

'Baptized in the name of the Lord'

Read Matthew 3:1–17

What is baptism? It is a public confession of faith in Christ. By baptism, believers symbolically show their union with Christ in his death, his burial and his resurrection. Going down into the water, we confess that we are crucified with Christ. The old man, being dead to the law through the body of Christ, is buried in the watery grave. Coming up out of the watery grave, we testify that we have been raised with Christ to the newness of life by the power of the Holy Spirit.

Who should be baptized? Baptism in the New Testament was never administered to anyone but believers. I refuse to baptize babies, or unbelievers, because it was never done in the New Testament. Only those who believe the gospel are to be baptized (Acts 2:41; 8:37). Show me one case in the Bible where any baby was ever baptized, and I will start baptizing babies tomorrow.

How is baptism to be performed? Some say, 'Sprinkle'. Some say, 'Pour'. The Bible says, 'Baptize'. The word 'baptize' means to immerse, to dip, or to plunge into water. Baptism is a burial of believers in water. Not until you can bury a man by sprinkling a few grains of sand in his face can you baptize a man by sprinkling a few drops of water on him. Immersion is not *a mode of* baptism. Immersion *is* baptism. Anything other than immersion is not baptism. Why be so dogmatic? Because I recognize the authority of the Word of God. Show me one case where baptism was administered by the apostles by 'sprinkling', and I will start sprinkling believers and quit baptizing them. But, unless you can find at least one example of 'baptism by sprinkling' in the New Testament, you must not tolerate such a practice. (Read Matt. 3:13–17; Acts 8:38; Col. 2:12.) Baptism is the immersion of believers in water as a public confession of faith in Christ.

Can a person be saved without baptism? The answer to that question is obvious. All of God's people are saved without baptism. We are saved, like that penitent thief, by grace alone (Eph. 2:8–9). Yet no saved person will refuse to obey Christ and follow him in baptism.

'By the grace of God I am what I am'

Read Isaiah 51:1–23

This is my testimony. This is my confession of faith. This is my hope. **'By the grace of God I am what I am.'** It is certain that I am not what I ought to be. I am not what I desire to be. And I am not what I hope to be. But, blessed be God, I am not what I once was. God has mercifully brought me up out of the deep miry clay and set my feet upon the Rock, Christ Jesus. He has saved my soul. And now it is my desire to extol and honour his matchless, free, sovereign and distinguishing grace, because 'By the grace of God I am what I am.' It is my heart's great joy to ascribe my salvation entirely to the grace of God.

This is my doctrinal confession. Do you want to know what is the sum and substance of my doctrine? Do you want to know the essence of all that I believe? It is just this: 'By the grace of God I am what I am.' Let me put it in such a way that you cannot mistake my meaning. Salvation is altogether the work of God's grace. Salvation is not in any degree whatsoever the work of man. Salvation is not by man's will, but by God's will. Salvation is not man's work, but God's work. Salvation is not accomplished by man's decision, but by the grace of God. Like Jonah, all of God's people have learned that 'Salvation is of the Lord!' (Jonah 2:9.) 'For by grace are ye saved through faith; and that not of yourselves: it is the gift of God: not of works lest any man should boast' (Eph. 2:8–9). '[God] hath saved us, and called us with an holy calling, not acording to our works, but according to his own purpose and grace, which was given us in Christ Jesus before the world began' (2 Tim. 1:9). Grace elected me. Grace redeemed me. Grace sought me. Grace gave me life. Grace revealed Christ in me. Grace gave me faith. Grace taught me to pray. Grace preserves me. From beginning to end, salvation is by the grace of God. With the apostle Paul, I freely and gladly renounce all human merit. I am not what I am as the result of anything good which God foresaw would be in me. Like all other men, there is nothing good in me by nature. I am not what I am as the result of anything I have done. Like all men, I was without strength. But 'By the grace of God I am what I am.'

'Rejoice in the Lord, O ye righteous'

Read Psalm 33:1–22

We have a very gracious God indeed. He makes delight a duty. He commands us to do that which is most pleasant. God commands his people to rejoice. Have you not read that commandment in the Scriptures? 'Rejoice evermore. Pray without ceasing. In everything give thanks: for this is the will of God in Christ Jesus concerning you' (1 Thess. 5:16–18). Again we are exhorted: 'Rejoice in the Lord alway: and again I say, Rejoice' (Phil. 4:4). If you are a child of God, you should be a person full of joy. You are chosen of God, redeemed by blood and regenerated by grace. Why shouldn't you rejoice? Is it possible for a man to know the love and grace of God and not rejoice? I do not suggest that you be light-hearted to the point of being frivolous. We must take life, and our responsibilities in it, seriously. I do not suggest that you should rejoice in your heartaches and sorrows. But I do say that men and women of faith can and should rejoice, even in the midst of their sorrows. I cannot rejoice in pain, but I can rejoice in my God, who sends me the pain. I am addressing you who are the people of God. Do you want a reason to rejoice?

Child of God, rejoice because your greatest trouble is past. Your sin and guilt are gone. Why shouldn't you rejoice? God took your sin and put it on his own Son, the Lord Jesus Christ. Christ took your sin and washed it away in his own precious blood. Oh, if you ever get hold of this, you will rejoice – God has put away your sin! God no longer charges you with sin. 'As far as the east is from the west, so far hath he removed our transgressions from us' (Ps. 103:12). Our God declares, 'I, even I, am he that blotteth out thy transgressions for mine own sake, and will not remember thy sins ... I have blotted out, as a thick cloud, thy transgressions, and, as a cloud, thy sins ... for I have redeemed thee' (Isa. 43:25; 44:22). 'There is therefore now no condemnation to them which are in Christ Jesus' (Rom. 8:1). 'Blessed is the man to whom the Lord will not impute sin' (Rom. 4:8). I can and will rejoice in my God, for he has put away my sin!

'Rejoice in the Lord, O ye righteous'

Read Revelation 21:1–27

You may well rejoice in the Lord because Satan, your soul's great enemy, is defeated. That fiend of hell who roars against your soul is a defeated foe. All he can do is roar. Christ broke the arm of his power at the cross. He has, once and for all, cast the accuser down. Satan has no power against your soul. He is bound by the chain of Christ's power. When our Lord died, he said, 'Now shall the prince of this world be cast out' (John 12:31). 'And the God of peace shall bruise Satan under your feet shortly' (Rom. 16:20).

You can rejoice in the midst of your many temptations because your indwelling sin, the old man of the flesh, is doomed. So long as we are here upon this earth, we shall have to put up with this old carnal nature. The lusts of the flesh will be with us so long as we live in this flesh. But that old man is doomed.

You may well rejoice because your God rules this world. That one who loved me and gave himself for me holds the reins of universal dominion. Everything in this world is ruled by the hand that was nailed to the tree for me. Surely, he will do me good. He will see to it that 'all things work together for good to them that love God, to them who are the called according to his purpose' (Rom. 8:28).

Rejoice! You live upon a bank which can never be broken. The bank of heaven, the treasury of infinite grace is open to you. 'Let us therefore come boldly unto the throne of grace that we may obtain mercy, and find grace to help in time of need' (Heb. 4:16).

Yes, you can rejoice, even in the midst of your trials, because you are not alone. The eye of the Lord is upon you. The Comforter is within you. Beneath you are the everlasting arms of divine grace and strength. And the Lord God himself is with you. 'The Lord is at hand' (Phil. 4:5). He promises, 'I will never leave thee, nor forsake thee' (Heb. 13:5).

If you are a believer, if you are in Christ, you may well rejoice because all your troubles will soon be over. We shall soon leave this world of sorrow and enter into that glory land, where 'God shall wipe away all tears from their eyes' (Rev. 21:4).

The Lord's Supper

Read Matthew 26:1–29

These verses of inspiration tell us several things about the Lord's Supper. It is a symbolic remembrance of Christ. Just as the Jewish Passover symbolically portrayed the deliverance of Israel from Egypt, the Lord's Supper symbolically reminds the children of God of our salvation and redemption by the righteous life and sacrificial death of the Lord Jesus Christ.

The elements to be used in observing the Lord's Supper are wine and unleavened bread. It is not proper to use grape juice or fizzy drinks. To use those things is to make a mockery of the ordinance. We use wine, because wine was used by our Lord when he instituted the Supper. Being fermented, all impurities are removed from the wine. Therefore it is a suitable representative of our Lord's precious blood, by which we are redeemed. As the wine was crushed from the grape in the winepress, so the blood of Christ poured out of his body when he was crushed in death as our Substitute in the winepress of divine justice. The unleavened bread represents the spotless humanity of Christ, his sinless body, which was sacrificed for us. The unleavened bread has no impurities in it, even as our Lord was without sin. As a man he lived in perfect righteousness for us. Only wine and unleavened bread can be used in the observance of the Lord's Supper, because this is the way it was done in the New Testament, and only wine and unleavened bread can truly represent the body and blood of Christ.

And the Lord's Supper is to be observed often by all true believers. No unbeliever is permitted to receive the Lord's Supper, because the unbeliever does not discern the Lord's body. But no believer is to be refused admittance to the Lord's Table. This is not an ordinance to be guarded by the local church. It is the Lord's Table, open to all the Lord's children, just as it was in the New Testament (Acts 20:1–7). We who believe are worthy to come to the Lord's Supper, because we are in Christ. In him we are worthy. And we are commanded to come often. Not to come would be disobedience to our Saviour.

'If any man sin'

Read Romans 7:1–25

The apostle John writes to us as the children of God in this world, and says, **'My little children, these things write I unto you, that ye sin not. And if any man sin, we have an advocate with the Father, Jesus Christ the righteous: and he is the propitiation for our sins: and not for ours only, but also for the sins of the whole world.'** These are two of the most precious, most comforting, most soul-cheering verses to be found in the whole Word of God. Yet they remind us of a very sad fact, which we must never forget.

All of God's children in this world, at their very best, are still sinners. 'My little children, these things write I unto you, that ye sin not.' Children of God, do not sin. We should never sin. We must oppose sin and resist it. It is an astonishing thing to realize that men and women who are loved of God, redeemed by the blood of Christ and regenerated by the power and grace of the Holy Spirit need to be urged not to sin. But the admonition is needed by us all: 'Do not sin!' Yet John knew very well that all of God's saints in this world do sin. Therefore he says, 'If any man sin.' The apostle uses gentle language, but he knew that we would sin. It was John who said, 'If we say that we have no sin, we deceive ourselves, and the truth is not in us' (1 John 1:8). So long as we live in this world, in this body of flesh, we shall sin. Sin is what we are by nature. Sin is mixed with all we do. Sin mars even our best deeds. 'We are all as an unclean thing; and all our righteousnesses are as filthy rags' (Isa. 64:6). All of God's people in this world have learned to confess, with the apostle Paul, 'I know that in me (that is, in my flesh) dwelleth no good thing' (Rom. 7:18). Every believer mournfully cries, 'O wretched man that I am!' (Rom. 7:24), because every believer knows himself to be a vile sinner.

'We have an advocate'

Read 2 Samuel 12:1–14

We do sin, but John assures us that our sins will never deprive us of our interest in Christ. Notice John's words: **'If any man sin, we have an advocate with the Father.'** Yes, my friend, though we do sin, we have an Advocate with the Father still. The text does not read, 'If any man sin, he has forfeited his advocate with the Father.' It says, 'We have an advocate,' sinners though we are! All the sin a believer ever has committed, or ever can commit, cannot destroy his interest in Christ. We may, any one of us, fall into some dreadful, shameful, sorrowful transgression. God forbid that it should ever happen. But there is no sin, no evil thought, imagination, or deed, of which you and I are not capable. Yet if we do sin, these horrible, treasonable acts can never tear us from our Saviour's heart. Aren't you glad that God 'hath not dealt with us after our sins; nor rewarded us according to our iniquities'? (Ps. 103:10.) Child of God, I tell you plainly that the Lord Jesus Christ will never forsake his wandering sheep! He will not leave his erring child! I say, do not sin. May God strengthen you with grace to resist sin and to hate evil. But when you do sin, do not despair. God still declares, 'I am the Lord, I change not; therefore ye sons of Jacob are not consumed' (Mal. 3:6). Mark this down as a solid pillar of gospel truth: notwithstanding all our sin, we are perfectly justified, accepted, righteous and beloved in Christ.

John also gives us a reason for this blessed assurance. God has provided his Son, the Lord Jesus Christ, as an advocate for his sinning people. **'We have an Advocate with the Father, Jesus Christ the righteous: and he is the propitiation for our sins.'** God will never charge his believing children with sin, because Christ has completely satisfied the justice of God for us, and he pleads the merits of his righteousness and blood for us in heaven.

'Made righteous'

Read Isaiah 64:1-12

The only righteous person in this world is that person who has been made righteous by God himself. Ony God can produce righteousness suitable to God and only God can make men righteous in his sight. How does God make sinners righteous?

God has made all of his elect righteous by imputing the righteousness of the Lord Jesus Christ to us. This imputed righteousness is an act of God's grace in redemption. Because the Lord Jesus Christ lived in righteousness upon the earth as our Representative and died under the penalty of God's law as our Substitute, the law and justice of God declare that we are righteous. The very righteousness of Christ, his perfect obedience to God as a man, has been imputed to us. That is to say, righteousness has been laid to our account. In exactly the same manner as our sins were imputed to Christ, his righteousness has been imputed to us. When God made Christ to be sin for us, he charged him with our sin. The Son of God became responsible to the law for the sins of his elect people. And the penalty of sin was exacted from him. He died under the wrath of God because of our sin. Even so, God having imputed the righteousness of Christ to us who believe, we have become responsible for righteousness in the sight of God's law. And we shall receive the just reward of the law for righteousness: eternal life and everlasting glory. As our works of sin were made to be our Lord's, so his works of righteousness have been made ours. As he received the reward of our sin, we must receive the reward of his righteousness. That is substitution.

Our righteousness before God is an unalterable fact of divine justice. It is perfect righteousness and it never varies in degree. In Christ we are righteous! Our righteousness is the righteousness of Christ, our Substitute. Child of God, can you realize this? Your standing, your acceptance with God never change. God is always well pleased with you in his Son! If you are truly one with Christ by faith, you are a righteous person.

'Thou thoughtest that I was ... as thyself'

Read Exodus 33:12 – 34:7

The God of heaven is not like men think he is. God is not helpless; he is almighty. God is not frustrated; he is sovereign. God is not subject to man's will; man is subject to God's will. God is not in your hands; you are in God's hands. 'Our God is in the heavens: he hath done whatsoever he hath pleased' (Ps. 115:3). God says, 'I am God, and there is none else; I am God, and there is none like me, declaring the end from the beginning, and from ancient times the things that are not yet done, saying, My counsel shall stand, and I will do all my pleasure ... I have spoken it, I will also bring it to pass; I have purposed it, I will also do it' (Isa. 46:9–11).

God Almighty does not want to save everyone in the world. Stop and think for a minute. If God really wanted to save everyone in the world, everyone in the world would be saved. He is God. God is not trying to save everybody. Almighty God never tries to do anything. Whatever God puts forth his hand to do is done. 'None can stay his hand' (Dan. 4:35). He is God. If God tried to save everybody, everybody would be saved. Who can thwart his purpose? Who can resist his power? Find me the man, or the demon, who can successfully thwart the purpose of God, resist the power of God and frustrate the grace of God, and I will worship him, for he is almighty.

The fact is God wants to save and does save some men. It has been God's purpose from eternity to save those people whom he has chosen, and God's eternal purpose cannot be defeated. God's elect people must and will be saved. God himself declares, 'It shall come to pass.' He does not say, 'It may come to pass.' He does not say, 'I hope it will come to pass.' He does not say, 'It will come to pass, if man will exercise his free will and bring it to pass; but if man does not give me permission, my hands are tied and I can do nothing.' Our God declares, 'It shall come to pass, that in the place where it was said unto them, Ye are not my people, there it shall be said unto them, Ye are the sons of the living God' (Hos. 1:10). I love the 'shalls' and 'wills' of Almighty God. He says, 'I will be your God, and ye shall be my people,' and he brings it to pass.

'Until he find it'

Read Matthew 18:1-14

I want you to picture the Lord Jesus Christ, our Shepherd, as he searches for his lost sheep. He leaves the ninety-nine in the wilderness, and goes out to search for his one lost sheep. He knows the sheep that is lost. He has a picture of it in his mind. He thinks little of the ninety-nine who need no Shepherd. His heart is all wrapt up in that one lost sheep. This one thought seems to possess his entire being: 'My sheep is lost!' Immediately, the search begins.

It is an *all-absorbing* search. That one lost sheep consumes the Shepherd's tender heart. He can neither eat nor sleep until he finds that lost sheep. The poor, lost, wandering sheep has no thought of the Shepherd, but the Shepherd seems to think of nothing else except that one lost sheep. The sheep belongs to him. He purchased it with his own precious blood and he will not lose it. The sheep is his responsibility. His honour as a Shepherd is bound up in the welfare of that sheep. And he loves his sheep. He cannot bear the thought of its being lost. The Shepherd knows all the pits into which the sheep might fall and all the wolves which thirst for its blood. And he knows that his poor sheep is both defenceless and senseless.

It is a *definite* search. The Shepherd goes after his sheep. He is seeking one, definite, particular sheep.

It is an *active* search. No hill is too difficult to climb. No mountain is too high. No precipice is too rocky. No valley is too low. No distance is too far. The Shepherd must have his sheep.

It is a *persevering* search. He will search for his lost sheep 'until he find it'.

It is a *personal* search. The Shepherd himself goes after his sheep. It is a glorious thought to think of Christ himself on the trail of his sheep. Sinners who will not come to Christ are pursued by the Son of God, pursued by the eternal Lover of men, until he finds them!

And it is a *successful* search. Of this one thing you may be sure: the Shepherd will find his lost sheep! Not one of those lost sheep, for whom the Lord Jesus Christ suffered and died will be lost for ever. He will find his sheep and bring it home rejoicing.

'When he hath found it'

Read Ezekiel 34:1-31

Picture that poor, lost sheep. He has fallen over the edge of a high cliff on a dark, stormy night. Overhead he sees the terrifying storm of God's wrath. The lightning seems to strike out at him, saying, 'The soul that sinneth, it shall die.' Below he sees the gaping jaws of hell opened wide to engulf him. He is losing his footing, slipping into hell. His very soul is terrified. That sheep is you and me. 'All we like sheep have gone astray; we have turned every one to his own way.' We were all lost and ruined by the fall of our father Adam (Rom. 3:12). We went astray as soon as we were born, speaking lies (Ps. 58:3). If left to ourselves, we would all surely perish. Silly sheep are helpless. They have no sense of direction. They have a will to roam and wonder, strayng further and further away. But they have no will to return to the Shepherd.

Just when the sheep is ready to perish for ever, Christ finds his lost sheep! What does he do? Does the Shepherd say, 'Now I have done all I can for you, the rest is up to you. You take the first step, and I will do the rest. If you will let me I will save you?' Nonsense! Our dear Shepherd reaches down with the long arm of his almighty, irresistible grace and lays hold of his perishing sheep and **'He layeth it on his own shoulders, rejoicing!'**

Now picture the sheep. The Good Shepherd has the sheep on his own shoulders, holding its four legs securely in the strong hands of his grace. This is a place of rest for the sheep. All the weight and burden of his soul is on the Shepherd's shoulders. And the sheep is secure. He is in the Shepherd's hands and upon the Shepherd's shoulders. He has nothing to fear (Deut. 1:30-31; John 10:27-29). Nothing can hurt the sheep until it first destroys the Shepherd. At last, the great, all-sufficient Shepherd brings his sheep home rejoicing. In that saved sheep, he sees of the travail of his soul and is satisfied. Imagine that – the Son of God rejoices in the salvation of sinners! This was the joy set before him, for which he endured the cross, despising its shame. Thank God for such a Shepherd as Christ is!

The pre-eminence of Christ (I)

Read Revelation 1:1-20

The apostle shows us in this text that it is the will, the pleasure and the determination of the Father's heart that his Son, the Lord Jesus Christ, be pre-eminent in all things and above all things. God has so highly exalted, honoured and magnified his Son that the only way any creature can exalt, honour and magnify the triune God is by exalting, honouring and magnifying the Lord Jesus Christ. So determined is the eternal, triune God to make Christ pre-eminent in all things that God can only be known and revealed to men by the knowledge and revelation of Christ. The only way God makes himself known is through the Son. And the only way God deals with men is through the Son. 'The Father loveth the Son, and hath given all things into his hand' (John 3:35).

We are trinitarians. We worship the one true and living God in the trinity of his sacred persons: the Father, the Son and the Holy Spirit. There are three distinct and separate persons in the Godhead. Yet these three divine persons are one God. The Father is the Father. The Son is the Son. And the Spirit is the Spirit. They are three distinct persons. Yet they are one God. There is no way to explain the doctrine of the Trinity, or even illustrate it, in human terms. We simply believe it, because it is plainly revealed in Holy Scripture. In the baptism of our Lord (Matt. 3:16-17) we see the three persons of the Godhead: the Father speaks from heaven, the Son is immersed in water and the Spirit descends upon him. Believers are commanded to be baptized in the name of the Father and of the Son and of the Holy Spirit (Matt. 28:19), three distinct persons. Yet our Lord says plainly, 'I and my Father are one' (John 10:30). 'He that hath seen me hath seen the Father' (John 14:9). The Word of God plainly states the doctrine of the Trinity in 1 John 5:7: 'There are three that bear record in heaven, the Father, the Word, and the Holy Ghost: and these three are one.' The Father, the Son and the Spirit are one in essence, one in purpose, one in character, one in power, and one in being. All true believers are trinitarians.

The pre-eminence of Christ (II)

Read Revelation 4:1-11

We know, worship and serve the triune God only as we know, worship and serve the Lord Jesus Christ. Thomas, with his hand in the pierced side of the crucified, risen Christ, said unto him, 'My Lord and my God' (John 20:28), and he was right in doing so. Paul says, 'In him dwelleth all fulness of the Godhead bodily' (Col. 2:9). What can he mean but this: in the God-man, Jesus Christ, all that God is – Father, Son and Holy Spirit – perpetually and eternally resides? 'You must know that you are never to separate in your thoughts God from Christ; always as you look upon Christ, so look upon God; or as you look upon God, look upon him no otherwise than as he is in Christ, not as if there were another God besides what Christ is; for there is no such thing' (Tobias Crisp). Jesus Christ our Saviour is God.

Everything God has ever done, is doing, or will ever do, he does through the mediation of his dear Son, the Lord Jesus Christ.

The covenant of grace was made before the world was with Christ the Mediator. That solemn compact of mercy, ordered in all things and sure, was made with Christ (Ps. 89:3-4, 19-37; 2 Sam. 23:5; 2 Tim. 1:9).

The world was created by God through Christ the Mediator. When Paul says, Christ is 'the firstborn of every creature' (Col. 1:15), he is simply declaring that Christ is the one out of whom creation was born. All things sprang from him. He is the original cause of all things, 'the beginning of the creation of God' (Rev. 3:14; John 1:1-3).

God's providential rule of the world is by Christ the Mediator (Dan. 7:13-14; John 17:2). In time, as the reward of his obedience and death as our Substitute, Christ took his place of dominion as a man. But this world has always been under the mediatorial rule of the Lord Jesus Christ, 'whose goings forth have been from old, from everlasting' (Micah 5:2). It is the mediatorial rule of the Lord Jesus Christ that preserves this world. He will not allow this world to be destroyed until all his elect are saved (2 Peter 3:9). Thanks be unto God, the God who rules this world is the pre-eminent Christ, the Friend of sinners!

The pre-eminence of Christ (III)

Read Revelation 5:1–14

Our Lord said, 'All things are delivered unto me of my Father: and no man knoweth the Son but the Father; neither knoweth any man the Father, save the Son, and he to whomsoever the Son will reveal him' (Matt. 11:27). God reveals himself to men only in Christ (John 1:18; 14:6). Christ is the Word, the revelation of God (John 1:1–3). All that we know of God is Christ. He is the brightness of the Father's glory and the express image of his person. In *the revelation of God*, Christ is pre-eminent.

In *the worship and service of God* Christ is pre-eminent. God deals with men only in and through his beloved Son, the Lord Jesus Christ, who said, 'No man cometh unto the Father but by me' (John 14:6; 10:9; Eph. 2:18; Heb. 7:25; 10:19). 'God will not speak to, nor will he be spoken to by any man apart from the Lord Jesus Christ' (Scott Richardson). The whole of our salvation is in Christ. He is made of God 'unto us wisdom, and righteousness, and sanctification, and redemption' (1 Cor. 1:30). And the only way we can approach God is in him. God will not receive any worship, prayer, sacrifice, or service offered to him by man, but through the merits and mediation of Christ (1 Peter 2:5). Everything done for God and offered to God must be performed and offered in the name of Christ with a conscious realization that we have no access to or acceptance with the eternal God but by Christ. All that God does for us is in Christ, too. All the blessings of grace and glory are freely bestowed by God upon his sinful people for Christ's sake and through his merits alone (Eph. 1:3–14;4:32).

And when this world is folded up like a worn-out garment, when time shall be no more, and all men stand before God *in judgement*, Christ will yet be pre-eminent. Even at the bar of judgement God will deal with men only in Christ. The Judge who will sit upon the great white throne in that day will be none other than the God-man, Christ Jesus our Lord (John 5:21–22; Rom. 14:1–12; 2 Cor. 5:10–11; Rev. 20:11–15). God has determined that in all things he must have the pre-eminence.

'The pre-eminence of Christ (IV)'

Read Revelation 7:1–17

Throughout the endless ages of eternity, the Lord Jesus Christ will have the pre-eminence. When all creation is brought to bow at the feet of Christ and acknowledge him as rightful Lord of the universe, God will be glorified (Col. 1:20; Phil. 2:9–11; 1 Cor. 15:24–28). In fulfilment of his last engagement as our Surety in the covenant of grace, the God-man Mediator will present all the universe to the triune God, and in all the universe God will be glorified. God will be all in all as the enthroned Christ reigns for ever and ever in the infinite splendour and majesty of his righteousness and glory.

What the sun is to our solar system, Christ, the Sun of Righteousness, is to heaven and eternity. He is the centre of heaven, the light of heaven, the life of heaven, the strength of heaven and the joy of heaven. Withdraw the sun from our solar system, and everything would be darkness, destruction and death. Withdraw Christ from heaven, and heaven itself would be hell! In heaven Christ is, and for ever shall be pre-eminent, because for all eternity Christ is all! Christ is for ever all our reward, all our joy, all our peace and all our love. In heaven's eternal bliss, Christ alone will fill our vision and Christ alone will have our praise (Rev. 4:9–11; 5:9–13). This is the ultimate end for which God said in the beginning, 'Let there be light.' This world was created by God, so that 'in all things he [the Lord Jesus Christ] might have the pre-eminence'.

As God the Father has given the Son alone pre-eminence, so must we. Let us honour the one true and living God in all things. There is only one way for us to do so. We must honour the Son, the Lord Jesus Christ (John 5:23–24). When I acknowledge my sin and my need of Christ, I honour him (Ps. 51:1–5; 1 John 5:7–10). When I trust Christ alone as my all-sufficient Substitute, I honour him (John 3:36). When I bow and surrender to Christ as my rightful, sovereign Lord, I honour him (Matt. 10:36–39). When I confess Christ before men, I honour him (Matt. 10:27–33). God delights to give his Son the pre-eminence. And God delights in those who give Christ alone pre-eminence in all things.

'The pre-eminence of Christ (V)'

Read Revelation 19:1-10

Christ alone has pre-eminence as the revelation of God, the Saviour of men, the Ruler of providence and the glory of heaven. God the Father gives Christ all pre-eminence. And God the Holy Spirit gives Christ alone pre-eminence. All the comfort, instruction and direction of God the Holy Spirit come to men from the Lord Jesus Christ (John 16:13).

The Holy Spirit, according to the disposition of the covenant of grace, is Christ's agent in this world. He does nothing of himself, speaks nothing of himself and receives nothing to himself. It is the Spirit's delight to do Christ's bidding in this world, even as it has been the Son's delight to do the Father's bidding. Christ is the Fountain of all grace. The Holy Spirit is the channel through whom all the blessings of grace come to us, but Christ is the Fountain. If you compare 1 Corinthians 12:11 with Ephesians 4:7–12 and Psalm 68:18–20, you will see that all the gifts of the Spirit are really the gifts of Christ, which he has bestowed upon the church for the glory of his own great name, for the furtherance of the gospel and for the spiritual welfare of his people.

Everywhere today men talk much about the Holy Spirit. We are told, 'This is the age of the Holy Spirit.' They talk much about the anointing of the Spirit, the baptism of the Spirit, the power of the Spirit and the presence of the Spirit, and say little about the person and work of the Son. This is all wrong. Those who preach the Holy Spirit and ignore Christ do not have the Holy Spirit. The Holy Spirit speaks only of Christ, and those who have the Spirit speak of Christ, only of Christ. Do not misunderstand me. Believers reverence, worship and honour the Holy Spirit. The Holy Spirit is God. But the only way to honour the Spirit is to honour Christ. This is the age of the Son. This is the age of Christ. This is the gospel day. It began when the Sun of Righteousness arose with healing in his wings. And God has determined in this day that Christ must have the pre-eminence.

'The pre-eminence of Christ (VI)'

Read Revelation 19:11-21

God the Holy Spirit speaks of and reveals Christ to men. He takes the things of Christ and shows them to us. In regeneration, he creates and forms Christ in us. He comforts our hearts by showing us what Christ has done for us and is yet doing on our behalf. He gives us assurance by applying the blood of Christ to our hearts and consciences. And he both reproves us for sin and leads us in the paths of righteousness by showing us the example Christ left for us to follow. When it was needed, the Holy Spirit even gave men the ability to preach the gospel of Christ in languages unknown to them. In the work of the Holy Spirit, Christ is pre-eminent. He is the centre and the object of the Spirit's ministry. He neither seeks nor receives any honour to himself. He promotes the honour of Christ.

To be baptized in the Spirit is to be baptized into Christ's death, resurrection and life. It is to be translated from death to life in Christ (1 Cor. 12:13; Gal. 3:27). The anointing of the Spirit is Christ in you, the hope of glory (Col. 1:27; 1 John 2:27). The gifts of the Spirit are the covenant blessings of God's grace, promised in eternity, purchased by the blood of Christ and bestowed upon men by the royal authority of Christ our King through the agency of his Spirit (Gal. 3:13–14). To be filled with the Spirit is to be filled with the character of Christ (Eph. 5:18–21). The power of the Spirit upon men is the power of the enthroned Christ (Luke 24:49). The blessed presence of the Spirit is the presence of Christ, made known to us by the Spirit (Matt. 18:20; 28:20; John 14:18,23). To walk in the Spirit is to walk in Christ, with Christ, like Christ, towards Christ and for Christ by faith (Gal. 5:16–24).

It may seem that this is an over-simplification of the Spirit's work. I readily acknowledge that there is much more involved in the work of the Holy Spirit than I have mentioned. But whatever else may be included in the ministry of the Spirit, it is the Spirit's determination 'that in all things Christ might have the pre-eminence'.

The pre-eminence of Christ (VII)

Read Revelation 20:1–15

The Lord Jesus Christ is everything to his Father. 'The Father loveth the Son, and hath given all things into his hand' (John 3:35). And his reason for doing so is 'that all men should honour the Son, even as they honour the Father. He that honoureth not the Son honoureth not the Father which hath sent him' (John 5:23). The Father loves, delights in, honours, exalts and magnifies the Son, having determined in all things to make the Son pre-eminent. Christ is to his Father what Benjamin was to Jacob, the Son of his love. His great love for his Son is seen in the place of pre-eminence over all things which the Son enjoys by the gift of his Father.

In his essential deity, as the second person of the holy Trinity, the Father gives nothing to the Son, because the Son is in every way equal to the Father and possesses all things equally as God with the Father and the Spirit. But in his mediatorial character and office, as the Representative of his people and as the reward of his covenant engagements, the Son was given all things by his Father (John 17:2) and has been given pre-eminence in all things. Christ is the pre-eminent object of his Father's affection (Prov. 8:30–31). Nothing is so dear to the Father as the Son. God delights in and is pleased only with his Son (Matt. 3:17). God is pleased with the righteousness of his Son and with the sacrifice of his Son, and he is pleased with believers in his Son and for the sake of his Son. Christ is the pre-eminent object of his Father's trust, too. The Father has entrusted everything to the hands of his Son: his people as a Surety (Eph. 1:12), his creation as a King (Ps. 2:7–8),his glory as the ultimate end of his work (1 Cor.15:28). The Father has made Christ pre-eminent by giving him the place of highest honour, majesty,power and dominion (Phil. 2:9–11; Heb. 1:3–9; 10:12–13). And God the Father has made Christ pre-eminent, giving the Son everything he asks of the Father (John 11:22). God the Father has devoted himself, his heart, his creation, his very being to the glory and honour of his Son, because he is determined 'that in all things Christ might have the pre-eminence'.

The pre-eminence of Christ (VIII)

Read Revelation 21:1–27

As it pleases the Father to give Christ pre-eminence in all things, it pleases every believer to know that Christ is pre-eminent. Nothing can more effectually comfort and challenge the believer's heart than the knowledge of Christ's pre-eminence. In Colossians 1:15–20, Paul gives us a picture of the Lord Jesus Christ, the Son of God, our Redeemer, our Saviour, our Friend, our glorious King, holding in his almighty hand all of creation. He who loved us and gave himself for us holds the whole world in his hand. He who died on the cross knows the most distant star by name. He not only knows it, but also guides it. Better still, he so controls that distant star and all things in God's creation that he makes everything serve the interest of his people (Rom. 8:28). The fact that Christ is pre-eminent assures us of four things.

1. The Lord Jesus Christ is an all-sufficient Saviour. In Paul's day, as in ours, there were some who taught that Christ alone is insufficient, inadequate, incapable by his own merits and grace to save his people. To dispel that heresy, Paul says, 'Christ is pre-eminent.' He is able to do exceedingly and abundantly above all that we ask or think.

2. The Lord Jesus Christ is a sovereign Saviour. He who died on Calvary now rules all things, and nothing can ever separate him from the people he loves. No harm shall befall his elect. No evil shall come upon his people. He will not allow even one to perish. To the trembling, fearful, anxious, fretful believer, Paul says, 'Let not your heart be troubled, Christ is pre-eminent.'

3. The Lord Jesus Christ is a rich and bountiful Saviour. He has all things, and he freely gives all things to his people as they need them. Paul says, to every believer, 'There is no need to worry about hard times or old age, Christ is pre-eminent.'

4. The Lord Jesus Christ is a Saviour worthy of our heart's trust and devotion. You can safely trust Christ in all things and give him the devotion of your heart, because he is pre-eminent. He to whom God the Father has given pre-eminence should have pre-eminence in the hearts of his people.

The pre-eminence of Christ (IX)

Read Revelation 22:1-21

In God's *creation* the triune God said, 'Let us make man in our image, and after our likeness' (Gen. 1:26). And Christ is the image of God, in whose likeness we were made, and the one by whom we were made (Col. 1:15). In the providential rule of the world Christ is pre-eminent (Col. 1:16). All things were made by him and for him. He upholds all things, sustains all things, rules all things and will have the praise of all things.

Christ is pre-eminent in *the book* of God (Luke 24:27). The Bible is a book about Christ. It speaks only of him. The Old Testament says, 'He is coming.' The four Gospels and Acts say, 'He has come.' The epistles and Revelation say, 'He is coming again.'

God has made Christ pre-eminent in *the church* (Col. 1:18). He is the Head (the seat of authority and the source of life) to his body the church. In salvation Christ is pre-eminent (Col. 1:14). He is our wisdom, righteousness, sanctification and redemption. Christ is our salvation. His mediatorial possessions, as the God-man our Saviour, display his pre-eminence (Col. 1:19). All the fulness of the eternal Godhead is in Christ. All the fulness of grace is in Christ. And all the fulness of the divine glory is in Christ.

In *the resurrection* Christ will be the pre-eminent one (Col. 1:18). He was the first one to be raised from the dead, and all who believe will be raised in his likeness.

And Christ is pre-eminent in *reconciliation* (Col. 1:20–22). We have broken God's law and offended his justice. But 'God was in Christ, reconciling the world unto himself, not imputing their trespasses unto them' (2 Cor. 5:19). By the blood of his cross Christ reconciled us to God. And in the ages to come Christ our Lord will reconcile all things to God (Isa. 45:22–25). He will clearly demonstrate the glory of God in all things. The whole creation of God will, in the end, show forth the praise of him by whom and for whom all things were created. 'Every creature' will say, 'blessing, and honour, and glory, and power, be unto him that sitteth upon the throne, and unto the Lamb for ever and ever' (Rev. 5:13).

'The pre-eminence of Christ (X)'

Read Philippians 2:1–11; Acts 2:22–36

Why must Christ have the pre-eminence? Why must all things be put under his feet? Why should he have no rival? Christ must have the pre-eminence in all things, because God the Father said that he must (Ps. 89:27). Why was Joseph made the prime minister of Egypt? Because Pharaoh wanted it that way. Why did Mordecai ride through the city in pomp and pageantry, while Haman led the horse? Because King Ahasurerus said that he must. It is only right for Christ to be pre-eminent, simply because the sovereign God has so ordained it!

Christ was born unto the place of pre-eminence (Isa. 9:6–7). He is the Firstborn in the family of God. As such he has a right to the Father's inheritance. He is the only begotten of the Father. Therefore he has rightful possession of all the Father's property.

Christ must have the pre-eminence because he has paid for it (Isa. 53:9–12). Any man who buys and holds the title to an estate is lord of that estate. And Christ both bought and holds title to God's creation. Therefore, he is Lord of all.

Christ alone deserves the pre-eminence. He has earned the right of pre-eminence by his obedience to the Father's will, having fulfilled all that was required of him as the Surety of the covenant (John 17:1–4). And he has earned the right of pre-eminence in the hearts of his people (Ps. 116:12). Who else has loved us so freely? Who other than Christ has done so much for us? Who but Christ has given us so much? Who else but Christ has been a faithful Friend to our souls?

Let every redeemed, justified, forgiven sinner say, with God our Father, 'Christ alone must have the pre-eminence!' As John Gill puts it, 'Christ ought to have the pre-eminence and first place in the affections of our hearts, in the contemplations of our minds, in the desires of our souls, and in the highest praises of our lips.' He who loved us, bought us with his blood and saved us by his grace has a rightful claim to pre-eminence in our hearts!

'He abideth faithful'

Read Psalm 78:1–39

Meditate today upon the faithfulness of God. It will be good medicine for your soul. 'It is of the Lord's mercies that we are not consumed, because his compassions fail not. They are new every morning: great is thy faithfulness. The Lord is my portion, saith my soul; therefore will I hope in him. The Lord is good to them that wait for him, to the soul that seeketh him' (Lam. 3:22–25). Child of God, in great faithfulness to us, the Lord our God has loaded us with all the benefits of his grace and mercy.

He chose us in eternal love. Before the world began, God loved us and determined to save us. He made for us a covenant. Through Christ Jesus our Head and Representative, God bestowed upon us all the blessings of his grace (Eph. 1:3–6).

In the fulness of time he redeemed us by the blood of Christ. 'Herein is love, not that we loved God, but that he loved us, and sent his Son to be the propitiation for our sins' (1 John 4:10).

Then 'According to his mercy he saved us' (Titus 3:5). At the time appointed, God sent his Spirit to us. He gave us life and faith in Christ. Yes, in Christ,

> There's pardon for transgressions past:
> It matters not how black their cast.
> And, Oh, my soul, with wonder view,
> For sins to come there's pardon too!

Here is another great benefit of grace: the Lord Jesus Christ is continually making intercession for us. The Son of God ever bears our names before the Father, pleading the merits of his own blood and righteousness for our eternal salvation. We need never fear wrath and condemnation from God, because 'We have an advocate with the Father, Jesus Christ the righteous: and he is the propitiation for our sins' (1 John 2:1–2).

Now add to all of these things God's wise and adorable providence on our behalf. God our Saviour so rules all things in providence that all things are benefits of grace to our souls!

'He was manifested to take away our sins'

Read Leviticus 16:1–34

The Lord Jesus Christ *bore all our sins* in his own body on the cross (1 Peter 2:24). Whatever my sins are, that I have committed in the past, that I am committing now, or that I ever shall commit in the future, Christ bore them all in his own body on the cursed tree. The blood of Christ is infinite. It is a boundless ocean, which swallows up and drowns all our sins. Many seem to think that some of our sins are under the blood, but others must be answered for by us at some future judgement. It is not so. All our sins were judged, condemned, punished and washed away at the cross.

Christ so completely bore our sins that he *bore them away*. He carried them up to the cross on his mighty shoulders and bore them until he bore them away. When his great work of redemption was done, our Lord had effectually put away the sins of his elect people. He annihilated them, so that they ceased to be. It is written: Christ has 'forgiven you all trespasses, blotting out the handwriting of the ordinances that was against us, which was contrary to us, and took it out of the way, nailing it to his cross' (Col. 2:13–14). 'And ye know that he was manifested to take away our sins: and in him is no sin' (1 John 3:5).

The Lord Jesus Christ *bore our sins alone*. It was Christ alone, 'who his own self bare our sins in his own body on the tree'. In order to redeem his elect and make atonement for our sins, Christ took our sins upon himself and bore them until he cried with a loud voice, 'It is finished!' Then and there our souls were redeemed. When the Son of God had finished his work, he had put away the sins of his people by the sacrifice of himself. 'This man, after he had offered one sacrifice for sins for ever, sat down on the right hand of God; from henceforth expecting till his enemies be made his footstool. For by one offering he hath perfected for ever them that are sanctified' (Heb. 10:11–14). Our sins were put away. And Christ had done it all alone. Nothing is needed and nothing can be added to the finished work of Christ. His one sacrifice for sin is sufficient and effectual.

'Them that are saved'

Read Exodus 28:1–38

In order to be saved God requires that you must have a perfect righteousness. That righteousness which God requires of sinners he has supplied for sinners, by the incarnation and obedience of his Son, the Lord Jesus Christ. As the Representative of God's elect, the Son of God perfectly obeyed the law of God as a man, establishing righteousness in the earth. This is the only righteousness there is in the world. If you would be saved, you must have the righteousness of Christ. Your own righteousness is filthy rags in the sight of a holy God. He will never accept your righteousness, but he does accept the righteousness of his Son. This perfect righteousness of the man Christ Jesus is imputed to every sinner who believes on him.

In order to be saved God requires that you must die. 'The wages of sin is death.' 'The soul that sinneth, it shall die.' That death which God requires of sinners he has provided for sinners, in the sin-atoning death of his Son, the sinner's Substitute. When Christ died as the Substitute for God's elect, bearing their sins in his own body on the tree, all of God's elect died in him. This sin-atoning sacrifice, which God has accepted, was made for every sinner who believes on the Lord Jesus Christ.

In order to be saved God requires that you must believe on his Son. You must rest your soul upon the merits of Christ's righteousness and shed blood for all your salvation. You must trust the doing and dying of the Lord Jesus Christ alone for salvation. If you will trust Christ, you can trust him. If you can trust Christ, you will trust him. If you do trust Christ as your Saviour and Lord, even that faith by which you trust him is a work of his grace in your heart. It is 'the gift of God, not of works, lest any man should boast'.

'The grace of God'

Read Psalm 85:1–13

The grace of God is in Christ. It comes to us through him. The grace of God is eternal. The grace of God is irresistible. The grace of God is effectual. The grace of God is everlasting. The grace of God is immutable. When we get to glory all of God's elect will gladly sing the sweet song of sovereign grace. The grace of God is sovereign, selective, saving, securing and satisfying. But what does it mean to be saved by grace?

To be saved by grace is to be saved *according to the purpose* of God. All who are saved in time were saved in God's eternal purpose of grace before the world began. Do you want the chapter and verse? 2 Timothy 1:9: God 'hath saved us, and called us with an holy calling, not according to our works, but according to his own purpose and grace, which was given us in Christ Jesus before the world began'. Are you a believer? Are you saved by the grace of God? Then give all praise to God. He loved you, chose you and determined to save you before the world was made!

To be saved by grace is to be saved *by the purchase* of God. Yes, God the Son came into this world as a man. By his righteous life of obedience to God's law, Christ merited salvation for all his people. By his sin-atoning sacrifice, pouring out his life's blood unto death, the Son of God cancelled the debt of our sins, redeemed us from the curse of the law and purchased peace, pardon and eternal glory for us.

To be saved by grace is to be saved *by the power* of God. We were dead, helplessly lost sinners. But God the Holy Spirit came to us in sovereign mercy and he gave us life! This life-giving power of the Holy Spirit is the irresistible grace of God by which the new birth is accomplished. We are born again by the power of God. To be saved by grace is to be saved *for the praise* of God. Why has God saved such worthless worms as we are? The only answer that can be found is this: 'To the praise of the glory of his grace' (Eph. 1:6).

What is love?

Read 1 Corinthians 13:1–13

1. **'Love suffereth long.'** Love is not vengeful, but forbearing. Love is not malicious, but forgiving.
2. **'Love is kind.'** What a blessed word – 'kind'! Let me be surrounded by kind, gentle, thoughtful, caring people. Let me be kind to those around me.
3. **'Love envieth not.'** Love does not envy the happiness, peace and prosperity of others, but rejoices in it.
4. **'Love vaunteth not itself.'** It is not rash. It does not promote, honour, exalt or pamper self.
5. **'Love is not puffed up.'** It is not self-centred, conceited or condescending towards other people.
6. **'Love doth not behave itself unseemly.'** It is neither flattering nor scornful.
7. **'Love seeketh not her own.'** Love does not look after self, but rather looks after its object.
8. **'Love is not easily provoked.'** It is not soon given to anger, or ill-temper.
9. **'Love thinketh no evil.'** Love is not suspicious of evil in others. It puts the best possible light on all actions and words.
10. **'Love rejoiceth not in iniquity.'** Love takes no pleasure in the sins and infirmities of others and mourns over personal sin.
11. **'Love rejoiceth in the truth.'** It rejoices in the faithfulness of men, the truth of God and the success of the gospel.
12. **'Love beareth all things.'** It bears the burdens, infirmities and cares of the one loved, and bears the reproach of Christ gladly.
13. **'Love believeth all things.'** Love is quick to believe the best and slow to receive the evil reports of men about its dear object.
14. **'Love hopeth all things.'** It hopes the best of its object and shuns to consider the worst.
15. **'Love endureth all things.'** For the sake of those loved, Christ and his people, love will willingly endure any hardship.
16. **'Love never faileth.'** True love never quits loving. It only grows deeper, stronger and firmer, even to eternity.

'With the temptation'

Read 1 Corinthians 10:1–14

1. The temptations we suffer have been endured by others before us. **'There hath no temptation taken you but such as is common to man.'** All of God's children in this world have had to face the same temptations as we face. They were men of like passions as we are. If they endured them, we should be able to endure them. Our Lord Jesus Christ, the God-man, endured the same temptations as we do. Because he was tempted in all points like as we are, yet without sin, he is touched with the feeling of our infirmities. It is comforting to me to know that my Saviour really does know exactly what I am going through and how I feel. He will never call upon us to endure anything for him that he has not already endured for us.

2. God is faithful to his tempted people. **'God is faithful, who will not suffer you to be tempted above that ye are able; but will with the temptation also make a way to escape, that ye may be able to bear it.'** Our God and heavenly Father rules this world with total control. Nothing happens except that which God has ordained for our good and his glory, even our temptations. And God will never allow us to be tempted above measure. In great faithfulness to our souls God graciously protects his own elect. With every temptation, God will give his own grace sufficient to bear it. Or else, he will make for us a way of escape, so that we shall not be consumed by it. He promises: 'My grace is sufficient for thee' (2 Cor. 12:9).

3. Every true believer will endure and overcome his temptations. Because God is faithful, none of his own elect will ever be destroyed by temptation. We all do fall, from time to time, under the strain of temptation, but we are not consumed. His grace raises us up, strengthens us and preserves us. True faith cannot be destroyed, but only proved and refined by temptation. 'Because greater is he that is in you, than he that is in the world' (1 John 4:4). 'Blessed is the man that endureth temptation: for when he is tried [having been proved] he shall receive the crown of life, which the Lord hath promised to them that love him' (James 1:12).

'I hope in him'

Read Lamentations 3:1–26

I hope in God's immutable *mercy*. Some people trust their works. Others place all confidence in their religion. But we who believe know that 'It is of the Lord's mercies that we are not consumed.' I am by nature a guilty, helpless sinner. I have no hope but in God, who 'delighteth in mercy' (Micah 7:18). God's mercies towards my soul are many: eternal mercy, redemptive mercy, saving mercy and daily mercy. All God's mercy is in Christ. All of God's mercy in Christ is immutable.

I hope in God's *unfailing love*. 'God is love' (1 John 4:16). 'Herein is love, not that we loved God, but that he loved us, and sent his Son to be the propitiation for our sins' (1 John 4:10). God's love is sure and unchangeable. He who so loved me that he gave his Son to redeem me will not withhold any good thing from me. This gives me hope. 'Because his compassions fail not,' the eternal God will never cease to love his own. This gives me hope.

God's unchanging *faithfulness* also gives me hope. 'Great is thy faithfulness!' This I know: God is faithful. 'If we believe not, yet he abideth faithful: he cannot deny himself' (2 Tim. 2:13). God is faithful to his purpose, faithful to his Word, faithful to his covenant, faithful to his people, and faithful to his Son. Divine faithfulness fills me with hope. I often doubt myself. I often question the motives and actions of men. But I cannot question or doubt the faithfulness of my God.

And I have hope because of God's inexhaustible goodness. Jeremiah said it, and we have often proved it: 'The Lord is good to them that wait for him, to the soul that seeketh him' (Lam. 3:26). God will do good and nothing but good for his own all the days of our lives and for all eternity. This is my hope, a good hope God has given me by his grace. Do you have a good hope?

Four bold challenges of faith

Read 2 Timothy 4:1–18

The believer's assurance does not depend upon his outward circumstances, his inward feelings, or his personal obedience. Our assurance rests entirely upon the person and finished work of Christ, as it is set forth in the Word of God. In this passage of Scripture, the apostle Paul breaks out into exultant praise. Having established the great truths of God's rich grace in Christ, he seems unable to restrain himself. Waving the palm branches of victory through Christ, this redeemed sinner defies all his enemies and glories in salvation by Christ, raising these four bold challenges.

1. '**If God be for us, who can be against us?**' The God of all power, of sovereign dominion, and eternal love is for us. He is for us in his sovereign providence, working all things together for our good. God is for us in his saving purpose, in electing love, predestinating grace, effectual calling, perfect justification and eternal glorification. He is for us in his substitutionary provision, sparing not his only Son. Let earth and hell unite in their rage against God's elect – we will not fear, for God is for us!

2. '**Who shall lay anything to the charge of God's elect?**' Nobody can! Satan cannot; he is defeated. The world cannot; it is condemned. The law cannot; it is honoured. God in justice cannot; 'it is God that justifieth'. God declares that we are perfectly righteous in Christ. He will never charge us with sin. 'Blessed is the man to whom the Lord will not impute sin!'

3. '**Who is he that condemneth?**' It is impossible that one of Christ's sheep should ever perish, because Christ died in our place. He was raised again for our justification. He finished the work of our redemption and sat down in heaven. Christ himself intercedes for us in glory.

4. '**Who shall separate us from the love of Christ?**' No power, no being and no act of men, of Satan, or of the demons of hell, can separate us from the Saviour's love.

'Thanks be unto God for his unspeakable gift'

Read Matthew 1:1–25

'Unto us a child is born, unto us a Son is given.' The appearance of God in human flesh was the embodiment of the gospel. Surely nothing but good could result from the miraculous birth of the God-man. Well did the angels sing, 'Glory to God in the highest, and on earth peace, good will toward men.' As we now frequently meditate upon the incarnation and birth of Christ, we are compelled to employ the apostle's language in our praise: 'Thanks be unto God for his unspeakable gift!' For thy Son, O Lord, we cannot give thanks enough. Words cannot be formed which would express the gratitude of our hearts.

Jesus Christ is the gift of God. We had no claim upon him. We felt no need of him. We did not desire him. But, freely, out of his abundant love and grace, God gave us his Son. 'For God so loved the world that he gave his only begotten Son.' God the Father gave us his Son in the covenant of grace. He gave us his Son in his condescending incarnation. God gave his Son at Mount Calvary. And God gave us his Son in the new birth. In giving us salvation and eternal life, God gave us Christ and all that he is, and all that he has done and all that he possesses. Christ is our salvation, our life and our all. And all who have him have him by the free gift of God.

As the gift of God, Jesus Christ is unspeakable. Who can describe the glorious Godhead and perfect humanity of Christ? The complex union of the God-man is a mystery beyond human understanding. We can only say, 'Great is the mystery of godliness, God was manifest in the flesh.' Is there a man who can adequately explain the vicarious life of Christ to accomplish our righteousness, or his substitutionary redemption to purchase our pardon? No. We can only say, 'Thanks be unto God for his unspeakable gift.'

But Jesus Christ is a gift of whom we shall speak very much. We shall speak of him to God in prayer and praise. We shall speak of him to men while we live. And we shall speak of him eternally among the hosts of heaven.

'He that feareth God and worketh righteousness, is accepted of him'

Read 2 Peter 1:1–21

Saving grace causes every believer to fear God. This is not a slavish fear, or morbid dread of punishment. Cain feared God's judgement. Pharaoh feared God's wrath. Judas feared God's punishment for sin in hell. Yet they were all lost. The fear of God produced by grace is a loving reverence for God. To fear God is to believe him, love him, seek his honour and endeavour to please him with a willing heart. This kind of fear is always produced by God's saving grace. Faith in Christ teaches us the fear of God.

The grace of God that brings salvation causes every believer to perform works of righteousness (Eph. 2:8–10). Works of righteousness have nothing to do with religious separation and isolation (Rom. 14:17). Most people think they are doing works of righteousness when they quit smoking, quit dancing, quit going to the films and quit playing cards. Those things may be all right, but they have nothing to do with works of righteousness. Works of righteousness are those things which God's people do with a willing heart for the benefit of others and for the glory of God. Works of righteousness are works of love, arising from a willing heart. Works of righteousness are works of self-denying generosity. Works of righteousness are works of love, kindness, thoughtfulness and charity towards men, and works of faith and devotion to God.

All who are saved by the grace of God fear God and do works of righteousness, and they are accepted with God. This is salvation, to be accepted with God. To be accepted with God is to be one with Christ. To be accepted with God means that God accepts me, accepts every gift I bring to him and accepts every work I endeavour to perform for him through the merits and mediation of Christ. To be accepted with God means that God will reward me with eternal glory in the Day of Judgement, because he has made me both sinless and perfectly righteous through the blood and righteousness of his Son. All who trust Christ are 'accepted in the beloved' (Eph. 1:6). Do you suppose God will accept you? If you are in Christ, he will.

Should believers celebrate Christmas?

Read Romans 14:1–23

No one knows the day of our Lord's incarnation. The Holy Spirit did not reveal it to us. And, as believers, we must not be brought into a bondage observance of any day. We must not honour one day above another. We do not observe holy days and sabbath days of any kind. To be sure, the world's observance of Christmas has little, if anything, to do with the worship and honour of Christ. For these reasons, and many others, some of the Lord's people conscientiously choose not to join in any form of Christmas celebration. I respect their opinions and convictions – I must, because I once shared them. While we must not look upon those who differ with us in scorn or contempt (Rom. 14:1–5), I believe it is best for us wisely to use this season of the year.

At this season of the year people everywhere are reminded of the fact that Jesus Christ lived and died in this world. Above all else, I have chosen to celebrate Christmas, because it gives me an open door for preaching the gospel for the honour of Christ and the salvation of men.

Another motive for celebrating this season of the year is the fact that it is a time of giving. It does my heart good to see men and women engaged in seeking the happiness of other people. Such a spirit should be encouraged and nourished, not dampened and reprimanded.

And Christmas is a time for the family. More so than at any other season of the year, families try to get together for Christmas. All the children come home with all their children. It is truly a happy time. I am for anything that promotes such family feelings.

Yes, I think that it is best for us to celebrate Christmas, not as a religious holy day, but for the remembrance of that blessed event when the Son of God assumed our nature, that he might live and die as our Substitute and accomplish our eternal redemption. December 25 is nothing to us. But Immanuel is everything to us. We will magnify our Lord, our Saviour, our King for his birth!

'Mine eyes have seen thy salvation'

Read Luke 2:1–40

I want you to behold Christ as God's salvation. The Lord Jesus Christ himself is God's salvation. It is good to see salvation in the work of Christ: his glorious incarnation, his life of righteousness, his effectual atonement, his mighty resurrection, his triumphant ascension and his gracious intercession. Without these things we could never have been saved. But it is our Lord's gracious person that makes all his work effectual. Had he not been a man like us, he could not have died as our Substitute. Had he not been God, his dying could never have availed for our redemption. It is who Christ is that gives virtue and merit to what he does.

My friend, Christ Jesus is the only salvation there is (John 14:6). The Holy Spirit tells us that Simeon was a 'just and devout man'. Yet he did not rely upon his goodness for acceptance with God. Simeon also observed the ceremonies and ordinances of worship as God prescribed them in his day. But he found no hope of salvation in the things he did (Rom. 3:20). He trusted Christ alone. When Simeon said, 'Mine eyes have seen thy salvation', he was saying that the Lord Jesus Christ is the whole of salvation (1 Cor. 1:30; 1 John 5:13). Christ is salvation. He that gets Christ gets full, complete, perfect salvation. When God gives his Son he gives all grace with his Son (Eph. 1:3), and will not withhold any good thing from those to whom his Son is given (Rom. 8:32).

Never forget, my friend, that the whole of salvation is in Christ. Do not expect to find any portion of it in yourself, or in the ordinances of the church, or in the works of the law, or in some pretended priest, or through doing penance for your sin. Christ alone is salvation. He does not need, nor will he accept, any help from man in the work of salvation. You must trust Christ alone in everything and for everything. I warn you that if you trust Christ for almost everything and yourself, your baptism, your good works, your speaking in tongues, or your experience for a little something, your hope is vain. Christ will be all, or he will be nothing (Gal. 5:2). Do you see this? Can you say with Simeon, 'Mine eyes have seen thy salvation'?

'The Word was made flesh'

Read Luke 1:1–56

No human mind can ever comprehend, nor earthly tongue describe, the great mystery of godliness: 'God was manifest in the flesh.' That baby born at Bethlehem is himself the eternal God. Though he was dependent upon the milk of his mother's breasts for life, he is God who formed the breasts that nourished him. Though Mary held him in her arms, he is God who upholds all things by the word of his power. Though he learned to walk and talk, and grew like any other child, he is the omniscient, immutable God. Though he lived as a man in wilful, voluntary, perfect obedience to the law, he is God who gave the law to Moses. Though he died under the penalty of the law as a man in the place of sinners, that man who died is God!

Why was Christ born? Why did the Son of God assume manhood? 'This is a faithful saying, and worthy of all acceptation, that Christ Jesus came into the world to save sinners' (1 Tim. 1:15). Athanasius said, 'Christ became what we are that he might make us what he is.' The Son of God became the Son of man for this purpose: that the sons of men might become the sons of God. A.W. Tozer put it like this: 'The awful majesty of the Godhead was mercifully sheathed in the soft envelope of human nature to protect mankind.'

Our Lord Jesus Christ, the Son of God, became a man because it was not possible for God to save sinners in any other way. In order to be our Saviour, it was necessary for God himself to become one of us, bone of our bone and flesh of our flesh. Were he only God, he could never suffer the punishment of sin as our Substitute. Were he only man, he could never satisfy the infinite wrath and justice of God against sin. But he who is both God and man in one glorious person both suffered and satisfied the penalty of the law as the sinner's Substitute.

Though I can neither understand nor explain the wonder and mystery of his person, I can and do trust that man who is God as my only, all-sufficient Saviour. Since God became a man and suffered in the place of men, he is able to save all who trust him.

'What think ye of Christ?'

Read John 1:1–34

Who do you think he is? Most people acknowledge that he was a prophet, a religious teacher, a good man, who promoted morality and truth and justice. Many would like to make his life of morality, self-sacrifice, self-denial and devotion a good example for men to live by. Even Nicodemus, a leader of the Jews, acknowledged, 'We know that thou art a teacher come from God' (John 3:2). But the Word of God declares that Jesus Christ was and is God the eternal Son. Mary's Son is also Mary's God, Mary's Lord and Mary's Saviour. The great, miraculous mystery that took place in Bethlehem two thousand years ago is just this: 'God was manifest in the flesh' (1 Tim. 3:16). Jesus Christ is more than just the fair, little baby of Bethlehem. He is 'over all, God blessed for ever' (Rom. 9:5).

Why did the Lord Jesus Christ come to this earth in human flesh? The answer to that question is plainly declared many times in the Bible: 'Thou shalt call his name Jesus, for he shall save his people from their sins' (Matt. 1:21). 'When the fulness of time was come, God sent forth his Son, made of a woman, made under the law, to redeem them that were under the law' (Gal. 4:4–5). 'This is a faithful saying, and worthy of all acceptation, that Christ Jesus came into the world to save sinners; of whom I am chief' (1 Tim. 1:15). Yes, the Son of God took upon himself human flesh, according to the will of God our Father, and came into this world as a man, to save sinners. He lived in righteousness to establish righteousness as a man, even the very righteousness of God which is imputed to every believer. He was made to be sin and died as the sinner's Substitute, in order to satisfy the law and justice of God against sin. He came to save sinners, to die as the sinner's Substitute, so that God might be just and yet justify all who believe.

Where is the Lord Jesus Christ now? Having finished the work which he came to do, he has ascended back to heaven, to reign as King of Kings and Lord of Lords, until he has put all his enemies under his feet. By his one great sacrifice for sin, he put away the sins of his people, redeemed and justified them, and now he ever lives to save all who come to God by him.

'Why did Christ come?'

Read Isaiah 61:1–11

1. Christ came into the world *to establish righteousness for us* as a man. He came to restore that which we lost in our sin and fall in Adam. He said, 'I restored that which I took not away' (Ps. 69:4). God required righteousness from us, perfect conformity to his holy law. But we are guilty. We have broken God's law. And we have no ability to live in righteous obedience to God's law, because we are sinful by nature. But the Lord Jesus Christ came as a man, without sin, to live as our Representative in perfect obedience to the law and will of God. Now by his obedience to God as our Representative, Christ established righteousness before God for his people. And it is written, 'By the obedience of one shall many be made righteous' (Rom. 5:19).

2. Christ came *to redeem his people* by dying as our Substitute under the wrath of God. Christ Jesus was born at Bethlehem as a man, so that he might die at Calvary in the place of sinners, according to the will of God our Father. At the appointed time our Lord was nailed to the cursed tree. God took all the sins of all his people and made them to be his Son's, so that by divine imputation the Son of God was made to be sin for us. God's law and justice found our sins upon Christ and punished him for sin as our Substitute. Since the law of God punished Christ for sin in our place, we are redeemed. All who believe, all God's elect, are fully pardoned through Christ's precious blood. 'Christ hath redeemed us from the curse of the law, being made a curse for us: for it is written, Cursed is everyone that hangeth on a tree' (Gal. 3:13).

3. Christ came *to glorify his Father* in the salvation of sinners. Since Christ Jesus lived in righteousness as our Representative and died under the curse of the law as our Substitute, satisfying the righteousness and justice of God for us, God's glory is revealed in the salvation of his elect. Christ Jesus lived and died for us, so that God could be both just and the Justifier of all who believe (Rom. 3:24–26).

'What did Christ accomplish?'

Read Daniel 9:16–27

1. He brought in an everlasting righteousness for us (Dan. 9:24). By his life of submission and obedience to the law of God as a man, the Son of God established righteousness in the earth. This righteousness was performed by Christ as our Representative before God. It is this righteousness, performed by Christ, which God imputes to believers. He declares us righteous by virtue of Christ's righteousness for us. We have no righteousness of our own, but we are made righteous before God in Christ.

2. Christ satisfied the justice of God as our Substitute. God demands the death of every transgressor. Every sinner must suffer the infinite wrath of God for sin. 'The wages of sin is death' (Rom. 6:23). And God always pays men their wages. 'The soul that sinneth, it shall die' (Ezek 18:20). When Christ hung upon the cross he died under the penalty of the law. He died as the object of God's wrath, because he was made to be sin for us. And by his death, he satisfied the claims of justice against us, so that those for whom he died are no longer under the sentence of death.

3. Jesus Christ our Saviour has put away the sins of his people by the sacrifice of himself. He took our sins upon himself and made them his own. Dying under the penalty of sin for us, Christ put away our sins. He drowned them in his precious blood. In so far as the law and justice of God are concerned, our sins, the sins of all who believe, the sins of God's elect do not exist! In Christ we are freed from all sin. 'Blessed is the man to whom the Lord will not impute sin' (Rom. 4:8).

4. By his life and by his death, the Lord Jesus Christ secured and guaranteed the eternal salvation of his people. God will save every sinner for whom Christ died upon the cross. Not one of God's elect will perish. By his life of righteousness as our Representative Christ merited the blessings of God for us, and by his sin-atoning death as our Substitute he silenced the claims of justice against us. All for whom Christ died shall live for ever in glory.

'Where is Christ now?'

Read Philippians 2:1–30

1. Christ Jesus is making intercession as our High Priest before God. 'He ever liveth to make intercession' (Heb. 7:25). We bow to no earthly priest. We worship at no earthly altar. We have but one Priest. He is Jesus Christ, the Son of God. He prays for us, for our eternal salvation, for our forgiveness, for our preservation in grace and for our spiritual, eternal welfare. And his prayers are always effectual. God will do for us all that his Son desires of him, because he pleads on our behalf his own blood and righteousness. Satan will not prevail over us, sin will not be charged to us, temptation will not reign over us and trials will not destroy us because Christ, our High Priest, makes intercession for us.

2. The Lord Jesus Christ is sovereignly ruling the affairs of this world for the salvation of God's elect. God has given him power (authority and dominion) over all flesh, that he should give eternal life to as many as God has given him (John 17:2). Christ is the sovereign Ruler of the universe. He governs all things, according to God's eternal purpose to this end: that he might give eternal life to all God's elect who were redeemed by his blood. Because all things are under the dominion of Christ, it is certain that 'He shall see of the travail of his soul, and shall be satisfied' (Isa. 53:11).

3. And the Lord Jesus Christ is saving all who come to God by him. 'This man, because he continueth ever, hath an unchangeable priesthood. Wherefore he is able also to save them to the uttermost that come unto God by him, seeing he ever liveth to make intercession for them' (Heb. 7:24–25). Yes, Christ Jesus is able (and willing too) to save every sinner who comes to God by him. He is an all-sufficient Saviour. His blood is sufficient to satisfy God's justice and wrath against you. His righteousness is sufficient to cover you and make you accepted before a holy God. Come to God by Christ, simply trusting his blood and his righteousness, and he will save you. 'For whosoever shall call upon the name of the Lord shall be saved' (Rom. 10:13). Call upon him now, in simple faith, and you will be saved.

'Christ, who is our life'

Read Colossians 3:1–24

Christ is the *source* of a believer's life. We have no life towards God by nature. By nature we were born in spiritual death (Rom. 5:12; Eph. 2:1–3). All spiritual life comes from Christ. The Lord Jesus Christ comes into the graveyard of fallen humanity and gives life to whom he will (John 5:21,24–25).

Christ is the *sum and substance* of the believer's life. He is not just an important part of our lives. The Lord Jesus Christ is our life! He lives in us, and we live in him! Spiritual life is a mystery. I cannot begin to explain the life of a believer. All I can say is 'Christ is our life.' 'Christ in you' is spiritual life. It is the life of Christ created in a man by the power of the Holy Spirit.

Christ is the *sustenance* of a believer's life. Just as your physical life is maintained by food and drink, the believer's life is maintained and sustained by daily feeding upon the life and death of Christ by faith (John 6:50–57).

Christ is the *solace* of a believer's life. There are times in the believer's life when the only comfort and consolation we have is Christ. And he is all the comfort we need. How sweet the solace of his presence!

Christ is the *standard* of a believer's life. Christ himself is the standard by which God's children live in this world. He is the example we follow. He teaches us how to love, how to forgive, how to suffer, how to bear reproach, how to pray and how to honour God. We strive in all things to walk in his steps.

Christ is the *security* of a believer's life. 'Your life is hid with Christ in God.' If Christ is my life, then my life is secure. Nothing can harm me until Christ is dethroned; and that cannot happen. Since Christ is my life, I must live.

And Christ is the *satisfaction* of a believer's life. Because Christ is my life, I can never be satisfied with this world, or with life in this world. My life will only be satisfied when I behold his face in righteousness and awake in his likeness (Ps. 17:15).

'Christ is all'

Read Philippians 3:3–21

Christ is all in *the salvation of God's elect*. Our election in eternity was in Christ. God has chosen us in him as our covenant Head. In the matter of our redemption Christ is all. He alone is our Redeemer. He bore our sin. He paid our debt. He satisfied the justice of God for us. And he did it all by himself. Christ is all in our justification too. We stand accepted and aquitted before God only by his righteousness and shed blood. His name is 'the Lord our Righteousness'. The quarrel between God and our souls was taken up by Christ and settled by Christ. And Christ is all in sanctification. We are positionally sanctified in Christ. We are progressively sanctified by the power of Christ. We shall be perfectly sanctified by the glorification of our bodies and souls with Christ. Salvation, from start to finish, is the work of Christ.

Christ is all in what we call *practical Christianity*. Christ alone gives me comfort and hope before God. Christ alone gives me strength for every trial and grace to persevere in the faith. Christ is all to be known, all to be chosen, all to be loved, all to be desired, all to be delighted in, all to be thought upon, all to be followed and all to be obeyed. We need no law but Christ and the example he has left for us to follow. Does any believer need a higher, more compelling motive for anything than Christ himself?

Christ is all *to be preached*. The Bible, in its entirety, is a book about Jesus Christ. No doctrine and no precept can be rightly understood apart from Christ. Christ is the key which unlocks the treasure chest of Holy Scripture. 'He is the treasure in that field, the marrow in that bone, the manna in that dew, the diamond in that ring, the milk in that breast (John 5:39).' (Philip Henry)

Christ is all *in heaven*. The foundation of that city is Christ. The gate to that city is Christ. The light of that city is Christ. The joy, bliss, and happiness of heaven is Christ. The praises of the redeemed in heaven for all eternity are the praises of Christ. The reward of God's saints in heaven is Christ himself. Heaven is Christ and Christ is heaven to my soul.

Index to Scripture Texts

Index to Scripture Texts